the Daily Cookie

TEMPTING TREATS FOR
THE SWEETEST YEAR OF YOUR LIFE

Anna Ginsberg

Andrews McMeel
Publishing, LLC

Kansas City · Sydney · London

Andrews McMeel Publishing, LLC
an Andrews McMeel Universal company
1130 Walnut Street, Kansas City, Missouri 64106

www.andrewsmcmeel.com

12 13 14 15 16 TEN 10 9 8 7 6 5 4 3 2 1

ISBN: 978-1-4494-2070-3

Library of Congress Control Number: 2012935507

www.cookiemadness.net

Book design Diane Marsh

A Hollan Publishing, Inc., concept

The author has taken steps to ensure that the recipes contained in this book can be made with a variety of brands of ingredients, though a few specific brand names are suggested. All brand names mentioned in this work are the registered property of their owners, and the author makes no claim to them.

ATTENTION: SCHOOLS AND BUSINESSES
Andrews McMeel books are available at quantity discounts with bulk purchase for educational, business, or sales promotional use. For information, please e-mail the Andrews McMeel Publishing Special Sales Department: specialsales@amuniversal.com

Contents

Introduction
iv

Getting Started
v

Ready to Bake!
xiii

Acknowledgments
402

Metric Conversions and Equivalents
403

Cookie Indexes
405

Index
417

Just the Facts
Writing this cookbook
was truly enjoyable,
but finding an event
for every day of the
year was a challenge.
While the dubiously
titled "national" food
holidays were always
fun to write about
and there was a food
holiday for every day
of the year, there
were days when a cer-
tain event or birthday
meant more to me
than a particular food
that was supposed
to be celebrated. For
instance, Bill Cosby's
birthday falls on
National Pecan Pie
Day and the first eye
bank opened on But-
terscotch Cookie Day.
As a Bill Cosby fan,
I chose his birthday
over National Pecan
Pie Day (but don't
worry, pecan bars are
represented else-
where!) and felt the
eye bank was more
interesting than but-
terscotch cookies. In
short, each day was
whatever resonated
at that particular
moment, which is
why I also listed a few
"Other Events on This
Day" should you find
that the birthday/
event/holiday I chose
for the cookie is not
your cup of tea.

Introduction

People often tell me they love to bake but are waiting for an occasion—a visiting relative, teacher apprecia-tion, Bunco party, or office baking contest. It's nice to have an occasion to bake, but should there always be one? We don't need an occasion to paint a picture, arrange a pot of flowers, or knit a scarf.

Since 2005, my excuse for baking has been a blog called *Cookie Madness*, where I committed to baking one batch of cookies a day. While I've expanded my repertoire to include pies, cakes, and other desserts, I've consistently posted a photo and recipe almost every day. I've also watched thousands of other baking blogs pop up, and have enjoyed the online camaraderie of people who would surely agree that homemade cookies are not only tasty and fun, but that baking them provides an instant feel-ing of accomplishment, gratification, and achievement. For every batch of cookies you pull out of the oven you get a tiny dose of positivity, and all those doses add up! Baking is an enjoyable way to relieve stress and create something in the process. It's cheaper than therapy, rewarding to the senses, and enhances all of life's little occasions. Thus, the goal of this book is to give every baker out there an occasion—silly or serious.

But then there's the question of what to do with all the goodies. Unless you have a house full of people, the solution is to share, and sharing can be kind of awkward at first. Whereas people who know you may be accustomed to having cookies dropped off at the door, others may appear bewildered and confused—as if perhaps they'd missed the note about some-one's birthday, a holiday, or event. "What's the occasion?" they may ask. This book answers it. Why wouldn't you make Snowballs on Polar Bear Day (page 66)? And how could you not show up at the office with Pretty Pink Melt-Aways when it's Barbie's birthday (page 78)? And finally, if anyone questions your choice of cookie for any given holiday, challenge them to come up with something better. Believe me, they'll try! And that's all part of the fun.

Getting Started

As a home baker, I'm always curious to know what brands of equipment and ingredients were used in testing. For this reason, I've occasionally listed specific names of brands I use on a regular basis. None of the recipes, as written in this book, were tested by a recommended brand's test kitchen, but rather at home in my little Texas kitchen where each cookie was photographed after being baked.

EQUIPMENT
MIXING BOWLS

You'll usually need only two bowls, one for mixing dry ingredients and another for the batter. My everyday mixing bowls are OXO Softworks plastic mixing bowls. They are lightweight and easy to knock around, plus they have a little spout that comes in handy for pouring bar cookie and brownie batter into pans. When I want to save a bowl by melting butter or chocolate in the same bowl used for the batter, I use microwave-safe mixing bowls. Emile Henry makes an earthenware set ranging from 1¾ to 5¾ cups in capacity, and Pampered Chef sells a deep 2-quart bowl they call a "batter bowl." It's dishwasher safe, has a spout, and can even be heated in both a microwave and regular oven should you wish to make a bowl-shaped cake.

BAKING SHEETS

The type of baking sheet you use may affect your results. I use heavy-duty, rimmed baking sheets called half sheet pans or jelly-roll pans, which are either 13 by 18 inches or 12 by 17 inches. While I did not use them for testing cookies in this book, insulated cookie sheets are also nice. The extra layer of air between the bottom layers helps distribute heat evenly and protects against burnt bottoms. Insulated sheets are especially helpful when making fatter, softer cookies and biscuits.

BAKING SHEET LINERS

Lining your baking sheets will help make cleanup easier. Instead of rubbing the pan with butter or spraying with nonstick cooking spray, I almost always line baking sheets with nonstick foil or parchment paper.

- Nonstick foil is relatively new, a bit more expensive, but very handy. It's especially useful for lining pans of bar cookies because it doesn't buckle or flip up.
- Parchment paper is now widely available. It comes in a 15-inch roll and is usually found near the foil. Lining your baking sheet with a sheet of parchment will protect the pan and make cleanup easier. Like nonstick foil, parchment paper can be used more than once. Just remove your cookies from the sheet of parchment, wipe off any excess grease, fold the paper, and stash it somewhere until you are ready to use it again.
- A Silpat is a nonstick silicone mat used to line baking sheets. It's a convenient and seemingly environmentally sound alternative to paper, but it does require a bit of care and needs to be cleaned by hand.

There are some cases when it's best to bake cookies on an ungreased, unlined pan. For instance, chocolate chip cookies with high ratios of butter and sugar tend to spread, so baking them on a slick surface may exacerbate the problem. In my experience, these types of cookies are usually better off on a slightly less slick surface, so if a recipe says to use an ungreased baking sheet, there's a reason.

METAL BAKING PANS

I bake bar cookies in an 8-inch square, 9-inch square, 9 by 13-inch, or 15 by 10-inch metal pan. Pans made of glass conduct heat differently, and using them may result in overbaked, dark edges and undercooked centers. If a glass pan is all you have or if you prefer using glass for aesthetic reasons, set your oven 25°F lower than the recipe directs. All of the recipes in this book are tested in metal pans.

MEASURING CUPS

For measuring dry ingredients, you will need a set of graduated measuring cups measuring from ¼ cup to 1 cup. A 1-cup glass measuring cup, preferably microwave-safe, is necessary for measuring liquids, and a 2-cup glass measuring cup (such as Pyrex) really comes in handy when you're making small amounts of glaze or drizzle or melting small amounts of chocolate.

MEASURING SPOONS

You will need a set of graduated measuring spoons with spoons measuring from ⅛ teaspoon to 1 tablespoon.

ROUND COOKIE CUTTER SET

Perfect for punching out sandwich cookies, mini piecrusts, and any circular cookie, a set of round cutters will really come in handy. Ateco makes a nice set with circles ranging from 1½ inches to 4½ inches.

#70 COOKIE SCOOP

This type of cookie scoop holds about a tablespoon of dough, and if you're striving for uniformity, it's a helpful tool. Invest in a stainless-steel or metal cookie scoop rather than a cheapo plastic scoop. It's worth it. That being said, for this book I measured with regular measuring teaspoons and tablespoons.

COOLING RACK

Placing a hot pan of cookies or bars on a cooling rack speeds up the cooling process and helps prevent condensation of steam, which may soften the edges of some cookies and bars and affect the cookie's texture. Buy a good, sturdy wire rack with lots of room underneath for air to circulate.

MICROWAVE OVEN OR DOUBLE BOILER

A microwave oven is a handy tool for melting chocolate. If you have neither a microwave nor a double boiler, you can create your own double boiler by setting a heatproof bowl over (but not touching) a shallow saucepan of hot water. I prefer using the microwave, and because modern microwaves are more powerful than ever, I use 50 percent power for melting chocolate. For white chocolate chips, butterscotch chips, or other chips that tend to have a high sugar content, I sometimes find that using an even lower setting on the microwave helps melt the chips smoothly. You may have to fiddle with the settings of your own microwave to find the perfect chocolate-melting power, but start low. If you have a microwave but it doesn't have a lot of power settings, try using the defrost setting to melt chocolate.

The microwave is also a lifesaver when it comes to melting butter. Place the butter in a microwave-safe bowl or measuring cup and heat on high, stirring every 30 seconds, until the butter is melted.

SIFTER

Sifting removes lumps and helps aerate flour. It's almost always necessary for cakes, but because I provide weights for most of the flour measurements, all you really need to do is fluff the flour with a spoon. If you don't have a sifter and need to sift something light such as confectioners' sugar, try using a sieve or a colander.

HEAT-RESISTANT SILICONE SPATULA SCRAPER

A good scraper will get batter off the sides of the bowl and so much more. In fact, it may become your most-used kitchen tool. I recommend a heavy-duty scraper with a wide, heat-resistant silicone head for stirring, scraping, and folding. Mine happens to be the Pampered Chef brand and I've put it to the test on many occasions. After having broken my share of scraping tools, this particular brand has proven to be quite durable. You can order Pampered Chef tools online, or better yet, from a friend who sells Pampered Chef. It always feels good to help out a friend and you get an awesome tool in return.

OVEN THERMOMETER

Keep an oven thermometer on hand to make sure your oven's temperature runs true. Over time, ovens tend to run faster and hotter, and cookies that once took you 15 minutes to bake are now done in 10. I speak from experience. For a few months, I noticed that everything I baked was ready in a little less than the minimum timed called for. Edges and tops browned before the inside of cookies were done and cakes were turning out dry. I stuck a $5 oven thermometer in the back of the oven and discovered the temperature was almost 50°F too hot!

HANDHELD ELECTRIC MIXERS AND STAND MIXERS

For quick small-batch cookies, I prefer using a handheld electric mixer rather than a stand mixer, but for large batches I pull out the stand mixer and attach the paddle. If you buy a stand mixer, treat yourself to a scraper attachment and never worry about stopping to scrape the bowl.

FOOD PROCESSOR

There are some appliances I could do without, but my food processor is essential. It's handy for chopping nuts, but where it really shines is in making crusts and types of dough where cold or room temperature butter needs to be cut into the flour. The alternative to a food processor is using your fingers or a pastry cutter, but a food processor makes the job so much easier and less messy. Plus it's also good for making cheesecake batter, crushing graham cracker crumbs, and shredding vegetables. I have a large Cuisinart processor and a small chopper/grinder.

SPICE AND NUT GRINDER OR OLD COFFEE GRINDER

Cuisinart makes some spiffy spice and nut grinders, but I've been using a little Krups Fast Touch coffee grinder for years.

KITCHEN SCALE

Once you start using a kitchen scale, you will find it indispensable. While you can certainly produce a great batch of cookies without one, having a scale will not only ensure that your measurements are accurate, but will save you from cleaning out a few more measuring cups. For instance, if you know that a cup of flour weighs 4.5 ounces, you can set your bowl on the scale, set the tare to zero, and pour 4.5 ounces directly into the bowl. If you tend to be a messy spoon-and-sweeper, a scale is for you.

Because flour, especially, varies so much depending on how you pack it into the cup, I've put the weight of the amount of flour I used next to all flour measurements.

MICROPLANE ZESTER

Removing the yellow part of a lemon's peel, the zest, is not the chore it used to be. A Microplane Zester makes the job easy. Microplane tools are available at most kitchen stores, and I've even seen them at my grocery store.

INGREDIENTS
FLOUR

Most of my recipes call for all-purpose flour. You may use bleached or unbleached, but I tested my recipes with unbleached. All-purpose flour should weigh between 4.25 to 4.75 ounces per cup, but this varies, depending on how heavy handed one is in measuring.

I measure flour by really fluffing it up and aerating it before scooping the cup in the bin of flour and leveling it carefully with a knife. When using a very light hand, I've come in at 4.25 ounces, and when using a heavier hand or shaking the cup, I've come it at over 5 ounces. While an ounce to a half-ounce difference in weight might not sound like a lot, the extra (or lack of) flour will affect the overall outcome of your cookie. For consistency and accuracy, I've used the weight of 4.5 ounces of flour for every cup.

In the past year I've become a huge fan of white whole wheat flour, which is made by the King Arthur Flour Company and sold at most grocery stores. If your store doesn't sell it, consider asking the manager to stock it, or just order some online. White whole wheat flour is milled from white spring wheat rather than traditional red wheat and has a milder flavor. With white whole wheat, you get a slightly nutty, nonoverpowering wheat flavor, along with the benefits of whole wheat.

This is also true for whole wheat pastry flour, which is made with softer, lower protein wheat that helps keep cookies tender. And if you're interested in the benefits of wheat without the flavor of wheat, look for Eagle Mills Ultragrain, which can be used cup for cup in place of regular all-purpose flour. While none of these recipes were tested with it, it generally works the same as all-purpose flour, though the batter or dough might require a little more liquid.

Other flours that appear in the book include barley flour, rice flour, and tapioca flour. Barley flour and tapioca flour can usually be found at your local health food store, while rice flour is sold at most mainstream grocery stores.

PREPARED COOKIE MIX

A handful of recipes call for cookie mix. The brand I use is Betty Crocker and it comes in a 1 pound, 1.5-ounce (or 17.5-ounce) pouch.

SUGAR

The main types of sugar used in this book are granulated sugar, light brown sugar, dark brown sugar, and confectioners' sugar. Every so often I mention a less commonly used sweetener such as coconut palm or turbinado sugar, but for the most part I stick with the big four. In most cases, substituting dark brown sugar for light brown sugar shouldn't cause any issues, other than making the cookies darker and perhaps somewhat sweeter, but be careful using brown sugar in place of granulated, as brown sugar may not only change the flavor, but also cause the cookie to spread and be a little bit softer. In a pinch, you can, however, substitute granulated sugar mixed with a little molasses for light brown sugar. Just add 2 tablespoons of molasses to a cup of granulated sugar, stir well, and then measure as you would the brown sugar.

If you need to substitute one of the sugars with an artificial sweetener, keep in mind the cookie will be different than one made with sugar. This is not to say you can't make a good cookie with some artificial stand-ins, but sugar plays an important role in the overall structure of a cookie, and replacing a cup of sugar that weighs 7 ounces with a sweetener weighing a fraction of that will change the composition of the dough. Experiment and learn from your mistakes!

LEAVENING AGENTS

Baking soda is an alkaline that neutralizes acidity. It is activated by acidic ingredients and moisture. Because baking soda is alkaline, it will reduce the acidity of your cookie batter. Cookie recipes with less acid tend to brown better, so in some cases, a bit of baking soda will help cookies develop a more golden hue.

Baking powder is a combination of baking soda and an acid. The most common type of baking powder is double-acting, which reacts first to moisture in the batter and again to the heat of the oven. Cookies made with baking powder do not spread as much and tend to rise higher more quickly than do those made with baking soda. They also do not brown quite as fast.

Cream of tartar is derived from a by-product of the wine-making process called argol. The argol is refined to make an acidic salt, which some companies mix with baking soda to make baking powder. Alone, cream of tartar is used as an acid to stabilize meringues or balance acid levels in batter.

Of course, I've already given leavening amounts for all of these recipes, so you shouldn't worry about it. The point is not to swap baking soda for baking powder or vice versa.

SALT

Salt used to be a pretty straightforward ingredient, but today we have table, kosher, fine sea, and coarse salt. What's the best choice? In the interest of keeping things simple, all recipes in this book have been tested with either Morton Kosher Salt or just regular table salt. The reason I mention the brand is that various kosher salts have different levels of saltiness. Some brands of kosher salt have larger crystals, so when you measure them by volume, you're actually using less salt. If you prefer the flavor of kosher salt, look for a brand that says it measures like table salt.

UNSALTED BUTTER

Recipes in this book call for unsalted butter. If regular (salted) butter is the only butter you have, feel free to use that instead, but reduce the amount of salt in the recipe by ⅜ teaspoon. Certain recipes say to omit the salt if using salted butter, so check the Baker's Notes. Also, unless a recipe calls for cold or melted butter, butter should be at room temperature. The ideal temperature of butter is between 67°F and 72°F (which may be cooler than the average kitchen), but you don't have to go to the trouble of measuring your butter temperature with a thermometer. Ideally, the butter should be cool on the outside, but just malleable enough to give when you beat it with a spoon.

SHORTENING AND OIL

Cookies made with shortening often have a superior texture and stay fresher longer. Shortening helps prevent spreading and, in some cases, makes cookies crisper and lighter tasting. When a recipe calls for shortening, you can use Crisco or a nonhydrogenated brand such as Spectrum. I tested my recipes with Crisco. The easiest way to measure shortening is with a scale: ½ cup should weigh 96 grams or 3.4 ounces.

For vegetable oil, you can use your favorite. I prefer light tasting olive oil for baking, but I also use canola, soybean, and grapeseed oils.

Not to be confused with hydrogenated coconut oil, natural or virgin coconut oil is becoming a popular fat alternative. When used in baking, some brands leave behind a very faint taste of coconut, while the flavor of coconut in less expensive brands tends to dissipate. I'm still kind of new to using coconut oil in baking, but so far the results have been pretty good.

EGGS

Most recipes call for large eggs, which weigh about 2 ounces and are a little less than 4 tablespoons (¼ cup) in volume. In some recipes, I call for "2 tablespoons lightly beaten egg," which equals about half an egg. If a recipe calls for raw egg, such as the case for royal icing, I use a pasteurized egg product called Safest Choice eggs. Also, unless otherwise specified, eggs should be room temperature. If you're in a hurry and need to bring an egg to room temperature quickly, put it in a bowl of very hot water and let it sit for about 5 minutes.

MILK

Unless otherwise indicated, all cookies and bars were tested with whole or 2% milk, with whole milk being the preferred choice for icings and glazes. If a very small amount of milk is called for in a cookie, it's usually acceptable to substitute low-fat or even nonfat milk, but in recipes such as frostings or fillings, the extra fat in the whole milk helps add richness and body.

PEANUT BUTTER

Most of the recipes in this book were tested with peanut butter such as Jif, Skippy, and Reese's. If freshly ground peanut butter is called for, I've indicated it in the recipe. Also, a handy way to measure peanut butter is to weigh it on your scale. Peanut butter weighs a little more than its volume. For example, an 8-ounce-volume cup of peanut butter will weigh about 9 ounces on a scale.

GOLDEN SYRUP

A terrific and flavorful alternative to corn syrup is Lyle's golden syrup or cane sugar syrup. Lyle's used to be a British specialty item, but for the past few years I've found it at my regular grocery store right next to the Karo.

CORN SYRUP
Corn syrup, not to be confused with the high-fructose corn syrup used in so many processed foods, is made from cornstarch and glucose. I use Karo light and dark.

MAPLE SYRUP
Pure maple syrup is more expensive than pancake syrup, but worth it! Its flavor is subtle, and when used in baking, it imparts maple undertones rather than a strong maple flavor. Pancake syrup, which many of us associate with maple, actually gets its flavor from an herb called fenugreek.

MOLASSES
For almost all cookie recipes, I use mild molasses. One recipe in the book (Mini Ginger Cookies, page 210) calls for dark, but you can substitute mild if that's all you have.

LIME AND LEMON ZEST
When a recipe calls for zest, use the outer part of the fruit; that is, use the yellow part of a lemon rather than the underlying white rind.

VANILLA EXTRACT
For most cookies, I use pure vanilla extract such as McCormick or Spice Islands. For icings or fillings or cookies where I really want the vanilla flavor to come through, I'll use Nielsen-Massey vanilla extract, or in some cases, their excellent vanilla bean paste. I rarely use imitation vanilla extract, though I do use artificial clear vanilla in icing recipes that need to be very white, such as Black and Whites (page 3). For Mexican vanilla, I like Nielsen-Massey, which has a unique flavor all its own.

UNSWEETENED COCOA POWDER
Two kinds of unsweetened cocoa powder are used in this book—Dutch-processed cocoa powder and "natural" cocoa powder. Dutch-processed cocoa, which Hershey markets as "extra dark," has had much of the natural acids removed and yields a deeper, darker, richer, chocolate flavor. Because it is more alkaline than natural cocoa, it may react differently with the leavening. Natural cocoa powder is more acidic. If a recipe calls for baking powder (an acid), it's usually safe to use either Dutch-processed or natural cocoa because the batter has enough acid. However, if baking soda is the only leavening, it's often best to use the natural kind. Situations vary, but there have been instances where I've substituted Dutch-processed cocoa for natural and have ended up with flat cookies. An example of that is the Tex-Mex Chocolate Chipotle Cherry Cookies (page 126).

CHOCOLATE CHIPS
I use extra-dark, dark, and semisweet chocolate chips interchangeably depending on my mood, but they all have flavor differences and you have to go with what you prefer.

NUTS
My theory is that people who don't appreciate nuts in cookies have eaten too many cookies with untoasted nuts. Toasted, they add rich flavor plus a little nutrition as well. Softer nuts such as pecans and walnuts are best in softer cookies and bars, while harder nuts such as almonds and pistachios work best in crisp or hard cookies such as biscotti.

If you don't have a certain type of nut and want to make a substitution, it's usually best to substitute a soft nut for another soft nut or a hard nut for another hard nut.

COCONUT

Unless indicated otherwise, recipes in this book were tested with the sweetened flaked coconut commonly found in the baking aisle of most grocery stores. If you try a cookie or bar and feel it is too sweet, try substituting unsweetened shredded coconut, which is often sold at specialty grocery stores or in the bulk bin or produce section of mainstream grocers.

Ready to Bake!

No matter how simple the recipe, always read it from start to finish. Have ingredients ready to go (chefs call this *mise en place*) so that all your ingredients make it into the bowl.

LINING PANS

I'm very fond of nonstick foil. It's a bit more expensive than regular foil, but it's easy to use and it lets you bypass nonstick cooking spray completely. To line a pan with foil, turn the pan over, tear off a large sheet of foil, and press the foil over the pan to make a mold. Flip the pan over and set the foil in the pan. You can do the same thing with regular foil, but spray the foil with flour-added baking spray once you've set it in the pan.

To line a pan with parchment, spray the pan with nonstick cooking spray or rub it with butter, then press the parchment paper into the pan and pat down so it covers bottom and sides. You can skip the greasing step if you want, but parchment paper tends to get unruly without something to help it cling to the sides of the pan. Now that we have nonstick foil, I rarely use parchment paper for lining anything other than baking sheets.

BRINGING BUTTER TO ROOM TEMPERATURE

The urge to bake cookies often strikes suddenly, which means you'll need to soften cold butter quickly. One way to do this is with a microwave. If you don't have a butter soften-

ing setting on your microwave, cut your butter into chunks, microwave on high for 10 seconds, then use a handheld electric mixer to beat it until creamy. Of course, if you have time, it's best to just leave the butter on the kitchen counter for a while.

TOASTING NUTS

To toast nuts, line a baking sheet with foil or parchment and spread the nuts evenly over the tray. Bake at 350°F for 6 to 8 minutes, or until aromatic. Let the nuts cool and crisp before you chop them and add them to cookie dough. If you're in a hurry or are making a small-batch recipe and only need about a handful of nuts, try toasting your nuts in a microwave. Using a high setting will undoubtedly burn them to a crisp, but try toasting a handful at 40 or 50 percent power. Lay the nuts flat on a paper towel and microwave for 1½ minutes. If your nuts are not aromatic, continue microwaving at 10-second intervals. Microwave toasting can save you some time, but you will need to adjust cook times for different sizes and varieties. I have a 1,000-watt microwave and can toast a handful of pecans in 1 minute and 40 seconds at 40 percent power. Again, play with the settings using different amounts of nuts. Microwave powers vary and nuts burn easily.

MIXING DRY INGREDIENTS

Sifting is not necessary for most of the recipes in this book. However, it is important to stir dry ingredients thoroughly. If you've ever bitten into a lump of baking powder, you understand why.

CREAMING

Many recipes ask you to beat the butter and sugar until creamy, the point being not only to mix those ingredients, but to create tiny air bubbles that will expand during baking. In cookies, you'll know you've creamed the butter and sugar when the mixture starts to appear smooth and fluffy or, in the case of a recipe with more sugar than fat, gritty, like paste, but free of any fat chunks. This can be done with a handheld electric mixer or a stand mixer fixed with a paddle. While a stand mixer creams butter and sugar faster, I am partial to a handheld mixer because I tend to make a lot of small-batch recipes. Be mindful of the temperature of the fat. If the butter is very cool and beaten until creamy, you'll usually get cookies with nicely rounded edges.

RACK POSITION

Recipes in this book are baked one sheet at a time on the center rack unless otherwise noted. If you'd prefer to bake two sheets at a time, adjust the racks to the lower two-thirds of your oven and bake on the lower two racks, rotating the sheets halfway through.

BAKING TIMES

Consider baking times a suggestion, as many ovens bake at different temperatures and thus at different speeds. If you notice that your cookies are too brown around the edges, chances are your oven runs hot. If this is the case, try reducing the temperature by 25°F. If your oven runs slow, it's probably best to just bake the cookies longer. Cookies

made in a convection oven generally need the temperature to be set at 25°F lower than indicated in the recipe. Whichever kind of oven you use, always preheat it for at least 20 minutes to ensure that the oven is at the recommended temperature when you begin baking. An oven thermometer set or hung inside your oven will help you determine the true heat of your oven.

COOLING

When you pull your cookies from the oven, they may appear slightly pale in the center. Five minutes after they've cooled, you may notice the paleness disappears. This is because cookies are still baking internally when you pull them from the oven. In most recipes, it's best to let the cookies sit on the baking sheet for a few minutes to finish their internal cooling process before transferring them to a cooling rack. It is especially important to let bar cookies cool completely. For some bars, it's best to not only cool them completely, but chill them before slicing and serving.

STREAMLINING THE BAKING PROCESS

- Keep your equipment in one place. Why not devote some shelf space to a baking sheet, two stackable bowls, measuring cups (neatly tucked inside the bowls), and measuring spoons?
- Keep ingredient basics at hand. Store your flour, granulated sugar, and brown sugar in decorative, airtight containers set conveniently on your counter. Or if you have pantry space, buy a plastic tub and keep your flour, salt, baking powder, and baking soda together in the tub on a shelf. If you are a chocoholic, you may want to designate a canister for your unsweetened cocoa powder.

- To take things a step further, group your most frequently used spices together in a little tub or plastic box. For instance, you might group cinnamon, nutmeg, cloves, and allspice together so you'll never have to go searching, and group the less frequently used items such as cream of tartar, espresso powder, and your sifter so they won't get lost in the shuffle. It sounds simplistic, but if you are not naturally organized and spend a lot of time just searching for ingredients and equipment, taking baby steps like these will help make baking more fun.

STORING AND PACKING COOKIES

Cookies tend to disappear quickly, but chances are you'll want to stash a few away. First, make sure your cookies are completely cool before covering. If they are placed in a sealed container while warm, the condensation will make them soft and moist. In some cases, warm cookies sealed in a bag may even take on the flavor of the plastic bag.

Keeping cookies in the cookie jar is also an option, but remember to keep your soft cookies away from your crisp cookies. The crisp cookies draw moisture from the soft cookies, leaving you with a bunch of softies.

My personal preference is to store cookies in the freezer. To freeze your cookies, place the cooled cookies in a resealable freezer bag, squeeze out any extra air, and then seal tightly. I like to place my bag of frozen cookies in a tin or container just to make sure they don't get crushed by other things in the freezer.

Bar cookies should be either frozen or stored in the refrigerator. If you have the option, bake a full batch, cut off what you need, then wrap the remainder in foil.

If you are baking your batches of cookies for a friend, there are dozens of ways to pack the cookies, but always keep freshness in mind. The Chinese take-out style of gift boxes are adorable, but seal your cookies in a bag before placing them in the box.

DIRECTIONS RUN-DOWN

Most recipes follow the same pattern.

First Step: Dry ingredients are mixed in a separate bowl. Directions usually say "medium-size" or "small," but you can use whatever size bowl you have on hand or just mix your dry ingredients on a big piece of foil.

Second Step: The fat is beaten or creamed with the sugar (page xiv).

Third Step: The mixer speed is either reduced or kept steady before adding the eggs. Beating the eggs on high speed will add more air to the batter, whereas blending them just until mixed will keep the air at a minimum. In a few recipes, the extra air is desirable, but in most recipes it's best to reduce the speed of the mixer and beat the eggs just until they're blended in.

Fourth Step: The flour mixture is added by hand or using the lowest speed of mixer. Even at the lowest speed, the beaters on a handheld electric mixer are a little rough on the dough, so if I'm making cookies with a handheld mixer, I put down the mixer and just stir in the flour with a spoon or my trusty silicone spatula scraper. If I'm using my stand mixer, I put the paddle attachment on low speed and carefully let the paddle do the mixing.

Fifth Step: Shape the cookies. You can make cookies any size you want, as long as you adjust the baking time and the distance between individual cookies on the baking sheet. The important thing is uniformity. I still struggle to make all my cookies the same size, but they look better when made the same size and they'll bake more evenly. Using a scoop (page vi) can help.

Sixth Step: Bake the cookies. Oven temperatures vary and if your oven is a little wonky, you tend to notice it. Or maybe it's the dough that's wonky. In any case, when I try a new recipe, I like to bake a few balls of dough as a test before committing to a whole dozen. And I've learned to view baking times as helpful suggestions rather than as absolutes. So use the times listed as guidelines and make sure to use your senses to tell when the cookies are ready. Okay, you probably knew that already, but I felt I had to add it, as I occasionally read recipe reviews where people mention something being terribly underdone or overdone and having to throw it out.

Seventh Step: Let the cookies cool. Most cookie recipes say to let cool on the baking sheet for a few minutes, then transfer to a wire rack to cool completely. As mentioned earlier, a wire rack lets the air circulate around each cookie so that it cools properly. Cookies that have been left on a baking sheet to cool completely might lose some of their crispness. In some cases, this is desirable, but in most cases cookies are left on the sheet for only a few minutes and then transferred to a cooling rack to cool completely. Bar cookies should be cut when completely cool. For a cleaner cut, I like to chill them.

THE MOST IMPORTANT NOTES

- I bake cookies on the center rack one sheet at a time or, in some cases, on the center and lower racks, in which case I rotate the baking sheets halfway through.
- Unless otherwise noted, ingredients are at room temperature when used.
- Flour is always weighed with a scale and measured by volume as well.

Now go bake some cookies!

Pomegranate Swirl Cheesecake Bars MAKES 16

POMEGRANATE SYRUP

¾ cup pomegranate juice

1 tablespoon granulated sugar

CRUST

6 tablespoons (3 ounces) unsalted butter, room temperature

⅓ cup firmly packed light brown sugar

¼ teaspoon salt

1 cup (4.5 ounces) all-purpose flour

FILLING

1 (8-ounce) package cream cheese, softened

¼ scant cup granulated sugar

1 large egg, room temperature

2 teaspoons freshly squeezed lemon juice

½ teaspoon vanilla extract

It takes about two pomegranates (1,200 seeds) to get a full cup of juice.

New Year's Day

Happy New Year! Double down on your good luck and follow those black-eyed peas with some pomegranate. With hundreds of pulpy little seeds, this legendary fruit symbolizes fertility, regeneration, and abundance. In Greece, it's customary to smash a pomegranate on the threshold—the more seeds dispersed, the more luck.

Other Events on This Day:
National Bloody Mary Day

1 **Make the pomegranate syrup:** In a small saucepan, bring the juice to a boil. As soon as it begins to boil, reduce the heat to a simmer. Simmer for about 10 minutes, or until you have ¼ cup of juice. Stir in the tablespoon of sugar. Bring to a quick boil, then reduce the heat and simmer for 2 to 3 minutes, or until you have about 2 tablespoons of syrup (it should be about the same consistency as pancake syrup). Put the syrup back into your measuring cup and set aside to let cool.

2 **Make the crust:** Preheat the oven to 350°F and place a rack in the center. Line an 8-inch square metal pan with nonstick foil, or line it with regular foil and spray the foil with flour-added baking spray.

3 In a large mixing bowl, using a handheld electric mixer, beat the butter, brown sugar, and salt on medium speed until creamy. By hand or using the lowest speed of the

mixer, add the flour and mix until evenly incorporated and crumbly. Press the batter into the pan and bake for 12 minutes, or until the edges are lightly browned. Let cool completely.

4 **Meanwhile, make the filling:** In a second mixing bowl, using a handheld electric mixer, beat the cream cheese and sugar on medium speed until smooth; reduce the speed and add the egg, lemon juice, and vanilla, beating just until blended. Pour the cheese mixture over the baked crust. Drop teaspoon-size puddles of pomegranate syrup over the top and pull a knife through the mixture to create a marbled effect. Bake for 20 to 25 minutes, or until the cheesecake appears set. Let cool completely in the pan, then chill for 3 hours, or until cold. Grasp the foil and lift the bars from the pan. Set on a cutting board and cut into sixteen squares.

National Science Fiction Day

Today we celebrate science fiction and the birthday of Isaac Asimov. Having come from Russia, his parents had no official record of his birth and declared it to be January 2, 1920. Asimov grew up to be a professor of biochemistry and the author of over five hundred science fiction works—many of which included futuristic food, such as food pellets, food prepared by robots, and food cooked with microwave radiation.

Robert Heinlein, another sci-fi master, wrote about prepackaged frozen food that could be heated up in seconds, as well as an apparatus called a "quickthaw" that could heat "synthosteaks." Heinlein's novel *Space Cadet*

Microwave Brownies MAKES 9

2 large eggs
½ cup granulated sugar
½ cup firmly packed light brown sugar
¾ teaspoon vanilla extract
¼ teaspoon almond extract
½ teaspoon salt
8 tablespoons (4 ounces) unsalted butter, melted
½ cup unsweetened natural cocoa powder
¾ cup (3.4 ounces) all-purpose flour
⅔ cup pecans or walnuts, chopped (optional)
⅓ cup semisweet chocolate chips

1 Grease and flour an 8-inch square glass microwave-safe baking dish. Line the bottom with parchment if desired.

2 In a mixing bowl, using a handheld electric mixer, beat the eggs at medium speed for 30 seconds. Add both sugars and continue beating for 1 minute, or until the mixture

is very light. Beat in the vanilla, almond extract, and salt. Stir in the melted butter and beat on low speed to blend. Beat in the cocoa powder. With a spoon, gently stir in the flour. Stir in the nuts (if using) and chocolate chips.

3 Heat uncovered in the microwave on high for 3 to 4 minutes, or until the brownies appear set. Baking times will vary with wattage. I use a 1,000-watt microwave oven and can tell the brownies are done when they feel firm all over but have a moist spot about 1¼ inches across in the center. If you have a turntable, there's no need to rotate the baking dish, but if you don't have a turntable, rotate once per minute. Let cool completely in the baking dish, then cut into nine squares.

Black and Whites

MAKES 7 LARGE COOKIES

COOKIES

1¼ cups (5.6 ounces) all-purpose flour

½ teaspoon baking soda

½ teaspoon salt

⅓ cup milk

2 teaspoons freshly squeezed lemon juice

1½ teaspoons vanilla extract

6½ tablespoons (3.25 ounces) unsalted
    butter, room temperature

½ cup granulated sugar

1 large egg, room temperature

ICING

1¾ cups confectioners' sugar, sifted

⅓ scant cup whole milk

1½ tablespoons heavy cream

1 teaspoon regular or clear vanilla extract

⅓ cup unsweetened dark cocoa powder,
    such as Hershey's Dark

1 teaspoon light corn syrup or golden syrup

was published in 1948, and although he didn't invent the microwave (they went on sale in 1947 and were 5½ feet tall and 750 pounds), he had the foresight to see them used in small spaces by your average human (or space cadet).

Other Events on This Day:
National Cream Puff Day

The Brooklyn Bridge Groundbreaking

On this day in 1870, construction began on one of the United States' oldest suspension bridges. Connecting the New York City boroughs of Manhattan and Brooklyn (then separate cities), the Brooklyn Bridge spans 5,989 feet across the East River with two large towers standing 276 feet tall.

In honor of the two boroughs connected by the bridge, here's my all-time favorite version of a New York classic. These fat and cakey vanilla cookies are sold all over New York City and are particularly popular upstate. I've adapted this recipe from one in *Gourmet* magazine because I always seem to find myself out of buttermilk. I also used my own icing, which calls for clear vanilla extract to keep it nice and white.

Other Events on This Day:
Festival of Sleep Day,
National Chocolate-Covered
Cherry Day

1 Preheat the oven to 350°F and place a rack in the center. Have ready two ungreased baking sheets.

2 **Make the cookies:** Mix the flour, baking soda, and salt together in a medium-size bowl; set aside.

3 Stir the milk, lemon juice, and vanilla together in a glass measuring cup or separate bowl.

4 In the bowl of a stand mixer fitted with a paddle attachment, or in a large mixing bowl, using a handheld electric mixer, beat the butter and sugar on medium speed for 2 minutes, or until very well mixed. Add the egg, beating until incorporated. With a mixing spoon or heavy-duty scraper, stir in the flour mixture and milk mixture alternately, beginning and ending with the flour mixture. Mix until smooth.

5 Using a ¼-cup measure, drop the batter about 3 inches apart onto the baking sheets. Bake one sheet at a time for 15 to 17 minutes, or until the cookies are puffy and golden and appear done. Transfer to a wire rack to cool completely.

6 **Make the icing:** Whisk the confectioners' sugar, milk, cream, and vanilla together in a mixing bowl until it is the consistency of glue. If the icing seems too thick, add more milk 1 teaspoon at a time as needed, whisking until smooth. Measure out about ⅓ cup of icing and set aside. Add the cocoa powder and ½ teaspoon of water to the remainder and stir until smooth. If the chocolate icing seems too thick, thin it with a little water or milk. Add the corn syrup to the chocolate icing. Spread the white icing over half of the top of each cooled cookie. Spread the chocolate over the other half. For more control of the icing, put one of the colors (let's say, chocolate) in a decorating bag fitted with a writing tip and use the writing tip to make a straight line down the middle. Cover all seven halves with chocolate. Let them set, then fill in the other half with the white icing.

Carrot Breakfast Cookies MAKES 10 LARGE COOKIES

1 cup (4.5 ounces) white whole wheat
   or all-purpose flour

½ teaspoon baking powder

¼ teaspoon salt

½ teaspoon ground cinnamon

⅓ cup vegetable oil

3 tablespoons granulated sugar

⅓ cup firmly packed dark
   brown sugar

1 teaspoon vanilla extract

1 large egg

½ teaspoon orange zest

½ cup old-fashioned or quick-cooking oats (not instant)

⅔ cup shredded or grated carrots

½ cup dried cranberries

⅓ cup toasted and chopped walnuts or pecans

It is believed that people with blue eyes have a single common ancestor.

1 Preheat the oven to 350°F and place a rack in the center. Line two baking sheets with parchment paper or nonstick foil.

2 Mix the flour, baking powder, salt, and cinnamon together in a small bowl; set aside.

3 In a large bowl, mix together the oil, both sugars, and the vanilla. When well mixed, add the egg and orange zest and beat for another 20 to 30 seconds. Add the flour mixture to the sugar mixture and stir until the flour is absorbed. Stir in the oats, carrots, cranberries, and nuts.

4 Using a ¼-cup measure, scoop up the dough and place on the prepared baking sheets, spacing about 3 inches apart. Bake one sheet at a time for 15 to 18 minutes, or until the cookies appear set. Let cool on the baking sheets for about 5 minutes, then transfer to a wire rack to cool completely.

National Eye Care Month

January is National Eye Care Month. Some handy tips: Block UV rays by wearing sunglasses, make sure to blink while starting at the computer, and keep lid margins clean.

Another thing to consider is diet. Studies show foods rich in carotenoids, lutein, and zeaxanthin antioxidants may improve vision by protecting the retina from the harmful effects of the free radicals in UV light. Good nutrition also plays a role in preventing macular degeneration, reduces the risk of cataracts, and helps form healthy tears.

You'll find eye nutrients in dark green leafy vegetables, carrots and yams, broccoli, citrus fruits, apricots, peaches, and mangoes. And herbs and spices may benefit the eyes as well. For healthy tears, try omega-3-rich foods such as flax, fish oil, and walnuts.

Other Events on This Day: **National Spaghetti Day, Trivia Day**

*Y*ou probably won't get a day off from work for this one, but today's unofficial crazy food holiday is National Whipped Cream Day. Aaron "Bunny" Lapin was born on this day in 1914. During the war, he sold Sta-Whip, a mixture of cream and vegetable oil that he eventually put in aerosol cans, for which he invented a special valve. His product, Reddi-wip, was distributed through local milkmen, but was so popular that sales went national in 1954.

Other Events on This Day:
National Bird Day

Chocolate Brownie Bites

MAKES 36

⅔ cup (3 ounces) all-purpose flour

½ teaspoon baking powder

⅛ teaspoon salt

2 large eggs

¾ cup granulated sugar

⅓ cup vegetable oil

3 ounces bittersweet chocolate, melted

2 teaspoons bourbon whiskey

½ teaspoon vanilla extract

⅓ cup toasted and chopped pecans

⅓ cup semisweet chocolate chips

Canned whipped cream, for topping

1 Preheat the oven to 350°F and place a rack in the center. Line thirty-six mini muffin cups with paper liners or spray the cups with flour-added baking spray.

2 Mix the flour, baking powder, and salt together in a small bowl; set aside.

3 In the bowl of a stand mixer fitted with a paddle or in a large bowl, using a handheld electric mixer on high speed, beat the eggs until fluffy. Gradually add the sugar, beating on high speed until slightly thickened. Beat in the oil, and then stir in the melted chocolate, bourbon, and vanilla.

4 By hand, gradually stir in the flour mixture, followed by the pecans and chocolate chips.

5 Divide the batter evenly among the prepared muffin cups. Bake for 11 to 12 minutes, or until the brownies appear set. Let cool in the pan for 15 minutes, then remove from the muffin cups and transfer to a wire rack to cool completely. When ready to serve, top with canned whipped cream.

Black Bean Brownies MAKES 16

1 (15.5-ounce) can black beans, drained and rinsed

3 large eggs

3 tablespoons vegetable oil or extra-light olive oil

¼ cup unsweetened natural cocoa powder

⅛ teaspoon salt

1¼ teaspoons vanilla extract

¾ cup granulated sugar

1 teaspoon instant espresso powder

½ cup bittersweet (60% cacao) chocolate chips

¾ cup pecans or walnuts, toasted and
    coarsely chopped

1 Preheat the oven to 350°F and place a rack in the center. Line an 8-inch metal baking pan with nonstick foil, or line it with regular foil and spray the foil with flour-added baking spray.

2 Puree the black beans in the bowl of a food processor or blender. Add the eggs, oil, cocoa powder, salt, vanilla, sugar, and espresso powder and process until smooth; stir in the chocolate chips and nuts.

3 Pour the mixture into the pan and bake for 30 minutes. The top should appear set and the edges should have pulled slightly away from the pan. Let cool completely in the pan, then chill the brownies, if desired. Grasp the foil, lift from the pan, set on a cutting board, and cut into sixteen squares.

One-Bowl Cranberry Oat Cookies MAKES ABOUT 48

8 tablespoons (4 ounces) unsalted butter

1 tablespoon pure maple syrup

1 cup granulated sugar

1 large egg

¼ cup 2% or whole milk

½ teaspoon vanilla extract

National Bean Day

It's Bean Day! No one knows the true origin, but speculation leans toward the fact that Gregor Mendel, who did genetics experiments using peas as subjects, died on this day in 1884.

Although Mendel used peas, I like black beans. A 1-cup serving contains nearly 15 grams of fiber and 15 grams of protein.

Other Events on This Day:
Apple Tree Day, Shortbread Day

Fannie Farmer Cookbook Published

On this day in 1896, *The Boston Cooking-School Cook Book*, later named *The Fannie Farmer Cookbook*, was published. Revolutionary for its time, it contained 1,849 recipes and was among the first to use standardized measurements such as "1 level teaspoon" and "1 cup."

In 1979 and then again in 1990, Marion Cunningham edited and revised *The Fannie Farmer Cookbook* with slightly more up-to-date dietary preferences; streamlined recipes; and conversational, encouraging prose.

Other Events on This Day:
Old Rock Day, Tempura Day

½ teaspoon orange zest

½ teaspoon baking soda

1 teaspoon ground cinnamon

½ teaspoon salt

1½ cups (6.8 ounces) white whole wheat or all-purpose flour

1¾ cups old-fashioned oats

½ cup toasted and chopped pecans

½ cup dried cranberries

1 Preheat the oven to 350°F and place a rack in the center. Have ready two ungreased baking sheets.

2 In a microwave-safe mixing bowl, microwave the butter on high for 30 seconds, or until melted. Coat a tablespoon with some of the melted butter, then use it to measure 1 tablespoon of maple syrup. Add the maple syrup to the mixing bowl, followed by the sugar, egg, milk, vanilla, and orange zest. Stir well with a mixing spoon, and then stir in the baking soda, cinnamon, and salt. Add the flour and stir until incorporated. Stir in the oats, pecans, and cranberries.

3 Drop rounded teaspoonfuls of batter onto the baking sheets, spacing about 2 inches apart. Bake one sheet at a time until the edges are browned, 10 to 12 minutes. Transfer to a wire rack to cool completely.

Baker's Notes: Modernizing the recipe even more, I made this in one bowl, used readily available maple syrup, and added orange and cranberries in place of raisins. These are small, slightly cakey rather than chewy, and approved by my oatmeal cookie–loving friends.

Peanut Browned Butter Banana Bacon Cookies

MAKES 20

9 tablespoons (4.5 ounces) unsalted
    butter, room temperature

1 cup dried banana chips

4 slices thin-sliced bacon

½ cup creamy or crunchy peanut butter

½ cup firmly packed brown sugar

½ cup granulated sugar

1½ teaspoons vanilla extract

1 large egg

1 tablespoon mild molasses

1 tablespoon whole or reduced-fat milk

½ teaspoon salt

¼ teaspoon baking soda

¼ teaspoon baking powder

1¾ cups (7.9 ounces) all-purpose flour

½ cup peanut butter chips

40 bite-size miniature peanut butter cups,
    halved, or 10 miniature cups, quartered

1 Preheat the oven to 350°F and place a rack in the center. Have ready two ungreased baking sheets.

2 In a large skillet, melt 1 tablespoon of the butter. When the butter has melted, add the banana chips and sauté until the butter starts to brown and the banana slices soak up some of the butter and brown a little around the edges. Transfer the banana chips to a paper towel and let cool, but not without tasting a few, of course! Wipe the skillet clean. Place the bacon in the skillet and cook until crisp. Drain on a paper towel, then chop the bacon into pieces.

3 In the bowl of a stand mixer fitted with a paddle attachment, or in a large mixing bowl, using a handheld electric mixer, beat the remaining 8 tablespoons of butter, peanut butter, and both sugars on medium speed until smooth. Beat in the vanilla, egg, molasses, and milk. Beat in the

Elvis's Birthday

While vacationing in Las Vegas, my husband and I somehow ended up in the middle of an Elvis-themed marathon. As we watched the runners cross the finish line in their capes, it occurred to me that while Elvis was a good singer, his legacy was more far-reaching than that of just about any entertainer I could think of. How did that happen? Was it Elvis himself or just the fact that his existence took place when the country needed an Elvis?

I've always liked Elvis, but honestly my fascination is mostly with his diet. Did he really fly to Denver in the middle of the night to satisfy a sandwich craving? Were his peanut butter and banana sandwiches fried in a full stick of butter? There are a lot of rumors, but it's a fact that he loved peanut butter and banana sandwiches, so today's cookie is for Elvis.

Other Events on This Day:
Man Watcher's Day, Show and Tell at Work Day

salt, baking soda, and baking powder, scraping the sides of the bowl to make sure the ingredients are evenly distributed. Add the flour and stir until mixed. Stir in the peanut butter chips, fried banana chips, and bacon pieces.

4 Scoop up rounded tablespoonfuls of dough and shape into balls about 1¾ inches in diameter. Arrange 3 inches apart on the baking sheets and pat the tops down slightly. Bake one sheet at a time for 12 to 14 minutes. Remove from the oven and immediately arrange about four peanut butter cup halves or quarters over the warm cookies (they'll kind of melt, then reset and adhere to the cookies). Let the cookies cool on the baking sheet for about 5 minutes, then transfer to a wire rack to cool completely. Serve the cookies when they are completely cool and the peanut butter cups have set.

Baker's Notes: This cookie was inspired by Elvis's peanut butter, banana, and bacon sandwiches that were fried in butter. Because I couldn't fry the whole cookie, I sautéed crisp dried banana chips in butter, then added them (along with some chopped crisp bacon) to the batter. As far as I know, Elvis never added chocolate to his sandwich, but I couldn't resist sticking a few chopped peanut butter cups on at the end.

Whole Wheat and Pecan Apricot Bars   MAKES 16

FILLING

¾ cup dried apricots, finely chopped

½ cup water

BASE

8 tablespoons (4 ounces) unsalted
    butter, room temperature

¼ cup granulated sugar

¼ scant teaspoon salt

1 cup (4.5 ounces) white whole wheat flour,
    sifted or fluffed up before measuring

TOPPING

1 cup lightly packed brown sugar
2 large eggs, well beaten
⅓ cup (1.5 ounces) whole wheat flour
½ teaspoon baking powder
½ teaspoon salt
¾ teaspoon vanilla extract
½ cup toasted and chopped pecans

1 **Make the filling:** Combine the apricots and water in a small saucepan. Bring to a quick boil, then reduce the heat and simmer uncovered for about 10 minutes, or until most of the water has soaked in. Drain the excess water (if any) and set aside to cool.

2 Preheat the oven to 350°F and place a rack in the center. Line an 8-inch metal pan with nonstick foil, or line it with regular foil and spray the foil with flour-added baking spray.

3 **Make the base:** In the bowl of a stand mixer fitted with a paddle attachment, or in a large mixing bowl, using a handheld electric mixer, beat the butter, sugar, and salt on medium speed until creamy. Stir in the flour to form a dough. Press the dough into the bottom of the prepared pan and bake for 20 minutes, or until the edges are lightly browned.

4 **Meanwhile, make the topping:** Beat the brown sugar and eggs together in a mixing bowl using an electric mixer on medium speed. Combine the flour, baking powder, and salt, and then with a spoon, stir the flour mixture into the egg mixture. Stir in the cooked apricots, vanilla, and pecans. Pour the apricot mixture over the baked base. Return the pan to the oven and bake for another 20 to 23 minutes, or until the bars appear set. Let cool completely in the pan. Lift from the pan, set on a cutting board, and cut into sixteen squares.

Other Events on This Day:
Static Electricity Day, Play God Day

In 1901, Texas history changed forever when a little well on Spindletop Hill, an area known for sulfur springs and bubbling gas, struck oil. The gusher spewed oil more than 100 feet in the air at a rate of 100,000 barrels per day until it was capped nine days later, making Beaumont, Texas, a boomtown.

Other Events on This Day:
Bittersweet Chocolate Day, Peculiar People Day

Chocolate Cookies with Oil MAKES 36

1½ cups plus 1 teaspoon (7 ounces) all-purpose flour

¾ teaspoon baking powder

⅛ teaspoon baking soda

¼ scant teaspoon salt

2 ounces unsweetened chocolate, chopped

2 large eggs

⅔ cup vegetable oil

½ cup firmly packed light brown sugar

¾ teaspoon vanilla extract

1½ cups semisweet or bittersweet chocolate chips

1 to 2 tablespoons lightly beaten egg, used only if needed

1 Preheat the oven to 350°F and place a rack in the center. Line two baking sheets with parchment paper or nonstick foil.

2 Mix the flour, baking powder, baking soda, and salt together in a medium-size bowl; set aside.

3 In the microwave, heat the chocolate for 1 minute at 50 percent power. Stir until melted. If chocolate is not fully melted after 1 minute, heat at 50 percent power for another 20 seconds. Stir and repeat until melted. Set aside to cool slightly.

4 In the bowl of a stand mixer fitted with a paddle attachment, or in a large mixing bowl, using a handheld electric mixer, beat the eggs on medium speed until foamy. Add the oil and brown sugar and continue beating for another minute. Beat in the vanilla. By hand, stir in the flour mixture, and then stir in the melted chocolate. The batter will be shiny and will pull away from the sides. Stir in the chocolate chips. At this point the dough should be be soft and crumbly, but you should be able to shape it. If not, add a tablespoon of lightly beaten egg to help bind the dough.

5 Scoop up rounded teaspoonfuls of dough and shape into balls. Arrange 2½ inches apart on the prepared baking sheets. Bake one sheet at a time for 10 to 12 minutes, or just until the cookies appear set. Let cool on the baking sheets for 3 minutes, then transfer to a wire rack to cool completely.

Baker's Notes: The texture of these cookies is a little different—slightly drier than fudgy chocolate cookies, but in a tasty and delicious way that complements the texture and sweetness of the chocolate chips. Don't leave them out.

Milk Chocolate Chunk Walnut Cookies MAKES 20

1½ cups plus 2 tablespoons (7 ounces)
    all-purpose flour

¾ teaspoons baking soda

¾ teaspoon salt

10 tablespoons (5 ounces) unsalted
    butter, room temperature

¾ cup firmly packed light brown sugar

1 large egg

¾ teaspoon vanilla extract

4 ounces milk chocolate, cut into chunks

¾ cup toasted and chopped walnuts

1 Preheat the oven to 350°F and place a rack in the center. Line two large baking sheets with parchment paper or nonstick foil.

2 Mix the flour, baking soda, and salt together in a small bowl; set aside.

3 In the bowl of a stand mixer fitted with a paddle attachment, or in a large mixing bowl, using a handheld electric mixer, beat the butter and brown sugar on medium-high speed for about 2 minutes, or until light and fluffy; reduce the mixer

JANUARY 11

National Milk Day

Today is National Milk Day. While not the official reason for Milk Day, today marks the anniversary of the death of Gail Borden and the day in 1878 when milk was first sold in glass bottles. Either way, it's a good day to celebrate one of America's favorite drinks and a good excuse to use milk chocolate.

Other Events on This Day:
Step in a Puddle and Splash Your Friend Day

speed to medium and beat in the egg and vanilla. By hand, or on low speed, stir in the flour mixture. Stir just until it is absorbed, being careful not to overbeat. Stir in the milk chocolate and walnuts.

4 Scoop up rounded tablespoonfuls of dough and shape into 1¼-inch balls. Arrange the balls about 2½ inches apart on the prepared baking sheets. Bake one sheet at a time for 10 to 12 minutes, or until the cookies appear done—the edges should be golden brown. Let cool on the baking sheets for 5 minutes, then transfer to a wire rack to cool completely. These cookies taste best when they've completely cooled and the milk chocolate has reset.

Baker's Notes: These cookies bake up dense, puffy, with a slightly sandy texture and a crisp edge. Like many other cookies, they turn out fatter and taller when made with chilled dough. I like to scoop up mounds of dough, chill them on baking sheets, transfer them to a zipper bag, refrigerate or freeze them, and then bake as needed.

HAL the Robot Becomes Fully Operational

On this day in 1992, HAL 9000, the sentient on board the *Discovery* space ship in *2001: A Space Odyssey*, became operational, trained to appreciate art, reproduce emotions, recognize speech, and (unfortunately) read lips. You'd never peg cool, calm HAL as one of the most villainous characters in movie history, but he made the American Film Institute's Top 50 Villians list in 2003. Cutting the brownies into rectangles instead of the usual squares and adding a bright red, round candy makes them look like HAL.

HAL-Shaped Frosted Fudge Brownies MAKES 24

BROWNIES

8 tablespoons (4 ounces) unsalted butter

1 cup granulated sugar

2 large eggs

1 teaspoon vanilla extract

½ cup (2.25 ounces) all-purpose flour

¼ teaspoon baking powder

¼ scant teaspoon plus an extra pinch of salt

⅓ cup unsweetened natural cocoa powder

½ cup toasted and chopped pecans

ICING

1⅓ cups confectioners' sugar, sifted

3 tablespoons (1.5 ounces) unsalted butter

2 tablespoons unsweetened natural or
    Dutch-processed cocoa powder

2½ tablespoons milk

¼ teaspoon vanilla extract

**Red candy-coated chocolates, such as M&M's,
or any small, round, red candies**

1 Preheat the oven to 350°F and place a rack in the center. Line an 8-inch metal pan with nonstick foil, or line it with regular foil and spray the foil with flour-added baking spray.

2 **Make the brownies:** In a microwave-safe mixing bowl, microwave the butter on high for 30 seconds, or until melted. Whisk in the sugar, then whisk in the eggs and vanilla. In a separate bowl, mix together the flour, baking powder, salt, and cocoa powder. Gradually add the flour mixture to the butter mixture. Stir in the pecans. Pour into the prepared pan and bake for 20 to 25 minutes, or until the brownies start to pull away from the edges from the pan. Remove from the oven and prepare the icing while the brownies are still warm in their pan.

Other Events on This Day:
**National Pharmacist Day,
Stick to Your Resolution Day**

3 **Make the icing:** Place the sifted confectioners' sugar in a medium-size heatproof mixing bowl and set it next to the stove.

4 Melt the butter in a small saucepan over medium heat. Add the cocoa powder and milk and bring just to a boil. When the mixture reaches a boil, remove from the heat. Pour the hot cocoa mixture into the bowl of sugar. Add the vanilla and stir with a wooden spoon until smooth. Work quickly so that icing won't start to set in the bowl. Pour over the warm brownies and let sit until the icing is firm and the brownies have cooled completely. Lift from the pan, set on a cutting board, trim the edges, and cut into twenty-four rectangles. Put a red candy on each rectangle. If it doesn't stick, melt a small bit of chocolate in the microwave and adhere the candy with the melted chocolate.

International Skeptics Day

*Y*ou may not believe me, and if you don't that's a perfect reaction for today, because it is International Skeptics Day—a day for those who follow the philosophy that true knowledge in just about any particular area is uncertain.

Skepticism is a healthy catalyst for progress. If it weren't for skeptics, we might still believe the Earth is flat, that you can really catch a cold by being in the rain, and that sitting too close to the TV ruins our eyes. Then again, being too skeptical has its drawbacks. Only an optimist would predict a good outcome after putting corn chips, peanut butter, and chocolate together.

Other Events on This Day:
National Rubber Ducky Day, Peach Melba Day

Sweet-and-Salty Corn Chip Candy   MAKES APPROXIMATELY 16 PIECES

2 cups miniature pretzels
½ cup corn chips, such as Fritos
½ cup lightly salted peanuts
8 tablespoons (4 ounces) unsalted butter
½ cup firmly packed light brown sugar
1½ cups semisweet chocolate chips

1 Preheat the oven to 350°F and place a rack in the center. Line a 9 by 13-inch pan with parchment paper or nonstick foil.

2 Break the pretzels up into thirds and fourths—you don't have to be precise. The point is to just break them rather than crush them. Next, break up the corn chips. Mix the corn chips, pretzels, and peanuts in the pan.

3 Melt the butter in a small saucepan over medium heat. When the butter is completely melted, stir in the brown sugar. Bring the mixture to a full boil and boil for 1 minute, stirring once or twice. Pour it over the pretzel mixture, then bake for 7 minutes.

4 Remove the pan from the oven and sprinkle the chocolate chips over the hot mixture. Return the pan to the oven for 1 minute to soften the chocolate, then remove it from the oven and spread the softened chocolate over the mixture. Let cool in the pan for about 1 hour, then chill until the chocolate is set and the candy holds together. When ready to serve, break the slab of candy into large chunks.

Kourabiedes MAKES 36

1 cup (8 ounces) unsalted butter, room temperature

⅓ cup confectioners' sugar, plus ⅔ cup for rolling

½ teaspoon salt

1 large egg yolk

2 tablespoons brandy

½ teaspoon vanilla extract

½ teaspoon baking powder

2 cups (9 ounces) all-purpose flour

½ cup finely chopped blanched almonds

36 whole cloves (optional)

1 In a stand mixer fitted with a paddle attachment, or in a large mixing bowl, using a handheld electric mixer, beat the butter and confectioners' sugar on medium speed for about 2 minutes, or until creamy. Beat in the salt, egg yolk, brandy, and vanilla. Beat in the baking powder, then by hand or with the lowest speed of a mixer, stir in the flour and almonds. Chill the dough for 30 minutes, or until it is thick enough to handle.

2 Preheat the oven to 325°F and place a rack in the center. Line two baking sheets with parchment paper or nonstick foil.

3 Shape tablespoonfuls of dough into crescents and place 1 inch apart on the prepared baking sheets. Insert a whole clove into center of each, if desired. Bake one sheet at a time for 25 to 30 minutes, or until lightly golden, taking care not to overbake or let the cookies brown. Transfer to a wire rack to cool completely, then roll in confectioners' sugar, if using.

Discovery of Aristotle's Lyceum

Aristotle's Lyceum was unearthed on this day in 1997. Findings included a large complex with a central courtyard and wrestling area that archaeologists have confirmed as belonging to the Lyceum, where Aristotle taught from around 334 to 323 BC. Also called the Peripatetic School, because students and teachers would stroll along the tree-lined grounds during the course of lectures, the Lyceum was renowned for its natural science program, extensive library, and museum. It was one of Athens's most important sites and the forerunner to our modern universities.

Other Events on This Day: **National Pastrami Sandwich Day, Dress Up Your Pet Day**

Coronation of Queen Elizabeth I

Q ueen Elizabeth I was crowned today in 1559, a date chosen by her personal astrologer, John Dee, and often called the "birth of a new age."

Although the coronation took place on the fifteenth, the festivities began on the preceding day with a procession through London. The queen was taken through the crowd-lined streets and the procession was punctuated with a series of five pageants recognizing attributes of the new, twenty-five-year-old regent. Elizabeth reigned for over forty-four years during a time called the "golden age of English history."

Other Events on This Day:
National Strawberry Ice Cream Day

Golden Sugar Cookies

MAKES 36

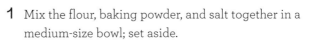

2¼ cups (10.1 ounces)
   all-purpose flour
½ teaspoon baking powder
¾ teaspoon salt
1 cup (8 ounces)
   unsalted butter,
   room temperature
½ cup granulated sugar
¾ cup confectioners' sugar
½ teaspoon vanilla extract
1 teaspoon lemon or orange zest
2 large egg yolks
Sparkling or coarse sugar, for sprinkling (optional)

> **Because sugar was known to blacken teeth, women wanting to look posh and upper class would darken their teeth with cosmetics.**

1 Mix the flour, baking powder, and salt together in a medium-size bowl; set aside.

2 In the bowl of a stand mixer fitted with a paddle attachment, or in a large mixing bowl, using a handheld electric mixer, beat the butter on medium speed until creamy. Beat in the granulated and confectioners' sugars and continue beating for another minute, or until very light and fluffy. Beat in the vanilla, zest, and egg yolks. By hand or using the lowest speed of a stand mixer, gradually add the flour mixture to form a soft dough. Chill the dough for 30 minutes.

3 Preheat the oven to 350°F and place a rack in the center. Line two baking sheets with nonstick foil or parchment paper.

4 Scoop up tablespoonfuls of dough and shape into balls. Arrange about 2½ inches apart on the prepared baking sheets and press down slightly with the bottom of a glass. Sprinkle the tops with sparkling or coarse sugar, if desired. Bake one sheet at a time for 15 to 18 minutes. Transfer to a wire rack to cool and crisp.

Glazed Bourbon Whiskey Cookies **MAKES 18**

COOKIES

1¼ cups (5.6 ounces) all-purpose flour

1½ teaspoons baking powder

¼ teaspoon baking soda

¼ teaspoon salt

1 teaspoon ground cinnamon

1 teaspoon freshly grated nutmeg

4 tablespoons (2 ounces) unsalted butter, room temperature

½ cup granulated sugar

2 large eggs

¼ cup bourbon whiskey

¾ cup toasted and chopped pecans

¾ cup raisins

GLAZE

1 tablespoon (0.5 ounce) unsalted butter, melted

1½ cups confectioners' sugar

3 tablespoons bourbon whiskey (or as needed)

1 If you plan to bake the cookies right away, preheat the oven to 350°F and place a rack in the center. Have ready two ungreased baking sheets.

2 **Make the cookies:** Mix the flour, baking powder, baking soda, salt, cinnamon, and nutmeg together in a medium-size bowl; set aside.

3 In the bowl of a stand mixer fitted with a paddle attachment, or in a large mixing bowl, using a handheld electric mixer, beat the butter and sugar on medium speed until light and fluffy. Add the eggs, one at a time, beating well after each addition. Using the lowest speed of the mixer or by hand, add the flour mixture and whiskey alternately to the creamed mixture. Stir in the pecans and raisins. At this point, you may bake the cookies right away or chill for 1 hour. Chilling the dough will thicken it slightly and give you nicer-looking mounds. (If you chill the dough, preheat the oven to 350°F before proceeding to the next step.)

JANUARY 16

Prohibition in Effect

On this day in 1920, Prohibition officially took effect.

We all know how that worked out. Citizens entertained themselves by drinking, dancing, and listening to jazz at speakeasies as crime increased and became organized. Profiting from less serious offenses such as alcohol consumption, gambling, and prostitution, the Mafia gained a stronghold, opening the door to more serious crimes.

As the years went by, it became readily apparent that Prohibition was not working, and it was repealed on December 5, 1933.

Other Events on This Day:

Spicy Foods Day, National Fig Newton Day

4 Scoop up rounded tablespoonfuls of dough and arrange 2 inches apart on the baking sheets. Bake one sheet at a time for 10 minutes, or until the edges are lightly browned and the cookies appear set. Transfer to a wire rack set over a paper towel and let cool completely.

5 **Make the glaze:** In a small mixing bowl, combine the melted butter and confectioners' sugar. Add the whiskey 1 tablespoon at a time until it is a drizzling consistency. Spoon over the cookies, letting the excess glaze fall onto the paper towel you've set under the rack.

Baker's Notes: These bake up like little mounds of cake and, when topped with the opaque glaze, are quite pretty. For this recipe, you can use regular raisins, but if you want to really be a gangster, soak them in whiskey overnight and drain before using.

Chocolate Chip Dream Bars   MAKES 32

BASE
12 tablespoons (6 ounces) unsalted butter, room temperature
¼ teaspoon plus a pinch of salt
¾ cup firmly packed light brown sugar
¼ teaspoon vanilla extract
1½ cups (6.8 ounces) all-purpose flour
2 cups semisweet chocolate chips

FILLING
2 large eggs
1 cup firmly packed light brown sugar
1 teaspoon vanilla extract
1 teaspoon baking powder
½ teaspoon salt
2 tablespoons all-purpose flour
1 cup toasted and chopped walnuts
1½ cups sweetened flaked coconut, plus an extra handful for topping

1 Preheat the oven to 375°F and place a rack in the center. Line a 9 by 13-inch metal pan with nonstick foil, or line it with regular foil and spray the foil with nonstick baking spray.

2 **Make the base:** In the bowl of a stand mixer fitted with the paddle attachment, or in a large mixing bowl, using a handheld electric mixer, beat the butter, salt, brown sugar, and vanilla on medium speed until smooth. By hand, stir in the flour. If you need to, use your fingers to mix it until it just barely comes together. Press the mixture into the bottom of the prepared pan and bake for 12 minutes, or until lightly browned. Let cool in the pan for about 15 minutes.

3 After the base has cooled slightly, scatter the chocolate chips over the crust. Press down the chips just enough that when you cover them with the filling, they won't get pulled all over the place.

4 **Make the filling:** In a mixing bowl, using a handheld mixer on medium speed, beat the eggs, brown sugar, and vanilla. Beat in the baking powder and salt, then add the flour and stir just until mixed. Stir in the walnuts and 1½ cups of the coconut. Drop spoonfuls of the filling over the chocolate chip–covered base and spread gently to cover the chocolate chips the best you can. Sprinkle the reserved handful of coconut over the top. Bake for 20 minutes. Let cool completely in the pan. Lift from the pan, set on a cutting board, and cut into thirty-two bars.

On this day in 1778, James Cook, explorer and captain in the Royal Navy, made the first recorded European visit to Hawaii.

While some say Captain Cook introduced the pineapple to Hawaii, others believe it reached Hawaii in the 1500s when a Spanish ship wrecked off the coast of the Big Island and certain provisions floated ashore. Cultivation of the pineapple did not begin until the 1880s, under the supervision of John Kidwell. In 1903, James Drummond Dole began canning pineapple, making it easily available around the world.

Other Events on This Day:
**Winnie-the-Pooh Day,
Thesaurus Day**

Hawaiian Bars MAKES 32

2 cups (9 ounces) all-purpose flour

½ teaspoon baking soda

½ teaspoon salt

12 tablespoons (6 ounces) unsalted
    butter, room temperature

1 cup firmly packed dark brown sugar

2 large eggs

2 teaspoons vanilla extract

¾ cup chopped dried pineapple chunks

8 ounces white chocolate, cut into chunks

½ cup unsweetened shredded coconut

½ cup toasted and chopped unsalted
    macadamia nuts (optional)

1   Preheat the oven to 325°F and place a rack in the center. Line a 9 by 13-inch metal pan with nonstick foil, or line it with regular foil and spray the foil with nonstick baking spray.

2   Mix the flour, baking soda, and salt together in a small bowl; set aside.

3   In the bowl of a stand mixer fitted with a paddle attachment, or in a large mixing bowl, using a handheld electric mixer, beat the butter and brown sugar on medium speed until creamy. Beat in the eggs, one at a time, and then beat in the vanilla. By hand or using the lowest speed of the mixer, stir in the flour mixture just until incorporated. Stir in the pineapple, white chocolate, coconut, and macadamia nuts (if using).

4   Pour into the prepared pan. Bake for 30 to 35 minutes, or until the bars appear set and the edges are lightly browned. Let cool completely in the pan. Lift out of the pan, set on a cutting board, and cut into thirty-two bars.

Hidden Happiness Cookies

MAKES 24

1 cup (4.5 ounces) all-purpose flour

1 teaspoon baking powder

⅜ teaspoon salt

8 tablespoons (4 ounces) unsalted
   butter, room temperature

1 cup firmly packed brown sugar

1 cup creamy peanut butter

2 large eggs

1 teaspoon vanilla extract

24 to 30 square chocolate candies,
   such as Hershey's Bliss

Confectioners' sugar, for rolling (optional)

1 Mix the flour, baking powder, and salt together in a medium-size bowl; set aside.

2 In the bowl of a stand mixer fitted with a paddle attachment, or in a large mixing bowl, using a handheld electric mixer, beat the butter and brown sugar on medium speed until fluffy. Beat in the peanut butter, then reduce the mixer speed to medium and beat in the eggs and vanilla. Scrape the sides of the bowl and continue beating until well mixed.

3 By hand, stir in the flour mixture. Chill the dough for 1 hour, or until you are ready to use it.

4 Preheat the oven to 350°F and place a rack in the center. Line two baking sheets with nonstick foil or parchment paper.

5 Scoop up tablespoonfuls of dough and mold each around a candy, hiding the candy the best you can. Arrange 2½ inches apart on the prepared baking sheets. Bake one sheet at a time for 12 to 14 minutes, or until the edges are lightly browned and the cookies look done. Transfer to a wire rack and let cool slightly, and then roll in confectioners' sugar, if desired.

Hunt for Happiness Week

Declared by Pamela Gail Johnson, author of *Don't Even Think of Raining on My Parade: Adventures of the Secret Society of Happy People*, January 16 through 22 is Hunt for Happiness Week—a week dedicated to seeking out things that give pleasure. Tips for celebrating include cultivating positive relationships, finding a new hobby, looking for humor in situations, and eating mood-enhancing chocolate.

Other Events on This Day:
National Popcorn Day

The discovery of cheese may have been a happy accident. Someone left the milk out, the vessel that contained the milk just happened to be made out of animal stomach, and the rennet from the stomach lining caused coagulation. The very hungry person who tasted the coagulated milk thought, "Not bad!" and went on to refine it—and thus began the art of cheese making. Today we have over five hundred recognized varieties of cheese, and the most popular of all is Cheddar.

Other Events on This Day:
**Penguin Awareness Day,
Meet the Beatles released
in 1964**

Cheddar Cheese Cookies

MAKES 72

1 cup (8 ounces) unsalted butter, room temperature
**2 cups freshly grated sharp Cheddar
    cheese (see Baker's Notes)**
¾ teaspoon salt
¼ teaspoon cayenne
¼ teaspoon garlic powder
2 cups (9 ounces) all-purpose flour
1 cup crispy rice cereal, such as Rice Krispies
72 pecan halves
Paprika, for dusting (optional)

1 Preheat the oven to 350°F and place a rack in the center. Have ready two ungreased baking sheets.

2 In the bowl of a stand mixer fitted with a paddle attachment or in a large mixing bowl, using a handheld electric mixer, beat together the butter and cheese on medium speed. As you beat, the cheese should soften and the mixture should turn orange. Beat in the salt, cayenne, and garlic powder. Blend the flour and cereal into the butter mixture.

3 Pinch off small pieces and shape into 1-inch balls. Arrange 2 inches apart on the baking sheets, and with a fork, gently make a crisscross pattern on each ball, flattening the dough slightly. Stick a pecan half in the center of each. Bake one sheet at a time for 10 to 12 minutes, then transfer to a wire rack to cool completely. Dust with paprika, if you feel like it.

Baker's Notes: Some Southern ladies make cheese straws, but my grandmother, Bessie, made her straws as rounds and stuck a pecan half in the center. For the best results, use freshly grated full-fat or premium Cheddar cheese. I've tried it with pre-grated Cheddar and the cheese just doesn't melt into the dough as it should. If you use salted butter, be sure to omit the added salt.

Caramel Nut Bars MAKES 32

CRUST

12 tablespoons (6 ounces) unsalted
butter, room temperature

½ teaspoon salt

¾ cup firmly packed light brown sugar

1 large egg

1½ cups (6.8 ounces) all-purpose flour

1 cup old-fashioned oats

TOPPING

1 (14-ounce) package caramel bits
(or unwrapped caramels)

⅓ cup half-and-half

1¼ cups lightly salted mixed nuts, roughly chopped

1 cup semisweet or dark chocolate chips

1 Preheat the oven to 350°F and place a rack in the center. Line a 9 by 13-inch metal pan with nonstick foil, or line it with regular foil and spray the foil with flour-added baking spray.

2 **Make the crust:** In the bowl of a stand mixer fitted with a paddle attachment, or in a large mixing bowl, using a handheld electric mixer, beat the butter, salt, and brown sugar on medium speed until creamy. Reduce the mixer speed to medium-low and beat in the egg. Stir in the flour and oats. With wet fingers, press the mixture into the baking pan and bake for 16 to 18 minutes, or until the crust appears fully set and is golden brown around the edges.

3 **Make the topping:** Combine the caramels and half-and-half in a small saucepan and cook over low heat, stirring constantly, until the caramels are melted. Pour over the crust. Sprinkle the nuts over the caramel. Sprinkle the chocolate chips over the nuts. Let cool in the pan for about 20 minutes, then chill until cold. Lift from the pan, set on a cutting board, and cut into thirty-two bars.

Squirrel Appreciation Day

These are in honor of the squirrels that live in our backyard and provide hours of entertainment for our dogs. Created by wildlife rehabilitator Christy Hargrove of Asheville, North Carolina, Squirrel Appreciation Day is a day to take the time to learn something about these agile, adaptable, and decidedly cute animals.

Other Events on This Day: **National Hugging Day, Clam Chowder Day**

Fact: There are more than three hundred species of squirrel and they are found in every continent except Antarctica and Australia.

National Blonde Brownie Day

Its origin is unknown, but today is National Blonde Brownie Day—your day to bake and enjoy the great American blondie.

Traditional brownies were all the rage in the early 1900s, but their chocolate-free cousins were around long before that. Blondies are perfect for packing in lunchboxes, but also look elegant on a plate, topped with ice cream and caramel sauce.

Other Events on This Day:
Answer Your Cat's Question Day

Kentucky Blondies MAKES 32

2 cups (9 ounces) unbleached all-purpose flour

1½ teaspoons baking powder

½ teaspoon salt

1 cup (8 ounces) unsalted butter

2 cups firmly packed brown sugar

2 large eggs

2 teaspoons vanilla extract

1 tablespoon Kentucky bourbon or apple
    juice, plus more for brushing on top

1 cup bittersweet chocolate chips

1 cup pecans, toasted and coarsely chopped

1 Preheat the oven to 350°F and place a rack in the center. Line a 9 by 13-inch metal pan with nonstick foil, or line it with regular foil and spray the foil with flour-added baking spray.

2 Mix the flour, baking powder, and salt together in a medium-size bowl; set aside.

3 In a large, microwave-safe mixing bowl, microwave the butter on high for 1 minute, or until it is completely melted and very hot. With a mixing spoon, beat together the melted butter and brown sugar. Let the mixture cool for 10 minutes, and then gently beat or whisk in the eggs, vanilla, and bourbon. Stir the flour mixture into the batter. Let the batter cool if it is still warm, and then stir in the chocolate chips and pecans.

4 Spread the batter in the pan and bake for about 35 minutes, or until golden and the edges start to pull away from the sides of the pan. Let cool in the pan for 1 hour or until completely cool. If desired, brush the top with extra bourbon. Grasp the foil, transfer to a cutting board, and cut into thirty-two squares. For a cleaner cut, chill for about 2 hours before cutting.

Baker's Notes: I prefer dense, nut-filled, noncakey blondies served at room temperature and brushed with a little extra bourbon.

No-Bake Peanut Butter Pie Bites MAKES 64

CRUST

1¼ cups chocolate cookie crumbs, such
    as Oreos (see Baker's Notes)

4 tablespoons (2 ounces) unsalted butter, melted

FILLING

4 ounces cream cheese, softened

½ cup confectioners' sugar

¼ cup creamy peanut butter

1 tablespoon whole or 2% milk

TOPPING

¼ cup heavy cream

3 ounces semisweet chocolate, chopped

Coarsely chopped salted peanuts, for garnishing

1 Line an 8-inch square pan with nonstick foil, or line it with regular foil and spray the foil with flour-added baking spray.

2 **Make the crust:** Stir the crumbs and butter together in a medium-size mixing bowl. Press tightly into the bottom of the prepared pan. Place the pan in the freezer for about 20 minutes to make a firm crust.

3 **Meanwhile, make the filling:** In a medium-size bowl, using a handheld electric mixer on medium speed, or by hand, beat the cream cheese and confectioners' sugar until smooth. Beat in the peanut butter and milk. Spread this mixture over the frozen crust. Chill in the refrigerator for about an hour, or until the peanut butter layer is firm.

4 **Make the topping:** In a saucepan, heat the cream just until it begins to simmer. Remove from the heat and add the chocolate. Let sit for about a minute, and then stir until the chocolate is melted and the mixture is very smooth. If the mixture is very hot, let it cool for about 5 minutes. Carefully spoon the chocolate over the peanut butter layer. If desired, sprinkle the top with chopped peanuts. Return the pan to the refrigerator and chill until set.

National Pie Day

Pie is so important to Americans that we have our own Pie Council, an organization dedicated to raising the enjoyment and consumption of pies. In fact, it was the Pie Council who declared this day a holiday. The goal, says the council, is to "share the warmth of the ultimate comfort food by giving the gift of pie to a friend or neighbor. Your generosity will be long remembered."

Other Events on This Day: **Measure Your Feet Day, National Hand Writing Day**

5 When ready to serve, grasp the foil, lift from the pan, set on a cutting board, and trim the edges with a chef's knife. Cut into sixty-four squares.

Baker's Notes: Because they are so rich, I cut these no-bake bars very small and serve them in miniature cupcake liners. For the chocolate cookie crumbs, I use whole chocolate sandwich cookies, filling and all, ground into crumbs.

National Compliment Day

National Compliment Day was started in 1998 by Kathy Chamberlin and Debby Hoffman. Praise and admiration go a long way in making both the receiver and the giver feel good, so imagine what would happen if we all gave two to five people a compliment on this day.

To reinforce the sincerity of your compliment, serve it up with the cookie of your choice and maybe you'll get a compliment back. Not that you're fishing for one . . .

Other Events on This Day:
Beer Appreciation Day, Eskimo Pie Patent Day

Fishing for Compliments Cookies MAKES ABOUT 24

1⅓ **cups (6 ounces) all-purpose flour**

2 **tablespoons cornstarch**

½ **teaspoon baking soda**

½ **teaspoon salt**

8 **tablespoons (4 ounces) unsalted butter, room temperature**

½ **cup lightly packed light brown sugar**

½ **cup granulated sugar**

2 **tablespoons heavy cream**

1 **large egg**

1 **teaspoon vanilla extract**

½ **cup lightly salted cashews**

1 **cup goldfish pretzels**

2 **ounces white chocolate, chopped**

1 Preheat the oven to 375°F and place a rack in the center. Have ready two ungreased baking sheets.

2 Mix the flour, cornstarch, baking soda, and salt together in a medium-size bowl; set aside.

3 In the bowl of a stand mixer fitted with a paddle attachment, or in a large mixing bowl, using a handheld electric mixer, beat the butter and both sugars on medium speed until light and creamy. Beat in the cream. Add the egg and continue beating on high speed for 30 seconds. Add the vanilla. By hand or using lowest speed of the mixer, stir in the flour mixture. Stir in the cashews, goldfish, and white chocolate.

4 Drop rounded teaspoonfuls of dough 2½ inches apart onto the baking sheets. Bake one sheet at a time for 7 to 9 minutes, or until the edges are browned and the centers appear set. Let cool on the baking sheets for about 4 minutes, then transfer to a wire rack to cool completely.

Dr. Keen's Scottish Shortbread

MAKES ONE 10 BY 15-INCH PAN

3½ cups (1 pound) all-purpose flour

¾ scant cup (4 ounces) rice flour

1 cup plus 2 tablespoons granulated
    sugar, plus more for sprinkling

½ teaspoon ground ginger

2 cups (1 pound) salted butter (see Baker's Notes)

1 teaspoon vanilla extract

1 Preheat the oven to 375°F and place a rack in the center. Grease and flour a 10 by 15-inch inch pan with rims at least ½ inch tall.

2 Mix the flour, rice flour, sugar, and ginger together in a large mixing bowl; set aside.

3 In a microwave-safe mixing bowl or cup, microwave the butter on high for 30 seconds, or until melted. Alternatively, melt it in a saucepan set over medium heat. Mix the vanilla with the melted butter. Add the butter to the flour mixture and stir with a wooden spoon until the flour is coated in butter. Allow the mixture to rest for about 10 minutes. Press the flour mixture into the prepared pan, packing it tightly to cover all nooks and crannies. Use a knife to flatten the top, making sure it's even. Sprinkle the top with sugar and bake for 10 minutes at 375°F.

4 Reduce the oven temperature to 350°F and bake the shortbread for another 18 to 20 minutes. Remove from the oven when golden brown all over. Use a knife or pizza cutter to cut through the shortbread to make rows about 1 inch wide down the length of the pan. Cut across these, spacing about 2 inches apart, to make shortbread fingers.

JANUARY 25

Robert Burns's Birthday

Robert Burns, the national poet of Scotland, was born on this day in 1759. A pioneer in the romantic, socialist, and liberalism movements, he wrote lighthearted poems with political undertones and symbols of Scottish nationalism, one of his most famous being "Address to a Haggis," which is recited at Scottish celebrations while bagpipes play and the dish is served. This recipe is from my friends, the Keens, who make large batches of shortbread for Christmas. Perfected through the years by the Keen family, the secret to the light, ethereal texture is rice flour.

Other Events on This Day:
National Irish Coffee Day, Dinner Party Day, Opposite Day

With the fork, prick holes all over the fingers. Transfer the pan to a cool place and allow it to cool completely.

Baker's Notes: Good-quality butter is a key ingredient, so use a top-shelf brand and don't even think about making this with margarine. I'm in the habit of using unsalted butter, but Dr. Keen makes his with salted and I wanted to stay true to the recipe. The Keens make large batches and share them with all their friends, but if you want a small batch for the family or whoever stops by, you can halve the recipe and make it in a 9-inch square metal pan.

JANUARY 26

Australia Day

It's Australia Day, mate! Commemorating the first settlement at Port Jackson in Sydney, Australia Day is a federal holiday celebrating Australian achievement, culture, and history. Festivities include public fireworks, a televised ceremony in Canberra saluting the Australians of the year, and citizenship ceremonies welcoming those who have been granted Australian citizenship. This recipe is from my friend Jesse in Melbourne, and I love it because it's simple and always results in a perfect, tight crumbed sponge.

Other Events on This Day:
National Peanut Brittle Day, Michigan joined the Union in 1837

Lamingtons MAKES 16

CAKE
3 large eggs, room temperature
7 tablespoons granulated sugar
⅛ teaspoon salt
½ teaspoon vanilla extract
¾ cup (3.4 ounces) all-purpose flour, sifted twice
2 tablespoons (1 ounce) unsalted butter, melted and cooled
⅓ cup raspberry or apricot preserves, room temperature

CHOCOLATE COATING
12 tablespoons (6 ounces) unsalted butter
12 ounces semisweet or dark chocolate, chopped
½ cup sweetened flaked or shredded coconut, for coating

1 Preheat the oven to 350°F and place a rack in the center. Line a 9-inch square metal pan with nonstick foil.

2 **Make the cake:** Place the eggs and sugar in the bowl of a stand mixer fitted with a whisk attachment. Beat on high speed for 8 minutes, or until thick, pale, and almost tripled in volume. Beat in the salt and vanilla.

3 Sift the flour for the third time over the mixture and fold in with a scraper or large spoon. Stir in the melted butter.

4   Pour the mixture into the prepared pan and bake for about 25 minutes, or until the cake is golden. Let it cool completely in the pan, then grasp the foil, lift from the pan, place on a cutting board, and cut the square horizontally so that you have two layers.

5   Spread preserves between the cut layers, stack the layers, then wrap tightly in plastic wrap or foil and put the cake in the freezer for 2 hours or until frozen. Make the chocolate coating before removing the cake from the freezer.

6   **Make half of the chocolate coating:** In a 2-cup microwave-safe measuring cup or in a deep microwave-safe bowl, heat half of the butter for 1 minute or until melted. Add half of the chocolate to the melted butter and stir until the chocolate melts from the heat of the butter. When the chocolate is no longer melting, return the measuring cup or bowl to the microwave and heat at 50 percent power, stirring every 20 seconds, until the mixture is smooth and all the chocolate is melted. Alternatively, you may make the whole batch of chocolate coating by melting the butter and chocolate together in the top of a double boiler.

7   Unwrap the frozen cake and set it on a cutting board. Using a large serrated knife, cut the cake into sixteen squares. Place the frozen cake squares on a wire rack placed over a foil-lined baking pan, then spoon chocolate coating over the squares, brushing down the sides to cover completely. Sprinkle with coconut and transfer the coated cakes to a baking pan lined with nonstick foil or parchment paper. When you run out of chocolate coating, make more using the remaining butter and chocolate. Chill the squares until set.

Baker's Notes: For best results, weigh your ingredients. Perfect sponge cakes are the result of precision and careful attention to detail, but having a scale is half the battle. A stand mixer fitted with a whisk attachment makes it easy to whip the egg and sugar mixture to its full volume, but a handheld mixer may also be used. The triple sifting ensures the flour will be light and not weigh down the eggs, while freezing the cake makes it easy to handle as you coat it with a mixture of melted butter and chocolate (as opposed to the traditional sugar and cocoa icing). You can make the chocolate coating all at once, but I find it easier to work with in small batches.

JANUARY 27

Chocolate Cake Day

Its origin is unknown, but Chocolate Cake Day is a holiday you just don't question. Americans love it, and we've perfected it over the years, as evidenced by its evolution. In the early 1800s, an American chocolate cake was usually a spice or vanilla cake meant to be accompanied by a chocolate beverage, such as cocoa. As years went by and baking ingredients were more readily available, bakers began to improvise, creating variations, including the richer and more chocolate-packed devil's food cake; mayonnaise cake; and chocolate cakes made with beets, sauerkraut, avocado, and pureed prunes. There's still nothing better than chocolate cake, except maybe chocolate cake in cookie form.

Other Events on This Day:
Thomas Edison patented the incandescent lamp in 1880

Chocolate Whoopie Pies   MAKES 24

COOKIES

1¾ cups (7.9 ounces) all-purpose flour

½ teaspoon salt

1½ teaspoons baking soda

½ teaspoon baking powder

¾ cup unsweetened natural cocoa powder

4 tablespoons (2 ounces) unsalted
      butter, room temperature

¼ cup (1.7 ounces) shortening

1 cup firmly packed light brown sugar

1 large egg

1 teaspoon vanilla extract

1 cup buttermilk

FILLING

1 cup (8 ounces) unsalted butter, room temperature

2 cups confectioners' sugar

1 (7.5-ounce) jar marshmallow crème,
      such as Marshmallow Fluff

2 teaspoon vanilla extract

1 Preheat the oven to 400°F and place one rack in the center and another in the lower third. Have ready two unlined, ungreased baking sheets. This is critical so the cookies don't spread too much.

2 **Make the cookies:** Mix the flour, salt, baking soda, baking powder, and cocoa powder together in a medium-size bowl; set aside.

3 Combine the butter and shortening in a large mixing bowl and beat with a handheld electric mixer on medium

speed until creamy. Add the brown sugar, increase mixer speed to high and beat until light and fluffy. Beat in the egg and vanilla. Using a heavy-duty scraper or large mixing spoon, add the buttermilk and flour mixture alternately, stirring until mixed. You should have a thick batter rather than a dough.

4 Drop heaping tablespoons of batter, spacing about 2½ inches apart, onto the ungreased baking sheets, twelve equal-size mounds per sheet. Bake on the center and lower racks for 11 minutes, rotating the sheets halfway through the baking process. Let cool on the baking sheets for a few minutes, then transfer to a wire rack to cool completely.

5 **Make the filling:** Beat the butter with an electric mixer until smooth. Stir in the confectioners' sugar until incorporated. Beat until smooth. Beat in the marshmallow crème and vanilla until light and fluffy, 2 to 3 minutes.

6 Drop generously rounded tablespoonfuls of filling onto twelve of the cookies. Cap with the remaining cookies.

Raspberry Thumbprint Scones MAKES 16

SCONES

6 tablespoons granulated sugar

1 teaspoon lemon zest

1 teaspoon orange zest

2 cups (9 ounces) all-purpose flour

1 tablespoon baking powder

½ teaspoon salt

3 tablespoons (1.5 ounces) cold unsalted butter, cut into chunks

1 large egg yolk

1 cup heavy or whipping cream, plus a little extra for brushing

¼ teaspoon vanilla extract

⅓ to ½ cup raspberry preserves, preferably seedless

JANUARY 28

Pride and Prejudice Published

On this day in 1813, *Pride and Prejudice* was published anonymously in England. Jane Austen began writing it in 1796 under the title *First Impressions*, submitted it to a publisher a year later, and was rejected. She continued to work on it off and on over the years until, finally, a publisher agreed to publish it as a three-volume set. The first edition sold out rapidly. Flash forward to October 2010, when a first edition was sold at Sotheby's London for a record £139,250.

In honor of the fact that tea time was one of Jane Austen's favorite rituals, not to mention the fact that January is National Tea Month, here's a treat that suits the occasion.

Other Events on This Day:
National Blueberry Pancake Day, National Kazoo Day

ICING

1 tablespoon (0.5 ounce) unsalted butter, melted

1 cup confectioners' sugar

1 teaspoon freshly squeezed lemon juice

1 tablespoon freshly squeezed orange juice

1 to 2 teaspoons whipping cream

1 Preheat the oven to 400°F and place a rack in the center. Line a baking sheet with nonstick foil or parchment.

2 **Make the scones:** In the bowl of a food processor, mix the sugar with the lemon and orange zest and pulse until you have a very fragrant sugar. Add the flour, baking powder, and salt to the sugar mixture and pulse to mix. Add the butter and pulse until the mixture is coarse.

3 Whisk the egg yolk, cream, and vanilla together in a bowl and add to the food processor. Process just until the mixture comes together, then transfer to a large, flat surface dusted with flour.

4 Knead once or twice to bring all the dough together, then divide the dough in half and shape each half into a rectangle about 6 by 3 inches. Cut each rectangle horizontally so that you have four squares, and then cut each square diagonally so that you have eight triangles. And finally, cut those triangles in half for a total of sixteen mini triangles. Arrange about 2 inches apart on the prepared baking sheet, and, with your finger, make an indentation in the center of each. Fill the indentation with preserves.

5 Brush the scones lightly with extra cream if you like, then bake for 14 minutes, or until the scones are nicely browned. Transfer to a wire rack and let cool completely.

6 **Make the icing:** Mix the butter and confectioners' sugar together in a small bowl or 2-cup Pyrex measuring cup; stir in the lemon juice, orange juice, and cream until you get a smooth icing that's a good consistency for drizzling. Drizzle the icing decoratively over the scones.

Baker's Note: I make them in a food processor, but they can also be prepared in a mixing bowl. Just cut the butter in with a pastry cutter or your fingers.

Pecan Dainties MAKES ABOUT 36

1 large egg white
1 cup firmly packed light brown sugar
¼ teaspoon vanilla extract
1 tablespoon all-purpose flour
⅛ teaspoon salt
1 cup toasted and finely chopped pecans

1 Preheat the oven to 350°F and place a rack in the center. Line two baking sheets with parchment paper or nonstick foil.

2 In a large mixing bowl, using a handheld electric mixer, beat the egg white on high speed until stiff peaks form. Gradually beat in the brown sugar. Stir in the vanilla, flour, and salt, and then stir in the pecans.

3 Drop heaping teaspoonfuls of batter about 2½ inches apart onto the prepared baking sheets. Bake the cookies one sheet at a time for 10 to 13 minutes, or until they appear dry and set. Transfer to a wire rack and let cool completely.

JANUARY 29

National Puzzle Day

Today is dedicated to crosswords, find-a-words, logic problems, and most of all, those thousand-piece puzzles that are impossible to do with a cat in the house, the jigsaw.

This recipe is from the late, great Helen Corbitt who supervised the Neiman Marcus tearoom for many years.

Other Events on This Day:
Salt Awareness Day in the United Kingdom

Fact: The jigsaw puzzle was invented in the mid-eighteenth century by John Silsbury, an engraver and mapmaker who attached a map to a piece of wood, then cut out each country. Teachers used his puzzles to teach geography.

Lone Ranger Premieres

In 1933, *The Lone Ranger* premiered on a Detroit radio station. A hit with children, the show picked up sponsors, including one for a cereal that advertised with the radio show for many years and underwent a name change from Cheerioats to Cheerios. During that period, Cheerios featured special promotions, such as deputy badges in the cereal box and boxes that could be folded into frontier towns.

Other Events on This Day:
National Escape Day, National Inane Answering Machine Message Day, National Croissant Day

Toasted Oat Breakfast Bars MAKES 16

8 tablespoons (4 ounces) unsalted butter

¼ teaspoon salt

3 cups miniature marshmallows

½ cup creamy peanut butter

½ cup nonfat dry milk powder

4 cups toasted oat cereal

⅓ cup dried cranberries

⅓ cup lightly salted or unsalted toasted peanuts

1 Line an 8-inch square pan with nonstick foil, or line it with regular foil and spray the foil with flour-added baking spray.

2 In a large, nonstick saucepan, melt the butter over medium heat. Add the salt and marshmallows and stir until the marshmallows are melted. Stir in the peanut butter and milk powder. Remove from the heat and stir in the cereal, cranberries, and peanuts. Place the mixture in the prepared pan and press down. Let cool completely in the pan, then lift from the pan, set on a cutting board, and score into 16 bars, using a large knife.

First Monkey in Space

On this day in 1961, a chimp named Ham blasted off in the Mercury capsule, reaching a distance of 155 miles. He'd been specially trained to pull levers in response to flashing lights, and he carried out his operations successfully. Though the capsule overshot the flight path, and it took three hours to find him, Ham was safe in his spacesuit and happily accepted an apple and an orange as a reward for his efforts.

Whole Wheat Banana Chocolate Chunk Walnut Cookies MAKES ABOUT 36

2 cups (9 ounces) white whole wheat flour

2 teaspoons baking soda

1 teaspoon salt

12 tablespoons (6 ounces) unsalted butter, room temperature

¾ cup firmly packed light brown sugar

¾ cup granulated sugar

2 very ripe bananas, mashed to make about 1 cup

2 large eggs

2 teaspoons vanilla extract

1 cup old-fashioned oats

¾ cup sweetened flaked coconut

6 ounces semisweet or dark chocolate, cut into
    chunks, or 1 cup dark chocolate chips

1 cup toasted and chopped walnuts

Other Events on This Day:
National Brandy Alexander
Day, Backwards Day, Bubble
Wrap Appreciation Day

1   Mix the flour, baking soda, and salt together in a medium-size bowl; set aside.

2   In the bowl of a stand mixer fitted with a paddle attachment, or in a large mixing bowl, using a handheld electric mixer, cream the butter and both sugars on medium speed for about 2 minutes. Stir in the banana, eggs, and vanilla. Stir in the flour mixture, ½ cup at a time, and then stir in the oats, coconut, chocolate, and walnuts. Chill the dough for 1 hour.

3   Preheat the oven to 325°F and place a rack in the center. Line two baking sheets with nonstick foil or parchment paper.

4   Spoon tablespoonfuls of dough about 2½ inches apart (nine to a sheet) onto the prepared baking sheets. Bake one sheet at a time until golden brown, 12 to 15 minutes. Let cool on the baking sheets for about 5 minutes. Transfer to a wire rack and let cool completely. The cookies taste best when they're completely cooled and the chocolate has solidified.

Banana Pudding Cookies

MAKES ABOUT 42

2¼ cups (10.1 ounces) all-purpose flour

1 teaspoon baking soda

½ teaspoon salt

1 cup (8 ounces) unsalted butter, room temperature

¾ cup firmly packed light brown sugar

¾ cup granulated sugar

1 (3.4-ounce) box instant banana pudding mix

2 large eggs

FEBRUARY 1

National Freedom Day

National Freedom Day was created in 1948 by Major Richard Wright, a former slave who believed a day should be set aside to celebrate freedom and promote peace. In commemoration of the day in 1865 when Lincoln signed a resolution leading to the Thirteenth Amendment, the date chosen was February 1, which also happens to kick off Black History Month. Celebrate National Freedom Day and the start of Black History Month with some soul food. My personal favorite is banana pudding, so here it is in cookie form.

Other Events on This Day:
The First Digital Learning Day Observed in 2012

2 teaspoons vanilla extract

1 cup quick-cooking oats (not instant)

4 ounces white baking chocolate, chopped

20 vanilla wafers, broken, or 8 graham cracker squares, broken

1 Preheat the oven to 350°F and place a rack in the center. Have ready two ungreased baking sheets.

2 Mix the flour, baking soda, and salt together in a medium-size bowl; set aside.

3 In the bowl of a stand mixer fitted with a paddle attachment, or in a large mixing bowl, using a handheld electric mixer, beat the butter and both sugars on medium speed until creamy, scraping the sides of the bowl often. Beat in the pudding mix, and then beat in the eggs and vanilla on medium-low speed. By hand or using the lowest speed of the mixer, add the flour mixture to the batter and blend until it is almost fully mixed in. Stir in the oats, white chocolate, and broken cookies, letting the cookies break a little more as you stir.

4 Scoop up tablespoonfuls of dough and make balls about 1 inch in diameter. Arrange about 2½ inches apart on the baking sheets. Press down slightly so that the tops are even. Bake one sheet at a time for 10 to 12 minutes, or until the edges are nicely browned and the cookies appear set. Remove from the oven and while they are still warm, using the tip of a spatula, gently nudge the edge of the cookies inward to add some crinkles and folds. Let cool on the baking sheets for about 5 minutes, then transfer to a wire rack to cool completely.

Groundhog Cookies MAKES ABOUT 12

1¾ cups (8 ounces) cups all-purpose flour

½ teaspoon baking powder

½ teaspoon salt

⅓ cup unsweetened natural cocoa powder

12 tablespoons (6 ounces) unsalted
    butter, room temperature

¾ cup granulated sugar

1 large egg

1 teaspoon vanilla extract

12 chocolate drops, such as Hershey's Kisses

24 white chocolate chips

12 raisins

1   Mix the flour, baking powder, salt, and cocoa powder together in a medium-size bowl; set aside.

2   In the bowl of a stand mixer fitted with a paddle attachment, or in a large mixing bowl, using a handheld electric mixer, beat the butter and sugar on medium speed until creamy.

3   Beat in the egg and vanilla extract. By hand or using the lowest speed of the mixer, stir in the flour mixture.

4   Transfer the dough to a sheet of waxed paper and divide it in half. Press each section into a ¼-inch slab and cover each section with a sheet of waxed paper. Stack your pressed dough on a baking sheet and chill for about 3 hours, or until very firm.

5   Preheat the oven to 350°F and place a rack in the center. Line two baking sheets with nonstick foil or parchment paper.

6   Remove one slab of cookie dough from the refrigerator. Using a heart-shaped cookie cutter (about 2¾ inches wide), cut the chocolate dough into hearts and arrange the hearts about 1 inch apart on the prepared baking sheets. Repeat with the remaining slab of dough.

Groundhog Day

Groundhog Day celebrates Punxsutawney Phil. Phil lives in a burrow called Gobbler's Knob and every year on February 2, in front of thousands of spectators, he comes out. If he sees his shadow, expect six more weeks of winter. If he does not see his shadow, spring is on the way. His fans, who claim that Phil is only one groundhog and that he gets his longevity by drinking "groundhog punch," contend that he's been making accurate predictions for more than 125 years.

Other Events on This Day:
Candlemas

7   Turn the baking sheets so that your hearts are all upside down. This is the groundhog's head.

8   Slice the chocolate kisses down the center vertically. Place half of each kiss to the side of each heart's point to make ears.

9   For the eyes, on each side of the face, stick a white chocolate chip point side down in the dough, not too far from the ears. Using scraps of chocolate dough, make tiny chocolate balls and stick them into the center of the white chip to make pupils. Use a raisin for the nose.

10 Bake the groundhogs one sheet at a time for about 12 minutes. Let cool on the baking sheets for 10 minutes, then transfer to a wire rack to cool completely.

Lunar New Year

The Lunar New Year begins the first day of the first month of the Chinese calendar, which means it can start as early as January 21 or as late as February 19. Like the Western New Year, the Lunar New Year is about starting fresh, but the Lunar New Year lasts for fifteen days, and each day corresponds to a particular ritual. On the last day, people carry lanterns to a parade, where men do a dance with a dragon made of bamboo, silk, and papers. At home, families hang paper lanterns and wish for peace and prosperity in the New Year.

Chinese Almond Cookies
MAKES ABOUT 48

3 cups (13.5 ounces) sifted all-purpose flour
1½ teaspoons baking soda
¾ teaspoon salt
1 cup (8 ounces) unsalted butter, room temperature
1 cup granulated sugar
1 large egg
¼ cup light corn syrup
1 tablespoon almond extract (see Baker's Note)
¼ teaspoon vanilla extract
48 whole almonds, blanched or with skins

1   Preheat the oven to 375°F and place a rack in the center. Line two baking sheets with parchment paper or nonstick foil.

2   Mix the flour, baking soda, and salt together in a medium-size bowl; set aside.

3   In the bowl of a stand mixer fitted with a paddle attachment, or in a large mixing bowl, using a handheld electric mixer, beat the butter and sugar on medium speed until light and creamy. Reduce the speed slightly and beat in

the egg, corn syrup, almond extract, and vanilla. Using the lowest speed of the mixer, stir in the flour mixture until it's completely incorporated.

4   Scoop up rounded teaspoonfuls of dough and arrange about 2½ inches apart on the prepared baking sheets. Top each cookie with a whole almond. Bake one sheet at a time for 10 to 12 minutes, or until the cookies are browned around the edges. Let cool on the baking sheets for about 4 minutes, then transfer to a wire rack to cool completely.

Baker's Note: A full tablespoon of almond extract gives these sugar cookies the flavor of the popular restaurant-style cookies.

Peanut Butter–Oat Candy Bar Cookies   MAKES 32

8 tablespoons (4 ounces) unsalted
    butter, room temperature

½ cup firmly packed light brown sugar

½ cup granulated sugar

½ cup creamy or crunchy peanut butter

1 large egg

½ teaspoon vanilla extract

½ teaspoon baking powder

½ teaspoon baking soda

³⁄₈ teaspoon salt

1 cup (4.5 ounces) all-purpose flour

1 cup quick-cooking or old-fashioned oats (not instant)

½ cup semisweet chocolate chips (optional)

½ cup (2.07 ounces) cold chopped nougat
    and caramel peanut candy bar, such
    as Snickers (see Baker's Note)

1   Preheat the oven to 350°F and place a rack in the center. Line two baking sheets with parchment paper.

2   In the bowl of a stand mixer fitted with a paddle attachment, or in a large mixing bowl, using a handheld electric

Other Events on This Day: **National Carrot Cake Day, Day the Music Died—RIP Buddy Holly, Ritchie Valens, and J. P. "the Big Bopper" Richardson, who died in a plane crash in 1959**

FEBRUARY 4

Snickers First Goes on Sale

Named after the Mars family's favorite horse, the Snickers candy bar went on sale today in 1930. Made with peanuts, nougat, and caramel coated in milk chocolate, the Snickers bar was second to the Milky Way bar, which was meant to be a candy version of a malted milk shake. Today, the Mars Company website calls Snickers the world's best-selling candy bar.

Other Events on This Day: **Create a Vacuum Day, Stuffed Mushroom Day, J. W. Goodrich introduced rubber galoshes to the public in 1824**

mixer, beat the butter and both sugars on medium speed until creamy. Beat in the peanut butter, then add the egg and beat for about 30 seconds. Beat in the vanilla, baking powder, baking soda, and salt. Stir in the flour, then stir in the oats, chips (if using), and chopped candy bars.

3 Scoop up tablespoonfuls of dough and shape into 1½-inch balls. Arrange about 2 inches apart on the prepared baking sheets.

4 Bake one sheet at a time for 11 to 13 minutes, or until the cookies are lightly browned and appear set. Let cool on the baking sheets for 5 minutes. Transfer to a wire rack to cool completely.

Baker's Note: To get ½ cup of candy bars, you'll need about 1½ full-size candy bars. They're easier to chop when cold.

FEBRUARY 5

World Nutella Day

In 2007, a couple of Americans living in Italy declared today World Nutella Day and encouraged people all over the world to get creative with Italy's popular chocolate hazelnut spread. Based on feedback from social media and blogs, the holiday has caught on.

Created in the 1940s and originally named *pasta gianduja*, the chocolate nut paste was made into loaves and wrapped in tinfoil so it could be sliced and put on bread. Because children were throwing away the bread and eating only the paste, Ferrero made the product spreadable and put it in a jar. The name was changed to Nutella, pronounced "new-tella," in 1964.

Double Chocolate Hazelnut Cheesecake Bars MAKES 16

12 chocolate sandwich cookies, such as Oreos
2 tablespoons (1 ounce) unsalted butter, melted
1 (8-ounce) package cream cheese, room temperature
1 cup sour cream
¼ cup firmly packed brown sugar
¼ cup granulated sugar
½ cup chocolate hazelnut spread, such as Nutella
⅓ cup unsweetened natural cocoa powder
½ teaspoon vanilla extract
1 teaspoon instant espresso powder
1 large egg, plus 1 large egg white
2 tablespoons cornstarch
2 teaspoons hazelnut liqueur (optional, but good)

1 Preheat the oven to 325°F and place a rack in the center. Line an 8-inch square metal pan with nonstick foil, or line it with regular foil and spray the foil with flour-added baking spray.

2 In the bowl of a food processor, process the cookies into crumbs. Add the melted butter and pulse to mix. Transfer the crumb mixture to the prepared pan and press tightly to make a crust. Set aside.

3 Wipe the processor bowl clean and add the cream cheese and sour cream; process until smooth, scraping the sides of the bowl as needed, then add both sugars, the chocolate hazelnut spread, and the cocoa powder, vanilla, and espresso powder; process until well mixed. Scrape the sides of the bowl, then add the egg, egg white, and cornstarch and pulse to mix. Add the hazelnut liqueur, if using, and pulse to mix again. Pour the mixture over the cookie crust.

4 Bake for 35 to 40 minutes. Let cool completely in the pan, then refrigerate for a few hours, or until well chilled. Grasp the foil, lift from the pan, set on a cutting board, and cut into sixteen squares.

Other Events on This Day:
**Chocolate Fondue Day,
Weatherman Day**

Apple Orange Bars MAKES 16

1 cup (4.5 ounces) all-purpose flour
1 teaspoon baking powder
¼ teaspoon salt
¼ teaspoon baking soda
6 tablespoons (3 ounces) unsalted butter
1 cup firmly packed light brown sugar
½ cup unsweetened applesauce
1 lightly beaten egg
1 teaspoon orange zest
1 teaspoon vanilla extract
½ cup toasted and chopped walnuts
Confectioners' sugar, for dusting (optional)

1 Preheat the oven to 350°F and place a rack in the center. Line an 8-inch square pan with nonstick foil.

2 Mix the flour, baking powder, salt, and baking soda together in a medium-size bowl; set aside.

FEBRUARY 6

Saint Dorothy's Day

The Feast of Saint Dorothy celebrates a young girl named Dorothy who was tortured for her Christian faith. On the road to her execution, a lawyer taunted her, saying to "send apples or roses" from the garden of her heavenly home. After her death, an angel appeared, with apples for the lawyer. He ate them, was converted, and died a martyr. Today, Saint Dorothy is the patron saint of brewers, brides, newlyweds, florists, gardeners, horticulturalists, and midwives.

3 In a large, microwave-safe mixing bowl, microwave the butter on high for 30 seconds, or until melted. Whisk in the brown sugar, applesauce, egg, orange zest, and vanilla. Using a spoon, stir in the flour mixture, followed by the walnuts.

4 Spread the mixture in the prepared pan and bake for 30 minutes, or until the edges are browned and the blondies appear set. Let cool completely in the pan. When completely cool, lift from the pan, set on a cutting board, and cut into sixteen squares. Dust with confectioners' sugar before serving.

FEBRUARY 7

The Beatles Come to America

Much to the delight of the three thousand–plus hysterical fans who'd gathered at the airport to greet them, the Beatles touched down at JFK on this day in 1964. Two days later they performed live on the *Ed Sullivan Show* for an estimated viewing audience of 73 million.

In honor of the Fab Four, here's a four-ingredient cookie. One of my all-time favorites, this recipe elevates mundane pantry staples to a treat worthy of serving to a crowd—especially a crowd of school kids. My daughter says these remind her of Nestlé Crunch bars.

Fabulous Four-Ingredient Bars MAKES 36

8 tablespoons (4 ounces) unsalted butter
1 cup semisweet chocolate chips
1 (10-ounce) package marshmallows
6 cups crispy rice cereal, such as Rice Krispies

1 Line a 9 by 13-inch pan with nonstick foil.

2 In a large, microwave-safe mixing bowl, microwave the butter on high for 30 to 60 seconds, or until melted. Add the chocolate chips to the melted butter and stir well. Microwave on high, stirring at 30-second intervals, until the mixture is melted and smooth. Add the marshmallows. Microwave on high for 30 seconds and stir until the marshmallows are completely melted. Stir in the cereal. Transfer the mixture to the prepared pan and spread evenly, pressing down slightly. Let cool and set. Lift from the pan, set on a cutting board, and cut into thirty-six squares.

Soft Trail Mix Cookies

MAKES ABOUT 72 SMALL COOKIES

- 1½ cups (6.7 ounces) white whole wheat or all-purpose flour
- ¾ teaspoon salt
- 1 teaspoon baking soda
- 1 teaspoon ground cinnamon
- 8 tablespoons (4 ounces) unsalted butter, room temperature
- ½ cup unsweetened applesauce
- ¾ cup firmly packed light brown sugar
- ½ cup granulated sugar
- 2 large eggs
- 1½ teaspoons vanilla extract
- 2 cups old-fashioned or quick-cooking oats (not instant)
- 1 cup trail mix (cranberries, raisins, sunflower seeds, nuts, pepitas)

Boy Scout Day

Today in 1910, Chicago's William Dickson Boyce filed papers to create the Boy Scouts of America. With the slogan "Do a Good Turn Daily" and the motto "Be Prepared," the goal of scouting was to build a better society by instilling values and teaching life skills to youth. The Boy Scouts of America celebrated their hundredth anniversary in 2010, and membership has grown to over 4.5 million.

Other Events on This Day:
Kite Flying Day, Molasses Bar Day

1 Preheat the oven to 350°F and place a rack in the center. Line two baking sheets with parchment paper or nonstick foil.

2 Mix the flour, salt, baking soda, and cinnamon together in a bowl; set aside.

3 In the bowl of a stand mixer fitted with a paddle attachment, or in a large mixing bowl, using a handheld electric mixer, beat the butter on medium speed until creamy. Beat in the applesauce and both sugars. Reduce the mixer speed to low and beat in the eggs and vanilla. By hand or using the lowest speed of the mixer, stir in the flour mixture. Stir in the oats and trail mix.

4 Drop rounded teaspoonfuls of dough about 2 inches apart onto the prepared baking sheets. Bake one sheet at a time for 10 to 12 minutes, or until lightly browned around the edges. Let cool on the baking sheets for 3 minutes, then transfer to a wire rack to cool completely.

Cinna-Brickle Cookies MAKES 24

I t's Toothache Day. Ouch. I'm not sure who came up with this "holiday," but just thinking about it makes me want to reach for the ibuprofen. That or candy. I can't decide. Either way, it's a day to think about proper dental care, which means brushing regularly, flossing, taking care of your gums, eating foods rich in calcium, and avoiding chewing tobacco and soda. As for sticky treats, I have this theory that the stickier the treat, the more you'll think about your teeth, and thus, the more likely you'll be to brush them.

Other Events on This Day:
Reading in the Bathtub Day, Bagels and Lox Day

1¼ cups (5.6 ounces) all-purpose flour

½ teaspoon baking soda

½ teaspoon plus a small pinch of salt

8 tablespoons (4 ounces) unsalted
    butter, room temperature

½ cup granulated sugar

½ cup firmly packed dark brown sugar

1 large egg

1 teaspoon vanilla extract

1 cup old-fashioned or quick cooking oats (not instant)

½ cup brickle chips (toffee chips)

¼ cup cinnamon chips, such as Hershey's

½ cup sweetened flaked coconut

1 Preheat the oven to 350°F and place a rack in the center. Line two baking sheets with nonstick foil or parchment paper.

2 Mix the flour, baking soda, and salt together in a medium-size bowl; set aside.

3 In the bowl of a stand mixer fitted with a paddle attachment, or in a large mixing bowl, using a handheld electric mixer, beat the butter and both sugars on medium speed until light and creamy. Reduce the mixer speed slightly and beat in the egg and vanilla, then beat in the oats, brickle chips, and cinnamon chips.

4 Drop heaping teaspoonfuls of dough about 2 inches apart onto the prepared baking sheets. Press down the tops slightly and sprinkle with coconut. Bake one sheet at a time for 8 to 10 minutes, or until lightly browned around the edges. Let cool on the baking sheets for 4 minutes, then transfer to a wire rack to cool completely.

Favorite Cream Cheese Brownies MAKES 16

FILLING

12 ounces cream cheese, softened

2 tablespoons sour cream, room temperature

3 tablespoons granulated sugar

1 teaspoon vanilla extract

1 large egg white, lightly beaten with a fork

BROWNIE BASE

1½ cups extra-dark or bittersweet chocolate chips

1 cup (8 ounces) unsalted butter

1½ cups granulated sugar

3 large eggs, room temperature

2 teaspoons vanilla extract

1 cup (4.5 ounces) all-purpose flour

½ teaspoon salt

1 Preheat the oven to 350°F and place a rack in the center. Line a 9-inch square metal pan with nonstick foil, or line it with regular foil and spray the foil with nonstick baking spray.

2 **Make the filling:** In the bowl of a stand mixer fitted with a paddle attachment, or in a large mixing bowl, using a handheld electric mixer, beat the cream cheese, sour cream, and sugar on medium speed until light and fluffy. Reduce the speed of the mixer and beat in the vanilla and egg white, beating just until mixed. Set aside (see Baker's Note).

3 **Make the brownie base:** Put the chocolate in a medium-size, microwave-safe bowl and melt in the microwave, using 50 percent power and stirring every 40 to 60 seconds. Set aside to cool slightly.

4 In the bowl of a stand mixer or in a large mixing bowl, using a handheld electric mixer on medium-high speed, beat the butter and sugar until creamy. Reduce the mixer speed and add the eggs, one at a time, followed by the

National Cream Cheese Brownie Day

In a perfect world, cream cheese brownies would have their own day. Oh, wait. They do, and it's today. For true cheesecake lovers, these thick and stately bars feature a generous layer of tart cream cheese nestled between two layers of brownies.

Other Events on This Day: In 1863, two of the world's most famous dwarfs, General Tom Thumb and Lavinia Warren, were married.

vanilla and melted chocolate. By hand or using the lowest speed of the mixer, stir in the flour and salt.

5 Scrape all but about 1 cup of the chocolate batter into the prepared pan and smooth it out. Spread the cream cheese filling over the chocolate mixture. Spoon the remaining chocolate batter over the cream cheese mixture. Pull a table knife through the layers of batter with a light lifting motion to create a marbled look.

6 Bake for about 50 minutes. Let cool completely in the pan, then chill for a few hours, or if you have the time, overnight. Lift the foil from the pan, set on a cutting board, peel back the foil, and cut with a chef's knife into sixteen squares.

Baker's Note: You can use the same stand mixer bowl for both batters. Make the filling first and scrape it into a separate bowl. Proceed with the chocolate batter, using the stand mixer bowl. You'll still use two bowls, but you won't have to thoroughly clean all the chocolate from the mixer bowl before mixing the white.

FEBRUARY 11

National Peppermint Patty Day

Peppermint Patty Day celebrates any and all forms of peppermint-flavored fondant enrobed in chocolate. My favorite is the York, invented by Henry C. Kessler for the York Cone Company.

Other Events on This Day: National Make a Friend Day, the first US hospital opened in 1752

One-Bowl Peppermint Patty Brownies MAKES 16

12 tablespoons (6 ounces) unsalted butter

½ cup unsweetened natural cocoa powder

1½ cups granulated sugar

½ tablespoon vanilla extract

2 large eggs plus 2 tablespoons of lightly beaten egg

½ teaspoon baking powder

½ teaspoon salt

1 cup (4.5 ounces) all-purpose flour

12 small peppermint patties

1 Preheat the oven to 350°F and place a rack in the center. Line an 8-inch metal pan with nonstick foil, or line it with regular foil and spray the foil with flour-added baking spray.

2 In a large, microwave-safe mixing bowl, microwave the butter on high for 30 seconds, or until melted. Add the cocoa powder and whisk until smooth, then whisk in the sugar and vanilla. Whisk in the eggs, one at a time. When eggs are well mixed, whisk in the baking powder, salt, and flour. Reserve about 1 cup of batter. Spread the remaining batter in the prepared pan.

3 Arrange the peppermint patties about ½ inch apart in a single layer over the batter. Spread the reserved batter over the patties. Bake for 45 to 50 minutes, or until the brownies begin to pull away from the sides of the pan. Test for doneness by inserting a toothpick in the center. It should come out with moist crumbs, as opposed to batter. Let cool completely in the pan, then chill until cold. Grasp the foil, lift from the pan, set on a cutting board, and cut into sixteen squares.

Baker's Notes: With big chunks of mint, these are for people who are truly crazy about peppermint patties. I make the brownies in an 8-inch pan, stir the cocoa in with the butter before adding to the batter, and always chill the brownies before slicing. The original version, which probably came from Hershey's, called for five eggs, so the "2 large eggs plus 2 tablespoons of lightly beaten egg" is pretty much the equivalent of two and a half large eggs. If you double the recipe, use a 9 by 13-inch pan and five eggs.

Sturdy Gingerbread Men
MAKES 15 TO 20, DEPENDING ON SIZE OF CUTTER

½ cup granulated sugar

½ cup mild molasses

1 teaspoon ground cinnamon

1 teaspoon ground cloves

1½ teaspoons ground ginger

½ teaspoon ground allspice

2 teaspoons baking soda

¼ teaspoon salt

FEBRUARY 12

Lincoln's Birthday

Abe Lincoln, sixteenth president of the United States, was born on this day in 1809. Celebrated by the American people, he is remembered for his voracious reading habits, natural intelligence, and the ambition that took him from a log cabin in Indiana to the White House.

Unlike Thomas Jefferson and Ben Franklin, Abe Lincoln wasn't terribly interested in food and his list of favorites is rather slim. High on that short list was gingerbread, and there are accounts of Lincoln fondly recalling his mother's. In honor of a Lincoln childhood favorite, here's another good ginger cookie.

Other Events on This Day: **Savannah, Georgia, founded by James Oglethorpe in 1733; the catcher's mask invented in 1878**

8 tablespoons (4 ounces) unsalted butter,
    cut up and at room temperature
1 large egg, lightly beaten
3 to 3½ cups (13.5 to 16 ounces) all-purpose flour

1 Place the sugar, molasses, cinnamon, cloves, ginger, and allspice in a 2- to 3-quart saucepan on medium heat. Bring to a boil, stirring often. When the mixture starts to boil, remove from the heat and stir in the baking soda. It will fizz up and become very airy. Stir in the salt and butter until the butter melts. Let cool slightly (about 3 minutes).

2 Transfer the slightly cooled mixture to a mixing bowl and stir in the lightly beaten egg. Add the flour, 1 cup at a time, until the mixture forms a dough. Divide the dough into two equal portions. Wrap tightly and chill until ready to use. The dough is easier to work with when cold; however, you can use it right away if necessary. Sometimes I roll it into two portions as mentioned, but sometimes I just flatten it into a big slab, put the slab on a baking sheet, and place it in the refrigerator to firm up even more before I cut the cookies.

3 When ready to cut, preheat the oven to 325°F and place a rack in the center. Line two baking sheets with parchment paper or nonstick foil.

4 Roll the dough into ⅜-inch-thick slabs and cut out shapes. The cookies thicken during baking, so keep that in mind when you are rolling out the dough.

5 Transfer the cutouts to the baking sheet, arranging them about 2½ inches apart. Bake one sheet at a time for 12 to 14 minutes, or until the cookies appear done. Transfer to a wire rack to cool completely.

Baker's Note: If you like icing on your gingerbread cookies, try the version on page 187 and use any food coloring you wish.

Three-Step Cookies MAKES 40

80 round butter crackers, such as Ritz
About ¾ cup creamy peanut butter
2½ pounds white candy melts or any type of white chocolate you are comfortable melting and dipping with

1 Using the crackers and the peanut butter, make forty little sandwiches.

2 Melt the white chocolate in a double boiler or a microwave-safe dish using a low setting and stirring every 30 seconds. If using candy melts, follow the directions on the package.

3 Dip the sandwiches in the melted chocolate or set them on a wire rack and drizzle the chocolate over the top so that it falls down the sides. Let the white coating set before serving.

Baker's Notes: I still remember the day my mom came home from some event and told me about these amazingly simple cookies made with Ritz crackers, peanut butter, and melted white chocolate. She eventually made them herself and served them with pride, even though she did have some trouble with the dipping process. It takes practice, but if you melt the white chocolate over a steady low heat or low power setting in the microwave, you shouldn't have any trouble. If you're using a new brand of white chocolate or are new to the process of melting it, I recommend melting a small amount in a smaller vessel for a practice test.

Strauss's "Blue Danube" Waltz

Instantly recognizable from carousels, advertising, and movies, Strauss's "The Blue Danube" was first performed on this day in 1867 in Vienna. Composed for a small ensemble of ten to twelve players, the waltz, which had words at the time, was not a success and Strauss is famously quoted as saying, "The devil take it." But he didn't stop playing it. Instead he removed the words and arranged it for a small orchestra to play at the 1877 World's Fair in Paris. It was a smashing success and eventually became world famous. In its honor, here's a cookie you can make in three easy steps.

Other Events on This Day:
Tortellini Day; the last original *Peanuts* strip appeared in the newspaper in 2000 (Charles M. Schulz died the day before)

Valentine's Day

Break out the chocolate, it's Valentine's Day! My favorite candies are truffles, so here's a version of that candy in brownie form.

I created this recipe years ago for a contest. It didn't win, but my friends liked it so much I kept making it. For the instant coffee, I use a brand with large granules such as Taster's Choice or Folgers Instant. If you use a finer ground instant coffee such as Starbucks Via, reduce the amount by half.

Other Events on This Day:
Ferris Wheel Day, Organ Donor Day, Arizona's statehood

Mocha Truffle Brownies

MAKES 48

BROWNIES

2 tablespoons instant coffee granules

2 tablespoons boiling water

1 cup (8 ounces) unsalted butter

2 cups (12 ounces) semisweet chocolate chips

3 ounces unsweetened baking chocolate

⅔ cup firmly packed light brown sugar

½ cup granulated sugar

3 large eggs

2 teaspoons vanilla extract

½ cup (2.25 ounces) all-purpose flour

1½ teaspoons baking powder

½ teaspoon salt

TRUFFLE TOPPING

1 cup (6 ounces) semisweet chocolate chips

1 tablespoon instant coffee granules

½ cup heavy whipping cream

4 tablespoons (2 ounces) unsalted butter, room temperature

1 cup confectioners' sugar, sifted

½ teaspoon vanilla extract

1 Preheat the oven to 350°F and place a rack in the center. Line a 9 by 13-inch pan with nonstick foil, or line it with regular foil and spray the foil with flour-added baking spray.

2 **Make the brownies:** Dissolve the coffee granules in the boiling water and set aside.

3 Melt the butter in a small saucepan set over medium heat. Reduce the heat to low and add 1½ cups of the chocolate chips and the baking chocolate. Stir until melted. Set aside to cool. Alternatively, you may do this step in the microwave by combining the butter, chocolate chips, and chocolate in a large microwave-safe bowl, heating at 50 percent power, and stirring every 30 seconds, until melted.

4 In a large mixing bowl, beat both sugars and the eggs with a handheld electric mixer on medium-high speed for 2 minutes. Stir in the melted chocolate mixture, vanilla, and dissolved coffee.

5 Combine the flour, baking powder, and salt and stir into the batter. Add the remaining ½ cup of chocolate chips and pour into the prepared baking pan. Bake for 20 to 23 minutes and let cool completely in the pan.

6 **Make the topping:** Place the chocolate chips and coffee in a large mixing bowl. Place the cream in a microwave-safe measuring cup and microwave on high for 1 minute, or just to boiling. Pour the hot cream over the chips and stir to melt the chips and dissolve the coffee. Let cool slightly, then chill for about 20 minutes, or just until the mixture is cold. Don't chill for too long or it will become stiff.

7 When the mixture is cold, beat for 2 minutes with a hand-held electric mixer on high speed; the mixture should lighten in color and fluff up a bit. Add the butter, 1 tablespoon at a time, and beat for 1 more minute. Add the confectioners' sugar and continue to beat for 2 minutes. Stir in the vanilla. Spread on top of the completely cooled brownies. Chill the brownies for about an hour, then let them come to room temperature before cutting and serving. As they chill, the icing will harden, but it will soften at room temperature. If you try to cut the icing while firm, it will crack a little. At room temperature, it is soft and trufflelike.

Orange Slice Cookies MAKES 36

2 cups (9 ounces) all-purpose flour

1 teaspoon baking powder

1 teaspoon baking soda

½ teaspoon salt

1 cup (6.8 ounces) shortening (see Baker's Note)

1 cup firmly packed dark brown sugar

1 cup granulated sugar

½ teaspoon vanilla extract

2 large eggs

53

by Crusaders. My favorite gum-drops for baking are the large orange gumdrops known as orange slices—a cross between candied fruit and gumdrops. Interestingly, a serving of three has 100 percent of the daily requirement of vitamin C.

Other Events on This Day:
Singles Awareness Day

1 cup sweetened flaked coconut

1 cup orange slice candies, finely chopped

2 cups old-fashioned or quick-cooking oats (not instant)

1 cup pecans, toasted and coarsely chopped

1 Preheat the oven to 350°F and place a rack in the center. Line two baking sheets with nonstick foil or parchment paper.

2 Mix the flour, baking powder, baking soda, and salt together in a medium-size bowl; set aside.

3 In a large bowl, using a handheld electric mixer on medium-high speed, beat the shortening and both sugars for 2 minutes, or until light and fluffy. Beat in the vanilla. Reduce the mixer speed slightly and beat in the eggs. By hand or using the lowest speed of the mixer, stir in the flour mixture, then stir in the coconut, orange slices, oats, and nuts.

4 Shape the dough into balls about 1½ inches in diameter and place 2½ inches apart on the prepared baking sheets. Press them down to make rounds a little over ½ inch thick. Bake one sheet at a time for 13 to 15 minutes, or until the cookies appear set. Let cool on the baking sheets for about 5 minutes, then transfer to a wire rack to cool completely. These taste better when they are completely cool.

Baker's Note: Vegetable shortening enhances the cookies' hearty, crispy-edged texture. Butter can be substituted, but the texture is not quite as light and the cookies are usually a little flatter.

FEBRUARY 16

The Opening of King Tut's Tomb

While many Egyptologists believed that all the ancient tombs had been found, archaeologist and Egyptologist Howard Carter had a feeling that the teen

Almond Toasts MAKES 24

2 large egg whites, room temperature

¼ cup granulated sugar

½ scant tablespoon honey

⅛ teaspoon salt

½ teaspoon almond extract

¼ teaspoon vanilla extract

½ cup minus 1 tablespoon (2 ounces) all-purpose flour

½ cup unsalted almonds, toasted and coarsely chopped

½ cup mixed dried fruit, such as apricots, raisins, and cranberries

1 Preheat the oven to 350°F and place a rack in the center. Line six muffin cups with paper liners and spray the liners with flour-added baking spray.

2 In the bowl of a stand mixer fitted with a whisk attachment or in a large mixing bowl, using a handheld electric mixer, beat the egg whites on high speed until stiff peaks form. Slowly add the sugar and continue beating until the sugar dissolves and the mixture is glossy. Beat in the honey, salt, almond extract, and vanilla. With a large spatula or spoon, fold in the flour. Fold in the almonds and dried fruit.

3 Spoon the mixture into the muffin cups about three-quarters of the way full. Bake for 20 to 25 minutes, or until the tops are browned. Let the pan cool slightly, then remove the muffins from the muffin cups and pull off the paper liners. Transfer to a wire rack to cool completely, then wrap loosely in foil and chill for about 4 hours, until very cold.

4 Reduce the oven temperature to 200°F. Lay the "muffins" on their sides, and using a large serrated knife, slice them into thin rounds. You should get at least three rounds and one stubby-looking top per muffin. Arrange the rounds in one big layer on a baking sheet and bake at 200°F for 1 hour to 1 hour and 15 minutes, or until dried out. They'll dry out even more as they cool, so if the centers aren't completely firm after the full baking time, take them out anyway. Let cool completely on a wire rack. Store in a tin or in a zipper bag, tightly sealed.

Baker's Notes: This thin, crunchy cookie is a cross between melba toast and mandel bread. I've made lots of variations by simply swapping out the nuts and using different blends

King Tutankhamen was quietly at rest in the desolate, arid Valley of the Kings. Carter searched for seven years, finding nothing. Finally, in November 1922, his team of laborers discovered a series of steps leading down to a sealed door. After months of digging and entering various passages, on February 16, 1923, Carter entered King Tutankhamen's burial chamber.

Other Events on This Day:
In 1968, the first 911 call was made from the mayor's office in Haleyville, Alabama, and answered at the police station.

of dried fruit or trail mix. This is the most basic version, and I've also included chocolate and ginger versions on pages 260 (Chocolate Nut Toasts) and 394 (Almond Ginger Toasts). If you like biscotti or dry cookies, I can almost guarantee you will be coming up with your own flavor combinations once you've mastered the first version. I kept the batch size fairly small because rather than just make one big batch of one flavor, I like to make a small batch of a particular flavor and second and third batches using variations.

FEBRUARY 17

Café au Lait Day

Today is Café au Lait Day, where we celebrate coffee with milk. Not to be confused with *caffè latte*, the Italian version served with espresso and steamed milk, the French café au lait is generally a fifty-fifty mixture of regular brewed coffee and steamed milk.

With or without milk, coffee has a few benefits worth keeping in mind. It's loaded with antioxidants, and the caffeine helps fight headaches by increasing dopamine, a chemical that counteracts pain. It also constricts swollen blood vessels in the brain associated with certain types of migraines.

Other Events on This Day:
Random Acts of Kindness Day

Easy Café au Lait Brownies
MAKES 12 TO 16

BROWNIE BASE
1 (12-ounce) pouch fudge brownie mix plus necessary
    ingredients as directed on the package

FILLING
1 tablespoon heavy whipping cream
1 tablespoon milk
1 teaspoon instant coffee granules
2½ tablespoons (1.25 ounces) unsalted
    butter, room temperature
1 cup confectioners' sugar

TOPPING
1 cup semisweet chocolate chips
⅓ cup heavy whipping cream

1 Preheat the oven to 350°F and place a rack in the center. Line an 8-inch square metal pan with nonstick foil, or line it with regular foil and spray the foil with flour-added baking spray.

2 **Make the brownie base:** Prepare the brownies as directed on the package and let cool in the pan.

3 **Make the filling:** In a small cup, stir together the cream, milk, and coffee to dissolve the coffee. In a medium-size bowl, stir together the butter and confectioners' sugar. Add the coffee mixture and stir well, then beat with a

handheld electric mixer on medium-high speed until very fluffy. If necessary, add a little more cream. Spread this over the cooled brownies and chill for about 30 minutes.

4 **Make the topping:** Combine the chocolate chips and cream in a microwave-safe bowl. Microwave on high for 30 seconds, and then stir until smooth. If the chips are not completely melted, repeat. Spread the melted chocolate mixture over the coffee mixture. Chill for about 30 minutes, or until the chocolate is set. Cut into twelve to sixteen brownies.

Frozen Mousse Balls
MAKES ABOUT 32

9 ounces milk chocolate, or 1½ cups
   milk chocolate chips

1 (12-ounce) tub frozen whipped
   topping, thawed

2 cups vanilla wafer or graham
   cracker crumbs

1 Melt the milk chocolate in the microwave in a large, microwave-safe bowl, using 50 percent power and stirring every 30 seconds, or until the chocolate is fully melted. Let the chocolate cool for about 10 minutes, and then fold in the whipped topping. Cover the bowl and chill for about 1 hour, or until thick enough to handle. Shape the mixture into 1-inch balls and then roll them in the crumbs. Lay the balls on a large, parchment-lined cake pan and freeze for a few hours, or until ready to eat. Serve frozen.

Fact: The name "Pluto" was proposed by an eleven-year-old British girl named Venetia Burney. A mythology enthusiast, Venetia believed the cold, dark planet should be named after Pluto, god of the underworld.

FEBRUARY 18

Discovery of Pluto

In 1930, while working nights in an unheated dome in the Lowell Observatory, Clyde Tombaugh discovered Pluto, and for many years after that it was considered a planet. In August 2006, the International Astronomical Union announced that Pluto would no longer be considered a planet, due to new rules that said a planet must clear the neighborhood around its orbit. Because Pluto's oblong orbit overlaps that of Neptune, it was disqualified. Pluto is now considered a dwarf planet.

Perfect for Pluto Day, here's a cookie that's not really a cookie, but rather a cold, dark treat you can pull out of your freezer. My daughter calls these chocolate mousse in ball form.

Other Events on This Day:
Drink Wine Day, National Battery Day

Crispy Mint Cookies MAKES 36

The National Confectioners' Association says today is Chocolate Mint Day. Not to be confused with Peppermint Patty Day celebrated just last week, today's food holiday honors the chocolate mint in other shapes, including Andes, created in 1921 by Andrew Kanelos. He called his store Andy's Candies, but discovered men didn't like giving their girlfriends candy with another guy's name on it, and changed his store to Andes Candies. The mints have been popular since the 1920s, and are currently part of the Tootsie Roll Industries.

Other Events on This Day:
Battle Creek Toasted Corn Flake Company founded, Edison patented the phonograph in 1878

2 cups (9 ounces) all-purpose flour

1½ teaspoons baking soda

½ teaspoon salt

8 tablespoons (4 ounces) unsalted butter

½ cup vegetable oil

½ cup granulated sugar

½ cup firmly packed light brown sugar

2 tablespoons beaten egg

1 teaspoon vanilla extract

½ cup crispy rice cereal, such as Rice Krispies

½ cup quick-cooking oats (not instant)

36 chocolate mint candies, such as Andes

1 Preheat the oven to 350°F and place a rack in the center. Line two baking sheets with parchment paper or nonstick foil.

2 Mix the flour, baking soda, and salt together in a medium-size bowl; set aside.

3 In the bowl of a stand mixer fitted with a paddle attachment, or in a large mixing bowl, using a handheld electric mixer, beat the butter on medium speed until creamy. Beat in the oil and both sugars until well mixed. Beat in the egg and vanilla. By hand or using the lowest speed of the mixer, add the flour mixture and stir until it's absorbed. Stir in the cereal and oats.

4 Scoop up teaspoonfuls of dough, shape into balls, and wrap each ball of dough around a mint, covering it as best you can without using too much dough. In the end you should get about thirty-six cookies. Arrange about 2½ inches apart on the baking sheets. Bake one sheet at a time for 10 minutes, or until lightly browned all over. Let cool on the baking sheets for 3 minutes, then transfer to a wire rack to cool completely.

Crispy Peanut Butter Balls   MAKES 70

- 3 cups crispy rice cereal, such as Rice Krispies
- 4 Butterfinger candy bars
- 2 cups creamy peanut butter
- 8 tablespoons (4 ounces) unsalted butter, room temperature
- 1 tablespoon vanilla extract
- 1 (1-pound) box confectioners' sugar
- ¼ teaspoon salt
- 1 pound dipping chocolate, or ½ pound white dipping chocolate and ½ pound milk chocolate

1   Line a 9 by 13-inch baking pan or a couple of large plates with nonstick foil or parchment paper.

2   In a resealable heavy-duty freezer bag, crush the cereal with a rolling pin. Repeat with the Butterfinger bars. Combine the cereal and candy in a large mixing bowl. Stir in the peanut butter, butter, vanilla, confectioners' sugar, and salt.

3   Scoop up level tablespoonfuls and roll into balls. Arrange the balls side by side on the lined pan and chill for an hour, or until very firm.

4   When ready to dip, melt the dipping chocolate according to the manufacturer's directions (I use 50 percent power in the microwave and stir every 30 seconds). Using a toothpick, spear a peanut butter ball and dip in the melted chocolate. Let the excess chocolate drizzle off, then place on the prepared baking pan. Repeat with a new toothpick per ball until all the balls are dipped. Let set in the refrigerator or at room temperature.

Baker's Notes: Make an assortment by dipping some in milk chocolate and others in white or dark chocolate.

FEBRUARY 20

Toothpick Day

On this day in 1872, Silas Noble and J. Cooley of Massachusetts were issued a patent on a toothpick manufacturing machine. Working as the Noble & Cooley Company, the two men were already successful manufacturers of military drums and toy drums. The toothpick-making machine allowed a small block of wood to be cut into tiny sticks with little waste.

Other Events on This Day: **Cherry Pie Day, Love Your Pet Day**

Erma Bombeck Born

Erma Bombeck started her journalism career in 1952 with a newspaper column called "Operation Dustbag," an eyebrow-raising topic, considering the fact that housekeeping was considered a serious affair. But World War II changed women's perspectives, and with 75 percent of women in the workforce, Erma's humor struck a chord. After taking a break to care for her family, she returned to journalism. Her newspaper column became syndicated, she wrote several books, spent eleven years on *Good Morning America*, and in 1978 was appointed to the President's Advisory Council for Women. A staunch supporter of the Equal Rights Amendment, Erma championed equality for women while maintaining her advocacy for housewives. Erma Bombeck died on April 22, 1996. In honor of her birthday and the title of one of her most famous books, here's a cherry-inspired biscotti recipe.

Other Events on This Day:
National Sticky Bun Day, Alka-Seltzer introduced in 1931, Lucy Hobbs became the first American woman to graduate from dental school in 1866

Cherry Coconut Pecan Biscotti MAKES 20

2¼ cups (10.1 ounces) all-purpose flour

½ teaspoon salt

1½ teaspoons baking powder

8 tablespoons (4 ounces) unsalted butter, room temperature

¾ cup granulated sugar

2 large eggs

½ teaspoon vanilla extract

1 teaspoon almond extract

½ cup chopped maraschino or dried cherries

¾ cup toasted pecans, chopped

1 Preheat the oven to 350°F and place a rack in the center. Line a large baking sheet with nonstick foil or parchment paper.

2 Mix the flour, salt, and baking powder together in a medium-size bowl; set aside.

3 In the bowl of a stand mixer fitted with a paddle attachment, or in a large mixing bowl, using a handheld electric mixer, beat the butter and sugar on medium speed until light and creamy. Beat in the eggs, one at a time, beating for 30 seconds after each addition, then beat in the vanilla and almond extract. By hand, stir in the flour mixture until incorporated. Stir in the cherries and pecans.

4 Transfer the batter to the prepared baking sheet and divide it in half. With dampened hands, mold each portion of batter into a log about 8 inches long and 3 inches wide. Place the logs side by side about 6 inches apart on the baking sheet. Bake for 35 minutes. Remove from the oven and transfer the baking sheet to a wire rack. Let the biscotti cool on the baking sheet for about 20 minutes. They don't have to be completely cool, just warm enough to touch comfortably.

5 Preheat the oven to 325°F. Transfer the logs to a cutting board. Using a serrated knife, cut slightly crosswise on the diagonal every ¾ inch. Cover loosely with a sheet of

Seize the moment. Remember all those women on the Titanic who waved off the dessert cart.

—Erma Bombeck

foil to prevent overbrowning and bake for 25 to 30 minutes, or until it is mostly dried out. If the biscotti are still a little tender in the middle, that's okay. They should crisp as they cool.

Baker's Notes: I learned how to make this many years ago before I could afford dried cherries, hence, the maraschino. Feel free to use whatever type of cherries you prefer.

Chocolate-Cherry Sour Cream Bars MAKES 32

BASE

1 (17.5-ounce) pouch oatmeal cookie
   mix, such as Betty Crocker

8 tablespoons (4 ounces) unsalted
   butter, room temperature

1 large egg

FILLING AND TOPPING

1 cup sour cream

¼ cup granulated sugar

1 large egg

½ teaspoon vanilla extract

1½ cups dried sour cherries or cherry-
   flavored dried cranberries

½ cup toasted and chopped pecans or walnuts

½ cup semisweet chocolate chips

FEBRUARY 22

George Washington's Birthday

George Washington was born on this day in 1732. Although he was commander in chief of the Continental Army, president of the United States, and has been called the father of our country, schoolchildren know him as the little boy who took a hatchet to his father's favorite cherry tree and admitted to the deed, saying, "I cannot tell a lie." For that, he earned a hug and the advice that telling the truth was more valuable than a thousand cherry trees.

Other Events on This Day:
Girl Scout's World Thinking Day, National Margarita Day

1 Preheat the oven to 350°F and place a rack in the center. Line a 9 by 13-inch metal pan with nonstick foil, or line it with regular foil and spray the foil with flour-added baking spray.

2 **Make the base:** In a large mixing bowl, stir together the cookie mix, butter, and egg until well mixed, moist, and slightly crumbly. Measure out about 1 cup of the mixture and set aside to use as the topping. Press the remainder into the prepared pan. Bake the crust for 15 minutes. Let cool to room temperature in the pan.

3 **Make the filling and topping:** In a medium-size bowl, mix together the sour cream, sugar, egg, vanilla, and dried cherries. Spread over the baked crust. Crumble the remaining oatmeal mixture over the top, and then sprinkle nuts and chocolate chips over the oatmeal mixture. Return the pan to the oven and bake for 25 minutes, or until the sour cream appears set and the edges are slightly brown. Let cool completely in the pan, then chill for about 2 hours, or until very cold and firm. Lift from the pan, set on a cutting board, and cut into thirty-two squares. Serve cold or at room temperature.

FEBRUARY 23

National Dog Biscuit Day

It's National Dog Biscuit Appreciation Day, so celebrate by buying a box or baking your own. My dog HAL (named after HAL from *2001: A Space Odyssey*) is crazy for pumpkin and these are his favorite. Making them is a lot of fun because you don't have to worry with precise measurements, butter temperatures, or amount of leavenings. If you feel the dough is too soft, throw in more rice flour. If it's too dry, just add water.

Hal's Pumpkin Biscuits
MAKES ABOUT 40

2 cups quick-cooking oats (see Baker's Notes)
1 cup (5.7 ounces) rice flour
2 large eggs
1 cup canned pumpkin (not pumpkin pie filling)

1 Preheat the oven to 350°F and place a rack in the center. Line two baking sheets with parchment paper or nonstick foil.

2 Mix all the ingredients together in a large mixing bowl. If the mixture seems too dry, add a little more pumpkin. If it's too wet, add more oats. Divide into four portions. Press one portion of the dough about ¼ inch thick on a piece of parchment paper or a flat surface. Using a small

cookie cutter, cut out your favorite shapes and transfer them to the lined baking sheets. Bake one sheet at a time for 20 minutes. Turn the cookies over and bake for another 20 minutes. Transfer to a wire rack and let cool completely.

Baker's Notes: Quick-cooking oats work best. If you'd like to see fewer oats mottled in the biscuit, grind them in the food processor before using. These stay fresh for a few days if sealed in a plastic bag, but I recommend keeping them in the freezer, in which case they'll stay fresh at least 2 months.

Peanut Butter Rocky Road Bars MAKES 16

BASE
8 tablespoons (4 ounces) unsalted butter

3 tablespoons unsweetened natural cocoa powder

1 cup granulated sugar

¾ cup (3.4 ounces) all-purpose flour

½ teaspoon salt

2 large eggs

½ teaspoon vanilla extract

TOPPING
¾ cup creamy peanut butter

2 cups miniature marshmallows

⅔ cup semisweet chocolate chips

⅓ cup lightly salted peanuts

Milk or dark chocolate, for melting and drizzling

1 Preheat the oven to 350°F and place a rack in the center. Line a 9-inch square pan with nonstick foil.

2 Make the base: In a microwave-safe mixing bowl, microwave the butter on high for 30 seconds, or until melted. Stir in the cocoa powder and let the mixture cool. When cool, stir in the sugar, flour, and salt and mix with a wooden spoon. Add the eggs, one at a time, and beat with the spoon, and then beat in the vanilla until the mixture

Other Events on This Day:
National Banana Bread Day, Play Tennis Day, Battle of the Alamo began in 1836

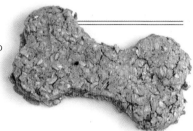

FEBRUARY 24

Introduce a Girl to Engineering Day

As part of National Engineering Week, February 19 through 25, today is Introduce a Girl to Engineering Day, when universities, businesses, and schools are encouraged to show kids in grades K through 12 the creative and collaborative aspects of engineering, spark curiosity about science, and showcase future careers.

Other Events on This Day:
Tortilla Chip Day

is well blended. Pour into the prepared pan. Bake for 20 minutes, or until the top appears set. Let cool in the pan for about 10 minutes.

3 **Make the topping:** Soften the peanut butter for 8 to 10 seconds on high in the microwave and spread it over the brownies. Sprinkle the marshmallows, chocolate chips, and peanuts over the peanut butter layer. Return the pan to the oven and bake for 3 to 4 minutes, or just until the marshmallows puff up. Let cool in the pan. If desired, melt some milk or dark chocolate in the microwave using 50 percent power. Drizzle the melted chocolate over the rocky road topping. Let cool completely and then chill. When chilled, lift from the pan, set on a cutting board, and cut into sixteen squares.

FEBRUARY 25

Chocolate-Covered Nuts Day

The latest news on food and nutrition says there are benefits to eating both nuts and dark chocolate—nuts for their high fiber content and omega-3, and chocolate for its heart-healthy flavonoids. I'm still waiting for a study on the benefits of *dulce de leche* and oatmeal cookie mix.

Other Events on This Day:
Samuel Colt received a patent for the revolving rifle in 1836

Chocolate Chip Pecan Dulce de Leche Bars MAKES 24

8 tablespoons (4 ounces) unsalted butter, room temperature
1 (17.5-ounce) pouch oatmeal cookie mix, such as Betty Crocker
1 large egg
¼ teaspoon ground cinnamon
1 cup dulce de leche, La Lechera Milk Caramel Spread, or thick sundae topping
½ cup toasted and chopped pecans
½ cup semisweet chocolate chips

1 Preheat the oven to 350°F and place a rack in the center. Line a 9-inch square metal pan with nonstick foil.

2 In a large mixing bowl, using a handheld electric mixer on low speed, mix the butter, cookie mix, egg, and cinnamon until you have a soft and crumbly dough. Press about three-quarters of the dough into the bottom of the prepared pan. Bake for 12 minutes, or until just set.

3 Spread the *dulce de leche* over the baked cookie dough. Stir the pecans and chocolate chips into the remaining oatmeal mixture and crumble over the *dulce de leche*. Return the pan to the oven and bake for another 15 to 17 minutes, or until the top is cooked. The bars will be jiggly, but will firm as they cool and chill. Let cool completely in the pan, then chill for 2 hours or until ready to serve. Using the foil as a handle, lift from the pan, set on a cutting board, and cut into twenty-four bars.

Josie's Chocolate Chip Cherry Pistachio Bars MAKES 16

8 tablespoons (4 ounces) unsalted
    butter, room temperature
½ cup firmly packed light brown sugar
½ cup granulated white sugar
1 large egg
¾ teaspoon vanilla extract
½ teaspoon baking soda
¼ teaspoon salt
1½ cups (6.7 ounces) all-purpose flour
1 cup semisweet chocolate chips
¾ cup shelled pistachios, toasted and chopped
⅔ cup dried cherries, chopped

Fact:
Pistachios
produce their
own salt.

1 Preheat the oven to 350°F and place a rack in the center. Line a 9-inch square metal baking pan with nonstick foil.

2 In the bowl of a stand mixer fitted with a paddle attachment, or in a large mixing bowl, using a hand-held electric mixer, beat the butter and both sugars on medium speed until creamy. Reduce the mixer speed slightly and beat in the egg and vanilla. Scrape the sides of the bowl and add the baking soda and salt,

FEBRUARY 26

National Pistachio Day

Pistachios aren't nuts. They're seeds disguised as nuts, or, more specifically, drupes. Recognizable by their deep green color and split shell, pistachios are grown all over the world. Iran produces the most, but California is the second-largest producer globally and grows 98 percent of the pistachios in the United States. The harvest begins in September, when the shells have turned yellow and split with an audible pop. Legend has it that those who hear the popping of pistachios are likely to have prosperity and good luck. Jam-packed with chocolate, fruit, and nuts, these easy bars were created by my friend Josie, in California.

beating until mixed. By hand or using the lowest speed of
the mixer, add the flour and stir until incorporated. Stir in
the chocolate chips, pistachios, and cherries.

3 Press the mixture into the prepared pan and bake for 30
minutes, or until the edges are browned and begin to pull
away from the sides. Let cool completely in the pan. Lift
from the pan, set on a cutting board, and cut into sixteen
squares.

FEBRUARY 27

International Polar Bear Day

International Polar Bear
Day honors a magnificent
animal whose existence is
threatened by climate change.
According to the World Wildlife Foundation, the decrease
in sea ice forces the bears to
have to swim farther to find a
suitable habitat and decreases
their major source of food.
Because their well-being is
a reflection on how global
warming affects the Earth,
scientists have taken a great
interest in studying polar bear
communities in the five nations
where they live: the United
States (Alaska), Canada, Russia,
Greenland, and Norway.

Other Events on This Day:
National Kahlúa Day

Snowballs

MAKES 30 SNOWBALLS OR 24 LARGE BEAR HEADS

**12 tablespoons (6 ounces) unsalted
  butter, room temperature**
**6 tablespoons confectioners' sugar,
  plus ½ cup for rolling**
½ teaspoon salt
2 teaspoons vanilla extract
1½ cups (6.8 ounces) all-purpose flour
1 cup toasted, ground pecans (see Baker's Notes)

1 Preheat the oven to 350°F and place a rack in the center.
Line two baking sheets with nonstick foil or parchment
paper.

2 In the bowl of a stand mixer fitted with a paddle attachment, or in a large mixing bowl, using a handheld electric
mixer, beat the butter and the 6 tablespoons of confectioners' sugar on medium speed until creamy. Beat in the
salt and vanilla. By hand or using the lowest speed of the
mixer, stir in the flour, and then stir in the pecans.

3 Scoop up tablespoonfuls of dough and roll into thirty
balls. Bake for 15 minutes. When cool, roll in the remaining confectioners' sugar.

4 **Variation:** To make your snowballs look like bears, proceed with the recipe, dividing the dough into thirty balls.
Divide each of six of those balls into four equal pieces, so
that you have twenty-four large balls and twenty-four little

dough pieces. For each large dough ball, divide a small dough piece into three parts, and shape two ears and a small snout. Attach these to the larger dough ball to make a polar head shape. Bake as directed and let cool completely. For the nose and eyes, stick on dried blueberries or chocolate mini chips, using a small dab of confectioners' sugar mixed with water.

Baker's Notes: Finely ground toasted pecans are what make these snowballs special. If you have a special nut-grinding attachment on your food processor, that's the way to go. However, I use an old coffee grinder reserved specifically for spices and nuts.

Stir-and-Bake Peanut Butter Protein Cookies MAKES 12

½ cup (2.3 ounces) white whole wheat
  flour or all-purpose flour

¼ cup vanilla-flavored protein powder

½ teaspoon salt

½ teaspoon baking soda

2 tablespoons (1 ounce) unsalted butter, room temperature

2 tablespoons unsweetened applesauce

5 tablespoons turbinado (raw) sugar

1 tablespoon mild molasses

½ teaspoon vanilla extract

¼ cup peanut butter

1 large egg

½ cup semisweet chocolate chips

1 Preheat the oven to 350°F and place a rack in the center. Line a baking sheet with nonstick foil or parchment paper.

2 Mix the flour, protein powder, salt, and baking soda together in a small bowl; set aside.

3 Beat the butter, applesauce, sugar, molasses, vanilla, and peanut butter together in a second bowl. Stir in the egg.

FEBRUARY 28

Linus Pauling's Birthday

Famous for promoting vitamin C, Linus Pauling is also known for figuring out the structure of protein. It started in 1948, while he was in bed recovering from a cold. Tired of reading mysteries and science fiction, he sketched a polypeptide chain on a piece of paper, then spent a few hours folding corners until he'd produced a model of an alpha-helix. Working with Robert Corey and Howard Branson, he continued to refine his model until he was sure it was correct. In 1951 he published a theoretical description of the structure of proteins. In 1954, Pauling was given the Nobel Prize for Chemistry.

Other Events on This Day:
Chocolate Soufflé Day,
Floral Design Day,
Public Sleeping Day

Add the flour mixture to the peanut butter mixture and stir until blended. Add the chocolate chips and stir.

4 Scoop up tablespoonfuls of dough and shape them into neat rounds. If you don't want to bake all the dough at once, just scoop up what you need and chill the rest. The cookies don't spread much or change shape much, so try to make the mounds of dough look nice rather than scruffy. Arrange the mounds evenly apart on the baking sheet and bake for 12 minutes, or until the cookies appear set. Transfer to a wire rack to cool completely.

Baker's Notes: These taste best when they are completely cooled and set. I use vanilla-flavored whey or soy protein powder from the bulk bin at the grocery store.

MARCH 1

Ohio Becomes a State and National Peanut Butter Lover's Day

On this day in 1803, Ohio joined the Union and became the seventeenth state. Coincidentally, it's also National Peanut Butter Day, and peanut butter is the main ingredient in one of Ohio's favorite sweets. Buckeyes are named after Ohio's state tree, a small tree that reaches 30 to 50 feet in height. Considered a good luck charm, it is said to resemble the eye of a buck. Squirrels love eating buckeyes, but humans should stick to the peanut butter type because buckeyes can be toxic to humans, cattle, and horses.

Buckeyes MAKES ABOUT 32

3 tablespoons white chocolate chips
 or white candy melts
1⅓ cups creamy peanut butter
2 tablespoons unsalted or salted
 butter, room temperature
½ teaspoon vanilla extract
1½ cups confectioners' sugar
½ pound dipping chocolate, such as almond bark,
 semisweet chocolate chips, or candy melts

1 Line a baking sheet or two plates with nonstick foil or parchment paper.

2 In the top of a double boiler, or in a microwave-safe bowl, melt the white chips for 1 minute, using low to 50 percent power and stirring every 30 seconds. Make sure not to use too high a heat or they will dry up and become grainy.

3 In a large mixing bowl, using a heavy-duty scraper or large mixing spoon, combine the peanut butter, butter, vanilla, melted chips, and confectioners' sugar. If the mixture is too soft, add more confectioners' sugar. If it seems dry, add more peanut butter.

4 Scoop up tablespoonfuls of dough and shape into equal-size balls. Arrange on the lined baking sheets and freeze until firm.

5 Grease a baking sheet or line it with nonstick foil. Melt the dipping chocolate in the microwave or in the top of a double boiler, according to the directions on the package. Using a toothpick or skewer, dip each ball into the chocolate, leaving just the very top of the ball exposed. Transfer to the prepared baking sheet and leave at room temperature until the chocolate sets.

Baker's Notes: If you have a scale, use it to measure your peanut butter. You'll get an accurate amount (12 ounces) and won't have to worry about messing up measuring cups.

Green Egg Cookies MAKES 18

1 (17.5-ounce) pouch sugar cookie
    mix, such as Betty Crocker
5 tablespoons plus 1 teaspoon unsalted
    butter, room temperature
1 large egg
1 (16-ounce) can vanilla frosting
A few drops of green gel or paste-type food coloring

1 Preheat the oven to 350°F and place a rack in the center. Have ready two ungreased baking sheets.

2 Prepare the cookies as directed on the bag for rolled cookies by mixing together the cookie mix, butter, and egg. Roll out the dough to ¼-inch thickness on a floured surface, and with a round cutter about 2½ inches in diameter, cut out eighteen circles. Arrange the circles 2 inches apart on the prepared baking sheets (nine per sheet). With your fingers, nudge the circles a little bit to make them less symmetrical and more like the white part of a fried egg. Bake one sheet at a time for 7 to 9 minutes (or use upper and lower racks and rotate the pans), until

Other Events on This Day: Salem Witch Trials began in 1692, Pig Day, Fruit Compote Day, Saint David's Day in Wales

MARCH 2

Dr. Seuss's Birthday

Happy birthday, Dr. Seuss! On this day in 1904, Theodor Seuss Geisel was born in Springfield, Massachusetts. Adored by children around the world, Geisel wrote and illustrated forty-four books, including *Green Eggs and Ham*. Dr. Seuss's birthday is also Read Across America Day.

These surreal looking cookies remind me of Dr. Seussland at Universal Studios. They're slightly exaggerated and out of proportion, but kids are crazy for them.

Other Events on This Day: Banana Cream Pie Day, Old Stuff Day

the cookies are lightly browned around the edges. Transfer to a wire rack to cool completely.

3 Shape the leftover dough into eighteen little balls and press down slightly to make circles. These will be the yolks. Bake the yolks for about 5 minutes, or until they appear done. Transfer to a wire rack and let cool completely.

4 Place one or two wire racks over paper towels and set the egg white–shaped cookies on the racks. Spoon about two-thirds of the white frosting into a small, microwave-safe bowl. Microwave on high for 5 to 10 seconds, stirring after 5 seconds, or just long enough that the icing is soft enough to fall off a spoon. Spoon the icing over the egg whites and let it set. Now make the green yolks. Using the green dye, tint the remaining one-third of the icing green. Soften in the microwave on high for 5 to 10 seconds and stir well. Place the yolk-shaped cookies on the wire rack and spoon the green icing over the yolks. Very carefully place a yolk on each white to make the green eggs. Leave at room temperature until the icing sets.

MARCH 3

Florida Becomes a State

On this day in 1835, President John Tyler signed a bill making Florida the twenty-seventh state. Because it is bordered on the west by the Gulf of Mexico and on the east by the Atlantic, some thought the Florida territory should be divided into two states—West Florida and East Florida.

Key Lime Cheesecake Bars MAKES 32

CRUST

12 tablespoons (6 ounces) unsalted butter

½ cup firmly packed dark brown sugar

½ teaspoon salt

1 teaspoon vanilla extract

2 cups (9 ounces) all-purpose flour

FILLING

1 (8-ounce) package cream cheese, softened

1 (14-ounce) can sweetened condensed milk

4 large eggs, room temperature

²/₃ cup key lime juice (bottled is fine)

1 tablespoon lime zest

½ cup (2.25 ounces) all-purpose flour

¼ teaspoon salt

Softened raspberry preserves, for garnishing

Congress decided it should be one, so Florida got both coasts plus the Florida Keys, a.k.a. "the American Caribbean." This particular cookie was inspired by a Key West favorite.

Other Events on This Day:
"The Star-Spangled Banner" adopted as the national anthem in 1931

1 Preheat the oven to 350°F and place a rack in the center. Line a 9 by 13-inch metal pan with nonstick foil, or line it with regular foil and spray the foil with flour-added baking spray.

2 **Make the crust:** In the bowl of a stand mixer fitted with a paddle attachment, or in a large mixing bowl, using a handheld electric mixer, beat the butter, brown sugar, salt, and vanilla on medium speed until creamy. By hand or using the lowest speed of the mixer, stir in the flour. Press the mixture into the bottom of the prepared pan and bake for 18 to 20 minutes. Let cool completely in the pan.

3 **Make the filling:** Beat the cream cheese until creamy and smooth. Add the sweetened condensed milk, eggs, and lime juice and zest and mix on low speed. Stir in the flour and salt. Pour the filling over the cooled crust. Return the pan to the oven and bake for 20 minutes.

4 Let cool in the pan for at least an hour and then chill. If you've lined the pan with foil, grasp the foil, lift from the pan, set on a cutting board, and cut into thirty-two bars. Garnish with the preserves. Store in the refrigerator.

Today in 1791, Vermont joined the Union and became the fourteenth state. Interestingly, this day also coincides with the beginning of Vermont's sugaring season, which begins in either late February or early March, when nights are cold and days are sunny and sap begins to flow. The process of making the syrup involves boiling and evaporating the sap with special equipment. Grade B maple syrup is darker, more robust, and often more expensive, whereas Grade A is lighter.

Other Events on This Day:
Hug a GI Day, Pound Cake Day

Maple Cream Sandwich Cookies   MAKES ABOUT 36

COOKIES

2⅓ cups (10.5 ounces) all-purpose flour

2 teaspoons baking powder

½ teaspoon salt

1 cup (8 ounces) unsalted butter, room temperature

½ cup very firmly packed brown sugar

6 tablespoons pure maple syrup

1 teaspoon maple flavoring

FILLING

4 tablespoons (2 ounces) unsalted butter, room temperature

1 cup confectioners' sugar

2 tablespoons pure maple syrup

Pinch of salt

1   Mix the flour, baking powder, and salt together in a medium-size bowl; set aside.

2   **Make the cookies:** In the bowl of a stand mixer fitted with a paddle attachment, or in a large mixing bowl, using a handheld electric mixer, beat the butter and sugar on medium speed until light and fluffy. Beat in the maple syrup and flavoring until combined. By hand or using the lowest speed of the mixer, gradually stir in the flour mixture. Divide the dough in half, shape each portion into a ball, and flatten slightly. Wrap in plastic wrap and chill for at least 1 hour, or until ready to use. When ready to bake, bring the dough to room temperature.

3   Preheat the oven to 375°F and place a rack in the center. Line two baking sheets with parchment paper or nonstick foil.

4   Roll out one portion of dough to about ⅛ inch thick on a lightly floured surface. Cut out cookies with leaf-shaped cookie cutters or with a 1¾- to 2-inch-diameter circle

cutter, dipped lightly in flour. Arrange about 1 inch apart on the prepared sheets. Bake one sheet at a time for 8 to 10 minutes, or just until the cookies start to brown. Let cool on the sheets for a few minutes, then transfer to a wire rack to cool completely.

5 **Make the filling:** Beat the butter with a handheld electric mixer set on medium-high speed. Add the confectioners' sugar, maple syrup, and salt and beat until smooth.

6 Spread the underside of one cookie with the filling, then top base to base with another cookie. Repeat until all the cookies are sandwiched.

Cherry Chip Cookies
MAKES ABOUT 28

1 cup (4.5 ounces) white whole wheat flour

½ teaspoon baking soda

¼ teaspoon baking powder

⅜ teaspoon salt

½ cup vegetable oil

½ cup granulated sugar

½ cup firmly packed light brown sugar

1 large egg

1 teaspoon vanilla extract

1 cup quick-cooking or old-fashioned oats (not instant)

1 cup extra-dark or dark chocolate chips

¾ cup dried cherries

½ cup almonds, toasted and chopped

1 Preheat the oven to 350°F and place a rack in the center. Line two baking sheets with parchment paper or nonstick foil.

2 Mix the flour, baking soda, baking powder, and salt together in a small bowl; set aside.

3 In the bowl of a stand mixer fitted with a paddle attachment, or in a large mixing bowl, using a handheld electric mixer, beat the oil and both sugars on medium speed until well mixed. Reduce the mixer speed slightly

Beginning of National Cheerleader Week

National Cheerleader Week starts today, so let's recognize cheerleaders for what they really are—dedicated athletes who exercise strength, flexibility, endurance, stamina, and tumbling skills for hours each week. Cheerleaders have their own rigorous competitions at local, regional, and national levels, including the National High School Cheerleading Championship (NHSCC) held every year in Orlando. In recognition of the energy it takes to be a cheerleader, here's a cookie to keep your energy levels up.

Other Events on This Day:
National Cheez Doodle Day

and beat in the egg and vanilla extract. By hand or using the lowest speed of the mixer, stir in the flour mixture. When the flour is incorporated, stir in the oats, chocolate chips, cherries, and almonds. The batter will be moist but slightly crumbly.

4 Scoop up tablespoonfuls of dough and pack each into a ball a little over 1 inch in diameter. Arrange 2½ inches apart on the prepared baking sheets and press down slightly to flatten the tops. Bake one sheet at a time for 12 to 15 minutes, or until the cookies are browned around the edges and appear set. Let cool on the baking sheets for 4 to 5 minutes, then transfer to a wire rack to cool completely.

Baker's Notes: This recipe calls for almonds, but feel free to use whatever type of nut you like. If you find the dough to be too crumbly and can't get it to bind together, add a teaspoon at a time of lightly beaten egg until the dough sticks. In most cases, you shouldn't have to.

MARCH 6

Oreos Introduced

Oreo Biscuits first went on sale today in 1912. Produced in the building that is now New York's Chelsea Market, the cookies came in flavors of lemon meringue and cream and were sold in round containers with glass tops. In 1920, the lemon flavor was dropped, and over the years, the name and design have been altered.

Other Events on This Day: Frozen Foods Day, Chocolate Cheesecake Day, Silly Putty went on sale in 1950, aspirin patented in 1899

Cookie Chunk Brownies
MAKES 16

8 tablespoons (4 ounces) unsalted butter

²/₃ cup plus 3 tablespoons semisweet chocolate chips

1½ ounces unsweetened chocolate

1 large egg, room temperature, plus 2 tablespoons
    lightly beaten egg

1½ teaspoons vanilla extract

½ cup plus 1 tablespoon granulated sugar

¼ cup plus 1 tablespoon (1.4 ounces) all-purpose flour

¾ teaspoon baking powder

⅜ scant teaspoon salt

1 teaspoon instant espresso powder or finely
    ground instant coffee, such as Starbucks VIA

9 chocolate sandwich cookies, broken
    up—not fully crushed

1 Preheat the oven to 350°F and place a rack in the center. Line an 8-inch metal pan with nonstick foil, or line it with regular foil and spray the foil with flour-added baking spray.

2 In a microwave-safe mixing bowl, microwave the butter on high for 30 seconds, or until melted. Add the ⅔ cup of chocolate chips and the unsweetened chocolate and microwave on high for 30 seconds; stir until the chocolate is melted. Let cool slightly.

3 In a large mixing bowl, whisk together the eggs, vanilla, and sugar. Scrape the melted chocolate mixture into the egg mixture and allow it to cool slightly.

4 Stir together the flour, baking powder, salt, and espresso powder and then add to the cooled chocolate mixture. Stir in the cookie chunks and remaining 3 tablespoons of chocolate chips. Pour into the prepared pan and bake for 20 minutes, then rap the baking sheet against the oven shelf to force the air to escape from between the pan and the brownie dough. Bake for 3 to 5 minutes more, or until a toothpick comes out clean. Do not overbake. Let cool in the pan, then chill the brownies thoroughly. Lift from the pan, set on a cutting board, and cut into sixteen squares.

Baker's Notes: Broken cookies add crunch, texture, and flavor to brownies. You can put them in just about any brownie recipe, but they're particularly good in this recipe, which is quite fudgy. It's adapted from a recipe by Ina Garten, who adapted hers from an old restaurant called the Soho Charcuterie. The original recipes were baked in giant batches, but because I bake these so often as a treat for our small family, I scaled it down to fit an 8-inch pan. The brownies are very rich, so you can cut them even smaller if you'd like.

Until the late nineteenth century, the trend in breakfast included eggs, sausage, and other protein-rich foods. Given how our lifestyles have changed, I'm thankful for the innovations of Post, Kellogg, and Perky, who all invented various forms of dry cereal. So happy National Cereal Day! While this holiday is certainly unofficial, March 7 is said to be the date cornflakes were invented.

Other Events on This Day:
Crown Roast of Pork Day, Alexander Graham Bell patented the telephone in 1876

Cereal Cookies MAKES ABOUT 30

½ cup old-fashioned or quick-cooking oats (not instant)

1¼ cups your favorite wheat flake cereal, such as Wheaties or Total

½ cup whole walnuts, toasted

6 tablespoons (3 ounces) unsalted butter, room temperature

½ cup lightly packed light brown sugar

½ cup granulated sugar

1 large egg

1¼ teaspoons vanilla extract

¼ teaspoon baking powder

¼ teaspoon baking soda

¼ teaspoon plus an extra pinch of salt

1¼ cups (5.6 ounces) all-purpose flour

¾ cup semisweet or dark chocolate chips

1 Preheat the oven to 350°F and place a rack in the center. Line two baking sheets with nonstick foil or parchment paper.

2 In the bowl of a food processor, process the oats until fine. Add the cereal and walnuts to the processor with the ground oatmeal and pulse until the cereal is finely crushed and the nuts are fairly well chopped.

3 In the bowl of a stand mixer fitted with a paddle attachment, or in a large mixing bowl, using a handheld electric mixer, beat the butter and both sugars on medium speed until creamy; add the egg and vanilla and beat on low speed just until the egg is mixed in. Add the baking powder, baking soda, and salt; stir well to mix. Scrape the sides of the bowl and stir in the flour. When the flour is incorporated, stir in the cereal mixture and chocolate chips.

4 Scoop up tablespoonfuls of dough and shape into 1-inch balls. Arrange about 2½ inches apart on the prepared baking sheets. Press down lightly to make ½-inch-thick rounds. Bake one sheet at a time for 15 minutes, or until the edges start to brown. Let cool on the baking sheets for 5 minutes, then transfer to a wire rack to cool completely.

Baker's Notes: I make these cookies with Wheaties, Total, or Grape-Nuts Flakes. You can use any flaked cereal, but the sweeter the flake the sweeter the cookie.

Chocolate Almond Shortbread MAKES 48

1 cup (8 ounces) unsalted butter, room temperature

¾ teaspoon salt

½ cup granulated sugar

1 teaspoon vanilla extract

¼ teaspoon almond extract

3 ounces semisweet chocolate, melted and cooled

1 ounce unsweetened chocolate, melted and cooled

2 cups (9 ounces) all-purpose flour

1 cup toasted almonds, very finely chopped

½ cup semisweet chocolate chips

Confectioners' sugar, for rolling (optional)

1 Preheat the oven to 350°F and place a rack in the center. Have ready an ungreased baking sheet.

2 In the bowl of a stand mixer fitted with a paddle attachment, or in a large mixing bowl, using a handheld electric mixer, beat the butter, salt, sugar, vanilla, and almond extract on medium speed until creamy. Beat in the chocolate, and then stir in the flour. Make sure the batter is cool, then stir in the almonds and the semisweet chocolate chips.

3 Shape the dough into 1-inch balls. Arrange 2 inches apart on the baking sheet and press down gently to make ⅜-inch-thick rounds. Bake for 10 minutes, or until set. Let cool on the baking sheet for about 5 minutes, then transfer to a wire rack to cool completely. Roll in the confectioners' sugar, if desired.

International Women's Day

*Y*our friends may not know it, so enlighten them with the fact that today is International Women's Day and bake a batch of cookies to celebrate. If you need a recipe, I have offered you over 350, but here's one more, and it is from my friend, Lisa. It's a very easy chocolate shortbread recipe featuring toasted almonds and chocolate chips. Expect a few recipe requests when you share these cookies. Omit the salt if using salted butter.

Other Events on This Day:
Peanut Cluster Day, Be Nasty Day

The plastic princess made her debut on this day in 1959. Barbie was invented by Ruth Handler, who noticed her daughter Barbara was more interested in paper dolls and make-believe than in mothering baby dolls. Modeled after a racy and ambitious German tobacco shop doll named Bild Lilli, Barbie was redesigned and introduced to little girls at the International Toy Fair in New York. The day of the toy fair marks her birthday.

Other Events on This Day:
Crabmeat Day, Day of Panic

Pretty Pink Melt-Aways MAKES 28

COOKIES

1 cup (8 ounces) unsalted butter, room temperature

½ cup confectioners' sugar

½ teaspoon salt

¾ teaspoon vanilla extract

½ cup cornstarch

1¼ cups (5.6 ounces) all-purpose flour

FROSTING

2 tablespoons (1 ounce) unsalted butter, melted

1½ cups confectioners' sugar

¼ teaspoon vanilla extract

1 or 2 tablespoons milk or half-and-half

2 to 3 drops red food coloring

Red sprinkles (optional)

1 **Make the cookies:** In the bowl of a stand mixer fitted with a paddle attachment, or in a large mixing bowl, using a handheld electric mixer, beat the butter and confectioners' sugar on medium speed until creamy. Beat in the salt and vanilla. By hand, stir in the cornstarch and flour. Chill the dough for about 30 minutes, or until easy to handle.

2 Preheat the oven to 350°F and place a rack in the center. Have ready two ungreased baking sheets.

3 Scoop up rounded teaspoonfuls of dough and shape into 1-inch balls. Arrange 2 inches apart on the baking sheets. Bake for 12 to 15 minutes, or until the edges are lightly browned. Let cool for 1 minute on the baking sheets, then transfer to a wire rack to cool completely.

4 **Make the frosting:** Combine the butter, confectioners' sugar, and vanilla and stir until well mixed. Add 1 tablespoon of milk, then add the remaining milk gradually until you get a smooth, drizzling consistency. Stir in the food coloring. Frost the cookies and decorate the tops with sprinkles, if you wish.

Scottish Oat Cookies MAKES 16

1¼ cups old-fashioned or quick-cooking
    oats (not instant)

¼ cup plus 2 tablespoons (1.8 ounces)
    all-purpose flour

¼ cup plus 2 tablespoons (1.8 ounces)
    whole wheat pastry flour

½ teaspoon baking powder

½ teaspoon baking soda

½ scant teaspoon salt

¼ cup firmly packed light brown sugar

2 tablespoons granulated sugar

9 tablespoons (4.5 ounces) cold unsalted butter

½ tablespoon golden syrup or light corn syrup

¼ teaspoon vanilla extract

4 ounces milk chocolate, such as Cadbury

1 Preheat the oven to 350°F, and place a rack in the center. Line two baking sheets with parchment paper or nonstick foil.

2 Process the oats in a food processor until fine; add the flours, baking powder, baking soda, and salt and pulse to mix. Add both sugars and pulse to mix again. Add the butter and process until the mixture is coarse and sand-like. Add the corn syrup and vanilla and pulse some more. The mixture will look very dry.

3 Transfer to a wide mixing bowl and shape into two big balls. Press each ball into a disk and place between sheets of waxed paper. Roll out one of the disks to about ¼-inch thickness. Cut out circles with a round cookie cutter about 2 inches in diameter. Arrange 2 inches apart on the prepared baking sheets. Bake for 12 minutes, or until the edges are lightly browned. Transfer to a wire rack to cool completely.

4 Melt the milk chocolate in a bowl set over a saucepan of barely simmering water. Spoon the melted chocolate over the cookies. When

First Successful Telephone Call Made by Alexander Graham Bell

On this day in 1876, Alexander Graham Bell shouted one of the most famous phrases in history, "Mr. Watson, come here, I want to see you," to his assistant, Thomas A. Watson. It was the first successful communication via telephone. In honor of Bell's Scottish heritage, today's cookie is a Scottish-style oatmeal cookie.

Other Events on This Day:
In 1785, Thomas Jefferson was appointed US minister to France.

the chocolate is partially set, drag a toothpick through it and make squiggly lines in the chocolate. Allow the chocolate to set at room temperature, or quick-set it in the refrigerator.

Baker's Notes: These are dense, crumbly, and crispy rather than chewy. Whole wheat pastry flour is softer than regular whole wheat and can usually be found in the bulk bin at big grocery stores. Omit the additional salt if using salted butter.

MARCH 11

Johnny Appleseed Day

T oday marks the anniversary of Johnny Appleseed's death in 1845. Born John Chapman on September 26, 1774, he was the son of a Massachusetts farmer. In his mid-twenties, Johnny became a nurseryman, and while most people think of him as a rag-tag guy walking the land, spreading apple seeds, he actually built nurseries, hired local managers, and sold trees on credit without pressing too hard for payment. A missionary for the Swedenborgian Church, Johnny went door-to-door seeking company, shelter, and food. He was a vegetarian, never married, and died in his sleep of pneumonia.

Other Events on This Day:
**Middle Name Pride Day,
Lawrence Welk born in 1903**

Apple Chip Oat Cookies
MAKES 32

1½ cups (6.8 ounces) all-purpose flour

1 teaspoon baking soda

1 scant teaspoon salt

1 teaspoon ground cinnamon

½ teaspoon freshly grated nutmeg

¼ teaspoon ground allspice

1 cup plus 2 tablespoons (10 ounces)
    unsalted butter, room temperature

¾ cup firmly packed light brown sugar

½ cup granulated sugar

¼ teaspoon lemon zest

1 large egg

1½ teaspoons vanilla extract

3 cups minus 2 tablespoons
    old-fashioned oats (not instant)

1 tablespoon toasted wheat germ

1 cup walnuts, toasted and chopped

½ cup dried apple chips (see Baker's Notes)

1 Preheat the oven to 375°F and place a rack in the center. Have ready two ungreased baking sheets.

2 Mix the flour, baking soda, salt, cinnamon, nutmeg, and allspice together in a bowl; set aside.

3 In the bowl of a stand mixer fitted with a paddle attachment, or in a large mixing bowl, using a handheld electric mixer, beat the butter and both sugars on medium speed until light and fluffy. Beat in the lemon zest, egg, and

vanilla. Gradually add the flour mixture to the butter mixture, mixing well. Stir in the oats, wheat germ, walnuts, and apple chips.

4 Shape the dough into 32 balls a little over 1 inch in diameter. Arrange about 2½ inches apart on the baking sheets, and press down slightly. Bake one sheet at a time for about 10 minutes, or until the cookies appear set. Let cool for 1 minute on the baking sheets, then transfer to a wire rack to cool completely.

Baker's Notes: These cookies are crisp and hearty, and the crunchy apple chips complement that texture. I like them because they add a subtle apple flavor rather than the strong flavor you often taste in baked goods labeled "apple." You can use store-bought apple chips (found in the chips aisle or dried fruit aisle) or make your own. To make your own, slice unpeeled apples about ⅛ inch thick or thinner (a mandoline does the job nicely), lay flat on a parchment-lined baking sheet, and bake in a preheated 225°F oven for about 3 hours, or until the edges start to brown and curl up. The apple chips will still be soft when you remove them from the oven, but they'll crisp as they cool.

Mint Thins MAKES 48 TO 56

COOKIES

1 cup (4.5 ounces) all-purpose flour

½ cup unsweetened dark cocoa powder, such as Hershey's Dark

⅛ teaspoon baking soda

⅜ teaspoon salt

8 tablespoons (4 ounces) unsalted butter, room temperature

1 cup granulated sugar

1 large egg

½ teaspoon vanilla extract

½ teaspoon peppermint extract

MARCH 12

Founding of the Girl Scouts

On this day in 1912, Juliette "Daisy" Gordon Low gathered eighteen girls from Savannah, Georgia, for the first Girl Scout meeting. Modeled after Lord Baden-Powell's UK Girl Guides, the goal of the US Girl Scouts was to bring girls out of the home and into the community through activities such as hiking, sports, and camping trips. According to Girl Scouts of the USA, more than 50 million US women today are former Girl Scouts.

COATING
12 tablespoons (6 ounces) unsalted butter
12 ounces dark chocolate, chopped

1 **Make the cookies:** In a small mixing bowl, mix together the flour, cocoa, baking soda, and salt. Set aside.

2 In the bowl of a stand mixer fitted with a paddle attachment, or in a large mixing bowl, using a handheld electric mixer on medium-high speed, beat the butter and sugar until creamy. Add the egg and beat for another minute, scraping the sides of the bowl often. Beat in both extracts. Using a mixing spoon, add the flour mixture and stir until fully blended. Divide the dough in half. On a large sheet of parchment paper or nonstick foil, press half of the dough into a slab about ¼ inch thick. Top with a second piece of parchment and place on a baking sheet. Repeat with the remaining dough, pressing into a ¼-inch slab and stacking it on the baking sheet. Set the baking sheet with the dough slabs in the refrigerator and chill for 1 hour or until firm.

3 Preheat the oven to 350°F and place a rack in the center. Line two baking sheets with parchment paper or nonstick foil.

4 Using a 1½-inch round cutter, punch out circles of dough, and arrange them 1 inch apart on ungreased baking sheets. Bake one sheet at a time for 10 to 12 minutes, or until the cookies appear set. Let the cookies cool for about 3 minutes on the baking sheets, then carefully transfer to a wire rack to cool completely.

5 **Make the coating:** When the cookies are cool, line the two baking sheets with parchment paper or nonstick foil and keep them handy. Melt 6 tablespoons of the butter in a large (2-cup) microwave-safe measuring cup. Add half (6 ounces) of the chocolate to the butter and stir to coat, then microwave chocolate and butter at 50 percent power, stirring every 30 seconds, until melted and smooth. Dip the

cookies in the melted chocolate mixture and place them on the prepared baking sheets. Melt the remaining butter and chocolate and repeat until all cookies are dipped. Chill the cookies for about 30 minutes or until the chocolate coating has set. Peel the cookies off the parchment (or foil) and store in an airtight container.

Baker's Notes: I made several versions of these and liked this one best. The key is using dark cocoa powder, just the right amount of peppermint extract (not to be confused with "mint" extract, which is almost always spearmint) and finding the right chocolate for coating. Mild dark chocolate or semisweet chocolate chips are closest to the Girl Scout version. The cookies do spread a bit, so expect your circles to be a little bigger when they come out of the oven.

Earl Grey Tea Cookies MAKES 24

8 tablespoons (4 ounces) unsalted
    butter, room temperature

½ cup confectioners' sugar

⅜ teaspoon salt

½ teaspoon orange zest

¾ teaspoon lemon zest

1 teaspoon Earl Grey tea leaves, finely crushed

2 tablespoons lightly beaten egg

1¼ cups (5.7 ounces) all-purpose flour

⅔ cup pecans, toasted and finely chopped

½ cup sweetened flaked coconut, plus an
    extra ¼ cup or more for rolling

1 In the bowl of a stand mixer fitted with the paddle attachment, or in a large mixing bowl, using a handheld electric mixer, beat the butter, confectioners' sugar, and salt on medium speed for about 2 minutes, or until light and creamy. Add the orange zest, lemon zest, crushed tea, and egg; beat at reduced speed until well blended. Add the flour and stir until mixed. Stir in the pecans and coconut.

MARCH 13

Happy Birthday, Earl Grey

British prime minister Charles Grey, the namesake for the famous tea made with bergamot oil, was born on this day in 1784. There are various stories on how the tea came to be, but the most plausible is that the recipe was given by an envoy from China. Other sources say the Grey family had the tea specially blended by a Chinese mandarin to suit the lime-heavy water of the family estate.

Other Events on This Day:
Ear muffs patented in 1877

2　Divide the dough in half and shape each portion into a log about 2 inches in diameter. Roll each log in extra coconut. Wrap in plastic wrap and chill for 3 hours, or place the rolls in the freezer and freeze for 1 hour. The dough is easier to slice when it's firm.

3　Preheat the oven to 350°F and place a rack in the center. Cut the logs into ⅜- to ¼-inch-thick slices and arrange about 1 inch apart on baking sheets. Bake one sheet at a time for 11 minutes, or until lightly browned around the edges. Let cool on the baking sheets for 2 minutes, then transfer to a wire rack to cool and crisp.

Baker's Note: The tea adds flecks of color to the dough, complements the orange flavor, and leaves a very faint and lingering taste. You can buy Earl Grey tea leaves in bulk from the grocery store or just crush up some tea from a bag.

Potato Chip Day

Potato chips were invented in 1853 by George Crum, the chef at an elegant restaurant in Saratoga, New York. As the story goes, a customer was unhappy with the thickness of his fries and sent them back to the kitchen. To show the customer a thing or two, Chef Crum made the fries so thin that they were too crispy to be eaten with a fork. Instead of teaching him a lesson, Crum made the restaurant patron very happy, so much so that other diners began requesting the chips. In 1860, Crum opened his own restaurant and set a bag of "Saratoga chips" on every table.

Other Events on This Day:
National Pi Day, Learn About Butterflies Day

Potato Chip Cookies
MAKES ABOUT 30

1 cup (8 ounces) unsalted butter, room temperature
½ cup granulated sugar, plus more for rolling
½ teaspoon salt
1 teaspoon vanilla extract
1¾ cups (8 ounces) all-purpose flour
¾ cup (1.5 ounces) finely crushed potato chips
⅓ cup pecans, toasted and finely chopped

1　Preheat the oven to 350°F and place a rack in the center. Line two baking sheets with nonstick foil or parchment paper.

2　In the bowl of a stand mixer fitted with a paddle attachment, or in a large mixing bowl, using a handheld electric mixer, beat the butter, sugar, and salt on medium speed until light and creamy. Beat in the vanilla extract. Reduce the speed to low and stir in the flour, potato chips, and pecans.

3　Scoop up dough by rounded teaspoonfuls and form 1-inch balls. Arrange 2 inches apart on the prepared baking sheets.

4 Rub the bottom of a drinking glass with butter. Sprinkle some sugar in a bowl and rub the glass in the sugar. Use the glass to press down the tops of the cookies so that they're about ¼ inch thick. Bake one sheet at a time for 10 to 12 minutes, or until the edges of the cookies are lightly browned. Let cool on the baking sheet for 5 minutes, then transfer to a wire rack to cool completely.

One-Bowl German Chocolate Chunk Cookies

MAKES 12

4 tablespoons (2 ounces) unsalted butter

2 ounces German's Sweet Chocolate
   (see Baker's Note)

⅔ cup granulated sugar

1 large egg, room temperature

½ teaspoon vanilla extract

¾ teaspoon baking powder

¼ teaspoon plus an extra pinch of salt

¾ cup all-purpose flour

½ cup semisweet chocolate chips

½ cup sweetened flaked coconut

½ cup toasted and chopped pecans

1 Preheat the oven to 350°F and place a rack in the center. Line two baking sheets with parchment paper or nonstick foil.

2 In a microwave-safe mixing bowl, melt the butter and chocolate in the microwave, using 50 percent power and stirring after 1 minute. Set aside to cool completely. Stir in the sugar, egg, and vanilla, then stir in the baking powder, salt, and flour until fully blended. Stir in the chocolate chips, coconut, and toasted pecans.

MARCH 15

Everything You Think Is Wrong Day

Today's holiday celebrates misconceptions, misnomers, preconceived notions, and prejudice. There are lots of things I was wrong about. One was German Chocolate Cake. I thought it was from Germany, but it was a "reader recipe" printed in a Dallas newspaper in 1957. In the ingredient list, the reader specified "German's Sweet Chocolate" which was a sweet chocolate formulated by a man named Samuel German who worked for the Walter Baker Chocolate Company. The cake recipe was so popular that newspapers around the country published it. General Foods later refined the recipe and renamed the cake German Sweet Chocolate Cake.

Other Events on This Day: **Maine joined the Union in 1820**

3 Scoop up generous tablespoonfuls of dough and shape into twelve large balls. Arrange 2 inches apart on the prepared baking sheets. Bake for 12 to 14 minutes, or until the cookies are cracked yet still soft; do not overbake. Transfer to a wire rack to cool completely.

Baker's Note: To get a sweet, yet still very chocolaty flavor, use German's chocolate.

MARCH 16

Visit Florence, Italy Day

I invented this holiday as an excuse to make some *cantucci*, but the truth is, this is a good time to visit Florence, Italy. Crowds are tolerable, the weather is cool yet sunny, and air fare is generally reasonable. If you can't make it to Florence quite yet but think it sounds fun, here's hoping a few pieces of *cantucci* (plus a little espresso) will take you there in spirit.

In Italy all cookies are biscotti and the twice-baked cookies we know as biscotti are actually *cantucci*, or the smaller-cut *cantuccini*. Cantucci can be made with butter, or oil, or without any fat at all. This version is the latter, so it's extra crunchy—hard, almost—and packed with flavor from the toasted almonds and sugar. I like to use the increasingly popular coconut palm sugar, which is dark and has a rich caramel flavor.

Other Events on This Day:
Freedom of Information Day

Palm Sugar Cantucci
MAKES ABOUT 20

1⅓ cups (6 ounces) white whole wheat or all-purpose flour
⅔ cup very firmly packed coconut palm sugar
¾ teaspoon baking soda
¼ teaspoon salt
2 large eggs
1 teaspoon vanilla extract
¾ cup whole almonds, toasted

1 Preheat the oven to 300°F and place a rack in the center. Line a baking sheet with parchment paper or nonstick foil.

2 Mix the flour, coconut palm sugar, baking soda, and salt together in a medium-size bowl; set aside.

3 In a second bowl, using a handheld electric mixer on medium-high speed, or a whisk, beat the eggs until light. Beat in the vanilla.

4 Blend the liquid ingredients into the dry ingredients by hand; the dough should be heavy and sticky.

5 Add the almonds. Using your hands, knead them into the dough so they are evenly distributed. The dough will be thick and crumbly. Wet your hands slightly and shape the dough into a log about 10 by 2½ inches. Place the log on the prepared baking sheet.

6 Bake the log for 40 to 50 minutes, or until it becomes very dark and aromatic. It will spread quite a bit in the oven. Remove from the oven and let cool on the baking sheet for 20 minutes, leaving the oven on. Transfer the log to a large cutting board. Using a serrated knife, cut crosswise slightly on the diagonal every ½ to ¾ inch. Place the cookies cut side up on the baking sheet. Bake for 20 to 30 minutes. Transfer to a wire rack to cool completely.

Irish Cream Cheesecake Brownies MAKES 20

FILLING

1 (8-ounce) package cream cheese, softened

¼ cup granulated sugar

¼ cup Irish cream liqueur

2 large egg whites

½ cup semisweet chocolate mini chips

BROWNIES

1 box brownie mix for a 9 by 13-inch pan, plus
    necessary ingredients as directed on the package

1 Preheat the oven to 350°F and place a rack in the center. Line a 9 by 13-inch metal pan with nonstick foil, or line it with regular foil and spray the foil with flour-added baking spray.

2 **Make the filling:** In a medium-size bowl, using a hand-held electric mixer on medium speed, beat the cream cheese and sugar. Beat in the Irish cream. Reduce the mixer speed and add the egg whites, beating only until they are mixed in and being careful not to beat in a lot of extra air. Stir in the chocolate chips. Set aside.

MARCH 17

Saint Patrick's Day

Saint Patrick's Day marks the death of Saint Patrick, who was famous for bringing Christianity to Ireland. St. Patrick's Day has been celebrated as a religious holiday for thousands of years. However, the first Saint Patrick's Day Parade was held in the United States. On this day in 1762, Irish soldiers serving the English militia marched through the streets of New York, playing music and bolstering Irish pride. Several other Irish organizations began holding their own parades after that, and through the years March 17 has evolved from a religious holiday to a day of celebrating Irish pride.

Other Events on This Day:
Absolutely Incredible Kid Day (founded by Campfire Girls and Boys)

3. **Make the brownies:** Prepare the brownie mix as directed on the package and pour all but ½ cup of brownie batter into the 9 by 13-inch pan. Pour the filling over the top. Drop spoonfuls of the reserved brownie batter over the filling. Bake the brownies for the length of time designated on the package. Let cool completely in the pan, then chill for 2 hours before slicing.

Baker's Notes: For convenience, I've designed this recipe for use with your favorite brownie mix. If you'd prefer using a scratch brownie, follow the directions for your favorite scratch brownie, but pour the Irish cream topping over the uncooked batter before baking. For testing, I used Pillsbury Family Size Chocolate Fudge Brownies.

National Lacy Oatmeal Cookie Day

My teenage babysitter used to make the best lace cookies. At the time, I didn't know what they were called, and I'm not so sure she did, either, but I remember that we'd say good-bye to my parents and head straight to the kitchen to make these thin, brittle cookies that she said were a secret family recipe. It wasn't until many, many years later that I learned they were lace cookies.

Other Events on This Day:
Stop, drop, and roll over! It's Sparky the Firedog's birthday. According to Sparky.org, he was born in 1951 and since then has taught millions of children the importance of fire safety.

Oatmeal Almond Lace Cookies MAKES ABOUT 28

½ cup (2.3 ounces) all-purpose flour

¼ teaspoon baking powder

¼ teaspoon salt

¼ teaspoon ground cinnamon

5½ tablespoons (2.75 ounces) unsalted butter, melted and cooled

2 tablespoons honey

½ cup granulated sugar

2 tablespoons heavy cream

1 tablespoon vanilla extract

½ cup old-fashioned oats

2 tablespoons almonds, toasted and finely chopped

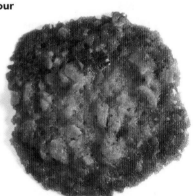

1. Preheat the oven to 350°F and place a rack in the center. Line two large baking sheets with nonstick foil or parchment paper.

2. Mix the flour, baking powder, salt, and cinnamon together in a small bowl; set aside.

3. In a medium-size mixing bowl, whisk together the cooled melted butter, honey, sugar, cream, and vanilla.

4 Add the flour mixture to the honey mixture and stir until blended, then stir in the oats and almonds.

5 Scoop up by rounded ¼ teaspoonfuls and drop twelve very small rounds on each prepared baking sheet. Make sure to space them at least 2 inches apart, as they will spread quite a bit. Bake for 6 to 8 minutes or until the edges are browned, but keep a close eye on the cookies because lace cookies don't always bake evenly. Watch the edges; the edges should be very brown, while the middles will still be fairly pale. Let cool completely on the baking sheets, then carefully peel the cookies off the liners.

Baker's Notes: These delicate cookies might take a little practice. For best results, keep the cookies very small and keep a close eye on them after the first 6 minutes of baking.

Mud Hen Bars MAKES 32

BASE
1½ cups (6.8 ounces) all-purpose flour
1 teaspoon baking powder
¾ teaspoon salt
8 tablespoons (4 ounces) unsalted
    butter, room temperature
½ cup granulated sugar
½ cup firmly packed light brown sugar
1 large egg
2 large egg yolks
1 teaspoon vanilla extract
16 large marshmallows, cut in half, or 1
    cup miniature marshmallows
1 cup semisweet chocolate chips
½ cup toasted and finely chopped pecans

TOPPING
2 large egg whites
1 cup firmly packed
    brown sugar
½ teaspoon vanilla extract

Swallows Return to Capistrano

For many years, today was the day thousands of cliff swallows returned to their summer home, an old Spanish mission in San Juan Capistrano, California. After wintering in Goya, Argentina, they'd make the long flight back to the town, arriving in the wee hours of the morning and increasing in numbers until flocks of birds filled the air. Unfortunately, most of the swallows have stopped returning to the old mission. Speculation is that urbanization has caused the swallows to look for more remote areas, but San Juan Capistrano still celebrates their swallows and continues to hold their weeklong La Fiesta de las Golondrinas, which includes a big parade.

1 Preheat the oven to 350°F. Line a 9 by 13-inch metal pan with nonstick foil, or line it with regular foil and spray the foil with gluten-free baking spray.

2 **Make the base:** Mix the flour, baking powder, and salt together in a medium-size bowl; set aside.

3 In the bowl of a stand mixer fitted with a paddle attachment, or in a large mixing bowl, using a handheld electric mixer, beat the butter and both sugars on medium speed until smooth. Beat in the egg, egg yolks, and vanilla. By hand or using the lowest speed of the mixer, stir in the flour mixture. Wet your hands with a little bit of water and use your fingers to press the dough to the edges of the pan. Press the marshmallows into the crust, spacing them evenly. Sprinkle on the chips, letting them land in the spaces between the marshmallows. Pat down slightly. Sprinkle with the pecans and pat down.

4 **Make the topping:** Beat the egg whites in a mixing bowl, using a handheld electric mixer on high speed, just until stiff peaks form. Gradually add the brown sugar, then beat in the vanilla. Spoon over the marshmallow topping and carefully spread to cover the marshmallows the best you can. Bake for 20 minutes, or until the top is golden brown. Let cool completely in the pan. For a cleaner cut, chill for about an hour before slicing; lift from the pan, set on a cutting board, and cut into thirty-two squares. If you left some of the edges uncovered by the topping, just trim them off and eat them.

Baker's Notes: You can make these with miniature or large marshmallows. I prefer the large because you can press them into the bottom crust, where they'll stick and not get dragged along as you spoon over the topping.

Birdseed Bars MAKES 16

1 cup raw sesame seeds

1 cup raw sunflower seeds

1 cup shredded unsweetened coconut

2 cups trail mix with dried fruit and nuts (not peanuts)

8 tablespoons (4 ounces) unsalted butter

Pinch of salt

¼ cup honey

½ cup firmly packed light brown sugar

1 Preheat the oven to 350°F and place a rack in the center. Line a 9-inch square pan with nonstick foil, or line it with foil and spray the foil with flour-added baking spray.

2 Spread the sesame and sunflower seeds on a rimmed baking sheet and bake for 4 to 6 minutes, keeping a close eye on them to make sure the seeds don't burn. Add the coconut and continue to bake for another 3 minutes. Remove from the oven and let cool.

3 Meanwhile, chop the trail mix slightly so that big chunks of such ingredients as apricot and Brazil nuts are no more than ½ inch across. In a large mixing bowl, mix together the toasted sesame seeds, sunflower seeds, coconut, and trail mix.

4 In a small saucepan, combine the butter, salt, honey, and brown sugar. Insert a candy thermometer and heat the mixture over medium heat, stirring once or twice, until it reaches 240°F (soft ball stage). Stir the honey mixture into the seed mixture.

5 Spread in the pan and press down, using a piece of nonstick foil or parchment to protect your fingers from the heat. Let cool completely in the pan, then chill for 1 hour. Lift from the pan, set on a cutting board, and score into sixteen bars or squares.

Baker's Notes: These nutrient-rich bars may remind you of the popular seed and nut

First Day of Spring and Big Bird's Birthday

Who's 8 feet 2 inches tall, has a teddy bear named Radar, and loves birdseed milkshakes? Big Bird, of course! How fitting it is that he should be born on the first day of spring. Technically, he's a little over forty, but it's generally agreed that he's perpetually six.

Now back to those birdseed milkshakes, I'm sure there's a recipe somewhere, but I think Big Bird might also like these birdseed cookies. They're high energy, and perfect for making with kids.

Other Events on This Day: **Mr. (Fred) Rogers born in 1928**

bars sold at airports and coffee shops. This recipe is better because you can tailor it to your specific tastes by varying the trail mix. Use 2 cups of your favorite variety or mix together apricots, raisins, and nuts to equal the 2 cups you need. Toasting is essential for flavor. I toast the seeds in the oven, but toasting in a large, dry skillet also works. Omit the additional salt if using salted butter.

California Strawberry Day

I t's National California Strawberry Day. While I haven't figured out the origin of this holiday, it's a fact that on this day in 1984, a section of Central Park was named Strawberry Fields, in honor of John Lennon. For either reason, it's a good day to try dried strawberries, which are becoming more commonplace. You can find them in the dried fruit section at many stores and in the bulk bins of some grocery stores.

Other Events on This Day:
National French Bread Day

Strawberries and Cream Cookies MAKES 18

1⅓ **cups (6 ounces) all-purpose flour**
3 **tablespoons cornstarch**
½ **teaspoon baking soda**
⅜ **teaspoon salt**
8 **tablespoons (4 ounces) unsalted butter, room temperature**
½ **cup firmly packed light brown sugar**
½ **cup granulated sugar**
1 **large egg**
¾ **teaspoon vanilla extract**
1 **tablespoon heavy cream**
1 **cup white chips**
½ **cup dried strawberries, chopped**

1 Preheat the oven to 350°F and place a rack in the center. Line two baking sheets with nonstick foil or parchment paper.

2 Mix the flour, cornstarch, baking soda, and salt together in a medium-size bowl; set aside.

3 In the bowl of a stand mixer fitted with a paddle attachment, or in a large mixing bowl, using a handheld electric mixer, beat the butter and both sugars on medium speed until creamy. Reduce the speed to medium and beat in the egg, vanilla, and cream. By hand or using the lowest speed of the mixer, add the flour mixture and stir just until blended. Stir in the white chips and strawberries.

4   Drop rounded tablespoonfuls of dough 2 inches apart onto the prepared baking sheets. Bake one sheet at a time for 12 to 13 minutes, or until the edges are nicely browned (the edges should brown faster than the center). Remove from the oven and, with the tip of a spatula, gently nudge the edge of the cookies inward to make wrinkles. Let cool on the baking sheets for about 5 minutes, then transfer to a wire rack to cool completely.

One-Bowl Thin and Buttery Chocolate Chip Cookies

MAKES ABOUT 22

8 tablespoons (4 ounces) unsalted
    butter, room temperature

½ cup firmly packed light brown sugar

6 tablespoons granulated sugar

1 teaspoon vanilla extract

1 large egg

½ teaspoon salt

½ teaspoon baking soda

1 tablespoon cornstarch

1 cup plus 1 tablespoon (5 ounces) all-purpose flour

1½ cups semisweet chocolate chips

1   Preheat the oven to 350°F and place a rack in the center. Have ready two ungreased baking sheets.

2   In the bowl of a stand mixer fitted with a paddle attachment, or in a large mixing bowl, using a handheld electric mixer, beat the butter, both sugars, and the vanilla on medium speed until light and creamy, about 2 minutes. Reduce the mixer speed to low and beat in the egg. When the egg is well blended, add the salt and baking soda and beat well, scraping the sides of the bowl once or twice and making sure the baking soda is well distributed throughout the batter. Add the cornstarch and stir until blended. Add the flour and stir until it is almost blended in. Add the chocolate chips and stir until all the flour disappears.

MARCH 22

Cornstarch Patented

Break out the champagne, because on this day in 1841, Orlando Jones was granted a patent for cornstarch. While Jones is credited for inventing the process of using alkali to speed up starch making, it was Thomas Kingsford who, in 1842, isolated kernels of starch from the corn kernel using technology he'd learned working at a wheat starch factory.

Other Events on This Day:
United Nations World Water Day

93

3   Drop rounded teaspoonfuls of dough about 2 inches apart onto the baking sheets. Bake one sheet at a time for 10 minutes, or until the edges are golden brown. The cookies should get very brown around the edges, but do take care not to burn the bottoms. Transfer to a wire rack and let cool completely.

Baker's Note: Cornstarch is often used as a thickener in sauces and gravies, but it can also enhance cookie recipes. In this recipe, it stands in for some of the flour, giving these flat and buttery cookies extra-crispy edges.

MARCH 23

First Elevator Installed

Built by the Otis Elevator Company, the country's first passenger elevator was installed on March 23, 1857, at 488 Broadway in New York City. It cost $300, had a speed of 0.67 feet per second, and is still in working condition today in the E. V. Haughwout Building in Soho. Today's cookies revolve around an elevator and a story by Peg Bracken, famous for her *I Hate to Cook Book*. As the story goes, Peg was eating these cookies in the elevator and offered one to its female operator. The elevator lady took a bite and told Peg she had a better recipe (generally, this might be considered rude, but I like to believe the lady was trying to be helpful). Upon trying the recipe, Peg Bracken agreed the elevator lady's version was better and went on to share the recipe.

Other Events on This Day:
National Chips and Dip Day

Better Than Elevator Lady's Cookies

MAKES ABOUT 24 LARGE COOKIES OR 32 SMALLER COOKIES

2 cups (9 ounces) all-purpose flour

2 teaspoons baking soda

¼ teaspoon salt

1 teaspoon ground cinnamon

½ teaspoon ground cloves

¾ teaspoon ground ginger

¼ teaspoon cayenne

1 teaspoon unsweetened natural cocoa powder

12 tablespoons (6 ounces) unsalted butter, room temperature

1 cup granulated sugar

1 large egg

¼ cup mild molasses

1   Mix the flour, baking soda, salt, cinnamon, cloves, ginger, cayenne, and cocoa powder together in a bowl; set aside.

2   In the bowl of a stand mixer fitted with a paddle attachment, or in a large mixing bowl, using a handheld electric mixer, beat the butter and sugar on medium speed until light. Reduce the mixer speed slightly and add the egg and molasses. By hand or using the lowest speed of the mixer, add the dry ingredients and mix until a dough forms.

3 Scoop up generously rounded tablespoonfuls and shape into balls a little over 1 inch in diameter (weighing about 1 ounce each). Arrange the balls of dough on a baking sheet (you don't have to worry about spacing at this point) and chill the dough for 2 hours.

4 When ready to bake, allow the dough balls to come to room temperature. Preheat the oven to 350°F and place a rack in the center. Line two baking sheets with parchment paper or nonstick foil. Space the balls of dough about 3 inches apart on the prepared baking sheets, and press down slightly so that tops are flat. Bake one sheet at a time for 8 to 10 minutes, or until the cookies are crackly and brown around the edges.

Baker's Notes: Peg liked the elevator lady's cookies, but I can't help wondering what would have happened if Peg had improved upon the recipe a bit more and challenged the elevator lady to a rematch. In this version, I've added a few of my favorite ginger cookie ingredients (cocoa for depth and cayenne for heat) and switched from shortening to butter. These are very thin, chewy, and flavorful. Peg made hers "walnut size" and got about thirty-two, but I make mine a bit larger.

Chocolate Peanut Raisin Clusters MAKES ABOUT 48

1⅓ cup semisweet chocolate chips

1 pound white or chocolate almond
    bark or white candy coating

1 cup raisins

12 ounces lightly salted peanuts (see Baker's Note)

1 Line two baking sheets with parchment paper or nonstick foil.

2 In a microwave-safe mixing bowl, combine the chocolate chips and almond bark. Microwave at 50 percent power for 1½ to 2 minutes, stirring every 30 seconds, until

MARCH 24

National Chocolate-Covered Raisin Day

In honor of Chocolate-Covered Raisin Day, here's a chocolate and raisin treat that may win you over if you are not yet a fan of chocolate-covered raisins. Almond bark, the inexpensive coating you find in the baking aisle of most supermarkets, helps these set nicely.

Other Events on This Day:
First automobile sold in 1898

melted. Alternatively, you may melt the mixture in the top of a double boiler. Stir the raisins and peanuts into the melted chocolate mixture.

3 Scoop up tablespoonfuls of batter and drop onto the baking sheets. Leave the candy at room temperature to set.

Baker's Note: These are so easy. Unsalted peanuts may be used, but I like the combination of sweet and salty, so I stick with lightly salted.

MARCH 25

International Waffle Day

*F*ire up the waffle iron and pull out the syrup, because today is International Waffle Day. Not to be confused with National Waffle Day, International Waffle Day ties in with an actual Swedish holiday known as Våffeldagen. Coinciding with Sweden's first day of spring as well as the Feast of the Annunciation, it's customary to make waffles in honor of both occasions. Hopefully, these count. They're kind of a cross between a waffle and a cookie. At our house, they're a popular breakfast at sleepovers.

Lemon-Blueberry Waffle Cookies MAKES ABOUT 30

2 cups (9 ounces) all-purpose flour
¾ teaspoon salt
2 teaspoons baking powder
½ teaspoon baking soda
1½ cups quick-cooking oats (not instant)
10 tablespoons (5 ounces) unsalted
   butter, room temperature
⅔ cup granulated sugar
2 large eggs
1 cup sour cream
1 teaspoon lemon zest
1 cup fresh or frozen (unthawed) blueberries

1 Preheat a waffle maker according to the manufacturer's directions.

2 In a mixing bowl, stir together the flour, salt, baking powder, baking soda, and oats; set aside.

3 In a second mixing bowl, using a handheld electric mixer on medium-high speed, beat the butter and sugar until creamy. Beat in the eggs, one at a time. By hand or using the lowest speed of the mixer, stir in the sour cream and lemon zest, followed by the dry ingredients. Stir in the blueberries.

4 Brush the waffle iron with oil. Drop generous tablespoonfuls of waffle batter on the waffle iron—if using a small waffle iron, you'll only be able to do two at a time. Close the waffle iron and bake the cookies for 3 to 6 minutes, or until they are set.

Baker's Note: These waffle "cookies" don't get that hard. In fact, they're more like miniature waffles you can eat with your hands.

Matzo Brittle with Spiced Pecan Topping
MAKES ABOUT 20 PIECES

SPICED NUTS
¼ cup confectioners' sugar

¼ teaspoon cayenne

¼ teaspoon salt

½ cup pecan halves

CANDY
3½ sheets unsalted matzos

1 cup (8 ounces) unsalted butter

¼ teaspoon salt

1 cup firmly packed light brown sugar

1 cup extra-dark chocolate chips, or 6 ounces
    of your favorite dark chocolate

½ cup pecans, toasted and finely chopped

1 Preheat the oven to 350°F and place a rack in the center. Line a 10 by 15-inch pan with nonstick foil.

2 **Make the spiced nuts:** Mix together the confectioners' sugar, cayenne, and salt. Splash the pecans with a little bit of water—just enough to dampen them—then roll them in the sugar mixture, dusting off any extra sugar. Spread on the prepared pan and bake for 7 minutes, or until fragrant and toasty. Remove from the pan and let cool.

3 **Make the candy:** In the same foil-lined pan, arrange the matzo so that it covers the whole pan. Break it up if you need to.

Other Events on This Day:
Pecan Day, commemorating the day in 1775 when George Washington planted pecan trees at Mount Vernon.

MARCH 26

Passover

Passover commemorates the exodus of the Israelites from Egypt during the reign of Pharaoh Ramses II. It is celebrated on the fifteenth day of the Jewish month of Nissan, which means its date of celebration changes every year on the Gregorian calendar. At any rate, this is a good day to try some new Passover recipes. This is one of my all-time favorites with a spicy twist.

Other Events on This Day:
Fire extinguisher patented in 1872

4. In a 3-quart saucepan set over medium heat, bring the butter, salt, and brown sugar to a boil; as soon as the mixture starts to boil, set a timer for 3 minutes. At 3 minutes, pour the hot sugar mixture over the matzo. Bake for 12 to 14 minutes. Let the pan cool for 1 minute.

5. Sprinkle chocolate chips over the top and let stand for another minute. Spread the chips over the brittle and sprinkle the toasted pecans over the melted chips. Let the brittle stand at room temperature for 30 minutes, then chill until firm. Break into about twenty pieces.

MARCH 27

Cherry Blossoms Planted in Washington, DC

On this day in 1912, First Lady Helen Taft and the wife of the Japanese ambassador, Viscountess Chinda, planted two of the first cherry blossom trees donated to Washington by Tokyo mayor Yukio Ozaki as a gesture of friendship. Three years later, the US government gave a gift of flowering dogwood trees to the people of Japan. In 1965, Lady Bird Johnson accepted 3,800 more trees, and then in 1981, the United States was able to reciprocate once again by giving Japanese horticulturists cuttings from the trees to replace some cherry trees in Japan that had been destroyed in a flood.

Other Events on This Day:
Spanish Paella Day

Sour Cherry Oatmeal Cookies MAKES 56

2½ cups (11.25 ounces) all-purpose flour

2½ teaspoons baking powder

1½ teaspoons baking soda

1 teaspoon salt

1 cup (8 ounces) unsalted butter, room temperature

2 cups firmly packed light brown sugar

2 large eggs

1½ teaspoons vanilla extract

2 tablespoons sour cream

1 teaspoon orange zest

1 teaspoon lemon zest

1½ cups old-fashioned oats

½ pound dried sour cherries or
   cherry-flavored cranberries

1. Mix the flour, baking powder, baking soda, and salt together in a medium-size bowl; set aside.

2. In a large mixing bowl, using a handheld electric mixer on medium-high speed, beat the butter and brown sugar until the mixture is creamy. Beat in the eggs, one at a time, beating for 30 seconds after each addition. Add the vanilla and sour cream; scrape the sides of the bowl. Stir in the orange and lemon zest.

3 Stir the flour mixture and oats into the creamed mixture, mixing just until combined. Stir in the cherries. Cover and chill for 2 hours up to overnight.

4 Preheat the oven to 350°F and place a rack in the center. Line two baking sheets with nonstick foil or parchment paper.

5 Drop rounded teaspoonfuls of chilled dough about 2½ inches apart onto the prepared baking sheets. Bake for 10 to 12 minutes, or just until the cookies appear browned around the edges and set. Let the cookies cool on the baking sheets for about 5 minutes, then carefully transfer to a wire rack to cool completely.

Baker's Notes: Sour cream complements the sour cherries and citrus and keeps these cookies soft and chewy. To make sure you get the right texture, scoop the dough by rounded teaspoonfuls and be careful not to make the cookies too large.

Chewy Jumbo Double Chocolate Cherry Cookies
MAKES 24 JUMBO COOKIES

3 cups (13.5 ounces) all-purpose flour

1 cup unsweetened natural cocoa powder

1½ teaspoons baking soda

1¼ teaspoons salt

1 cup (8 ounces) unsalted butter, room temperature

½ cup (3.4 ounces) shortening

1½ cups granulated sugar

1 cup firmly packed light brown sugar

1½ teaspoons vanilla extract

½ teaspoon cherry or almond extract

3 large eggs

2 cups semisweet or extra-dark chocolate chips

1 cup dried cherries

1½ tablespoons sparkling sugar, for
　　sprinkling (more or less if desired)

MARCH 28

"C Is for Cookie" first performed on Sesame Street

Written by Joe Raposo, "C Is for Cookie" (along with "Rubber Duckie" and "Bein' Green") is one of *Sesame Street*'s most memorable songs. The song had been released earlier on *The Muppet Alphabet Album*, but it was on this day in 1972 that Cookie Monster performed it on *Sesame Street*.

Like the big, flat, cookies whose crumbs flew all over the place when Cookie Monster sang, these cookies are big, sturdy, and irresistible. Because today is also Black Forest Cake day and because "c" is also for cherries, I threw in some dried cherries.

1 Preheat the oven to 325°F and place a rack in the center. Line two large baking sheets with parchment paper or nonstick foil.

2 Mix the flour, cocoa powder, baking soda, and salt together in a bowl; set aside.

3 In the bowl of a stand mixer fitted with a paddle attachment, or in a large mixing bowl, using a handheld electric mixer set at medium-high speed, beat the butter and shortening until creamy, increasing the speed to high if necessary. Beat in both sugars, the vanilla, and the cherry extract. Scrape the sides of the bowl and beat for another minute, or until creamy. Add the eggs and beat for 30 seconds, or until the eggs are mixed in.

4 Add the flour mixture to the butter mixture and stir with a mixing spoon, or mix on the lowest speed of the mixer, until most of the flour is incorporated. Add the chocolate chips and cherries and continue to stir until the remaining flour mixture is incorporated and the chips are mixed in.

5 Using a ¼-cup measure, scoop up the dough and arrange the mounds about 3½ inches apart (six to a sheet) on the prepared baking sheets. Sprinkle a tiny pinch of sparkling sugar (if using) on top of each dough ball. Bake two sheets at a time on the center and lower rack for 15 to 17 minutes, or until the cookies appear set. Halfway through the baking process, rotate the baking sheets so that each sheet bakes for half the time on center rack.

6 Let cool on the baking sheets for 5 minutes, then lift with a metal spatula and transfer to a wire rack to cool and set.

Baker's Notes: These large cookies are perfect for bake sales. This version uses chocolate chips, but white chips work well, too, or use a combination of both. Cherry extract adds a hint of extra cherry flavor, but because cherry extract can be hard to find, almond makes a great substitute.

Viennese Raspberry Bars MAKES 16

BASE

8 tablespoons (4 ounces) unsalted
    butter, room temperature

¼ cup granulated sugar

2 large egg yolks

1 teaspoon vanilla extract

¼ teaspoon salt

1 cup (4.5 ounces) all-purpose flour

FILLING

¾ cup raspberry preserves, preferably
    seedless, softened (see Baker's Notes)

½ cup semisweet chocolate chips

TOPPING

2 large egg whites

½ cup granulated sugar

¼ teaspoon vanilla extract

⅓ cup pecans or walnuts, toasted and finely chopped

1 Preheat the oven to 350°F and place a rack in the center.
Line a 9-inch square metal pan with nonstick foil.

2 **Make the base:** In the bowl of a stand mixer fitted with a
paddle attachment, or in a large mixing bowl, using a handheld electric mixer, beat the butter, sugar, egg yolks, vanilla,
and salt on medium speed until creamy. Stir in the flour. If
necessary, use your hands to mix all the ingredients, but be
careful not to overmix. Press into the bottom of the prepared
pan and bake for 18 to 20 minutes, or until lightly browned
around the edges. Let cool in the pan for about 10 minutes.

3 **Add the filling:** Spread the preserves over the crust, then
sprinkle the chocolate chips over the preserves.

4 **Make the topping:** In a large bowl, using a handheld
electric mixer, beat the egg whites on high speed until
stiff peaks begin to form. Beat in the sugar and vanilla.
Stir in the nuts. Spread the egg white mixture over the

Beethoven's First Public Performance

On March 29, 1795, Ludwig
van Beethoven gave his
first public performance in
Vienna at a charity event for
widows and orphans. A rising
star of the day, Beethoven
continued to gain popularity
with Vienna's elite. To make
ends meet, he gave private
lessons to young girls, a few of
whom became famous pianists
themselves.

Vienna's pastries are as
famous as its musical heritage,
with rich buttery dough-
based cookies, cheese-filled
Kuchen (cakes), and fruit
strudel. This little cookie,
far less complicated than
a strudel, pays tribute to
some of the most well-known
characteristics of Viennese
pastry.

Other Events on This Day:
**Lemon Chiffon Day, Smoke
and Mirrors Day, Dr. John
Pemberton brewed the first
batch of cola in 1886**

filling. Return the pan to the oven and bake for 22 to 25 minutes, or until the topping appears golden and set. Let cool completely in the pan. For a cleaner cut, chill before slicing. Lift from the pan, set on a cutting board, and cut into sixteen squares or bars.

Baker's Notes: To soften the preserves, heat them for 5 to 10 seconds in the microwave. Make sure the preserves and crust are cool when topping with the chocolate chips; otherwise the chips start to melt and things get messy.

First Starbucks Opens

On this day in 1971, two Seattle teachers and a writer opened a coffee shop and named it after a character in *Moby-Dick*. Originally selling only roasted coffee beans, teas, and coffee-making equipment, the store was located at 2000 Western Avenue. In 1975 it relocated to 1912 Pike Place, but it wasn't until 1984 when Starbucks, which by then had six locations, started selling espresso drinks. As of today, there are over seventeen thousand Starbucks operating in fifty different countries.

Other Events on This Day:
National Doctors' Day, Hot Dog Day, Secretary of State William H. Seward agreed to purchase Alaska from Russia for $7.2 million in 1867

Espresso Toffee Bars MAKES 36

2 cups (9 ounces) all-purpose flour
1 cup firmly packed light brown sugar
¾ teaspoon salt
1 teaspoon instant espresso powder
1 cup (8 ounces) unsalted butter, room temperature
1 large egg yolk
½ teaspoon vanilla extract
½ cup (4 ounces) toffee bits
2 cups semisweet chocolate chips, or 10 to 12
    ounces semisweet chocolate, chopped
²/₃ cup sliced almonds, toasted and chopped,
    or ²/₃ cup slivered almonds, toasted

1 Preheat the oven to 350°F and place a rack in the center. Line a 10 by 15-inch metal pan with nonstick foil or parchment paper.

2 In the bowl of a stand mixer fitted with a paddle attachment, or in a large mixing bowl with a wooden spoon, mix together the flour, sugar, salt, and espresso powder. Cut the butter into chunks and add it to the flour mixture along with the egg yolk and vanilla. If using a stand mixer, mix on low speed until soft and crumbly. If using a wooden spoon, beat until the mixture comes together, and then use your hands to finish mixing until moist and crumbly. Alternatively, you may mix all dry ingredients in the food processor, add the butter, egg, and vanilla, and then pulse

until moist and crumbly. Stir in the toffee bits. Press the mixture evenly into the prepared pan and bake for 15 to 20 minutes, or until the edges are lightly browned.

3 Melt the chocolate in the microwave, using 50 percent power, stirring at 1-minute intervals until smooth, or in the top of a double boiler. Spread the melted chocolate over the bars. Sprinkle the top with almonds. Set the pan on a rack and let cool in the pan for about 1 hour. Chill for about 30 minutes or until chocolate is set. To serve, lift from the pan and set on a cutting board. If cold, bring to room temperature. Using a large chef's knife, cut into 36 bars.

Baker's Notes: Toffee bits and lots of brown sugar give these bars a sweet, deep caramel flavor. For best results, make sure you use the right size pan. A 10 by 15-inch jelly-roll works much better than a 9 by 13-inch pan because the dough is spread thinner and the bars bake up slightly crispier. If you make them in a 9 by 13-inch pan the bars will be thicker and won't have the crispy, slightly chewy texture. Alternatively, you can use two 9-inch square pans, or halve the batch and bake it in a 9-inch square pan.

Island Cookies MAKES 30

1¼ cups quick-cooking oats, finely ground
    in a coffee grinder after measuring
1 cup (4.5 ounces) all-purpose flour
1 teaspoon baking powder
¼ teaspoon salt
8 tablespoons (4 ounces) unsalted
    butter, room temperature
¾ cup firmly packed light brown sugar
¾ cup granulated sugar
1 large egg
1 teaspoon rum extract (see Baker's Note)
½ cup dried pineapple, chopped
2⅔ cups sweetened flaked coconut
⅔ cup pecans, toasted and finely chopped

MARCH 31

The United States Takes the Virgin Islands

In 1917, for a fee of $25 million, the United States took possession of the Danish West Indies and renamed them the Virgin Islands. Consisting of St. Thomas, St. Croix, St. John, and about fifty other small islands, the Virgin Islands are about 65 kilometers east of Puerto Rico at the end of the Greater Antilles. The United States wanted the islands because of their strategic location in relation to the Panama Canal.

1 Preheat the oven to 350°F and place a rack in the center. Line two baking sheets with parchment paper or nonstick foil.

2 Mix the ground oats, flour, baking powder, and salt together in a bowl and set aside.

3 In the bowl of a stand mixer fitted with a paddle attachment, or in a large mixing bowl, using a handheld electric mixer, beat the butter and both sugars on medium speed until creamy. Beat in the egg and extract and continue beating for another minute. By hand or using the lowest speed of the mixer, stir in the flour mixture, followed by the dried pineapple, coconut, and pecans. The dough will be thick.

4 Shape into 1-inch balls and arrange 2 inches apart, flattening them slightly on the baking sheet. Bake one sheet at a time for 12 to 15 minutes, or until the edges are golden brown. Transfer to a wire rack to cool completely.

Baker's Note: Containing over 2½ cups of coconut, these chewy cookies are for coconut lovers. If you don't have rum extract, use vanilla extract.

APRIL 1

April Fools' Day

This might be my least favorite holiday ever, but there's no getting around it. Someone's going to try to fool you, so you might as well come back with an April Fools' Day cookie. My suggestions include the Ketchup Cookies from Henry Heinz's birthday (page 316), Black Bean Brownies from National Bean Day (page 7), Pork and Beans Bars (page 222), or Pat's Breakfast Cookies with the mysterious chopped bacon (page 275). Or you can take a more subtle approach and make these "apple" bars.

Mock Apple Crumb Pie Bars MAKES 16

BASE

¾ cup firmly packed light brown sugar

¾ cup old-fashioned oats

1½ cups (6.8 ounces) all-purpose flour

⅜ teaspoon baking soda

¼ teaspoon salt

9 tablespoons (4.5 ounces) cool unsalted butter, cut into 1-inch chunks

FILLING

2 cups water

1 cup granulated sugar

2 teaspoons cream of tartar

30 round butter crackers, such as Ritz

½ teaspoon ground cinnamon

1 tablespoon freshly squeezed lemon juice

¼ cup toasted and chopped pecans

Other Events on This Day: The White House hosted the first Egg Roll on its lawn in 1871

1   Preheat the oven to 350°F and place a rack in the center. Line a 9-inch square metal pan with nonstick foil, or line it with regular foil and spray the foil with flour-added baking spray.

2   **Make the base:** In the bowl of a food processor, combine the brown sugar, oats, flour, baking soda, and salt. Add the butter and pulse until the mixture is coarse and crumbly. Reserve about ¾ cup for the topping; pat the remaining into the bottom of the pan. Set aside.

3   **Make the filling:** Combine the water, sugar, and cream of tartar in a 2- to 3-quart saucepan. Set the pan over medium heat and bring to a boil. Add the crackers and boil for 5 minutes, or until the mixture is thick and looks like chunky applesauce. Spoon the cracker mixture over the crust and sprinkle with the cinnamon and lemon juice. Sprinkle the reserved crumbs on top, and then sprinkle the pecans over the crumbs. Bake the bars for 35 to 40 minutes, or until the top is lightly browned. Let the bars cool completely in the pan before slicing. When ready to serve, grasp the foil, lift from the pan, and set on a cutting board. Cut into sixteen squares.

Baker's Note: These bars were inspired by an old pie recipe that called for Ritz crackers instead of apples. If you've seen that recipe but never wanted to commit to a whole pie or just couldn't find the logic in swapping out apples for crackers, here's your excuse to try it.

Peanut Butter and Jelly Day

Some say peanut butter and jelly was made famous by soldiers in WWII, while others say the combo has been around since the early 1900s, when peanut butter was served with sweet toppings. No matter, it's the perfect day for baking these cookie bars, which capture one of America's most popular flavor combinations.

Other Events on This Day:
Children's Book Day, World Autism Day

Peanut Butter and Jelly Bars MAKES 32

2 cups (9 ounces) all-purpose flour, sifted
   or fluffed before measuring
¾ teaspoon baking powder
¾ teaspoon salt
11 tablespoons unsalted butter, room temperature
1 cup plus 2 tablespoons firmly
   packed dark brown sugar
1 teaspoon vanilla extract
1 large egg
1 large egg yolk
1 cup creamy peanut butter
¾ cup strawberry or raspberry jam or jelly
½ cup quick-cooking or old-fashioned oats (not instant)
½ cup lightly salted peanuts, coarsely chopped
½ cup peanut butter chips

1 Preheat the oven to 350°F and place a rack in the center. Line a 9 by 13-inch metal pan with nonstick foil, or line it with regular foil and spray the foil with flour-added baking spray.

2 Mix the flour, baking powder, and salt together in a medium-size bowl; set aside.

3 In the bowl of a stand mixer fitted with a paddle attachment, or in a large mixing bowl, using a handheld electric mixer, beat the butter and brown sugar on medium speed until creamy. Beat in the vanilla, egg, and egg yolk. Stir in the peanut butter. By hand or using the lowest speed of the mixer, stir in the flour mixture.

4 Reserve about 1⅓ cups of the dough and spread the rest in the bottom of the prepared pan. If you're having trouble spreading it, dampen your fingers with a little water and push the dough to the edges.

5 Spread the jam over the dough. Add the oats to the reserved peanut butter dough and drop little clumps of

it all over the top—some jam will show through. Sprinkle the peanuts over the top. Bake for 25 minutes, or until the edges are lightly browned. Remove from the oven and immediately sprinkle the peanut butter chips across the top. Let cool completely in the pan, then lift from the pan, set on a cutting board, and cut into 32 squares.

Baker's Notes: For a moist and rich bar, make sure to measure your flour with a light hand or to weigh 9 ounces. I like to weigh the peanut butter (9 ounces) as well.

Hard-Boiled Egg Chocolate Chip Cookies MAKES 16

2¾ cups (12.4 ounces) all-purpose flour

1 teaspoon salt

½ teaspoon baking soda

1 cup (8 ounces) cold unsalted
    butter

¾ cup granulated sugar

½ cup firmly packed light
    brown sugar

2 hard-boiled eggs, shells
    removed

1 teaspoon vanilla extract

1 cup semisweet chocolate chips

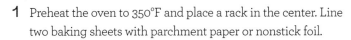

1 Preheat the oven to 350°F and place a rack in the center. Line two baking sheets with parchment paper or nonstick foil.

2 Combine the flour, salt, and baking soda in a food processor and pulse to mix. Add the butter and pulse until the mixture appears coarse and crumbly. Add both sugars and the hard-boiled eggs. Pulse again until the mixture is mealy looking. Add the vanilla and pulse until the mixture just begins to come together. Transfer the mixture to a bowl and stir in the chocolate chips—you may need to use your hands to knead it all together; the dough will be thick. You will see egg whites in the dough—they'll disappear as the cookies bake.

Easter's Coming

This recipe came about when my friend Rita, a pastry chef in Europe, pointed out that hard-boiled eggs were often used there in certain butter cookies. Curious to see how they'd work in American recipes, Rita, another baker friend named Katrina, and I tried adding it to chocolate chip dough, oatmeal dough, and double chocolate dough. The favorite was the chocolate chip version. I like making eight large cookies, but Katrina makes sixteen small ones. These are even better made with European-style butter, such as Plugra or Kerrygold.

Other Events on This Day: Don't Go to Work Unless It's Fun Day, Apple iPad first released for sale in 2010

3   Shape the dough into sixteen large balls. Arrange about 4 inches apart on the baking sheets and press down so that the tops are even. Bake one sheet at a time for 15 to 20 minutes, or until the cookies are lightly browned around the edges. Let cool on the baking sheets for 5 minutes, then transfer to a wire rack to cool completely. The texture gets better as the cookies cool. It's even better if you freeze the cooled cookies and then thaw them.

APRIL 4

Dutch-Processed Cocoa Powder Invented

On this day in 1828, Casparus van Houten Sr. was granted a patent for the hydraulic cocoa press, a device that squeezed the cocoa butter out of cocoa mass, leaving behind a "press cake" that could be pulverized into cocoa powder. Years later, his son Coenraad van Houten (who is often credited with patenting the device, when in fact it was his father) improved upon the cocoa powder by treating it with alkaline salts and creating a powder that could mix easily with water. This process is known as Dutching.

Other Events on This Day:
Cordon Bleu Day, Tell a Lie Day

Dutch Chocolate Chunk Cookies   MAKES 24

8 ounces 70% dark chocolate, chopped

1 cup (4.5 ounces) all-purpose flour

¼ cup Dutch-processed cocoa powder

1 teaspoon baking powder

½ teaspoon salt

5 tablespoons (2.5 ounces) unsalted butter, room temperature

½ cups firmly packed light brown sugar

½ cup granulated sugar

2 large eggs

1 teaspoon vanilla extract

1 cup extra-dark or semisweet chocolate chips

1 cup walnuts, toasted and chopped

5 chocolate sandwich cookies, such as
    Oreos, broken into chunks

1   In a microwave-safe bowl, melt the chocolate for 1 minute, using 50 percent power and stirring every 30 seconds until melted. Let cool slightly.

2   Mix the flour, cocoa, baking powder, and salt together in a medium-size bowl; set aside.

3   In the bowl of a stand mixer or in a medium-size bowl, using a handheld electric mixer, beat the butter on medium speed until creamy. Beat in both sugars. Reduce the mixer speed and beat in the eggs, one at a time. Add the vanilla. Stir in the melted chocolate. Using the lowest speed of the mixer, stir in the flour mixture. Making sure the dough is not too

warm from the melted chocolate, stir in the chocolate chips, walnuts, and sandwich cookie chunks.

4 Chill the dough for 30 minutes, or until it is easy to handle.

5 Preheat the oven to 350°F and place a rack in the center. Line two baking sheets with nonstick foil or parchment paper.

6 Shape the dough into 1½-inch balls and arrange 2 inches apart on the prepared baking sheets.

7 Bake one sheet at a time for 8 to 10 minutes, or until the cookies appear set—the centers should still be soft. Let cool on the baking sheets for 10 minutes, then transfer to a wire rack to cool completely.

Raisin and Spice Bars MAKES 36

2 cups (9 ounces) all-purpose flour

¼ teaspoon baking soda

½ teaspoon salt

1 teaspoon ground cinnamon

½ teaspoon freshly grated nutmeg

½ teaspoon ground allspice

¼ teaspoon ground cloves

½ teaspoon ground ginger

⅔ cup (4.5 ounces) shortening

½ cup granulated sugar

¼ cup mild molasses

1 large egg

2 tablespoons water

1 tablespoon cider vinegar

1½ cups raisins

¾ cup pecans, toasted and chopped

1 Preheat the oven to 375°F and place a rack in the center. Grease a 10 by 15-inch jelly-roll pan or line it with non-stick foil.

APRIL 5

National Raisin and Spice Bar Day

It's National Raisin and Spice Bar Day! Declared neither by Congress nor any other specific organization, this is just a day chosen at random to celebrate a flavor combination that all too often gets overshadowed by chocolate and vanilla. Adapted from Mary Margaret McBride's *Encyclopedia of Cooking*, this is my favorite raisin spice bar. It's neither too cakey nor too thick, but more like a dense and crumbly thin bar. Shortening is key to the great texture.

Other Events on This Day:
US National Park Service established in 1916

2 Mix the flour, baking soda, salt, cinnamon, nutmeg, all-spice, cloves, and ginger together in a bowl; set aside.

3 In the bowl of a stand mixer fitted with a paddle attachment, or in a large mixing bowl, using a handheld electric mixer, beat the shortening and sugar on medium speed until well mixed. Beat in the molasses, and then beat in the egg, water, and vinegar. With a spoon or using the lowest speed of the mixer, stir in the flour mixture; when it's almost blended in, add the raisins and pecans and stir until all the flour disappears. Press the batter into the pan, stretching it to the edges. Bake the bars for 20 minutes, or until the edges are browned. Let cool in the pan. If you lined the pan with foil, lift from the pan and set on a cutting board. Cut into thirty-six bars.

April Is National Pecan Month

On this day in 2001, Senator Max Cleland from Georgia asked his colleagues in Congress to join him in recognizing the whole month of April as National Pecan Month. Hey, I'm on board! They're a good source of protein and fiber, they're loaded with vitamins and minerals, and they are now being looked at for their cholesterol-lowering properties. But those are all just bonus points, because what makes pecans great are their taste and texture and the fact that they go with just about anything.

Other Events on This Day:
Teflon invented in 1938

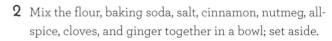

White Chocolate Mango Pecan Cookies MAKES 24

1⅓ cups (6 ounces) all-purpose flour

½ teaspoon baking soda

⅜ teaspoon salt

3 tablespoons cornstarch

8 tablespoons (4 ounces) unsalted
    butter, room temperature

½ cup firmly packed light brown sugar

½ cup granulated sugar

1 large egg

¾ teaspoon vanilla extract

1 tablespoon heavy cream

⅔ cup pecans, lightly toasted

3½ ounces white chocolate, chopped

½ cup finely chopped dried mango

1 Preheat the oven to 375°F and place a rack in the center. Line two baking sheets with nonstick foil or parchment paper.

2 Mix the flour, baking soda, salt, and cornstarch together in a medium-size bowl; set aside.

110

3 In the bowl of a stand mixer fitted with a paddle attachment, or in a large mixing bowl, using a handheld electric mixer, beat the butter and both sugars on medium speed until creamy. Beat in the egg, vanilla, and cream. By hand or using the lowest speed of the mixer, add the flour mixture to the butter mixture. When the flour mixture is absorbed, stir in the pecans, white chocolate, and mango.

4 Drop rounded tablespoonfuls of dough 2½ inches apart onto the baking sheets. Bake one sheet at a time for 12 to 13 minutes. Transfer to a wire rack to cool completely.

Baker's Note: In these cookies, pecans are paired with dried mango. I use the slightly sweetened Philippine Mango chunks by Mariani.

Pareve Brownies MAKES 16

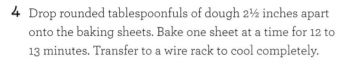

1¼ cups granulated sugar

2 large eggs

1 large egg yolk

½ cup plus 2 tablespoons vegetable oil

½ cup plus 2 tablespoons matzo cake meal

¾ cup unsweetened natural style or Dutch-
processed cocoa powder

1 teaspoon instant espresso powder

¼ teaspoon plus an extra pinch of salt

⅔ cup walnuts or pecans, toasted and finely chopped

⅓ cup pareve or vegan semisweet
chocolate chips (optional)

1 Preheat the oven to 325°F and place a rack in the center. Line an 8-inch square metal baking pan with nonstick foil.

2 In the bowl of a stand mixer fitted with a paddle attachment, or in a large mixing bowl, using a handheld electric mixer, beat the sugar, eggs, and egg yolk on medium speed for about 2 minutes or until light. Beat in the vegetable oil, cake meal, cocoa powder, and espresso powder and continue mixing until smooth. Beat in the salt and walnuts, and then stir in the chocolate chips. Pour into the prepared pan.

Another
Passover Treat

Passover dates change, but these brownies are good any time of year! Plus you can never have too many Passover recipes, right? To go with your Matzo Brittle (page 97), here's an unleavened brownie made with matzo cake meal in place of flour.

Other Events on This Day:
World Health Day

3 Bake the brownies for 28 to 32 minutes, or just until they appear set. For this recipe, it's important not to overbake. Let cool completely in the pan. Grasp the foil, lift from the pan, set on a cutting board, and cut into sixteen squares.

Baker's Notes: Espresso powder gives these unleavened brownies a rich deep flavor. If you can't find matzo cake meal, put a little regular matzo or matzo meal in a small coffee grinder and grind it until it is very fine.

Ponce de Léon Lands in Florida

After searching for the Fountain of Youth on the island of Bimini in the Bahamas, Ponce de Léon crossed the Gulf Stream and landed somewhere near St. Augustine on what many believe to be this day in 1513. Shortly after being named governor and establishing a colony, Ponce de Léon was killed by a Native American arrow.

Although Columbus first brought oranges to America, it was Ponce de Léon (who'd traveled with Columbus on the famous voyage in 1492) who planted the first crop of Florida oranges.

Other Events on This Day:
National Empanada Day

Orange Sugar Cookies MAKES 24

2 cups (9 ounces) all-purpose flour
1½ teaspoons baking powder
½ teaspoon salt
1 cup (8 ounces) unsalted butter, room temperature
1¼ cups granulated sugar
2 teaspoons orange zest
1½ teaspoons lemon zest
1 large egg, room temperature
1 teaspoon vanilla extract
3 tablespoons freshly squeezed orange juice
Coarse sugar or sprinkles, for garnishing

1 Preheat the oven to 350°F and place a rack in the center. Line two baking sheets with parchment paper or nonstick foil.

2 Mix the flour, baking powder, and salt together in a bowl; set aside.

3 In the bowl of a stand mixer fitted with a paddle attachment, or in a large mixing bowl, using a handheld electric mixer, beat the butter and sugar on medium speed until very light and creamy—about 3 minutes. Beat in the zest. Reduce the mixer speed and beat in the egg, vanilla, and orange juice. Scrape the sides of the bowl. By hand or using the lowest speed of the mixer, add the flour mixture and stir until blended.

4 Scoop up heaping tablespoonfuls and roll into large balls. Arrange about 2½ inches apart on the prepared baking sheets. Press down the tops slightly and sprinkle with the coarse sugar, or just top with some sprinkles. Bake one sheet at a time for 10 to 12 minutes, or until the edges are lightly browned. Let cool on the baking sheets for about 4 minutes, then transfer to a wire rack to cool and crisp.

Sour Cream Blueberry Pie Bars MAKES 16

BASE

¾ cup plus 2 tablespoons (4 ounces) all-purpose flour

¾ cup old-fashioned oats

½ cup firmly packed light brown sugar

½ teaspoon salt

6 tablespoons (3 ounces) cold unsalted butter, cut up

FILLING

6 tablespoons granulated sugar

½ cup regular sour cream

1¼ tablespoons all-purpose flour

¼ teaspoon vanilla extract

1 teaspoon freshly squeezed lemon juice

⅛ teaspoon salt

1½ cups fresh blueberries

¼ cup chopped pecans or almonds

1 Preheat the oven to 350°F and place a rack in the center. Line an 8-inch square metal pan with nonstick foil.

2 **Make the base:** Combine the flour, oats, brown sugar, and salt in a food processor. Pulse to mix, then add the butter and pulse until the mixture is a coarse meal. Set aside about ⅔ cup, then press the rest into the bottom of the prepared pan. Bake for 10 minutes to set the crust.

3 **Make the filling:** Mix the sugar, sour cream, flour, vanilla, lemon juice, and salt together in a bowl. Add the blueberries and stir to coat. Spread over the crust. Sprinkle

APRIL 9

Great American Pie Festival

The Great American Pie Festival is held every year during the first part of April, and includes competitions among amateur, independent, and commercial pie bakers. Pies are baked and judged on-site, and spectators are invited to stroll around and taste the goods, watch cooking demonstrations, and participate in activities such as the pie-eating contest.

It's also National Almond Cookie Day, so here's my favorite pie in bar form and with a smattering of almonds just to cover all the bases.

Other Events on This Day:
Winston Churchill Day

113

the reserved base and nuts over the filling. Bake for 30 minutes. Let cool in the pan. Chill for an hour, then lift the foil from the pan, set on a cutting board, and cut into sixteen squares.

Founding of the ASPCA

On this day in 1866, shocked by the cruelty toward animals he'd witnessed during his travels, Henry Bergh founded the American Society for the Prevention of Cruelty to Animals. The ASPCA quickly became the model for more than twenty-five other humane organizations in the United States and Canada. By the time Bergh died in 1888, thirty-seven of the thirty-eight states had passed anti-cruelty laws.

Show your pet some love by putting his or her face on a sugar cookie. First, find a good photo of your pet. Next, search the web for a company that will transfer it to edible paper. I've used a company called Sugarcraft, but there are others.

Other Events on This Day:
Golfer's Day, National Sibling Day, Cinnamon Crescent Day

Put-Your-Pet-on-a-Cookie
MAKES 12

COOKIES

3 cups (13.5 ounces) all-purpose flour

1 teaspoon baking powder

½ teaspoon salt

1 cup (8 ounces) unsalted
   butter, room temperature

1 cup granulated sugar

1 teaspoon vanilla extract

¼ teaspoon orange extract

1 large egg

ROYAL ICING

2 large pasteurized egg whites

3 cups confectioners' sugar

½ teaspoon clear or regular vanilla extract, or
   2 teaspoons of freshly squeezed lemon juice

2 to 3 tablespoons warm water, or as needed

1 Preheat the oven to 375°F and place a rack in the center. Line two baking sheets with nonstick foil or parchment paper.

2 **Make the cookies:** Mix the flour, baking powder, and salt together in a bowl; set aside. In the bowl of a stand mixer fitted with a paddle attachment, or in a mixing bowl, using a handheld electric mixer, beat the butter and sugar on medium speed until light and fluffy. Beat in the vanilla and orange extract. Reduce the mixer speed and add the egg, beating just until it's mixed in. By hand, stir in the flour mixture. The dough should be thick enough to roll at this point, but if it's not, chill for 1 hour.

3   Roll out the dough on a lightly floured surface to about
    ⅜ inch thick. Cut into 3-inch-diameter circles and arrange
    about 2½ inches apart on the prepared baking sheets.
    Bake one sheet at a time for 10 minutes, or until the edges
    begin to turn golden brown. Transfer to a wire rack to
    cool completely.

4   **Make the royal icing:** In a medium-size mixing bowl,
    combine the egg whites and confectioners' sugar and
    beat with a handheld electric mixer on low speed or whisk
    until well blended. Add the vanilla, then add warm water
    1 tablespoon at a time until you get a consistency that's
    thick enough to pipe. Transfer to a decorating bag fitted
    with a round writing tip or to a zipper bag with the corner
    snipped off. Pipe circles as neatly as you can around the
    rim of each cookie. Thin the icing that's left in the bowl
    with a little more water. Add to the piping bag and pipe
    into the center of your circles (the rims will act as dams),
    spreading until you get a clean white layer. While the ic-
    ing is still soft, carefully add your photo transfer.

Baker's Note: Put a photo on a cookie and your cookie will
be the belle of the cookie ball, even if all the other cookies
are ornately decorated masterpieces. Just ice your sugar
cookies with royal icing, peel the edible transfer from its
backing, and adhere it to the cookie.

Spicy Comets   MAKES 32

1 cup (8 ounces) unsalted butter,
    room temperature

¾ teaspoon salt

⅓ cup granulated sugar

2 teaspoons vanilla extract

1 teaspoon almond extract

¾ teaspoon ground allspice

¾ teaspoon ground cardamom

½ teaspoon ground cinnamon, plus
    more for sprinkling (optional)

2 cups (7.5 ounces) sifted cake flour

Halley's Comet Approaches Earth

Today 1986, Halley's Comet approached the Earth at a distance of 63 million kilometers on its outbound journey. Approaching the Earth every seventy-five years, it is the only comet visible to the naked eye, and might only be seen twice in a human lifetime. Unfortunately, during the 1986 visit, viewing circumstances were the poorest they'd been in two thousand years, due to urban light pollution and the fact that the comet and the Earth were on opposite sides of the sun—a big disappointment for people who'd traveled all the way to the Andes for prime viewing! The next pass won't be until 2061.

Other Events on This Day:
National Cheese Fondue Day

2 cups cornflakes, crushed after measuring
1 cup very finely chopped and toasted pecans
Confectioners' sugar, for sprinkling

1 Preheat the oven to 350°F and place a rack in the center. Line two baking sheets with parchment paper.

2 In the bowl of a stand mixer fitted with a paddle attachment, or in a large mixing bowl, using a handheld electric mixer, beat the butter, salt, sugar, vanilla, almond extract, allspice, cardamom, and ½ teaspoon of cinnamon on medium speed until creamy. Using the lowest speed of the mixer or by hand, stir in the cake flour, followed by the cornflakes and pecans.

3 Shape the dough into about 32 balls approximately ¾ inch in diameter. Arrange on the prepared baking sheets (these don't spread much). Bake for 20 to 25 minutes. Let cool slightly and then roll in confectioners' sugar while warm. Sprinkle with some extra cinnamon, if you feel like it.

Baker's Notes: Polverone means "dust," which describes the texture of one of Mexico's famous cookies. Made properly, a polverone should shatter in your mouth. Keys to good polverones include not overhandling the dough and using flour with less gluten (such as cake flour) or incorporating nuts and/or cereal.

APRIL 12

Launch of Space Shuttle Columbia

The space shuttle *Columbia* was first launched on this day in 1981. It orbited the Earth thirty-six times before landing at Edwards Air Force Base, at which point navy captain Robert L. Crippen made his famous statement, "What a way to come to California."

In memory of the space shuttle and its first launch,

Candy-Coated Chocolate Cookies MAKES ABOUT 36

1¾ cups (8 ounces) all-purpose flour
¾ teaspoon salt
1 teaspoon baking soda
8 tablespoons (4 ounces) unsalted butter, room temperature
½ cup shortening (see Baker's Notes)
¾ cup granulated sugar
½ cup firmly packed light brown sugar
1½ teaspoons vanilla extract

1 large egg

¾ cup plain candy-coated milk or dark chocolates

⅓ cup semisweet chocolate chips (optional)

1 Mix the flour, salt, and baking soda together in a medium-size bowl; set aside.

2 In the bowl of a stand mixer fitted with a paddle attachment, or in a large mixing bowl, using a handheld electric mixer, beat the butter, shortening, and both sugars on medium speed until creamy. Beat in the vanilla and egg. Continue beating for another minute, or until fluffy. Reduce the mixer speed to low and gradually add the flour mixture. Stir in the candy-coated chocolates and chocolate chips. Chill the batter for about an hour.

3 Preheat the oven to 350°F and place a rack in the center. Have ready two ungreased baking sheets.

4 Drop rounded teaspoonfuls of batter 2½ inches apart onto the baking sheets. Bake one sheet at a time for 12 to 14 minutes. Let cool on the baking sheets for about 2 minutes, then transfer to a wire rack to cool completely.

Baker's Notes: Shortening gives these cookies a crispy texture. For a wrinkly, crinkly look, tap the edges of the warm cookies inward with the tip of your spatula.

Crème Brûlée Bars MAKES 36

CRUST

1 (17.5-ounce) pouch sugar cookie
   mix, such as Betty Crocker

1 (4-serving size) box French vanilla
   instant pudding mix

2 tablespoons light or dark brown sugar

8 tablespoons (4 ounces) unsalted butter, melted

FILLING

2 (8-ounce) packages cream cheese, softened

½ cup sour cream

½ cup granulated sugar

here's a cookie packed with astronaut-approved candy.

Other Events on This Day:
National Licorice Day

Thomas Jefferson's Birthday

Happy birthday, Thomas Jefferson, one of the founding fathers of the United States, and loved by food enthusiasts for introducing us to pasta, French fries, and ice cream. Another favorite of Jefferson's was crème brûlée, so for his birthday, here it is in cookie form. This recipe is adapted from a winning recipe by Jeanne Holt of St. Paul, Minnesota, who used Betty Crocker cookie mix to create a crème brûlée–inspired bar cookie.

The touch of brilliance to this recipe is the addition of toffee bits, which stand in for what would otherwise be a burnt sugar top.

Other Events on This Day:
Peach Cobbler Day, the first elephant arrived in the United States from India in 1796

2 large eggs
3 large egg yolks
2½ teaspoons vanilla extract
⅓ cup toffee bits

1 Preheat the oven to 350°F and place a rack in the center. Line a 9 by 13-inch metal pan with nonstick foil or spray it with flour-added baking spray.

2 **Make the crust:** In a large mixing bowl, stir together the cookie mix, pudding mix, sugar, and butter to form a soft dough. Press the dough in the bottom of the prepared pan.

3 **Make the filling:** In the bowl of a stand mixer fitted with a paddle attachment, or in a large mixing bowl, using a handheld electric mixer, beat the cream cheese, sour cream, and sugar on medium speed until smooth. Add the eggs, egg yolks, and vanilla; beat until smooth. Spread the mixture over the crust and bake for 30 to 35 minutes. Remove from the oven and immediately sprinkle with the toffee bits. Let cool for 30 minutes to an hour in the pan, then chill for about 3 hours, or until very cold.

APRIL 14

Atom Split

Physicists Sir John Douglas Cockcroft and Ernest Walton split the nucleus of an atom today in 1932. Working under the direction of physicist Ernest Rutherford, they used a particle accelerator to bombard lithium with protons, creating two alpha particles. In 1951 they were awarded a Nobel Prize.

In light of the fact that it's also Pecan Day, this is my pecan-covered take on an old recipe called Split Seconds, a jam-filled cookie not unlike the butter-rich type you'd find in

Split-Second Pecan Cookies MAKES 48

2 cups (9 ounces) all-purpose flour
½ teaspoon baking powder
¾ teaspoon salt
12 tablespoons (6 ounces) unsalted butter, room temperature
⅔ cup granulated sugar
1 large egg
¾ teaspoon vanilla extract
¼ teaspoon almond extract
½ cup finely chopped pecans
⅓ cup of your favorite preserves

1. Preheat the oven to 350°F and place a rack in the center. Line two baking sheets with parchment paper or nonstick foil.

2. Mix the flour, baking powder, and salt together in a medium-size bowl; set aside.

3. In the bowl of a stand mixer fitted with a paddle attachment, or in a large mixing bowl, using a handheld electric mixer, beat the butter and sugar on medium speed until light and fluffy. Reduce the mixer speed slightly and beat in the egg, vanilla, and almond extract. By hand or using the lowest speed of the mixer, add the flour mixture and stir until incorporated.

4. Divide the dough into four portions and shape each into a skinny log about 12 inches long and ¾ inch wide. Roll the logs in the pecans. Place 4 inches apart on the prepared baking sheets, two logs per sheet. With your fingers, press a long indentation down the center of the logs and fill with your favorite preserves. Bake one sheet at a time for 15 to 20 minutes, or until the logs begin to brown around the edges. Let cool on the baking sheets for 2 minutes. Using a serrated knife, cut crosswise slightly on the diagonal every ¾ inch. Carefully separate into individual cookies and transfer to a wire rack to cool completely.

Europe. The name comes from the fact that they're relatively quick, and you split the dough down the center and fill it with your all-time-favorite jam or preserves.

Other Events on This Day:
Ex-Spouse Day, National Look Up at the Sky Day, Noah Webster copyrighted his first edition of his dictionary in 1818, Abraham Lincoln shot in 1865, the *Titanic* sank in 1912

No-Sharing Chocolate Chip Cookies MAKES 3 GIANT COOKIES

¾ cup plus 1 teaspoon (3.4 ounces) all-purpose flour

¼ teaspoon baking soda

⅛ teaspoon baking powder

¼ teaspoon salt

4 tablespoons plus 2 teaspoons (2.33 ounces) unsalted butter, room temperature

¼ cup firmly packed light brown sugar

2 tablespoons granulated sugar

1 large egg yolk

APRIL 15

Tax Day

Lighten the mood with a batch of cookies, and don't share them with anyone. You've done enough sharing this year, right? Here's the perfect batch size for today.

½ teaspoon vanilla extract

½ teaspoon water

⅔ cup semisweet chocolate chips

1 Preheat the oven to 375°F and place a rack in the center. Have ready an ungreased baking sheet.

2 Mix the flour, baking soda, baking powder, and salt together in a small bowl; set aside.

3 In a medium-size mixing bowl, using a handheld electric mixer on medium-high speed, beat the butter and both sugars until creamy. Add the egg yolk, vanilla, and water and beat on medium or low speed just until the mixture is blended. With a big spoon, stir in the flour mixture, stirring only until mixed. Stir in the chocolate chips.

4 Shape the dough into three giant mounds, 5 inches apart, on the baking sheet. Press down the tops slightly. Bake for 8 minutes at 375°F, then reduce the heat to 325°F and continue baking for another 5 to 8 minutes, or until the cookies appear set. Let cool on the baking sheet for about 5 minutes, then transfer to a wire rack to cool completely.

Baker's Notes: Measure the flour carefully, and use more chocolate chips if you want.

Other Events on This Day: **Glazed Ham Day; on this day in 1947, playing in an exhibition game for the Brooklyn Dodgers, Jackie Robinson became the first black player in major-league history**

Stress Awareness Day

Maybe you've had too much going on to notice, but the whole month of April is "Stress Awareness Month" and April 16 is Stress Awareness Day. Sponsored by a nonprofit called the Health Resource Network (HRN), the goals of Stress Awareness Month include reminding people of the dangers of stress and dispelling the many myths related to stress.

Rum Scotchies MAKES ABOUT 60

1⅓ cups (6 ounces) all-purpose flour

1 teaspoon baking soda

½ teaspoon salt

½ teaspoon ground cinnamon

1 cup (8 ounces) unsalted butter, room temperature

¾ cup granulated sugar

¾ cup firmly packed light brown sugar

1½ teaspoons rum extract

2 large eggs

3 cups old-fashioned oats

¾ cup pecans, toasted and chopped

1½ cups butterscotch chips

1 Preheat the oven to 350°F and place a rack in the center. Have ready two ungreased baking sheets.

2 Mix the flour, baking soda, salt, and cinnamon together in a medium-size bowl; set aside.

3 In the bowl of a stand mixer fitted with a paddle attachment, or in a large mixing bowl, using a handheld electric mixer, beat the butter and both sugars on medium speed until light and creamy. Beat in the rum extract. Scrape the sides of the bowl, then reduce the mixer speed slightly and beat in the eggs. By hand or using the lowest speed of the mixer, stir in the flour mixture. Stir in the oats, pecans, and butterscotch chips.

4 Scoop up rounded teaspoonfuls of batter and shape into balls. Arrange on the baking sheets, spacing about 2 inches apart. Bake one sheet at a time for 8 to 10 minutes, or until the edges are nicely browned. Let cool on the baking sheets for about 5 minutes, then carefully transfer to a wire rack to cool completely.

Rum extract is my twist on this classic comfort cookie. You might not peg it as rum right away (or at all) when tasting. It just makes the cookies taste slightly different than usual and in a good way.

Other Events on This Day: **Eggs Benedict Day; in 1862, President Lincoln signed an act abolishing slavery in Washington, DC**

Mini Tofu Chocolate Pies MAKES ABOUT 40

CRUST

1½ cups graham cracker crumbs

3 tablespoons granulated sugar

6 tablespoons (3 ounces) unsalted butter, melted

TOPPING

1½ cups semisweet chocolate chips

9 ounces silken tofu (see Baker's Note)

3 tablespoons brewed coffee

1 tablespoon vanilla extract

Rest in Peace, Benjamin Franklin

Benjamin Franklin died today in 1790. Known best for his experiments with electricity and for writing *Poor Richard's Almanac*, Franklin is credited with inventing bifocals, and is said to have introduced the colonies to tofu. In a letter from London dated January 11, 1770, he told his friend about a cheese made in China, along with instructions on how to make it. He called it "Tau-fu."

1   Preheat the oven to 325°F and place a rack in the center. Line about forty miniature muffin cups with paper liners or spray with flour-added baking spray.

2   **Make the crust:** In a large mixing bowl or the bowl of a food processor, mix the graham cracker crumbs, sugar, and butter. Scoop up heaping teaspoonfuls of the crumbs and divide evenly among the mini muffin cups. Press down tightly. Bake for about 4 minutes, keeping a close eye on them to make sure they don't burn.

3   **Make the topping:** In a microwave-safe bowl, melt the chocolate chips, using 50 percent power and stirring every 30 seconds. In the food processor or blender, puree the tofu until smooth. Add the melted chocolate, coffee, and vanilla, and continue to puree until smooth, scraping the sides of the food processor. Drop a teaspoonful of the filling into the center of each graham cracker–lined cup. Let the cups cool, then chill for 2 hours, or until set.

Baker's Note: These are mini versions of a very rich, vegetarian chocolate pie made with tofu. Make sure you use silken tofu for a smooth texture.

APRIL 18

Animal Crackers Day

Tiny animal-shaped cookies date back to medieval Germany, where master bakers made them at Christmas as edible decorations. In the mid-1800s, factories began churning out animal crackers and the cookies became quite popular—even more so in the late 1800s with cookies inspired by the P. T. Barnum circus. In 1902, the crackers officially became Barnum's Animal Crackers and were packaged in boxes similar to the ones we have today, and with a string that could be used as a handle or to hang the box from a Christmas tree.

Gluten-Free Cheddar Animal Crackers   MAKES ABOUT 84

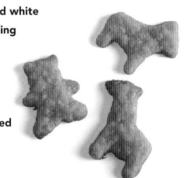

2 tablespoons tapioca flour

¾ cup (4.2 ounces) firmly packed white
     rice flour, plus more for rolling

1 tablespoon cornstarch

¾ teaspoon salt

¼ teaspoon paprika

⅛ teaspoon mustard powder

4 tablespoons (2 ounces) unsalted
     butter, room temperature

8 ounces grated Cheddar
     (see Baker's Notes)

3 to 4 tablespoons ice-cold water

1 Combine the tapioca flour, rice flour, cornstarch, salt, paprika, and mustard powder in the bowl of a food processor. Add the butter and pulse until the mixture is mealy and coarse. Add the cheese and pulse until well mixed and crumbly. Add 3 tablespoons of cold water and pulse until the mixture begins to come together. Pinch between your fingers to test. Add the remaining water if necessary.

2 Preheat the oven to 350°F and place a rack in the center. Have ready two ungreased baking sheets.

3 Dust a work surface generously with rice flour. Break off a portion of the dough and roll or pat into a ⅛-inch-thick slab. Cut as many animals as you can, and using a flat metal spatula, lift the shapes and arrange them about 1 inch apart on the baking sheets. Bake one sheet at a time for 8 to 10 minutes, or until the cookies appear slightly puffed and brown around the edges. Let cool on the baking sheets for about 5 minutes, then transfer to a wire rack to cool completely. The crackers should crisp as they cool.

Baker's Notes: These crackers are best when made with premium full-fat cheese. I've tested with 2% or low-fat, and they just don't get crisp. For the tiny animal cutters, I used the Noah's Ark Mini Metal Cutter Set by Wilton.

Cherry Amaretto White Chunk Cookies MAKES 30

¼ cup (1.7 ounces) shortening

4 tablespoons (2 ounces) unsalted
    butter, room temperature

½ cup firmly packed light brown sugar

½ cup granulated sugar

2 tablespoons amaretto-flavored liquid coffee creamer

1 large egg

2 teaspoons vanilla extract

1½ cups all-purpose flour

½ teaspoon baking powder

½ teaspoon baking soda

Other Events on This Day: Chicago hosted the first Woman's World's Fair in 1925

APRIL 19

Amaretto Day

Today's food holiday is Amaretto Day, celebrating the elegant Italian liqueur we associate with almonds, but which is actually made with apricot kernels and a blend of other ingredients that give it a bittersweet flavor. Amaretto di Saronno is named for its place of origin, Saronno, Italy, where it is said to have been created by a beautiful innkeeper who made it as a thank-you gift for the artist who used her as his muse. Years later, her recipe was rediscovered and made famous by an Italian family that has kept the blend a closely guarded secret. To really celebrate Amaretto Day, you'll need to serve these with a glass of liqueur. The cookie is more of a nod to the drink. There's no actual amaretto in it; the liquid coffee creamer is amaretto flavored.

Other Events on This Day:
Anniversary of the first Boston Marathon in 1897

½ teaspoon salt
¾ cup quick-cooking oats
5 ounces white chocolate, chopped
½ cup almonds, toasted and chopped
½ cup dried cherries, chopped

Fact: Amaretto di Saronno's beautiful square bottle was designed in the 1970s by a master glass maker from Murano, Venice.

1 Preheat the oven to 350°F and place a rack in the center. Have ready two ungreased baking sheets.

2 In the bowl of a stand mixer fitted with a paddle attachment, or in a large mixing bowl, using a handheld electric mixer, beat the shortening, butter, and both sugars on medium speed until fluffy. Beat in the coffee creamer, egg, and vanilla extract.

3 Combine the flour, baking powder, baking soda, and salt and stir into the sugar mixture. Stir in the oats, white chocolate chunks, nuts, and cherries.

4 Drop rounded tablespoonfuls of dough onto the baking sheets, spacing about 2½ inches apart. Bake one sheet at a time for 10 to 12 minutes, or until golden brown around the edges. Let cool on the baking sheets for about 4 minutes, then transfer to a wire rack to cool completely.

APRIL 20

The Curies Discover Radium

Marie and Pierre Curie isolated radium today in 1898. Working with a radioactive uranium-containing ore called pitchblende, they theorized that there was another element in the ore and continued to refine the pitchblende until they isolated tiny amounts of radium. In 1911, Marie was awarded with the Nobel Prize.

Radium Chip Pistachio Cookies MAKES ABOUT 42

2¼ cups (10.1 ounces) all-purpose flour
1 teaspoon baking soda
½ teaspoon salt
1 cup (8 ounces) unsalted butter, room temperature
¾ cup firmly packed light brown sugar
¾ cup granulated sugar
1 (3.4-ounce) box instant pistachio pudding mix
2 large eggs
1½ teaspoons vanilla extract

½ teaspoon almond extract

1 cup quick-cooking oats (not instant)

1½ cups semisweet chocolate chips

⅔ cup pistachios, toasted, unsalted, roughly
   chopped (see Baker's Note)

1 Preheat the oven to 350°F and place a rack in the center.
   Have ready two ungreased baking sheets.

2 Mix the flour, baking soda, and salt together in a medium-
   size bowl; set aside.

3 In the bowl of a stand mixer fitted with a paddle attachment, or in a large mixing bowl, using a handheld electric
   mixer, beat the butter and both sugars on medium speed
   until creamy, scraping the sides of the bowl often. Beat in
   the pudding mix, and then beat in the eggs, vanilla, and
   almond extract, using the medium-low speed of the mixer.
   By hand or using the lowest speed of the mixer, add the
   flour mixture to the batter and stir until it is almost fully
   mixed in. Stir in the oats, chocolate chips, and pistachios.

4 Scoop up tablespoonfuls of dough and shape into balls
   about 1 inch in diameter (about 42 balls). Arrange about
   2½ inches apart on the baking sheets. Press down slightly
   so that tops are even. Bake one sheet at a time for 10 to
   12 minutes, or until the edges are nicely browned and the
   cookies appear set. Remove the cookies from the oven,
   and while they are still warm, using the tip of a spatula,
   gently nudge the edges of the cookies inward to add
   some crinkles and folds. Let cool on the baking sheets
   for about 5 minutes, then transfer to a wire rack to
   cool completely.

Baker's Note: To toast the raw pistachios, spread
them on a baking sheet and bake at 350°F for about
7 minutes or until they are aromatic and slightly
browned around the edges.

Unlike the images
depicted in cartoons, radium
does not emit a green glow.
Disappointing, I know. But
that shouldn't stop you
from making cookies with a
lovely green hue, courtesy of
pistachio pudding mix.

Other Events on This Day:
**Pineapple Upside-Down Cake
Day**

San Jacinto Day

Everyone remembers the Alamo, but Texans also observe San Jacinto Day, an official state holiday commemorating the day in 1836 when General Sam Houston and his army defeated General Antonio López de Santa Anna's army in a battle that lasted 18 minutes. Three weeks later, Santa Anna signed a peace treaty that eventually led to Texas becoming an independent republic.

This cookie was inspired by one I tasted at a holiday cookie contest held at a cooking store called Faraday's in Austin, Texas. It was submitted by Michael Hedgedus. Over the years, it's become one of my all-time favorite chocolate cookies—fun to serve, because people aren't expecting the rush of heat at the end.

Other Events on This Day:
Chocolate-Covered Cashews Day, Seattle's Space Needle opened in 1962

Tex-Mex Chocolate Chipotle Cherry Cookies
MAKES ABOUT 32

2 cups (9 ounces) all-purpose flour

½ cup unsweetened natural cocoa powder

1 teaspoon baking soda

½ teaspoon salt

1 tablespoon ground cinnamon

½ teaspoon chipotle powder

¼ teaspoon freshly grated nutmeg

1 cup (8 ounces) unsalted butter, room temperature

¾ cup granulated sugar

½ cup firmly packed light brown sugar

¼ cup honey

1 tablespoon vanilla extract

2 large eggs

1 cup pecans, toasted and roughly chopped

2 cups extra-dark chocolate chips

⅔ cup dried cherries

1 Preheat the oven to 375°F and place a rack in the center. Line two baking sheets with parchment paper or nonstick foil.

2 Mix the flour, cocoa powder, baking soda, salt, cinnamon, chipotle powder, and nutmeg together in a medium-size bowl; set aside.

3 In the bowl of a stand mixer fitted with a paddle attachment, or in a large mixing bowl, using a handheld electric mixer, beat the butter, both sugars, honey, and vanilla on medium speed until creamy. Reduce the mixer speed slightly, and then add the eggs, one at a time. By hand or using the lowest speed of the mixer, slowly incorporate the flour mixture into the batter. Stir in the pecans, chocolate chips, and cherries. Chill the batter for about 15 minutes.

4 Scoop up tablespoonfuls of dough and shape into balls a little over 1 inch in diameter. Arrange about 2½ inches

apart on the prepared baking sheets. Bake one sheet at a time for about 10 minutes, or until the cookies appear set. Let cool on the baking sheets for about 5 minutes, then transfer to a wire rack to cool completely.

Brazil Nut Cookies MAKES 48

1¾ cups plus 2 tablespoons (8 ounces)
    all-purpose flour

2 tablespoons cornstarch

½ teaspoon baking powder

1½ teaspoons baking soda

½ generous teaspoon salt

1 cup (8 ounces) unsalted butter, room temperature

1 cup firmly packed light brown sugar

1 cup granulated sugar

1 large egg

1½ teaspoons vanilla extract

2 cups flaked cereal

6 ounces dark chocolate, cut into chunks, or
    1 cup bittersweet chocolate chips

¾ cup flaked sweetened or unsweetened
    shredded coconut

1 cup Brazil nuts, coarsely chopped

1   Preheat the oven to 350°F and place a rack in the center. Have ready two ungreased baking sheets.

2   In a small bowl, thoroughly stir together the flour, cornstarch, baking powder, baking soda, and salt.

3   In the bowl of a stand mixer fitted with a paddle attachment, or in a large mixing bowl, using a handheld electric mixer, beat the butter on medium speed until creamy. Add both sugars and continue beating for another minute, or until very light. Reduce the mixer speed to low and beat in the egg and vanilla. By hand or using the lowest speed of the mixer, add the flour mixture and stir until incorporated, then stir in the cereal, chocolate, coconut, and Brazil nuts. The batter will seem fairly dry.

Earth Day

Earth Day was conceived in 1970 by Senator Gaylord Nelson, an environmental activist who planned it as a national teach-in to raise awareness on environmental issues. In 1990, Denis Hayes, a coordinator for the original Earth Day, took it global by forming a large network that has grown to include over 175 countries.

Representing the rainforest and the complex growing environment Brazil nuts need to thrive, here's a cookie that might spur conversations for Earth Day.

Other Events on This Day:
Girl Scout Leader Day

4 Scoop up tablespoonfuls of dough and shape into 1-inch balls. Arrange about 2½ inches apart on the baking sheets. Press down the tops slightly. Bake one sheet at a time for 10 to 13 minutes, or until the edges are lightly browned and the cookies appear set. Let cool on the baking sheets for about 3 minutes, then transfer to a wire rack to cool completely.

Baker's Notes: The batter will seem somewhat dry when you add the cereal and nuts, but the resulting cookie is sweet and light. You can use whatever type of flaked cereal you like.

APRIL 23

Administrative Professionals Day

The original National Secretaries Week was held June 1 through 7, 1952, with Wednesday being the actual Secretaries Day. In 1955, the date was changed to the last week of April, keeping Wednesday the special day. In 1981, the name changed to Professional Secretaries Week, and later became Administrative Professionals Day.

In honor of all the administrative professionals, and the fact that today is also Cherry Cheesecake Day, here's the perfect treat to take to the office.

Other Events on This Day:
William Shakespeare was born in 1564

Mini Cherry Cheesecakes MAKES 18

BASE
1½ cups graham cracker crumbs (see Baker's Note)
1 tablespoon granulated sugar
6 tablespoons (3 ounces) unsalted butter, melted

FILLING
2 (8-ounce) packages cream cheese, softened
½ cup granulated sugar
2 large eggs, room temperature
2 tablespoons freshly squeezed lemon juice
½ teaspoon vanilla extract
1 (21-ounce) can cherry pie filling

1 Preheat the oven to 350°F and place a rack in the center. Line eighteen muffin cups with cupcake liners and set aside.

2 **Make the base:** Mix together the crumbs, sugar, and butter. Divide the crumb mixture evenly among the lined cups and press down firmly.

3 **Make the filling:** Beat the cream cheese and sugar with a handheld electric mixer on medium-high speed in a large mixing bowl until light and creamy. Reduce the mixer speed and add the eggs, lemon juice, and vanilla; beat until smooth, being careful not to beat in extra air.

Fill each baking cup with about 3 tablespoons of the cheesecake mixture. Bake the cheesecakes for 17 to 19 minutes, or until they appear set—a crack may form. Let cool in the muffin pans for about 10 minutes, then transfer to a wire rack to cool completely. Chill thoroughly, then top with the cherry pie filling.

Baker's Note: If you are short on time, use eighteen whole vanilla wafer cookies (or Oreos!) instead of making the crust.

Hazelnut Chocolate Marshmallow Puffs MAKES 16

8 large marshmallows

About ⅓ cup chocolate hazelnut spread

1 (8-ounce) can refrigerated crescent
   dinner rolls (see Baker's Notes)

2 tablespoons melted unsalted butter

2 tablespoons granulated sugar

1 teaspoon ground cinnamon

1 Preheat the oven to 375°F and place a rack in the center. Line two baking sheets with nonstick foil or parchment paper.

2 Cut the marshmallows in half horizontally so that you have sixteen little rounds. Working with one round at a time, cut each marshmallow in half again horizontally and sandwich a heaping ¼ teaspoon of Nutella between the split marshmallow rounds. Repeat until you have sixteen little marshmallow and Nutella sandwiches.

3 Open the crescent dough and separate it into eight triangles. Cut each triangle in half to make sixteen smaller triangles.

4 Working one triangle at a time, place one of your little marshmallow sandwiches in the center of the triangle of dough. Bring the corners up and over the marshmallow and pinch all the seams to hide the marshmallow. Place on a prepared baking sheet. Repeat with remaining dough triangles and marshmallows until you have sixteen little bundles, eight to a sheet. With a pastry brush, paint the

APRIL 24

Pigs-in-a-Blanket Day

Today is Pigs-in-a-Blanket Day, celebrating the snack most often comprised of a little sausage wrapped in some sort of dough. Of course, it varies by location. In some countries (such as England) a pig-in-a-blanket is meat wrapped in more bacon, while other cultures wrap meat or other vegetables in phyllo dough or puff pastry. Where I grew up, the meat was wrapped in dough from a can of crescent rolls. This marshmallow-filled version was inspired by an old recipe, where the marshmallows magically disappear after baking, leaving you with a chewy, buttery, cinnamon pastry.

Other Events on This Day:
Library of Congress established in 1800

129

melted butter over the dough. Mix the sugar and cinnamon and sprinkle generously over each round. Bake one sheet at a time for 10 to 12 minutes, or until the dough is golden and appears cooked. Let cool slightly on the pan, then serve while slightly warm or at room temperature.

Baker's Note: Keep a close eye on the puffs after the first 10 minutes. You can use full or reduced-fat crescent rolls.

APRIL 25

ANZAC Day

A NZAC Day is a day of remembrance celebrated in Australia and New Zealand to honor those who died while serving in the Australian and New Zealand Army Corps. It's also a perfect day for making cookies similar to the type made by army wives who put them in care packages for their loved ones. ANZAC biscuits are easy to make, travel well, and stay fresh for a long time.

Other Events on This Day:
Zucchini Bread Day, World Penguin Day, Plumber's Day

ANZAC Biscuits MAKES 24

1 cup (4.5 ounces) all-purpose flour
¼ teaspoon salt
½ teaspoon baking soda
¼ teaspoon ground cinnamon
1 cup old-fashioned oats
1 cup firmly packed light brown sugar
4 tablespoons (2 ounces) unsalted butter, melted
3 tablespoons water
¾ teaspoon vanilla extract
2 tablespoons golden syrup (see Baker's Note)
½ cup shredded sweetened coconut

1 Preheat the oven to 325°F and place a rack in the center. Line two baking sheets with nonstick foil or parchment paper.

2 Mix the flour, salt, baking soda, and cinnamon together in a medium-size bowl. Stir in the oats and sugar. When the dry ingredients are well mixed, add the butter, water, vanilla, and golden syrup and mix just until blended. Stir in the coconut.

3 Drop generously rounded teaspoonfuls of batter 2 inches apart onto the prepared baking sheets. Press down the tops slightly. Bake one sheet at a time for 12 minutes, or until almost set. Let cool on the baking sheets for 2 to 3 minutes, or until firm. Transfer to wire racks to cool completely.

Baker's Note: Golden syrup is light cane syrup with a golden color and caramel flavor. It can usually be found near the corn syrup under the brand name Lyle's.

Caramel Pretzel Blondies

MAKES 16 SMALL SQUARES

BLONDIES

½ cup pecan halves (see Baker's Note)

2 teaspoons unsalted butter

¼ cup vegetable oil

1 cup firmly packed light brown sugar

1 large egg

¾ teaspoon vanilla extract

½ teaspoon salt

¾ cup all-purpose flour

1 teaspoon baking powder

⅔ cup broken miniature pretzels

TOPPING

⅓ cup caramel bits, or 1½ ounces (about 7)
   unwrapped caramels

1 tablespoon heavy cream

1 Preheat the oven to 350°F and place a rack in the center. Line an 8-inch square metal pan with nonstick or regular foil.

2 **Make the blondies:** Put the pecans in the pan and toast in a 350°F oven for 7 minutes, or until aromatic and toasted. Remove from the oven and add the butter, tossing to coat. Transfer to a separate bowl or small plate.

3 In a large mixing bowl, whisk together the oil, sugar, and egg. Whisk in the vanilla and salt. In a separate bowl, mix together the flour and baking powder, then add to the batter and mix until blended. Stir in the pecans and ⅓ cup of the broken pretzels.

4 If you used regular foil to line the pan, spray it with flour-added baking spray. Spread the mixture evenly in the pan. Scatter the remaining pretzels over the top of the bars. Bake for 22 to 25 minutes, or until the bars appear set and the edges are browned. Let cool completely in the pan.

National Pretzel Day

Pretzels are one of the world's oldest snack foods. Invented around AD 610 by monks who shaped dough scraps into the shape of a child's arms folded in prayer, the three holes represent the Christian trinity. Those, of course, were the soft pretzels. As for the hard type, legend says they were invented in the seventeenth century in Pennsylvania when a baker fell asleep while the pretzels were baking in the hearth. He was about to throw them out, but tasted one anyway and decided they were quite good. They also stayed fresh longer, which probably made them even more popular.

Other Events on This Day:
**Hug an Australian Day,
National Richter Scale Day**

5 **Make the topping:** In a 2-cup microwave-safe measuring cup or bowl, combine the caramel and cream. Microwave for 20 to 30 seconds on high or just until the cream boils. Stir until the caramel melts, microwaving and stirring at additional 10-second intervals if necessary. Drizzle the caramel mixture over the bars. If the caramel seems too thick to drizzle, transfer it to a small resealable heavy-duty freezer bag, snip a tiny bit off the corner of the bag, and pipe the caramel on top.

Baker's Note: Toasting the pecans in the same pan you use to bake the bars saves a baking sheet.

APRIL 27

Museum of Natural History Opens

On this day in 1871, the American Museum of Natural History opened to the public in New York City. Located along the west side of Central Park, the museum houses the single largest collection of dinosaur fossils in the world.

Other Events on This Day: **Morse Code Day, Tell a Story Day**

Dinosaur Food (a.k.a. Cereal Puffs) MAKES 20

1 tablespoon unsalted butter, plus more
    for greasing your hands
20 large marshmallows
1½ tablespoons creamy peanut butter
4 cups chocolate and peanut butter puff
    cereal, such as Reese's Puffs

1 In a large, microwave-safe mixing bowl, microwave the butter on high for 30 seconds, or until melted. Add the marshmallows and heat for another minute on high to puff and soften the marshmallows. Remove from the microwave and stir until melted. Add the peanut butter and stir until smooth. Add the cereal and stir to coat.

2 Rub butter all over your hands. Scoop up ¼-cup-size blobs of cereal mixture and shape into balls. Set the balls on a large sheet of nonstick foil or parchment paper and let set for about 30 minutes.

Handheld Blueberry Pies MAKES ABOUT 36

1 pint fresh or frozen blueberries

⅓ cup granulated sugar

1 tablespoon all-purpose flour

1½ tablespoons water

2 teaspoons freshly squeezed
   lemon juice

Pinch of ground cinnamon

⅛ teaspoon vanilla extract

1 (14.1-ounce) package
   refrigerated unroll-
   and-bake piecrust

Fact: Blueberries are known for their high antioxidant content.

1 In a medium-size saucepan, mix together the blueberries, sugar, flour, water, lemon juice, and cinnamon. Bring to a boil over medium heat. Reduce the heat to a simmer and cook for about 7 minutes, stirring often. Remove from the heat and stir in the vanilla. Let cool completely or cover and keep chilled until you are ready to use it.

2 Preheat the oven to 375°F and place a rack in the center. Spray 36 mini muffin cups with flour-added baking spray.

3 Unroll one round of piecrust dough to make a 12-inch circle. Using a 2-inch round cookie cutter, cut out circles and press them as neatly as you can into the prepared muffin cups.

4 Put a small spoonful of blueberry mixture in the center of each cup. Bake for 15 to 17 minutes, or until the crusts are browned. Let cool completely in the pans, then unmold by loosening with the tip of a knife. Repeat with the remaining piecrust dough and filling.

National Blueberry Pie Day

The first thing I make during blueberry season is blueberry pie, but for parties and get-togethers, I've taken to making it in cookie form. These little pies are cute either plain or topped with a little whipped cream.

Other Events on This Day:
Vaccine for yellow fever developed in 1932

133

On this day in 2011, Prince William married Kate Middleton in Westminster Abbey. What we didn't get to see was the cake. Rumor has it that the groom's cake was a children's favorite called Biscuit Cake, a mixture of broken cookies and fruit held together by melted chocolate and similar to a British cookie called Chocolate Tiffin.

Other Events on This Day:
Zipper Day

Chocolate Tiffins MAKES 24

BOTTOM AND TOP LAYERS

3 tablespoons (1.5 ounces) unsalted butter

6 ounces semisweet chocolate, chopped

MIDDLE LAYER

5½ tablespoons (2.75 ounces) unsalted butter

6 ounces semisweet chocolate, chopped

1 tablespoon golden syrup or light corn syrup

16 graham cracker squares, broken into pieces,
or a heaping cup of bear grahams

¼ cup toasted and chopped pecans

⅓ cup dried sour cherries or cherry-
flavored cranberries

1 Line a 9-inch loaf pan with nonstick foil, or line it with regular foil and spray the foil with flour-added baking spray.

2 **Make the first layer:** In a small, microwave-safe mixing bowl, microwave the butter on high for 30 seconds, or until melted. Add the chocolate and stir until it has melted as much as it can. It probably won't melt all the way, so return it to the microwave and heat on 50 percent power for another 30 seconds to 1 minute and stir until fully melted. Spoon half of this melted chocolate over the bottom of the prepared pan to make an even layer of chocolate. Chill the pan to set the chocolate. Set the bowl of the remaining melted chocolate aside.

3 **Make the middle layer:** In a second microwave-safe mixing bowl, microwave the butter on high for 30 seconds, or until melted. Add the chocolate and stir until fully or partially melted. If necessary, return to the microwave and heat on 50 percent power for 30 to 60 seconds. Stir until completely melted. Stir in the golden syrup, broken graham crackers, nuts, and cherries. Carefully spoon this mixture over the thin layer of set chocolate in the pan. Press down as evenly as possible. Return the pan to the refrigerator and start on layer three.

4 **Make the top layer:** Soften the remaining chocolate mixture in the first bowl in the microwave by heating at 50 percent power for about 30 seconds. Spread it over the cookie mixture to make a flat top. Return the pan to the refrigerator and chill for about 3 hours, or until set. Grasp the foil, lift from the pan, and cut into squares.

Baker's Notes: In England they make these with digestive biscuits, but I like using graham crackers or little bear-shaped crackers. You may start to worry there are too many cookies, but in this case the chocolate and butter are so rich that you need all those light cookies to balance out the richness.

Old-Fashioned Oatmeal Cookies MAKES ABOUT 60

2 cups (9 ounces) all-purpose flour

1 teaspoon baking soda

1 teaspoon baking powder

1 teaspoon salt

2 teaspoons ground cinnamon

1 cup (8 ounces) unsalted butter, room temperature

1 cup firmly packed dark brown sugar

1 cup granulated sugar

2 teaspoons vanilla extract

2 large eggs

3 cups quick-cooking or old-fashioned
    oats (not instant)

1 cup raisins

$^2/_3$ cup toasted and chopped walnuts

1 Preheat the oven to 350°F and place a rack in the center. Line two baking sheets with nonstick foil or parchment paper.

2 Mix the flour, baking soda, baking powder, salt, and cinnamon together in a medium-size bowl; set aside.

3 In the bowl of a stand mixer fitted with a paddle attachment, or in a large mixing bowl, using a handheld electric

National Oatmeal Cookie Day

It's National Oatmeal Cookie Day, so celebrate one of America's favorite cookie flavors by making a batch from scratch.

Oatmeal cookies, which some believe evolved from Scottish oatcakes or bannocks, became popular in America after the founding of Quaker Oats in the mid-nineteenth century. In fact, Quaker featured one of the earliest American recipes for oatcakes in an ad dated 1908. The recipe had just three ingredients— ½ pound of butter, two eggs, and 3 cups of oats.

mixer, beat the butter and both sugars on medium speed until creamy. Reduce the mixer speed slightly and beat in the vanilla and eggs. When well mixed, stir in the oats, raisins, and nuts.

4 Drop tablespoons of batter about 2½ inches apart onto the prepared baking sheets. Bake for 8 to 10 minutes, or until golden brown. Let cool on the baking sheets for about 2 minutes, then transfer to a wire rack to cool completely.

MAY 1

Kentucky Derby

Founded by Colonel Meriwether Lewis Clark Jr. and held every year at Louisville's Churchill Downs, the Kentucky Derby has been called "the Greatest Two Minutes in Sports." Today commemorates the first race, held on May 17, 1875. Since then, wearing a big hat, drinking mint juleps, and eating a special pie made with pecans, bourbon, and chocolate at the derby has become a tradition.

These handheld pies with a cream cheese crust are similar to the famous pie named after the derby. In the South they're called tassies.

Other Events on This Day:
May Day

Mini Kentucky Derby Tarts MAKES 36

DOUGH
8 tablespoons (4 ounces) unsalted butter, softened
3 ounces cream cheese
1 cup (4.5 ounces) all-purpose flour

FILLING
1 large egg
¾ cup firmly packed light brown sugar
1 tablespoon bourbon
1 tablespoon unsalted butter, melted
¼ teaspoon vanilla extract
Pinch of salt
¼ cup pecans, toasted and finely chopped
¼ cup semisweet chocolate chips or mini chips

Fact:
To win the Triple Crown, a horse must win the Kentucky Derby, Preakness, and Belmont Stakes.

1 Preheat the oven to 325°F and place a rack in the center. Grease thirty-six mini muffin cups with shortening or spray with flour-added baking spray.

2 **Make the muffin dough:** Beat the butter and cream cheese in a medium-size bowl until light and creamy. Add the flour and stir just until mixed in. At this point, the dough should be a tad sticky, so chill it for 10 minutes or just until firm enough to handle.

3. **Meanwhile, make the filling:** Mix the egg, sugar, bourbon, butter, vanilla, and salt together in a medium-size bowl. Stir in the pecans and chocolate chips.

4. Remove the dough from the refrigerator and divide it into thirty-six equal-size pieces. Roll each into a ball and press each ball into a muffin cup so that it comes slightly up the sides. Divide the filling evenly among the mini muffin cups (about 1 teaspoon per cup). Bake for about 25 minutes, or until set. Let cool for about 10 minutes in the mini muffin cups, then gently loosen the edges with the tip of a knife and remove from the cups. Serve warm or let cool completely before serving.

Mice MAKES 36

11 tablespoons (5.5 ounces) unsalted
    butter, room temperature
²/₃ cup granulated sugar
¼ teaspoon salt
1 teaspoon vanilla extract
1 large egg yolk
2 cups (9 ounces) all-purpose flour
1 to 2 tablespoons of cream or as needed (optional)
1 large egg, lightly beaten with 2 teaspoons of water
Sliced almonds
Chow mein noodles or pieces of fiber cereal
Chocolate mini chips, or currants, or chopped
    dried cranberries, or raisins

1. Preheat the oven to 350°F and place a rack in the center. Line two baking sheets with parchment paper or nonstick foil.

2. In the bowl of a stand mixer fitted with a paddle attachment, or in a large mixing bowl, using a handheld electric mixer, beat the butter and sugar on medium speed until light. Beat in the salt and vanilla. Reduce the mixer speed to low and beat in the egg yolk. Add the flour

MAY 2

Children's Book Week

It's Children's Book Week! In honor of the star character of a beloved cookie-inspired book, If You Give a Mouse a Cookie, here's a cookie to make with the kids. Consider the almonds, currants, and chow mein noodles suggestions and decorate these mice with whatever ingredients you have in the pantry.

Other Events on This Day:
National Truffle Day

½ cup at a time, stirring by hand or using the lowest speed of the mixer until fully mixed. The dough should be slightly dry, yet not so dry that it falls apart. If your dough is too dry to easily mold, add cream 1 tablespoon at a time until the dough is malleable.

3   Scoop up tablespoonfuls of dough and shape into little ovals with a pointy end. Arrange about 2 inches apart on the prepared baking sheets. Brush the dough with a little beaten egg. Attach almonds for ears and a chow mein noodle or piece of cereal for a tail, and use chocolate mini chips or currants to make the eyes. For the nose, use another currant or a small piece of chopped dried cranberry.

4   Bake one sheet at a time for 15 to 20 minutes, or until slightly browned. Transfer to a wire rack and let cool completely.

National Teacher Day

National Teacher Day dates back to 1944, when a teacher in Arkansas began writing to political and educational leaders, encouraging them to proclaim a day for teachers. Eleanor Roosevelt, a recipient of one of those letters, believed in the cause, and in 1953, persuaded Congress to declare a National Teacher Day for that year. In the late 1970s, the National Education Association lobbied for another National Teacher Day.

Thanks to various organizations, we now celebrate National Teacher Week the first week of May, and National Teacher Day that Tuesday. I asked my daughter what the perfect Teacher Day cookie was and she suggested something with apples. I felt it should be chocolate, so we compromised and made this cakey bar cookie.

Chocolate-Apple Spice Bars   MAKES 24

BASE

2 cups (9 ounces) all-purpose flour

2 tablespoons unsweetened natural cocoa powder

1½ teaspoons baking soda

¾ teaspoon salt

½ teaspoon ground cinnamon

8 tablespoons (4 ounces) unsalted butter, room temperature

1½ cups granulated sugar

2 large eggs, lightly beaten

1 teaspoon vanilla extract

2 cups unsweetened applesauce

½ cup semisweet chocolate chips

TOPPING

1 tablespoon granulated sugar

⅔ cup pecans, toasted and finely chopped

1 cup semisweet chocolate chips

1 Preheat the oven to 350°F and place a rack in the center. Line a 9 by 13-inch metal pan with nonstick foil.

2 **Make the base:** Mix the flour, cocoa powder, baking soda, salt, and cinnamon together in a bowl; set aside.

3 In the bowl of a stand mixer fitted with a paddle attachment, or in a large mixing bowl, using a handheld electric mixer, beat the butter and sugar on medium speed until creamy. Reduce the mixer speed to low and beat in the eggs, one at a time. Beat in the vanilla and applesauce. Stir in the flour mixture by hand, then stir in the chocolate chips. Pour the batter into the pan.

4 **Make the topping:** Mix together the sugar, pecans, and chocolate chips and sprinkle evenly over the base. Bake for 25 to 30 minutes. Let cool completely in the pan before cutting into bars.

Double Chocolate Raspberry Chipotle Bars MAKES 16

8 tablespoons (4 ounces) unsalted butter

1 cup (4.5 ounces) all-purpose flour

3 tablespoons unsweetened natural cocoa powder

¾ cup old-fashioned oats

⅓ cup granulated sugar

2 tablespoons firmly packed light brown sugar

½ teaspoon salt

¼ teaspoon baking soda

1 cup extra-dark chocolate chips

¾ cup toasted and finely chopped walnuts or pecans

½ cup raspberry preserves

½ teaspoon chipotle powder (see Baker's Note)

1 Preheat the oven to 350°F and place a rack in the center. Line an 8-inch square metal pan with nonstick foil, or line with regular foil and spray with flour-added baking spray.

2 Melt the butter in the microwave or on the stovetop over low heat, then set aside to cool to room temperature. In

Other Events on This Day: **Lumpy Rug Day, World Press Freedom Day**

MAY 4

International Firefighters' Day

Today is International Firefighters' Day, so take a batch of cookies to your local firehouse. If you feel strange about dropping cookies off at the fire station, try the alternative. Make something with a little heat to it and serve it up with a reminder of the significance of the date.

Other Events on This Day: **Candied Orange Peel Day**

a large mixing bowl, combine the flour, cocoa powder, oats, sugars, salt, and baking soda. Stir very well. Add the cooled melted butter and mix until crumbly. Stir in ⅔ cup of the chocolate chips and ½ cup of the nuts. Press about half of the oat mixture into the bottom of the pan.

3 Stir together the preserves and chipotle powder, then spread over the oat mixture. Crumble the remaining oat mixture over the top and gently press down. Sprinkle with the remaining chocolate chips and nuts.

4 Bake for 30 to 35 minutes or until set. Let cool completely, then chill for at least 1 hour. Cut into sixteen bars.

Baker's Note: If your chipotle has been in the pantry a while, ½ teaspoon should give you just the right amount of heat. If your chipotle powder is brand new, consider reducing the amount slightly, as fresh chile powder is almost always quite a bit hotter. Chipotle powder varies in strength, but even if the filling is very fiery, it will be tempered by the rich sugar and chocolate.

Cinco de Mayo

Not just an excuse to drink margaritas, Cinco de Mayo is a Mexican holiday marking the day in 1862 when Mexico defeated the French army at the battle of Puebla. Celebrated across the United States and in some regions of Mexico, it has evolved into a celebration of Mexican heritage, and many people hold gatherings and barbecues. If you're going to a Cinco de Mayo party and want to take along something fun, here's a cookie made with a popular Mexican snack.

Cinco de Mayo Pepita Crunch Cookies MAKES 36

½ cup toasted, salted pepitas (see Baker's Note)

¾ cup old-fashioned or quick-cooking oats (not instant)

¾ cup cornflakes

½ cup flaked sweetened coconut

1¾ cups (8 ounces) all-purpose flour

1½ teaspoons baking soda

½ teaspoon salt

8 tablespoons (4 ounces) unsalted
      butter, room temperature

½ cup firmly packed light brown sugar

½ cup granulated sugar

2 tablespoons lightly beaten egg

2 teaspoons vanilla extract

½ cup vegetable oil

3 ounces white chocolate, finely chopped

1 Preheat the oven to 350°F and place a rack in the center. Have ready two ungreased baking sheets.

2 Combine the pepitas and oats in a food processor and process until coarsely ground. Add the cornflakes and coconut and pulse about twenty times, or until the mixture is fairly uniform but there are still some flecks of cornflakes. Set aside.

3 Mix the flour, baking soda, and salt together in a medium-size bowl; set aside.

4 In the bowl of a stand mixer fitted with a paddle attachment, or in a large mixing bowl, using a handheld electric mixer, beat the butter and both sugars on medium speed until creamy. Add the egg and vanilla and beat for another 30 seconds, then beat in the oil. Add the flour mixture and stir by hand until it is almost mixed in. Add the pepita mixture and white chocolate and stir until fully blended.

5 Scoop up tablespoonfuls of dough and shape into 1-inch balls. Press the balls lightly to make ½-inch-thick rounds and arrange them about 2 inches apart on the baking sheets.

6 Bake one sheet at a time for 12 to 14 minutes, or until the edges are lightly browned. Let cool for about 1 minute on the baking sheets, then transfer to a wire rack to cool completely.

Baker's Note: Toasted, salted pepitas (pumpkin seeds; Spanish for "little seeds") add flavor and help make these cookies light and crisp. In this case, the term "pepita" refers to the kernel of the pumpkin seed rather than the whole seed. You can find roasted, salted pepitas at Mexican grocery stores or in the bulk bins of specialty health food stores.

Other Events on This Day:
Oyster Day

It's National Accordion Day! Created by the CIA (Confédération internationale des accordéonistes), and it honors the date the accordion was patented in Germany.

Accordion Treats became famous when Gerda Roderer made an accordion fold in some aluminum foil and baked long, fingerlike cookies in the pleats. Her recipe went on to become a household favorite.

Other Events on This Day:
Tourist Appreciation Day,
International No-Diet Day

Accordion Cookies MAKES 48

12 tablespoons (6 ounces) unsalted butter, softened

¾ cup granulated sugar

2 large eggs, room temperature

1 teaspoon vanilla extract

½ scant teaspoon salt

1 cup (4.5 ounces) all-purpose flour

½ cup toasted and finely chopped
    walnuts or pecans (optional)

1 Preheat the oven to 325°F and place a rack in the center. Have ready one large ungreased baking sheet. Cut two pieces of nonstick foil exactly 3 feet long. Fold one of the foil sheets lengthwise to double it, making sure the nonstick side faces out. Fold crosswise into 1-inch pleats to make an accordion-pleated pan liner with 24 folds. Repeat with a second sheet of foil and place both foil accordion pan liners on the baking sheet. Spray the accordion pans with nonstick cooking spray.

2 In the bowl of a stand mixer fitted with a paddle attachment, or in a large mixing bowl, using a handheld electric mixer, beat the butter and sugar on medium speed until creamy. Reduce the mixer speed slightly and beat in the eggs, vanilla, and salt. Stir in the flour and nuts (if using) by hand, mixing well.

3 Drop a rounded teaspoonful of dough into each fold of the foil. Don't worry about spreading it, as it will spread during baking. Bake 12 to 15 minutes, or until golden brown all along the edges. Let the cookies sit in the folds for about 2 minutes, and then carefully remove the cookies from the foil pleats and let cool on a wire rack. Meanwhile, turn the accordion pan liners over, spray with cooking spray, and repeat the process using the remaining dough.

Baker's Note: You can garnish these with confectioners' sugar or a light glaze, or dip half of each cookie in melted chocolate.

Sparkling Star Cutouts   MAKES 60

3 cups (13.5 ounces) all-purpose flour

1½ teaspoons baking powder

1 scant teaspoon salt

12 tablespoons (6 ounces) unsalted butter, softened

1 cup granulated sugar

1 large egg

3 tablespoons heavy cream

1¼ teaspoons vanilla extract

½ teaspoon almond extract

Sparkling sugar, for topping

1 Preheat the oven to 350°F and place a rack in the center. Have ready two ungreased baking sheets.

2 Mix the flour, baking powder, and salt together in a bowl; set aside.

3 In the bowl of a stand mixer fitted with a paddle attachment, or in a large mixing bowl, using a handheld electric mixer, beat the butter and sugar on medium speed until creamy. Reduce the mixer speed slightly and beat in the egg. When the egg is incorporated, beat in the cream, vanilla, and almond extract. By hand or using the lowest speed of the mixer, stir in the flour mixture until absorbed.

4 On a floured surface, roll out a portion of the dough to about ¼-inch thickness. Using a star cutter (or any cutter), cut shapes and arrange about 2 inches apart on the prepared baking sheets. Sprinkle with sparkling sugar. Bake one sheet at a time for 8 to 10 minutes, or until the cookies have nicely browned edges. Let cool on the baking sheet for about 2 minutes, then transfer to a wire rack to cool completely.

National Astronomy Day

Astronomy Day is a shifting holiday that occurs on a Saturday between mid-April and mid-May. Founded in 1973 by Doug Berger, president of the Astronomical Society of Northern California, National Astronomy Day was created to encourage people in urban areas to look to the skies. Backed by several astronomical organizations, this is a day to invite your friends over for viewing parties or to teach kids how to identify the North Star.

Other Events on This Day: **Roast Leg of Lamb Day, Home Brewers Day**

Mother's Day

Moms love flowers, so why not pull out the old cookie press and make some edible ones? If you don't have a cookie press and are considering buying one, the brand I use is Kuhn Rikon. It's affordable, easy to clean, and comes with a booklet with tips on how to use the press.

Other Events on This Day:
National Coconut Cream Pie Day, Coca-Cola first served in 1886

Lemon Spritz MAKES ABOUT 30

2 cups (9 ounces) all-purpose flour

¾ teaspoon baking powder

¼ scant teaspoon salt

13 tablespoons (6.5 ounces) unsalted butter, room temperature

¾ cup granulated sugar

2 egg yolks

1 teaspoon vanilla extract

1 teaspoon lemon zest

1 Preheat the oven to 350°F and place a rack in the center. Have ready two clean, cold, ungreased baking sheets. Do not line them, as the dough needs to stick to the sheet as you press it from the cookie press.

2 Mix the flour, baking powder, and salt together in a small bowl; set aside.

3 In the bowl of a stand mixer fitted with a paddle attachment, or in a large mixing bowl, using a handheld electric mixer, beat the butter and sugar on medium speed until creamy. Beat in the egg yolks, vanilla, and zest and continue beating for 1 minute, scraping the bowl once or twice. By hand or using the lowest speed of the mixer, beat in the flour mixture until incorporated.

4 Fill the cookie press with dough and use the flower tip. Hold the press perpendicular to the baking sheet with the end of the press up against the sheet. Press one click and pull the press upward. Repeat, spacing the cookies about 2 inches apart. Bake for 10 to 13 minutes, or until the cookies start to brown around the edges. Let cool on a baking sheet for about 2 minutes, then carefully transfer to a wire rack to finish cooling.

> **Baker's Note:** To make the cookies look more like flowers, place a dried cranberry in the center before baking.

Carrot Cake Eyeballs

MAKES ABOUT 50

1 (8-ounce) package cream cheese, softened

4 tablespoons (2 ounces) unsalted butter,
    room temperature

2 cups confectioners' sugar

Pinch of salt

1 teaspoon freshly squeezed lemon juice

1 (18.25-ounce) box carrot cake mix, prepared and
    baked according to package directions, cooled

1 pound white melting candy, such as
    Candy Melts from Wilton

Candy-coated chocolates in blue, green, and brown

1   In a large mixing bowl, combine the cream cheese and
    butter. Beat with a handheld electric mixer until creamy.
    Reduce the mixer speed to low and beat in the confection-
    ers' sugar, salt, and lemon juice.

2   Remove the cake from the pan and place it in a large mix-
    ing bowl. Mash it up the best you can with a spoon. Stir in
    the cream cheese frosting and continue mixing until it all
    comes together.

3   Scoop level tablespoonfuls of the cake mixture and shape
    into balls. Arrange the balls on the prepared pan and
    chill for 3 hours.

4   Lay a few sheets of nonstick foil or parchment
    on a flat surface or a place that's convenient for
    letting the cake balls set. Melt the candy coating as
    directed on the package.

5   Spear one chilled cake ball with a toothpick and quickly im-
    merse it in one swift motion in and out of the melted white
    chocolate. Using a second toothpick, gently push the ball off
    the first toothpick onto the parchment paper. Press a candy-
    coated chocolate in the center of the ball to cover the mark
    where the tooth pick was (this will be the pupil of the eye).
    Repeat with remaining cake balls. Let the balls remain on the
    parchment paper at room temperature until the coating is set.

The First Eye Bank Opened

R. T. Patton and Aida Breckinridge opened America's first eye bank today in 1944. The Eye-Bank for Sight Restoration was created to facilitate the transfer of human eye tissue from donor to patient. Since its founding, the eye bank has saved the vision of more than forty-four thousand people.

Other Events on This Day:
National Butterscotch Brownie Day

Clean Up Your Room Day

Today is Clean Up Your Room Day, but since the holiday doesn't specify which room, let's say it's the pantry and make cookienola! This recipe was inspired by a Pillsbury Bake-Off recipe where a baking genius named Wanda Riley used refrigerated peanut butter cookie dough to make granola. I've made it for bake sales, but since then I've branched out and created new flavors using scratch cookie dough. Here's an oatmeal version. Make the base dough, add oats, bake it as you would granola, then add odds and ends from the pantry.

Because I make one pan at a time, I use only half of the "Oat Dough" portion of the recipe and save the rest for cookies or more granola.

Other Events on This Day:
National Shrimp Day, Chococat's birthday

Cookienola   MAKES 1 POUND

OAT DOUGH

8 tablespoons (4 ounces) unsalted butter

¾ cup (3.4 ounces) all-purpose flour

½ teaspoon baking soda

¼ teaspoon salt

½ teaspoon ground cinnamon

⅓ cup firmly packed light brown sugar

⅓ cup granulated sugar

1 large egg

½ teaspoon vanilla extract

1¼ cups old-fashioned oats

COOKIENOLA

¼ teaspoon ground cinnamon

¾ cup old-fashioned oats

½ cup shredded sweetened coconut (optional)

½ cup pecan halves

½ cup slivered almonds

½ cup golden raisins

½ cup cranberries

½ cup candy-coated dark chocolates

1 **Make the oat dough:** Melt the butter in a small saucepan and heat until it begins to turn brown around the edges. Set aside to cool. Meanwhile, mix together the flour, baking soda, salt, and cinnamon in a small bowl; set aside.

2 In a large mixing bowl, beat together the cooled melted browned butter, both sugars, the egg, and the vanilla. By hand, stir in the flour mixture, then add the oats and stir until mixed. Cover the bowl and chill for 1 hour, or until the dough is thick enough to crumble.

3 Preheat the oven to 325°F and set a rack in the center. Line a large baking sheet with nonstick foil.

4 **Make the cookienola:** Remove half of the dough from the refrigerator (see sidebar) and crumble it into a large mixing bowl. With a mixing

spoon or your fingers, work in the cinnamon, oats, and coconut. Add the pecans and almonds. Crumble the mixture over the prepared baking sheet, making sure you have plenty of crumbs and that there aren't too many stray oats. Bake the oatmeal mixture for 18 to 20 minutes, stirring every 5 to 7 minutes. Turn off the oven and let the granola sit in the closed oven for about 15 minutes, then place the pan on a wire rack to cool (and crisp) the granola completely.

5 When completely cool and crisp, toss with raisins, cranberries, and candy-coated chocolates. Store in a tightly sealed bag, or bag individually as gifts.

Monster Cookies MAKES 24

6 tablespoons (3 ounces) unsalted butter, softened
⅔ cup firmly packed light brown sugar
⅔ cup granulated sugar
1 cup creamy or crunchy peanut butter
¼ teaspoon salt
½ teaspoon pure maple syrup or mild molasses
1½ teaspoons baking soda
2 large eggs
1¼ teaspoons vanilla extract
3 cups old-fashioned oats
1 cup candy-coated chocolates
½ cup semisweet chocolate chips

1 Preheat the oven to 350°F and place a rack in the center. Line two baking sheets with parchment paper or nonstick foil.

2 In a large mixing bowl, stir together all ingredients in the order listed. Scoop up generously heaping tablespoonfuls of dough and shape into balls about 2 inches in diameter. Arrange at least 3 inches apart on baking sheets and flatten the tops slightly. Bake one sheet at a time for 13 to 15 minutes, or until the edges are lightly browned. Let cool on the baking sheets for 5 minutes, then transfer to a wire rack to cool and crisp.

MAY 11

Twilight Zone Day

You are about to celebrate another strange holiday—a holiday not only of sight and sound, but of cookies. Welcome to National Twilight Zone Day. The origin is a mystery, but I've gotten enough pleasure thinking back on the old episodes that I am all for May 11's being dedicated to the show that unlocked the door to the imagination.

Other Events on This Day:
Receptionists' Day

Marking the birth of Florence Nightingale, today is International Nurses Day. It's also Nutty Fudge Day, so hopefully the nurses in your life like chocolate. These were pretty much the holy grail of dessert bars for me as a kid. For a while, there was a packaged mix version called Fudge Jumbles, and thus the bars appeared more frequently at school parties and events, but then Fudge Jumbles were discontinued and I stopped seeing them on cookie trays. Luckily, I'd started doing some scratch baking on my own around that time and found the old recipe they were based on, chocolate revel bars.

Other Events on This Day:
**National Limerick Day,
Katharine Hepburn's birthday
(b. 1907)**

Nutty Fudge Revel Bars   MAKES 32

BASE

2½ cups (11.25 ounces) all-purpose flour

1 teaspoon baking soda

1 teaspoon salt

1 cup (8 ounces) unsalted butter, softened

2 cups firmly packed light brown sugar

2 large eggs

2 teaspoons vanilla extract

3 cups old-fashioned or quick-
    cooking oats (not instant)

FILLING

1½ cups semisweet chocolate chips

1 (14-ounce) can sweetened condensed milk

2 tablespoons unsalted butter

¼ teaspoon salt

1 cup toasted and chopped walnuts

2 teaspoons vanilla extract

1   Preheat the oven to 350°F and place a rack in the center. Line a 10 by 15-inch jelly-roll pan with nonstick foil, or line it with regular foil and spray the foil with flour-added baking spray.

2   **Make the base:** Mix the flour, baking soda, and salt together in a small mixing bowl; set aside.

3   In the bowl of a stand mixer fitted with a paddle attachment, or in a large mixing bowl, using a handheld electric mixer, beat the butter and brown sugar on medium speed until creamy. Reduce the mixer speed and add the eggs and vanilla. By hand or using the lowest speed of the mixer, stir in the flour mixture and the oats. Set aside.

4   **Make the filling:** In a small saucepan, combine the chocolate chips, sweetened condensed milk, butter, and salt. Heat over medium-low heat until the mixture is melted. Stir in the walnuts and vanilla.

5 Spread two-thirds of the oatmeal batter in the prepared pan and press down to form a crust. Cover with the filling and spread evenly. Drop clumps of the remaining oatmeal batter over the filling. Bake for 25 to 30 minutes. Let cool completely in the pan. Lift from the pan, set on a cutting board, and cut into thirty-two squares.

Apple Crumb Bars MAKES 16

BASE

¾ cup firmly packed light brown sugar

¾ cup old-fashioned oats

1½ cups (6.8 ounces) all-purpose flour

⅜ teaspoon baking soda

¼ teaspoon salt

9 tablespoons (4.5 ounces) unsalted
    butter, room temperature

FILLING

2 to 3 small Granny Smith apples, peeled,
    cored, and thinly sliced or chopped

2 teaspoons freshly squeezed lemon juice

½ teaspoon ground cinnamon

½ cup granulated sugar

1½ tablespoons cornstarch

½ cup water

½ teaspoon vanilla extract

1 tablespoon unsalted butter

½ cup chopped pecans

1 Preheat the oven to 350°F and place a rack in the center. Line a 9-inch square metal pan with nonstick foil or just spray the pan with flour-added baking spray.

2 **Make the base:** In a bowl or food processor, combine the brown sugar, oats, flour, baking soda, and salt. Cut in or process the butter until the mixture is coarse and crumbly. Reserve about ¾ cup for the topping; pat the remaining into the bottom of the prepared pan. Set aside.

MAY 13

Cardinal Richelieu Invents the Table Knife

Tired of watching people pick their teeth with daggers, Cardinal Richelieu is said to have invented the table knife on this day in 1624.

To celebrate, here is apple pie in bar cookie form! Make sure you cut them with a knife rather than, oh, a spoon or a fork, to commemorate the invention of the table knife.

Other Events on This Day:
National Apple Pie Day

3 **Make the filling:** Toss the apples with 1 teaspoon of the lemon juice and arrange in a fairly even layer across the crust. Sprinkle with the cinnamon.

4 In a small saucepan, combine the sugar, cornstarch, and water and stir well. Cook over medium heat, whisking or stirring constantly, until the mixture begins to boil and thicken. It will go from cloudy to translucent. Remove from the heat and stir in the vanilla, butter, and remaining teaspoon of lemon juice. Pour over the apples. Sprinkle the reserved crumbs on top, then sprinkle the pecans over the crumbs.

5 Bake for 35 to 40 minutes, or until the top is lightly browned. Let the bars cool completely in the pan before slicing. For a cleaner cut, chill before slicing, then serve at room temperature.

MAY 14

George Lucas's Birthday

George Lucas was born in Modesto, California in 1944.

He is best known for *Star Wars*, which broke box office records, won seven Academy Awards, and changed the course of moviemaking forever.

Is it a blondie or a brownie? These two bars aren't actually at war with each other, but work quite nicely together to make one big bar that gives you the best of both worlds.

Other Events on This Day: **National Buttermilk Biscuit Day, Charles Darwin began writing *On the Origin of Species* in 1856**

Bar Wars MAKES 24

BROWNIE BATTER

8 tablespoons (4 ounces) unsalted butter
1½ cups granulated sugar
½ cup plus 1 tablespoon natural cocoa powder
1 teaspoon vanilla extract
2 large eggs, room temperature
½ teaspoon baking powder
¼ teaspoon salt
1 tablespoon water
1 cup plus 2 tablespoons (4.9 ounces) all-purpose flour
⅔ cup semisweet chocolate chips

BLONDIE BATTER

8 tablespoons (4 ounces) unsalted butter
1 cup firmly packed light brown sugar
1½ teaspoons vanilla extract
1 large egg, room temperature
½ teaspoon baking powder
⅛ teaspoon baking soda
¼ teaspoon salt
1 cup (4.5 ounces) all-purpose flour
⅔ cup walnuts, toasted and chopped

1   Preheat the oven to 350°F and place a rack in the center. Line a 9 by 13-inch metal pan with nonstick foil.

2   **Make the brownie batter:** In a large, microwave-safe mixing bowl, microwave the butter on high for 30 seconds, or until melted. With a mixing spoon, beat in the sugar, cocoa powder, vanilla, and eggs. When fully mixed, stir in the baking powder, salt, and water; gradually stir in the flour, followed by the chocolate chips. Spread the batter across the bottom of the prepared pan.

3   **Make the blondie batter:** Rinse the mixing bowl from the brownie batter (or choose a fresh, microwave-safe mixing bowl, if you prefer) and use it to melt the butter in the microwave on high for 1 minute. With a mixing spoon, beat in the brown sugar, vanilla, and egg. When fully mixed, stir in the baking powder, baking soda, and salt; gradually stir in the flour and walnuts. Drop blobs of blondie batter over the brownie batter and carefully spread so the blobs come together to make one layer covering the chocolate.

4   Bake for 35 to 38 minutes, or until a toothpick inserted all the way through to the chocolate batter comes out clean. Let cool in the pan, or let cool to room temperature and then chill, if desired (I like to cut the bars while they're cold). Grasp the foil, lift from the pan, set on a cutting board, and cut into twenty-four bars.

Chocolate chip cookies were invented in the 1930s by Ruth Wakefield, who co-owned the Toll House Inn. Because the two-hundred-year-old inn had been an actual toll house, Ruth created new desserts based on traditional colonial recipes, one of which was a cookie called the Butter Drop Do. As the story goes, Ruth went to the kitchen to bake up a batch of the butter drops. Upon discovering she was out of her usual baking chocolate, Ruth cut up a bar of semisweet chocolate given to her by Mr. Andrew Nestlé. Instead of melting throughout the cookie, the chocolate stayed in chunks. The cookies were a hit and became a very popular item at the inn.

A few years later, Nestlé and Wakefield reached an agreement, part of which was that Ruth would receive a lifetime supply of chocolate in exchange for allowing Nestlé to print the recipe on the back of the chocolate bars. After experimenting with ways to make it easier to use, such as scoring the bars and selling them with little chopping tools, Nestlé introduced the chocolate as "morsels" in 1939.

Like a house wine, everyone needs a "house chocolate chip cookie." Chewy, bumpy, and packed with chocolate chips, this recipe is a reliable favorite.

Other Events on This Day:
Police Officer's Memorial Day

House Chocolate Chip Cookies   MAKES ABOUT 30

1⅓ cups (6 ounces) all-purpose flour

½ teaspoon baking soda

½ teaspoon baking powder

½ teaspoon salt

1 stick (4 ounces) unsalted butter, room temperature

½ cup firmly packed dark brown sugar

½ cup granulated sugar

1 large egg, room temperature

1 teaspoon vanilla extract

1½ cups extra-dark chocolate chips

1 cup toasted and chopped walnuts

1 Preheat the oven to 350°F and place a rack in the center. Have ready two ungreased baking sheets.

2 Stir the flour, baking soda, baking powder, and salt together in a medium-size bowl; set aside.

3 In the bowl of a stand mixer fitted with a paddle attachment, or in a large mixing bowl, using a handheld electric mixer, beat the butter on medium-high speed until it is creamy. Add both sugars and continue beating on medium-high speed, scraping the sides of bowl often, until creamy. Reduce the speed to medium-low, and mix in the egg and vanilla—mixing only until the egg is blended in. Add the flour mixture and stir until incorporated. Add the chocolate chips and nuts.

4 Drop generously rounded tablespoons of dough about 2½ inches apart onto the baking sheets. Bake one sheet at a time for 12 minutes, or until golden around the edges and set. Transfer to a wire rack to let cool completely.

Iced Root Beer Cookies

MAKES 42

COOKIES

1¾ cups (8 ounces) all-purpose flour

½ teaspoon baking soda

½ teaspoon salt

8 tablespoons (4 ounces) unsalted butter, softened

1 cup firmly packed light brown sugar

1 large egg

¼ cup light sour cream

2 teaspoons root beer extract, such as Watkins

1 teaspoon vanilla extract

ICING

6 tablespoons (3 ounces) unsalted butter, softened

2 cups confectioners' sugar

1 teaspoon root beer extract, such as Watkins

1 to 2 tablespoons hot water

MAY 16

Root Beer Invented

On this day in 1876, Charles Elmer Hires sold his root beer to the public at the United States Centennial Exposition in Philadelphia. Originally sold in packets requiring water, root beer wasn't sold premixed until 1893.

This recipe is adapted from one from the Watkins Company. For testing, I used Watkins brand extract because that's what our grocery store carries, but you may use any brand.

Other Events on This Day: **Corn Fritter Day, Love a Tree Day**

1 **Make the cookies:** Mix the flour, baking soda, and salt together in a bowl; set aside.

2 In the bowl of a stand mixer fitted with a paddle attachment, or in a large mixing bowl, using a handheld electric mixer, beat the butter and brown sugar on medium speed until creamy. Reduce the mixer speed slightly and beat in the egg, sour cream, root beer extract, and vanilla, mixing just until blended. By hand or using the lowest speed of the mixer, add the flour mixture and mix until incorporated. Cover the bowl with plastic wrap and chill the dough for 1 hour, or until ready to use.

3 Preheat the oven to 375°F and place a rack in the center. Line two baking sheets with parchment paper or nonstick foil.

4 Drop rounded teaspoonfuls of dough about 2 inches apart onto the prepared baking sheets. Bake one sheet at a time for 6 to 8 minutes, or until very lightly browned. Let cool on the baking sheets for about 5 minutes, then transfer to a wire rack to cool completely before topping with the root beer icing.

5 **Make the icing:** In a medium-size mixing bowl, using a handheld electric mixer on low speed, beat the butter and confectioners' sugar together until creamy, slowly increasing the speed to medium-high as the butter and sugar come together. Beat in the root beer extract. Add the hot water 1 tablespoon at a time, beating until you get a smooth, drizzling consistency. Drizzle over the cookies. Alternatively, add a little less water and spread the icing.

Cherry Cobbler Day

Fruit cobblers were popular with American settlers, and like most dishes of that time, open to improvisation. While they always include some sort of fruit filling, the crust on a cobbler may be anything from rich pastry dough to oatmeal dough, to plain biscuits or slices of bread. The shape of a cobbler varies depending on what type of bowl you use. They can be made as minis, circles, rectangles, fancy casserole dishes, or in this case, in bar form.

Other Events on This Day:
Pack Rat Day

Cherry Cobbler Bars   MAKES 16

¾ cup plus 2 tablespoons (4 ounces) all-purpose flour

¾ cup old-fashioned oats

½ cup firmly packed light brown sugar

⅛ teaspoon salt

¼ teaspoon baking soda

¼ teaspoon ground cinnamon

6 tablespoons (3 ounces) cold unsalted
   butter, cut into small pieces

¾ cup cherry preserves, softened or room
   temperature (see Baker's Note)

½ teaspoon almond extract

¼ cup sliced or slivered almonds

1 Preheat the oven to 350°F and place a rack in the center. Line an 8-inch metal pan with nonstick foil, or line it with regular foil and spray the foil with flour-added baking spray.

2 In the bowl of a food processor, combine the flour, oats, brown sugar, salt, baking soda, and cinnamon. Pulse the processor once or twice to mix the dry ingredients, and then add the butter and pulse until the mixture is coarse. Pour about two-thirds of the crumb mixture into the prepared pan and press down to make a crust.

3 Mix together the softened preserves and almond extract, then carefully spread over the crust. Sprinkle the remaining crumb mixture over the cherry mixture. Sprinkle the almonds over the top.

4 Bake for 25 minutes, or until the edges are lightly browned. Let cool completely in the pan. Lift from the pan, set on a cutting board, and cut into sixteen bars.

Baker's Note: These are worthy of the best cherry preserves you can find. Cherry pie filling also works.

One-Bowl Honey and Oat Cookies MAKES 28

8 tablespoons (4 ounces) unsalted
    butter, room temperature

1 cup granulated sugar

¾ teaspoon vanilla extract

¼ cup honey

1 large egg

1 teaspoon baking soda

½ teaspoon salt

½ teaspoon ground cinnamon

1½ cups (6.8 ounces) all-purpose flour

1 cup old-fashioned oats

½ cup sweetened flaked coconut (see Baker's Note)

½ cup toasted pecans

1 Preheat the oven to 375°F and place a rack in the center. Line two baking sheets with parchment paper or nonstick foil.

2 In the bowl of a stand mixer fitted with a paddle attachment, or in a large mixing bowl, using a handheld electric mixer, beat the butter and sugar on medium speed until creamy. Beat in the vanilla, honey, and egg. Scrape the sides of the bowl and beat in the baking soda, salt, and cinnamon. When fully mixed, stir in the flour until fully blended, and then stir in the oats, coconut, and pecans.

3 Drop rounded teaspoonfuls of batter 2 inches apart onto the prepared baking sheets. Bake one sheet at a time for 10 to 12 minutes. Let cool on the baking sheets for a few minutes, then transfer to wire rack to cool completely.

MAY 18

No Dirty Dishes Day

If you're prone to throwing dishes in the sink with the hope that a magic fairy will come along and either clean them or transport them to the dishwasher, this holiday is for you. The origin is unknown, but I have a feeling whoever thought it up must have played the role of "magic fairy" at some point and needed a fun, nonthreatening way to convince people around her (or him) to clean the heck up and stop leaving piles of dishes in the sink; or worse, in the living room or on the table.

Other Events on This Day:
International Museum Day

Baker's Note: For even more flavor, toast the coconut along with the pecans before using. Coconut doesn't usually take as long as pecans, so toast the pecans as you normally would (I toast pecans at 350°F for 6 to 8 minutes), and throw the coconut on the baking sheet during the last 5 minutes.

MAY 19

National Devil's Food Cake Day

If you have time to bake a devil's food cake, go for it. If not, here's a simple cookie that's almost as much fun to serve as the cake. Frost and decorate with sprinkles for a real kid pleaser.

This recipe is adapted from a book my grandmother gave me called *The Modern Housewife*. It was published during the 1940s and is so well loved that my copy is held together with masking tape and paper clips. Back then, these cookies were made with melted shortening, and you can still make them with the shortening today for a taller, slightly fatter, and more rounded cookie.

Other Events on This Day:
Boys & Girls Clubs Day

Devil's Food Chocolate Cake Cookies MAKES 30

COOKIES
**8 tablespoons (4 ounces) unsalted butter,
   or ½ cup (3.4 ounces) shortening**
2 squares unsweetened chocolate, chopped
1 cup firmly packed light brown sugar
1 large egg
½ cup whole or 2% milk
1 teaspoon vanilla extract
½ teaspoon baking soda
½ teaspoon salt
1¾ cups (8 ounces) all-purpose flour

FROSTING
1½ cups confectioners' sugar, sifted
4 tablespoons (2 ounces) butter, room temperature
⅓ cup unsweetened natural cocoa powder
1 teaspoon vanilla extract
2 tablespoons whole milk
Sprinkles, for decorating

1 Preheat the oven to 350°F and place a rack in the center. Have ready two ungreased baking sheets.

2 **Make the cookies:** Combine the butter and chocolate in a microwave-safe mixing bowl and microwave at 50 percent power for 1 minute. Stir well. Repeat until the chocolate is fully melted. Set aside and let cool completely.

3 When cool, whisk in the brown sugar, followed by the egg, milk, vanilla, baking soda, and salt. Add the flour gradually until you have a thick, sticky batter.

4. Drop well-rounded teaspoonfuls of batter about 2½ inches apart onto the prepared baking sheets. Bake one sheet at a time for 10 to 12 minutes, or until the tops appear set. Transfer to a wire rack and let cool completely.

5. **Make the frosting:** In a mixing bowl, using a handheld electric mixer, beat the confectioners' sugar and butter together at medium speed until creamy. Beat in the cocoa powder and vanilla. Add the milk 1 tablespoon at a time until you get a nice spreading consistency. Spread the frosting on the cookies and decorate with sprinkles.

Double Raisin Rum Ice-Cream Sandwiches MAKES 8

1 cup raisins

½ cup rum

½ cup water

7 tablespoons (3.5 ounces) unsalted butter, room temperature

¾ cup granulated sugar

2 tablespoons honey

1 large egg

1 teaspoon vanilla extract

1¾ cups (8 ounces) all-purpose flour

½ teaspoon baking powder

½ teaspoon baking soda

½ teaspoon salt

¼ teaspoon ground cinnamon

1 pint vanilla or rum raisin ice cream

1. Preheat the oven to 350°F and place a rack in the center.

2. Place the raisins, rum, and water in a small saucepan and bring to a gentle boil. Boil for about 5 minutes, or until the liquid has evaporated. Pat the raisins dry.

3. In a mixing bowl, using a handheld electric mixer, beat the butter and sugar until creamy. Add the honey, egg, and vanilla and beat for 1 minute, or until light.

MAY 20

Dolley Madison's Birthday

*B*orn on this day in North Carolina in 1768, First Lady Dolley Madison was so famous for her hospitality that food companies put her name on products. There are the famous Dolly Madison Snack Cakes, a Dolly Madison Bakery, Dolly Madison Popcorn, and even a Dolly Madison Wine—all with the *e* missing from the first name. But Dolley Madison had another claim to fame, and that was serving ice cream in the White House.

In honor of Dolley Madison's birthday, here's a cookie with ice cream in the middle.

Other Events on This Day:
Be a Millionaire Day, Pick Strawberries Day

4 Mix together the flour, baking powder, baking soda, salt, and cinnamon. Add to the butter mixture and stir until the flour mixture is incorporated.

5 Stir in the rum-soaked raisins.

6 Drop rounded tablespoonfuls of batter (eight per sheet) about 3 inches apart onto two ungreased baking sheets. Bake one sheet at a time for 12 minutes. Let cool on the baking sheets for 5 minutes, then transfer to a wire rack to cool completely. With a ⅓-cup measuring scoop, scoop out ice cream and sandwich between pairs of cookies.

Baker's Notes: Ice-cream sandwiches call for cookies that are dense and firm enough to hold the ice cream, but not too hard, either. This cookie makes the perfect ice-cream sandwich base, plus it's also a good excuse to break out the rum. Rather than soak the raisins overnight, I boil them in the rum and let the liquid evaporate.

MAY 21

National Strawberries and Cream Day

"Hello, my name is Strawberries and Cream and I'll be your cookie today."

Today we recognize two important holidays: Strawberries and Cream Day and Wait Staff Appreciation Day. No, make that three. It's also National Memo Day, so to celebrate I suggest you go out to eat, order something with strawberries, then leave a tip and a memo saying, "Thanks for the great service, Happy Wait Staff Appreciation Day!"

Other Events on This Day:
Memo Day, Wait Staff Appreciation Day

Strawberry Malt Swirl Brownies MAKES 16

BROWNIES

3 ounces semisweet chocolate, chopped

4 tablespoons (2 ounces) unsalted butter

1 large egg

6 tablespoons granulated sugar

1 teaspoon vanilla extract

⅓ cup (1.5 ounces) all-purpose flour

TOPPING

½ cup white chocolate chips

1 (8-ounce) package cream cheese, softened

¼ cup granulated sugar

½ teaspoon vanilla extract

1 large egg

½ cup strawberries, frozen and thawed
   (see Baker's Note)

1 tablespoon malted milk powder

1 Preheat the oven to 350°F and place a rack in the center. Line an 8-inch square metal pan with nonstick foil.

2 **Make the brownies:** Place the chocolate and butter in a microwave-safe mixing bowl and microwave on high for 30 seconds. Stir and repeat until melted and smooth. Beat in the egg, followed by the sugar and vanilla. Stir in the flour. Pour into the prepared pan and bake for 18 minutes; the brownies won't be fully cooked at this point, just slightly set. Let cool completely in the pan.

3 Preheat the oven again, but this time only to 325°F.

4 **Make the topping:** In the microwave, melt the white chips in a small bowl, using 50 percent power and stirring every 30 seconds.

5 Meanwhile, in a mixing bowl, beat the cream cheese and sugar until smooth. Beat in the vanilla and egg, and then stir in the melted white chips. In a separate bowl, mash the strawberries. Measure out ¼ cup of mashed strawberries and mix them with 1 cup of the white batter so that you have a pink batter. Add the malt powder to the pink batter. Pour most of the pink batter across the partially baked cookie crust. Drop spoonfuls of the remaining white batter over the pink batter, and then drop little gobs of remaining pink batter over the white for a rippled look. Using a half-teaspoon measure, drop bits of what's left of your mashed strawberries over the top and gently drag a knife through so that you have hues of pink, white, and red.

6 Bake for 25 minutes, or until the top is set but not dry. Let cool for 2 hours in the pan, or until the top is cool. Chill thoroughly before serving.

Baker's Note: Freezing and thawing fresh strawberries makes them softer and easier to mash. Otherwise, just use thawed frozen strawberries.

Buy a Musical Instrument Day

It's Buy a Musical Instrument Day, so if you've entertained the thought of playing an instrument or just need some new equipment for your band, today's the day to go to the music store and buy it. Consider buying some lessons, too.

My great-grandmother owned a music store, and she and my grandmother, who worked at the store during the summer, were too busy cleaning instruments to spend time in the kitchen. They did have a nice collection of recipes they never got around to making, though. Known as Goodie Bars, this is one I resurrected from their mess of clippings. The saltiness of the peanuts helps balance the sweetness, but I like to counter the sweetness even more by using dark chocolate chips and slightly less maple filling. I've also updated it with microwave directions, but if you prefer, you can use a double boiler.

Other Events on This Day:
Vanilla Pudding Day

BASE AND TOPPING
4 tablespoons (2 ounces) unsalted butter

1 cup dark chocolate chips

1 cup butterscotch chips

1 cup creamy peanut butter

1 cup lightly salted peanuts

FILLING
4 tablespoons (2 ounces) unsalted butter

2 tablespoons evaporated milk

2 tablespoons cook-and-serve vanilla pudding mix

1¾ cups confectioners' sugar

½ teaspoon maple flavoring

1 Line a 9-inch square pan with nonstick foil, or line it with regular foil and spray the foil with flour-added baking spray.

2 **Make the base and topping:** In a large, microwave-safe mixing bowl, microwave the butter on high for 30 seconds, or until melted. Add the chocolate chips and butterscotch chips and toss to coat with the butter. Microwave the chips and butter at 50 percent power stirring every 30 seconds until melted. Stir in the peanut butter. Spoon half of the mixture into the bottom of the pan and spread all the way to the edges. Chill for about an hour, or until set and very firm. Add the peanuts to the remaining mixture and set aside.

3 **Make the filling:** In a small, nonstick saucepan, melt the butter over medium heat, but do not bring to a boil. Remove from the heat and stir in the evaporated milk and pudding mix. With a wooden spoon or heat-resistant scraper, stir over medium-low heat for about 1 minute, being careful not to let it boil. It should look like thick vanilla pudding. Remove from the heat and gradually stir in about half of the confectioners' sugar and the maple flavoring. Stir in the remaining confectioners' sugar. The consistency

should be that of thick frosting or soft fudge. Let cool for about 10 minutes. Remove the firm chocolate layer from the refrigerator and spoon the filling over the chocolate, spreading evenly. Chill for 1 hour or until very firm.

4 The remaining chocolate mixture will be a little stiff. Microwave at 50 percent power for about 30 seconds; stir well and spoon over the pudding mixture. Return the pan to the refrigerator and chill for about 2 hours, or until fully set. Lift from the pan, set on a cutting board and, with a chef's knife, cut into sixteen squares. Cut those squares on the diagonal to make thirty-two triangles.

Baker's Notes: Be sure to cook-and-serve pudding, rather than instant. Make sure to not boil the filling, or it will separate.

Sweet Potato Pie Bars MAKES 32

CRUST

1½ cups plus 1 tablespoon (6.8 ounces)
   all-purpose flour

½ teaspoon salt

½ cup granulated sugar

½ cup firmly packed light brown sugar

1 teaspoon ground cinnamon

12 tablespoons (6 ounces) unsalted butter,
   cut up and at room temperature

FILLING

1 (15.5-ounce) can mashed sweet potatoes

4 tablespoons (2 ounces) butter, melted

1 (14-ounce) can sweetened condensed milk

2 large eggs, beaten

1 teaspoon ground cinnamon

⅛ teaspoon freshly grated nutmeg

½ teaspoon orange zest

¼ teaspoon salt

½ teaspoon vanilla extract

⅔ cup finely chopped nuts

MAY 23

South Carolina Joins the Union

South Carolina, which joined the Union in 1788, is nicknamed "the Palmetto State" for its official state tree. It's also called the Rice State, and in the 1930s people called it the Iodine State, due to its rich supply of iodine in fruits, vegetables, and milk.

South Carolina's rich history and coastal resorts make it a popular destination for tourists interested in history, outdoor recreation, and good food. Known as "low country cuisine," South Carolina specialties include crab; catfish; gumbo and rice dishes; and rich, sweet desserts, such as coconut cake and sweet potato pie.

Other Events on This Day:
Taffy Day, World Turtle Day

1. Preheat the oven to 350°F and place a rack in the center. Line a 9 by 13-inch metal pan with nonstick foil.

2. **Make the crust:** Combine the flour, salt, both sugars, and the cinnamon in the bowl of a food processor; add the butter and pulse until the mixture is crumbly. Set aside a heaping half-cup of the mixture, then place the rest in the prepared pan and press into the bottom.

3. **Make the filling:** Rinse the food processor bowl. Process the cooked sweet potatoes, melted butter, sweetened condensed milk, eggs, cinnamon, nutmeg, orange zest, salt, and vanilla until smooth. Pour evenly over the crust.

4. Toss the reserved flour mixture with the nuts and sprinkle over the sweet potato mixture. Bake for 30 to 35 minutes, or until set. Let cool in the pan. When completely cool, lift from the pan, set on a cutting board, and cut into thirty-two squares.

Escargot Day

Another unofficial food holiday, this is a day to encourage all your friends to try snails. You have a couple of options. Treat them to lunch at the nearest French bistro or the kinder option: bake them some snail-shaped cookies.

My friend Lisa gave me this recipe, saying it was one of her family's favorites. Lisa makes the cookies as spirals, rather than snails. Either way, it's a tasty cookie and the dough is very easy to work with. If you are very precise with your measuring and cutting, you should get about 60 snails. I tend to cut mine a bit thicker and get 50.

Cinnamon Snail Cookies
MAKES 50 TO 60

8 tablespoons (4 ounces) unsalted butter, room temperature
4 ounces cream cheese, softened
¼ teaspoon salt
⅓ cup plus 2 tablespoons granulated sugar
1¼ cups (5.6 ounces) all-purpose flour
1½ teaspoons ground cinnamon
Chocolate mini chips or currants for eyes

1. In the bowl of a stand mixer fitted with a paddle attachment, or in a large mixing bowl, using a handheld electric mixer, beat the butter, cream cheese, salt, and 2 tablespoons of the sugar on medium speed until light and creamy. By hand or using the lowest speed of the mixer, add the flour. On a sheet of nonstick foil or parchment paper, pat the dough into a small rectangle. Cover and chill for 1 hour, or until the dough is firm enough to roll.

2 In a small bowl, stir together the remaining ⅓ cup of sugar and the cinnamon.

3 On a lightly floured surface, roll the dough into a 15 by 12-inch rectangle. Sprinkle the cinnamon sugar over the dough. Starting from a long side, roll into a tight spiral. Brush the last ½ inch of dough with water to help seal the edge. Cut the log in half crosswise. Slide the logs onto the prepared baking sheet; cover with plastic wrap and freeze the dough for about 30 minutes, so that it can be sliced.

4 Preheat the oven to 400°F and place a rack in the center. Have ready a large ungreased baking sheet.

5 Remove one log from the freezer. With a serrated knife, cut the log crosswise into ¼-inch-thick slices. Arrange the spirals about 2 inches apart on a baking sheet and let them come to room temperature. Carefully loosen each spiral to form a snail's head. Add one chocolate mini chip for the eye.

6 Arrange ½ inch apart on the baking sheet. Bake for 12 minutes, or until lightly browned. Transfer to a wire rack to cool completely. Repeat with the remaining log.

Coffee Lover's Biscotti MAKES 20

2 large eggs

2 tablespoons instant coffee crystals, such
    as Folgers (see Baker's Note)

½ cup granulated sugar

¼ cup vegetable oil

1 teaspoon vanilla extract

¼ teaspoon salt

1 teaspoon baking powder

1¾ cups (8 ounces) all-purpose flour

1 cup toasted walnuts or pecans

⅓ cup chocolate-covered espresso beans, or
    chopped chocolate with espresso beans

Other Events on This Day:
Samuel Morse sent the first telegraph in 1844

MAY 25

Geek Pride Day

Celebrated in conjunction with the *Star Wars* release date, Geek Pride Day recognizes our geeky friends. Stereotypically, a geek is focused on computers and technology, but a geek can also be someone who is seriously into quilting, metallurgy, foraging, art, taxidermy, stamps, comic books, or food and wine. Not to be confused with nerds, who have very high IQs and are considered "brainy" and good at math, geeks can be of average intelligence—they're just really interested in something.

1 Preheat the oven to 300°F and place a rack in the center. Line a large baking sheet with nonstick foil or parchment paper.

2 In the bowl of a stand mixer fitted with a paddle attachment, or in a large mixing bowl, using a handheld electric mixer, beat the eggs on medium speed for about 1 minute, or until foamy. Add the coffee and beat until it starts to dissolve, then beat in the sugar and continue beating for another minute. Beat in the oil, vanilla, salt, and baking powder, making sure there are no stray lumps of baking powder. By hand or using the lowest speed of the mixer, stir in the flour, then stir in the nuts and chocolate espresso beans. The dough will be pretty soft, but it should be firm enough to mold. If not, add a small amount of flour.

3 Divide the dough in half. With damp hands, form each portion into a log about 7 by 3 inches directly on the prepared baking sheet, spacing the logs 4½ inches apart. Bake for 30 minutes, or until the logs are light brown. Let cool completely on the baking sheet that's been set on a wire rack. I usually let the logs cool for a full hour.

4 Preheat the oven to 275°F and place a rack in the center. Cut crosswise slightly on the diagonal every ¾ inch. You should get about 10 biscotti per log and 2 little nubby scraps from the end. Place cut side down on the prepared baking sheet. Bake for about 20 minutes, or until the cookies appear dry. Transfer to a wire rack to let cool completely.

Baker's Note: If you can't find the beans or want something a little different, try chopping up a bar with espresso beans mixed in. Endangered Species makes a good one.

Blueberry Cheesecake Bars MAKES 32

CRUST

6 tablespoons (3 ounces) unsalted butter, melted and cooled

¼ teaspoon salt

⅔ cup firmly packed light brown sugar

2 cups (9 ounces) all-purpose flour

FILLING

⅓ cup blueberry preserves

⅔ cup fresh blueberries

1 tablespoon freshly squeezed lemon juice

Small pinch of ground cinnamon

TOPPING

2 (8-ounce) packages cream cheese, softened

⅔ cup granulated sugar

2 teaspoons freshly squeezed lemon juice

½ teaspoon lemon zest

1 teaspoon vanilla extract

2 large eggs

National Blueberry Cheesecake Day

The world's been eating cheesecake for thousands of years, but domestication of the blueberry, a fruit native to North America, was not until 1908, so it's safe to say blueberry cheesecake is a modern day food of American origin. Celebrate an American original with your own cookie version of cheesecake. This recipe calls for a mixture of store-bought blueberry preserves and some fresh blueberries.

Other Events on This Day:
Sally Ride Day

1 Preheat the oven to 350°F and place a rack in the center. Line a 9 by 13-inch metal pan with nonstick foil or just spray with flour-added baking spray.

2 **Make the crust:** In a large mixing bowl, stir the cooled melted butter, salt, sugar, and flour together to make a somewhat crumbly dough. Press into the bottom of the prepared pan and bake for 15 minutes. Let cool in the pan.

3 **Make the filling:** In a microwave-safe mixing bowl, soften the preserves for about 10 seconds, microwaving on high. Stir in the berries, lemon juice, and cinnamon. Pour the mixture over the cooled crust.

4 **Make the topping:** Rinse the mixing bowl (or use a new one) and combine the softened cream cheese and sugar. Beat with a handheld electric mixer on medium speed until creamy and smooth. Beat in the lemon juice, lemon

zest, and vanilla. Lower the mixer speed slightly and add the eggs, one at a time, beating just until mixed. Pour the cheese mixture over the berries. Bake for 28 to 30 minutes, or until the edges are slightly browned. Let cool completely in the pan, then chill thoroughly. To serve, lift from the pan, using the foil as a handle. Set on a cutting board and score into thirty-two bars.

Three Little Pigs Movie Released

On this day in 1933, United Artists released Walt Disney's *Three Little Pigs*. The film won an Academy Award for Best Short Subject: Cartoons in 1934. In 2007, the Library of Congress selected it for the National Film Registry.

Celebrate the release of *Three Little Pigs* by making some *biscochitos*, Mexican cookies typically made with lard and spices such as cinnamon and anise.

They are known in other countries by different names, such as *polverones* and *biscochos* and *mantecosos*. They are the state cookie of New Mexico.

Other Events on This Day:
Grape Popsicle Day, Sunscreen Day

Biscochitos MAKES ABOUT 42

3 cups (13.5 ounces) all-purpose flour
1½ teaspoons baking powder
½ teaspoon salt
1 cup (6.8 ounces) shortening (or lard)
¾ cup plus 2 tablespoons granulated sugar
1 large egg
1 teaspoon vanilla extract
1 to 4 tablespoons of milk, or as needed
1 teaspoon ground cinnamon

1 Preheat the oven to 350°F and place a rack in the center. Have ready two ungreased baking sheets.

2 Mix the flour, baking powder, and salt together in a medium-size bowl; set aside.

3 In the bowl of a stand mixer fitted with a paddle attachment, or in a large mixing bowl, using a handheld electric mixer, beat the shortening and ¾ cup of the sugar on medium speed until creamy. Beat in the egg and vanilla. By hand or using the lowest speed of the mixer, stir in the flour mixture until you have a thick dough. If it seems too dry, add milk 1 tablespoon at a time until it feels easier to manage. Flour a work surface and roll a portion of the dough about ¼ inch

thick. Using a flower- or pig-shaped cutter, cut a shape and place it on a prepared baking sheet. Continue until all your dough is cut. Mix together the cinnamon and remaining 2 tablespoons of sugar. Sprinkle over the cutouts. Bake one sheet at a time for 9 to 12 minutes, or until the cookies appear set—the edges don't brown much. Let cool on the baking sheets for about 4 minutes, then transfer to a wire rack to cool completely.

Baker's Note: If you'd like to make the cookies more authentic, add 1 teaspoon of ground anise seeds or use 1 teaspoon of anise extract in place of the vanilla.

Jazzy Gelatin Spritz Cookies MAKES 60

1½ cups (12 ounces) unsalted butter,
   room temperature

1 cup granulated sugar

1 (3-ounce) box
   fruit-flavored gelatin

1 large egg

1 teaspoon vanilla extract

1 teaspoon salt

1 teaspoon baking powder

3½ cups (16 ounces) all-
   purpose flour

Fact: The birthplace of Jell-O is Leroy, New York, where you can visit the Jell-O Gallery.

1 Preheat the oven to 400°F and place a rack in the center. Have ready two clean, cold, ungreased baking sheets.

2 In the bowl of a stand mixer fitted with a paddle attachment, or in a large mixing bowl, using a handheld electric mixer, beat the butter and sugar on medium speed until creamy. Add the gelatin powder and beat until well mixed. Reduce the mixer speed slightly and beat in the egg and vanilla. Beat in the salt and baking powder, making sure they are well distributed and that there aren't any stray lumps of baking powder. Add the

MAY 28

Invention of Jell-O

The history of Jell-O dates back to 1845, when inventor and philanthropist Peter Cooper, known for designing the Tom Thumb Locomotive, patented a product that was set with gelatin. The patent changed hands over the years, and fruit flavors were added. Eventually an advertising campaign that involved sending representatives into the field to demonstrate the product and distribute cookbooks proved very successful. The Jell-O Company was born. This recipe was recommended by more than a few friends who say it's a regular on their Christmas cookie tray.

Other Events on This Day:
Jazz Day, Hamburger Day

MAY 29

End of the Middle Ages Day

Grab your paintbrushes, microscopes, and T-squares because today celebrates the beginning of the Renaissance; or to be more precise, the end of the Middle Ages. On May 29, 1453, the city of Constantinople fell to the Ottoman Empire. Byzantine scholars left the city and continued their studies in other places, such as Italy. Viewed as a rebirth of classical studies, the term "Renaissance" was coined many years later.

For this holiday you can make a medieval dessert such as gingerbread, or look to Florence, birthplace of the Renaissance and where Catherine de Médicis's Italian chefs helped popularize rich and creamy desserts.

This cookie originated in Austria, but made its way to Tuscany and is served around the holidays.

Other Events on This Day:
National Coq au Vin Day

---

flour gradually, stirring with a spoon or with the lowest speed of the mixer. Fill a cookie press and press shapes onto the baking sheets about 2 inches apart. Bake one sheet at a time for 7 to 10 minutes. Transfer to a wire rack to cool completely.

Oat Florentines   MAKES 48

½ cup sliced almonds

12 tablespoons (6 ounces) unsalted butter, melted

2 cups quick-cooking oats (not instant)

1 cup granulated sugar

⅔ cup (3 ounces) all-purpose flour

¼ cup golden syrup or light corn syrup

¼ cup milk

2 teaspoons vanilla extract

¼ teaspoon plus an extra pinch of salt

4 ounces semisweet chocolate, chopped

1 Preheat the oven to 350°F and place a rack in the center. Line two baking sheets with parchment paper or nonstick foil.

2 In a dry skillet, toast the almonds over medium-high heat, pushing the almonds around just until they start to brown a little and become fragrant. Remove from the heat and let cool.

3 Meanwhile, mix the melted butter, oats, sugar, flour, golden syrup, milk, vanilla, and salt together in a mixing bowl and stir well. Crush the cooled almonds and add to the batter.

4 Drop teaspoonfuls of batter 3 inches apart onto the prepared baking sheets. Using the back of the teaspoon, gently flatten each drop and shape into a round just about 2 inches in diameter. Bake one sheet at a time for 6 to 8 minutes, or until the edges are golden brown.

5 Let the cookies cool on the baking sheets for about 15 minutes, and then peel the liner away from the cookies. Line a baking sheet with fresh parchment paper.

6 Place the chocolate in a microwave-safe bowl and heat in the microwave on 50 percent power, stirring every 30 seconds, until melted. Turn the cookies over, and using the back of a spoon or a pastry brush, brush the chocolate over the bottom of the cookies. Place chocolate side up on the lined baking sheet and leave at room temperature until the chocolate sets.

Baker's Note: These cookies come out of the oven rather pale with dark edges, so keep an eye on the edges to determine when they are done. And make sure you use nonstick foil or parchment paper.

Chocolate Almond Oat Cookies MAKES 14

½ cup whole almonds

½ cup old-fashioned oats

⅓ cup sweetened flaked or shredded coconut

8 tablespoons (4 ounces) unsalted
    butter, melted and cooled

½ cup firmly packed light brown sugar

½ cup granulated sugar

1 large egg

1 teaspoon vanilla extract

1½ cups (6.8 ounces) bread flour

½ teaspoon baking powder

½ teaspoon baking soda

¼ teaspoon ground cinnamon

½ teaspoon salt

1 (6-ounce) bar dark or semisweet chocolate, chopped

1 Preheat the oven to 350°F and place a rack in the center. Spread the almonds over half of a large baking sheet. Spread the oats over the other half of the baking sheet. Bake the almonds and oats for 4 minutes, then lay the

MAY 30

Memorial Day

Memorial Day was officially proclaimed in May in 1868 by General John Logan, national commander of the Grand Army of the Republic. It was first observed on May 30 of that year, when flowers were placed on the graves of Union and Confederate soldiers at Arlington National Cemetery. Today we celebrate Memorial Day on the last Monday in May. It is a day to remember those who died, while spending time with family and friends. According to a soldier friend of mine, this cookie was a favorite among her battalion.

Other Events on This Day:
Mint Julep Day, Water a Flower Day

coconut on the baking sheet and bake for another 4 minutes, or until the almonds are aromatic and toasted and the oats and coconut are lightly toasted. Remove from the oven and let cool. Chop the almonds.

2 In a medium-size bowl, stir the melted butter and sugars together until smooth. Stir in the egg and vanilla, being careful not to overbeat. Mix together the bread flour, baking powder, baking soda, cinnamon, and salt and stir into the sugar mixture. Stir in toasted oats, almonds, coconut, and the chocolate chunks.

3 Using a packed ¼-cup measure, shape the dough into balls. At this point, you can chill the balls of dough until you are ready to bake them, or you can bake them right away. If you chill the dough, the cookies will be fatter.

4 Preheat the oven to 350°F and place a rack in the center. Line two baking sheets with parchment paper.

5 Arrange the balls of dough about 3 inches apart on the prepared baking sheets and press down the tops slightly. Bake for 12 to 15 minutes, or until the edges are nicely browned. Let cool on the baking sheets for about 3 minutes, then transfer to a wire rack to cool completely. These taste best when completely cool.

Baker's Notes: Bread flour gives these cookies a thick outer shell and soft inside. Toasting the almonds and oats adds depth of flavor. The dough is dry, so you might have to knead it with your hands a bit to get all the nuts and oats to stay in.

National Macaroon Day

Whether you favor the elegant Parisian type spelled "macaron;" the light, dry, coconut type; or the rich and chewy condensed milk version, today's all about enjoying macaroons. I'm a big fan of

Easy Macaroons MAKES 48

1 (14-ounce) can sweetened condensed milk

1 large egg white

5¼ cups sweetened flaked coconut

2 teaspoons Mexican or regular vanilla extract

½ teaspoon almond extract

1. Preheat the oven to 350°F and place a rack in the center. Line two baking sheets with nonstick foil or parchment paper.

2. Mix the sweetened condensed milk, egg white, coconut, vanilla, and almond extract in a large bowl.

3. Drop rounded teaspoonfuls of batter about 2 inches apart onto the baking sheets. Bake for 15 to 18 minutes, or until lightly browned around the edges. Carefully transfer to a wire rack and let cool completely.

all three, but the ease of the condensed milk version usually reels me in. When baked, the condensed milk takes on a *dulce de leche* quality. Vanilla, coconut, and almond extract create a pleasant array of flavors in a chewy, almost candylike cookie.

Other Events on This Day:
World No Tobacco Day

Ring Cookies MAKES 26

1½ cups (6.8 ounces) all-purpose flour

½ teaspoon baking powder

½ teaspoon salt

8 tablespoons (4 ounces) unsalted
    butter, room temperature

²/₃ cup granulated sugar

3 large egg yolks

1 teaspoon vanilla extract

Pinch of freshly grated nutmeg

Cinnamon sugar or sprinkles

1. Preheat the oven to 375°F and place a rack in the center. Line two baking sheets with nonstick foil or parchment paper.

2. Mix the flour, baking powder, and salt together in a medium-size bowl; set aside.

3. In the bowl of a stand mixer fitted with a paddle attachment, or in a large mixing bowl, using a handheld electric mixer, cream the butter and sugar on medium speed until light. Add the egg yolks, vanilla, and nutmeg, beating

JUNE 1

National Doughnut Day

National Doughnut Day is a floating holiday that occurs the first Friday in June. The date varies, so consider this a reminder and mark your calendar for this holiday, which was created by the Salvation Army to honor women who served doughnuts to soldiers during WWI. If it's not yet doughnut day, here's a cookie you can make to tide you over.

until light and fluffy. By hand or using the lowest speed of the mixer, add the flour mixture.

4 Shape into 1-inch balls. Push your thumb through the center of each ball and shape the dough into a ring. Dip the top of each ring in cinnamon sugar or sprinkles. Arrange about 2 inches apart on the prepared baking sheets. Bake for 10 to 12 minutes, or until golden brown. Transfer to a wire rack to cool completely.

Rocky Road Day

June is National Candy Month, but today we honor one particular favorite, Rocky Road. Known primarily as an ice cream flavor, Rocky Road was invented by William Dreyer, who introduced it in 1929 right after the stock market crashed. Dreyer is said to have named it partially as an allusion to tough times, as well as for its bumpy texture.

Other Events on This Day:
I Love My Dentist Day, Bubba Day

Rocky Road Bars MAKES 24

1 cup (8 ounces) unsalted butter
1 cup unsweetened natural cocoa powder
½ cup firmly packed light brown sugar
4 large eggs, cold
1½ cups granulated sugar
1½ teaspoons vanilla extract
½ teaspoon salt
1 cup (4.5 ounces) all-purpose flour
2 cups miniature marshmallows
1 cup semisweet chocolate chips
1¼ cups toasted and chopped walnuts

1 Preheat the oven to 350°F and place a rack in the center. Line a 9 by 13-inch metal pan with nonstick foil.

2 In a small saucepan, melt the butter over medium heat. Reduce the heat to low and stir in the cocoa powder until smooth. Add the brown sugar and stir until blended. Remove from the heat.

3 In a large mixing bowl, whisk the eggs for about 1 minute or until frothy, then whisk in the sugar and the vanilla. Using a large silicone scraper or mixing spoon, stir in the chocolate mixture, followed by the salt and the flour.

4 Pour the batter into the prepared pan and bake for 25 minutes, or until a toothpick inserted in the center comes out clean or with moist crumbs. Remove from the oven and sprinkle with the marshmallows, chocolate chips, and walnuts.

5 Return the pan to the oven for 2 minutes, or just until the marshmallows puff up. Let cool completely in the pan, then chill for about 1 hour or until the top is firm. For an even cleaner cut, freeze for about 30 minutes before cutting. To serve, lift from the pan, using the foil as a handle, set on a cutting board, and cut into 24 bars.

Baker's Notes: If you attempt to cut the bars before they're fully cooled, they'll be gooey. Once chilled, they're sturdy and you can cut them and package them or arrange them on a tray. My favorite way to serve them is cut into 48 wedges and sitting in cute cupcake liners.

Mud Bars MAKES 30

2 cups semisweet chocolate chips
1¾ cups butterscotch chips
1 cup creamy or crunchy peanut butter
2 cups dry roasted, lightly salted peanuts
2 cups miniature marshmallows

1 Line a 9-inch square pan with nonstick foil.

2 Combine the chocolate chips, butterscotch chips, and peanut butter in a large saucepan; heat on medium-low heat, stirring often, until melted. Remove from the heat and stir in the peanuts and marshmallows.

3 Spread the mixture in the prepared pan and chill for at least 2 hours. Grasp the foil, lift from the pan, set on a cutting board, and cut into 30 pieces. The mud should remain stored in the refrigerator and will keep for a couple of months in an airtight container.

Casey at the Bat Published

The most famous poem in baseball history was published today in 1888. Now known to be penned by Ernest Thayer, *Casey at the Bat* first appeared in the *San Francisco Examiner* with the author credited as "Phin." It didn't get much attention until a comedian performed the poem in front of an audience that included many ball club members. The poem's popularity grew and other people recited it, including the baseball player Mike "King" Kelly, who did a Vaudevillian parody.

This recipe is from my friend Amy, a teacher who said this candy was always a very popular teacher's gift.

Other Events on This Day:
Egg Day, Repeat Day

National Trails Day

After all that talk about rocky roads and mud (see June 2 and 3), it seems fitting that today's holiday is dedicated to trails. Created by the American Hiking Society, National Trails Day is a day designed to raise awareness of the wide variety of benefits that trails provide and encourage folks to get out and hike, bike, horseback ride, do some sort of maintenance project, row a boat, or participate in a fair. In any case, this is the kind of day where you need a rugged cookie that tastes good and keeps you going.

Other Events on This Day:
Hug Your Cat Day, Old Maid Day

Dried Cherry Chocolate Trail Bars   MAKES 16 OR 24

1 cup (4.5 ounces) white whole wheat
     flour (see Baker's Notes)
½ teaspoon baking powder
¼ teaspoon salt
8 tablespoons (4 ounces) unsalted
     butter, room temperature
1 cup firmly packed brown sugar
¼ cup granulated sugar
2 tablespoons pure maple syrup
1 teaspoon vanilla extract
1 large egg
1½ cups quick-cooking oats
1¼ cups flaked rice cereal, such as Special K
1 cup toasted and chopped pecans
½ cup semisweet chocolate chips
½ cup dried cherries, roughly chopped

1 Preheat the oven to 350°F and place a rack in the center. Line a 9 by 13-inch metal baking pan with nonstick foil.

2 Mix the flour, baking powder, and salt together in a medium-size bowl; set aside.

3 In the bowl of a stand mixer fitted with a paddle attachment, or in a large mixing bowl, using a handheld electric mixer, beat the butter and both sugars on medium speed until creamy. Add the syrup, vanilla, and egg and stir until mixed. By hand, stir in the flour mixture. When blended, stir in the oats, cereal, pecans, chocolate chips, and cherries. Press tightly into the pan.

4 Bake for 25 to 28 minutes, or until the top is lightly browned. Let cool in the pan for about 20 minutes. While still warm, lift from

the pan, set on a cutting board, and score into sixteen fat or tewnty-four thin bars, but do not separate. Let the bars cool completely before serving.

Baker's Notes: All-purpose flour can be substituted for white whole wheat, and if you don't have any flaked rice cereal, use corn or wheat. And of course all the nuts, chocolate chips, and cherries are variable as well.

Apple Chip Biscotti MAKES ABOUT 32

1 cup freeze-dried apple chips

2 cups (9 ounces) all-purpose flour

1½ teaspoons baking powder

½ teaspoon salt

½ teaspoon ground cinnamon

¼ teaspoon freshly grated nutmeg

⅛ teaspoon ground allspice

⅛ teaspoon ground cardamom

⅔ cup granulated sugar

4 tablespoons (2 ounces) unsalted
    butter, room temperature

1 large egg

⅓ cup apple juice

1 teaspoon vanilla extract

1 cup toasted and chopped walnuts

1 Preheat the oven to 350°F and place a rack in the center. Line a large baking sheet with nonstick foil or parchment paper.

2 Pulse the apple chips in the bowl of a food processor to crush them, then transfer to a large mixing bowl.

3 Pulse the flour, baking powder, salt, cinnamon, nutmeg, allspice, cardamom, and sugar in the food processor. Add the butter and pulse until the mixture is crumbly. Add the egg, apple juice, and vanilla and pulse until a soft dough forms. Transfer the dough into the bowl with the apple chips, then add the walnuts.

Apple II Day

A few friends count today among the most important in their lives. On this day in 1977, Apple co-founder Steve Wozniak introduced the 8-bit Apple II computer. The Apple II was innovative for its time. It had a color display, eight expansion slots for adding additional memory, was capable of doing spreadsheets (which up until that time was a lengthy task), and its BASIC language was built in so that it could run right out of the box. In honor of the Apple II, make a cookie with apples!

Other Events on This Day:
National Gingerbread Day, World Environment Day

4 Transfer the dough to a clean, flat surface and knead once or twice to distribute the apple chips and nuts. Divide the dough in half and shape each half into a 12 by 2½-inch log. Arrange the logs lengthwise on the prepared baking sheet, spacing them about 5 inches apart. Bake at 350°F for 20 minutes. Let cool on the baking sheet for 20 minutes.

5 Reduce the oven temperature to 300°F.

6 Carefully transfer the baked logs to a cutting board. Using a serrated knife, cut crosswise slightly on the diagonal every ¾ inch. Place cut side down on the baking sheet and bake until the biscotti are dry, about 30 minutes. Transfer the biscotti to a wire rack to cool and crisp.

JUNE 6

National Applesauce Cake Day

Applesauce cake is moist, spicy, easy to make, and inexpensive. If you've never made one, today's a good day to sift through some recipes and give it a try. Of course, if you'd rather make it in bar form, I've got just the recipe.

These bars are adapted from a cake recipe put out by Stokely. The original version called for shortening and it works beautifully, but I've also had great results with vegetable oil.

Other Events on This Day:
National Yo-Yo Day

Applesauce Cake Bars with Cream Cheese Frosting MAKES 16

BASE

1¼ cups (5.6 ounces) all-purpose flour

½ cup granulated sugar

⅛ teaspoon baking powder

¾ teaspoon baking soda

¾ teaspoon salt

½ teaspoon ground cinnamon

¼ teaspoon ground cloves

¼ teaspoon ground allspice

¼ cup shortening or vegetable oil

¼ cup water

1 cup unsweetened applesauce

2 tablespoons lightly beaten egg

⅓ cup walnuts, toasted and coarsely chopped

⅓ cup raisins (optional)

CREAM CHEESE FROSTING

3 tablespoons (1.5 ounces) unsalted butter, room temperature

3 ounces cream cheese, softened

¼ teaspoon vanilla extract

1¼ cups confectioners' sugar

1. Preheat the oven to 350°F and place a rack in the center. Line a 9-inch square metal pan with nonstick foil, or line it with regular foil and spray the foil with flour-added baking spray.

2. **Make the base:** Mix the flour, sugar, baking powder, baking soda, salt, cinnamon, cloves, and allspice together in a large mixing bowl. Stir in the shortening and mash it around so that it coats the flour. Add the water, applesauce, and egg and beat until well mixed. Stir in the walnuts and raisins, if using.

3. Pour into the prepared pan and bake for 25 minutes, or until a toothpick inserted in the center comes out clean. Let cool in the pan.

4. **Make the frosting:** Beat the butter and cream cheese together in a medium bowl until creamy. Beat in the vanilla and confectioners' sugar until the mixture is creamy and smooth. Spread over the cooled bars. When ready to serve, lift from the pan, set on a cutting board, and cut into sixteen bars.

Baker's Note: This is a small, everyday-size batch. For a crowd or large family, just double the recipe and bake in a 10 by 15-inch pan.

Granola MAKES 4½ CUPS

½ cup slivered almonds

½ cup coarsely chopped pecan halves

1⅔ cups old-fashioned oats

3 tablespoons shredded sweetened or unsweetened coconut

⅛ teaspoon salt

2 tablespoons firmly packed light or dark brown sugar

2 tablespoons pure maple syrup

1 tablespoon honey

2 tablespoons vegetable oil

½ teaspoon vanilla extract

½ cup golden raisins

½ cup dried apricots, chopped

½ cup raisins

Virginia Apgar's Birthday

Happy birthday, Dr. Virginia Apgar! Born in 1909, Apgar was an American anesthesiologist who developed a method for assessing the well-being of newborns. Using the initials in her last name, she applied five simple criteria: Appearance, Pulse, Grimace, Activity, and Respiration. Each criterion was assigned a score of 1 to 2, so the highest APGAR score a baby could get would be 10.

1 Preheat the oven to 250°F and place a rack in the center. Line a large rimmed baking sheet with nonstick foil or parchment paper, or just rub the pan lightly with some extra vegetable oil.

2 In a large bowl, mix the almonds, pecans, oats, coconut, and salt.

3 In a 1- or 2-cup microwave-safe measuring cup, stir together the brown sugar, maple syrup, honey, and vegetable oil. Heat in the microwave on high for 30 to 50 seconds, or until boiling; stir to dissolve the sugar slightly. Stir in the vanilla. Pour the hot syrup mixture over the oat mixture and stir until evenly coated. Pour the oat mixture onto the prepared baking sheet, spreading as evenly as possible and pressing down slightly to create a thin, tightly packed layer.

4 Cover loosely with a large piece of foil and place in the oven on the center rack. Set a timer for 40 minutes. Check the granola to make sure it's browning evenly. Give it a stir, re-cover with the foil, and bake for another 35 minutes, for a total baking time of 75 minutes. Let cool completely on the pan. The granola will crisp as it cools, so don't worry if it doesn't seem crisp right out of the oven. When cool, break up the bigger clumps into smaller clumps. Toss with the golden raisins, apricots, and raisins.

JUNE 8

Best Friends Day

A few years ago, my daughter and a friend declared "Best Friends Day" and marked it as a day in early June. Little did they know, there is actually a Best Friends Day in early June, and an International Friendship Day in August that has been observed since 1935. The point of today's Best Friends Day is to cherish the person or the

Chocolate Peanut Butter Swirl Brownies with Banana MAKES 36

1½ cups (6.7 ounces) sifted all-purpose flour

2 tablespoons unsweetened natural cocoa powder

½ teaspoon salt

12 tablespoons (6 ounces) unsalted butter

2½ cups extra-dark chocolate chips

3 ounces bittersweet chocolate (70% cacao), chopped

1 large ripe banana

178

2 cups firmly packed light brown sugar

4 large eggs

1 teaspoon vanilla extract

1 cup lightly toasted and chopped walnuts

3 tablespoons creamy peanut butter,
    plus more for garnishing

1 teaspoon vegetable oil

1 Preheat the oven to 325°F and place a rack in the center. Line a 9 by 13-inch metal pan with nonstick foil, or line it with regular foil and spray the foil with flour-added baking spray.

2 Mix the flour, cocoa powder, and salt together in a small bowl; set aside.

3 Melt the butter in a saucepan over medium-low heat. Reduce the heat to low and add 1½ cups of the chocolate chips and the chopped bittersweet chocolate. Stir until the chocolate is melted. Remove from the heat and let cool slightly.

4 Meanwhile, in the bowl of a stand mixer fitted with a paddle attachment, or in a large mixing bowl, using a handheld electric mixer, mash the banana. Add the sugar, eggs, and vanilla and beat on medium speed until the mixture is smooth. Add the melted chocolate to the banana mixture and stir until combined. Add the flour mixture and stir by hand until incorporated. If the batter is still fairly warm, let it cool slightly, then add the remaining cup of chocolate chips and the walnuts. Pour the batter into the pan, spreading all the way to the edges.

5 In a small bowl or custard cup, soften the 3 tablespoons of peanut butter for about 5 seconds on HIGH in the microwave. Stir in the vegetable oil. Drop about eight small blobs of the peanut butter mixture across the top of the brownie batter. Drag a knife through the peanut butter splotches to make a rippled or marbled pattern.

people who've been a constant presence through good times and bad.

This recipe was inspired by a blue-ribbon-winning baker named Gloria, who convinced me that adding mashed banana to brownie batter was a good idea.

Other Events on This Day:
Name Your Poison Day

6 Bake the brownies for 40 to 45 minutes, or until a toothpick inserted in the center comes out clean. Remove the pan from the oven. Drop extra bits of peanut butter over the peanut butter swirls to cover any holes that appeared during baking. Let cool in the pan, then chill thoroughly. Grasp the foil, lift the brownies from the pan, set on a cutting board, and cut into thirty-six squares.

Baker's Note: The vegetable oil keeps the peanut butter from drying out as the brownies bake.

JUNE 9

National Strawberry Rhubarb Pie Day

Of unknown origin, this "national" holiday celebrates the combination of tart, crisp rhubarb and sweet, juicy strawberries baked into pie. Cookie bakers may go the "bar" route, of course.

Other Events on This Day: Secretariat won the Belmont Stakes (June 9, 1973), Donald Duck made his debut in 1934

Strawberry Rhubarb Pie Bars MAKES 32

FILLING
1½ cups frozen unsweetened rhubarb
1½ cups sliced fresh strawberries
½ cup granulated sugar
1 tablespoon key lime juice
2 tablespoons cornstarch

CRUST
1½ cups (6.8 ounces) all-purpose flour
1 cup firmly packed light brown sugar
½ teaspoon baking soda
½ teaspoon salt
½ teaspoon ground cinnamon
12 tablespoons (6 ounces) unsalted
     butter, room temperature
1½ cups old-fashioned oats

1 Preheat the oven to 350°F and place a rack in the center. Line a 9 by 13-inch metal pan with nonstick foil.

2 **Make the filling:** Combine the rhubarb, strawberries, sugar, and lime juice in a large saucepan. Cover; cook over medium heat for about 3 minutes. Remove the cover and cook, stirring constantly, for about another minute, or until the rhubarb has thawed and the sugar is dissolved. Add the cornstarch and continue cooking, stirring constantly, until the sauce is bubbly and translucent. Remove from the heat.

3 **Make the crust:** Combine the flour, brown sugar, baking soda, salt, and cinnamon in the bowl of a food processor. Add the butter and pulse until the mixture is coarse and crumbly. Add the oats and pulse to mix. Reserve 1½ cups of the crumb mixture for the topping; press the remaining crumb mixture onto the bottom of the pan. Spread the filling over the crust. Sprinkle with the reserved crumb mixture.

4 Bake for 30 to 35 minutes, or until golden brown. Let cool completely in the pan. Lift from the pan, set on a cutting board, and cut into thirty-two bars.

Baker's Note: Frozen rhubarb works well and you can find it all year round.

Black Cow Brownies (a.k.a. Root Beer Glazed Brownies)

MAKES 16

1 cup (4.5 ounces) all-purpose flour

2 tablespoons Dutch-processed cocoa powder

Pinch of salt

4 ounces unsweetened chocolate, chopped

8 tablespoons (4 ounces) unsalted
    butter, room temperature

1 cup granulated sugar

½ cup firmly packed light brown sugar

¾ teaspoon vanilla extract

¼ teaspoon root beer extract, such as Watkins

⅓ cup golden syrup or light corn syrup

3 large eggs, room temperature

½ cup semisweet chocolate chips

DRIZZLE

1 teaspoon melted unsalted butter

½ cup confectioners' sugar

1 to 2 teaspoons milk

¼ teaspoon root beer extract, such as Watkins

National Black Cow Day

The black cow was invented today in 1893. A frosty mix of root beer and chocolate ice cream, the idea for the drink is often credited to Frank J. Wisner, owner of a gold mining company, who also produced a line of soda water for the citizens of the Cripple Creek gold mining district. According to some, Wisner's idea was inspired by the glow of the full moon on snow-capped Cow Mountain, which resembled a dark mountain capped in ice cream.

1   Preheat the oven to 350°F and place a rack in the center.
Line a 9-inch square metal pan with nonstick foil, or line
it with regular foil and spray the foil with flour-added baking spray.

2   Mix the flour, cocoa powder, and salt together in a bowl;
set aside.

3   In a microwave-safe bowl, melt the chocolate at 50 percent power, stirring every 30 seconds, until smooth. Set
aside to cool for 5 minutes.

4   In the bowl of a stand mixer fitted with a paddle attachment, or in a large mixing bowl, using a handheld electric
mixer, beat the butter and both sugars on medium speed
until creamy. Beat in the vanilla, root beer extract, and
golden syrup. When creamy, beat in the eggs, one at a
time, beating thoroughly after each addition.

5   Beat in the melted chocolate, scraping the sides of the
bowl. Gradually stir in the flour mixture. When fully blended, stir in the chips. Pour into the prepared pan and bake
for 35 minutes, or until the brownies appear set. Let cool in
the pan for 1 hour, or until the brownies are cool enough to
transfer to the refrigerator. Chill for 1 or 2 hours.

6   **Make the drizzle:** In a small bowl or a 2-cup Pyrex measuring cup, mix together the butter and confectioners'
sugar. Add the milk, starting with 1 teaspoon, and the root
beer extract. Stir well. Add more milk as needed to give
the icing a drizzling consistency. Drizzle from a spoon
held high over the brownies. Leave at room temperature
for the icing to set.

7   Grasp the foil, lift from the pan, set on a cutting board,
and cut into sixteen squares.

Macadamia White Chocolate Pineapple Cookies   MAKES ABOUT 40

COOKIES

2½ cups (11.3 ounces) all-purpose flour

1 teaspoon baking powder

1 teaspoon salt

12 tablespoons (6 ounces) unsalted
   butter, room temperature

1 cup granulated sugar

1 teaspoon vanilla extract

2 large eggs

½ cup chopped macadamia nuts

½ cup chopped dried pineapple

½ cup white chips, or 3 ounces white
   chocolate, chopped

GLAZE

1 tablespoon (0.5 ounce) unsalted butter, melted

1½ cups confectioners' sugar

3 tablespoons pineapple juice

Pinch of salt

1   Preheat the oven to 350°F and place a rack in the center. Have ready two ungreased baking sheets.

2   **Make the cookies:** Mix the flour, baking powder, and salt together in a bowl; set aside.

3   In the bowl of a stand mixer fitted with a paddle attachment, or in a large mixing bowl, using a handheld electric mixer, beat the butter and sugar on medium speed until light and creamy. Beat in the vanilla, scraping the sides of the bowl often. Reduce the speed of the mixer and add the eggs, one at a time, mixing just until blended. By hand or using the lowest speed of the mixer, add the flour mixture and stir until it is absorbed and you have a soft but easy-to-handle dough. Stir in the macadamia nuts, pineapple, and white chocolate.

King Kamehameha Day

Hawaiians honor King Kamehameha I today. Known as "the Napoleon of the Pacific," King Kamehameha established the Unified Kingdom of Hawaii in 1810. The holiday honoring him was proclaimed by his grandson, King Kamehameha V, in 1871, and when Hawaii became a state in 1959, it was officially proclaimed by the state legislature.

If you can't make it to Hawaii for Kamehameha Day, celebrate at home with some Hawaii-inspired cookies. This recipe is from my friend Lisa, who had the idea to put macadamia nuts and dried pineapple in her favorite soft, fat, dense sugar cookie.

Other Events on This Day: **Corn on the Cob Day, German Chocolate Day, *E.T.* opened in 1982**

4 Drop level teaspoonfuls of dough about 2 inches apart onto the baking sheets. Bake for 10 minutes, or until the edges are nicely browned, then transfer to a wire rack to cool completely.

5 **Make the glaze:** Mix together the melted butter and confectioners' sugar in a small bowl. Stir in the pineapple juice and a pinch of salt. Drizzle a little glaze over each cookie and leave at room temperature to let the icing set.

National Peanut Butter Cookie Day

It's National Peanut Butter Cookie Day, so celebrate the quintessentially American cookie by baking a big batch for your friends. These cookies are made with the salt-free peanut butter you grind fresh in the store.

Other Events on This Day:
Machine Day, Red Rose Day

Not-So-Classic Peanut Butter Crisscross Cookies

MAKES 36

8 tablespoons (4 ounces) unsalted
   butter, room temperature
½ cup firmly packed light or dark brown sugar
½ cup plus 2 tablespoons granulated sugar
1¼ cups natural, freshly ground, no-salt-added
   peanut butter (see Baker's Note)
1 large egg
½ teaspoon chipotle powder
1¼ teaspoons salt
½ teaspoon baking soda
1 teaspoon Mexican or regular vanilla extract
1½ cups (6.8 ounces) all-purpose flour
⅔ cup peanut butter chips, such as Reese's
1 teaspoon ground cinnamon

1 Preheat the oven to 350°F and place a rack in the center. Line two baking sheets with parchment paper or nonstick foil.

2 In the bowl of a stand mixer fitted with a paddle attachment, or in a large mixing bowl, using a handheld electric mixer, beat the butter on medium speed until creamy. Gradually add the brown sugar and ½ cup of the granulated

sugar and continue beating on medium-high speed for about 2 minutes, or until the mixture is light and creamy. Beat in the peanut butter and egg. Scrape the sides of the bowl and beat in the chipotle powder, salt, baking soda, and vanilla. When well blended, add the flour and stir until incorporated. Stir in the chips.

3   Stir the remaining 2 tablespoons of granulated sugar with the cinnamon. Shape the dough into 1-inch balls. Roll the balls in the cinnamon sugar and arrange about 2½-inches apart on the prepared baking sheets. Flatten the balls with a fork dipped in water, making crisscross patterns.

4   Bake for 10 to 12 minutes, or until ever-so-slightly browned around the edges—do not overbake. Let cool on the baking sheets for about 5 minutes, then transfer to a wire rack to cool completely.

Baker's Note: If your store doesn't sell freshly ground peanut butter, mainstream peanut butter works fine, too. Just make sure to reduce the salt to ¾ teaspoon.

Almond-Topped Shortbread Bars (a.k.a. Almond Pie Bars)
MAKES 32

CRUST

2 cups (9 ounces) all-purpose flour

⅓ cup granulated sugar

½ teaspoon salt

8 tablespoons (4 ounces) unsalted butter, room temperature

TOPPING

½ cup light corn syrup

⅓ cup firmly packed light brown sugar

3 tablespoons unsalted butter

¼ cup heavy whipping cream

1½ cups sliced almonds, toasted

½ teaspoon almond extract

¼ teaspoon vanilla extract

Fact:
George Washington Carver discovered over three hundred uses for the peanut in the 1800s. Because he believed food was a gift from God, Carver didn't patent peanut butter.

JUNE 13

Father's Day

Father's Day is a floating holiday that occurs the third Sunday in June. It can be difficult to keep track of, so consider this a reminder to start thinking about treats for Dad.

My dad's pretty easy to please when it comes to desserts. For a while he loved almond toffee and almond crunch bars, but after years of making him the same treats, I started branching off into other almond-inspired desserts, such as this one. It's the next best thing to almond toffee!

1 Preheat the oven to 350°F and place a rack in the center. Line a 9 by 13-inch metal pan with nonstick foil, or line it with regular foil and spray the foil with flour-added baking spray.

2 **Make the crust:** In the bowl of a food processor, combine the flour, sugar, and salt and pulse a few times to mix. Add the butter and pulse until the mixture is coarse. Press into the bottom of the prepared pan and bake for 15 minutes.

3 **Meanwhile, make the topping:** Combine the corn syrup, brown sugar, butter, and cream in a 2-quart saucepan and heat over medium heat just until the mixture starts to boil. Remove from the heat and stir in the almonds, almond extract, and vanilla. Pour over the baked crust and bake for 12 minutes. Let cool completely in the pan. When cool, lift from the pan, set on a cutting board, and cut into 32 squares.

JUNE 14

Flag Day

Proclaimed in 1916 by President Wilson, today commemorates the date in 1777 when the Second Continental Congress adopted the United States flag. Sewn by Betsy Ross, the original flag had thirteen white stars in a blue background and thirteen alternate red and white stripes. Between 1777 and 1960, the flag has been altered twenty-seven times to add additional stars.

Other Events on This Day:
Strawberry Shortcake Day

Flag Cookies MAKES ABOUT 24

1 cup (8 ounces) unsalted butter, room temperature
3 ounces cream cheese, softened
¼ teaspoon salt
1 cup granulated sugar
1 large egg yolk
1 teaspoon vanilla extract
2½ cups (11.3 ounces) all-purpose flour
Your favorite icing, or see June 15

1 In the bowl of a stand mixer fitted with a paddle attachment, or in a large mixing bowl, using a handheld electric mixer, beat the butter, cream cheese, and salt on medium speed until fluffy. Scrape the sides of the bowl and beat in the sugar. Beat for about 2 minutes, then add the egg yolk and vanilla and beat just until mixed. By hand, stir in the flour to make a thick dough—it should be moist but not too sticky. Divide it in half and shape into two balls. Press the balls into disks and chill until firm enough to roll and cut.

2 Preheat the oven to 350°F and place a rack in the center. Line two baking sheets with parchment paper or nonstick foil.

3 Press or roll out the dough about ⅜ inch thick. If you have a flag-shaped cookie cutter, cut out your flags. Otherwise, roll out the dough and cut out your own small rectangles, using a knife. Arrange about 2 inches apart on the prepared sheets. Bake one sheet at a time for 10 minutes, or until the cookies appear set. Let cool on the baking sheets for about 5 minutes, then transfer to a wire rack to cool completely. Decorate with red, white, and blue icing.

Baker's Notes: This sugar cookie base is perfect for Flag Day because you can cut it in rectangles and it won't spread too much. To decorate, use colored icings from the grocery store or dye your favorite icing red, white, and blue and decorate with piping bags. Omit the additional salt if using salted butter.

Smiley Face Cookies MAKES 12

COOKIES

3 cups (13.5 ounces) all-purpose flour

1 teaspoon baking powder

½ teaspoon salt

1 cup (8 ounces) unsalted butter, room temperature

1 cup granulated sugar

1 teaspoon vanilla extract

½ teaspoon almond extract

1 large egg, lightly beaten

ICING

3¾ cups (1 pound) confectioners' sugar, sifted

½ teaspoon cream of tartar

3 large pasteurized egg whites

1½ teaspoons clear vanilla extract

Water, as needed

Black and yellow food coloring paste

National Smile Power Day

You know that old saying about how it takes fewer muscles to smile than to frown? I never believed it, so I finally looked it up on Snopes .com. It is correct (sort of). No one agrees on the muscle count, but Snopes went on to say that people typically smile more than frown, therefore the smiling muscles are used more often and smiles take less effort. On the flip side, if you're a chronic frowner, then frowning takes less effort?

Other Events on This Day:
In 1752, Benjamin Franklin put a key on a kite and showed that electricity and lightening were related

1 **Make the cookies:** Mix the flour, baking powder, and salt together in a medium-size bowl; set aside.

2 In a mixing bowl, beat the butter and sugar until light and fluffy. Beat in the vanilla and almond extract. Reduce the mixer speed and add the egg, beating just until it's mixed in. By hand or using the very lowest speed of the mixer, add the flour mixture. The dough should be thick enough to roll at this point, but if it's not, then chill for 1 hour.

3 Preheat the oven to 375°F and place a rack in the center. Roll out the dough on a lightly floured surface to about ½ inch thick. Cut the cookies into circles and arrange about 3 inches apart on ungreased baking sheets. Bake the cookies for 8 to 10 minutes, or until the edges begin to turn golden brown in color. Let cool completely on a wire rack set over paper towels.

4 **Make the icing:** In a large mixing bowl, using a handheld electric mixer on low speed, beat the confectioners' sugar, cream of tartar, egg whites, and vanilla until smooth. Increase the speed to medium and add water 1 teaspoon at a time until the icing is of piping consistency. Dye about 1 cup of it black, transfer it to a heavy-duty zipper bag, seal the bag, and set aside. Add a little more water to the remaining icing until it is just slightly thicker than school glue, but not runny. Dye it yellow, or divide it and dye it different colors.

5 Spoon yellow icing over the cookies and let the icing set. Snip off a small corner of the zipper bag and pipe black eyes and smiles. Let the icing set.

Baker's Note: This is a basic royal icing recipe with a large yield. For best results, add any extra water very slowly. If you accidentally add too much, add a bit more sugar.

Caramel Corn MAKES 6 CUPS

4½ to 5 cups popped popcorn
¼ cup lightly salted peanuts or nut of choice
6 tablespoons packed dark brown sugar
3 tablespoons light corn syrup
2½ tablespoons (1.25 ounces) unsalted butter
1 teaspoon mild molasses
½ teaspoon vanilla extract
⅛ teaspoon baking soda
⅛ teaspoon salt

1 Preheat the oven to 250°F and place a rack in the center. Rub a large roasting pan generously with butter.

2 Combine the popcorn and peanuts in a large mixing bowl and set aside.

3 In a small saucepan set over medium heat, mix together the sugar, corn syrup, butter, and molasses and bring to a boil. From the time the mixture starts to boil, continue at a gentle boil for 5 minutes, stirring occasionally. Remove from the heat; stir in the vanilla, baking soda, and salt; then pour over the popcorn and toss to coat.

4 Spread the mixture in the prepared pan and bake for 1 hour, stirring every 15 minutes. Remove from the oven and stir once or twice, then let cool in the pan, breaking up any clumps. Store in a tin or another tightly covered container.

Caramel Corn Cookies MAKES 24

¾ cup (3.4 ounces) all-purpose flour
½ teaspoon baking soda
½ teaspoon baking powder
½ teaspoon salt
½ cup melted coconut oil, cooled to lukewarm
½ cup firmly packed dark brown sugar
½ cup granulated sugar
1 large egg
¾ teaspoon vanilla extract

Cracker Jack Invented

Cracker Jack was introduced at the World's Fair in 1893. It's a classic American snack and the prize in the box never gets old. However, if you want to make your own caramel corn, here's my favorite recipe. This caramel corn is a good starter recipe, perfect for making for just yourself or the family. If you get really good at it, you can double or triple the recipe.

For those who want to try it in a cookie, I've also included a recipe that some say tastes like the popular snack. My take on the cookie includes coconut oil, but if you don't have any, feel free to substitute shortening.

Other Events on This Day:
Fudge Day, First Ladies Day Celebrated in 1883

1 cup quick-cooking oats (not instant)

¾ cup crispy rice cereal

½ cup sweetened flaked coconut

½ cup chopped, lightly salted peanuts

Caramel Corn, for topping

1 Preheat the oven to 350°F and place a rack in the center. Line two baking sheets with parchment paper or nonstick foil.

2 In a small bowl, mix together the flour, baking soda, baking powder, and salt; set aside.

3 In the bowl of a stand mixer fitted with a paddle attachment, or in a large mixing bowl using a handheld mixer on medium-high speed, beat the coconut oil and both sugars for about 2 minutes or until well mixed. Reduce the speed to medium-low and beat in the egg and vanilla. By hand, stir in the oats, then stir in the flour mixture until incorporated. Stir in the cereal, coconut, and peanuts.

4 Scoop up level tablespoons of dough and shape into balls a little over 1 inch in diameter. Arrange about 2½ inches apart on the prepared baking sheets and press to make ½-inch-thick rounds. Press one or two pieces of caramel corn in the center or each cookie and bake for 11 to 13 minutes or until golden. Let cool on the baking sheets for 3 minutes, then carefully transfer to a wire rack to cool completely.

JUNE 17

Eat Your Vegetables Day

Today is National Eat Your Vegetables Day, geared to raise awareness of the vitamins, minerals, fiber, and great flavor of vegetables.

Carrot and Oat Cookies

MAKES ABOUT 24

¾ cup (3.25 ounces) whole wheat pastry flour

½ teaspoon baking soda

¼ teaspoon salt

1 teaspoon ground cinnamon

½ cup firmly packed light brown sugar

¼ cup granulated sugar

¼ cup vegetable oil

2 tablespoons pure maple syrup

⅓ cup carrot baby food

½ teaspoon vanilla extract

1½ cups old-fashioned oats

½ cup golden raisins

½ cup toasted and chopped pecans

1 Preheat the oven to 350°F and place a rack in the center. Line two baking sheets with parchment paper or nonstick foil.

2 Mix the flour, baking soda, salt, and cinnamon together in a bowl; set aside.

3 Mix both of the sugars, the vegetable oil, maple syrup, carrot baby food, and vanilla together in a large mixing bowl. Add the flour mixture and stir until blended. Stir in the oats, followed by the raisins and pecans, and let sit for 10 minutes. Scoop up tablespoonfuls of dough and arrange about 2½ inches apart on the prepared baking sheets.

4 Bake for 12 to 14 minutes. Let cool on the baking sheets for 5 to 8 minutes, then carefully transfer to a wire rack to cool completely.

Quick Cherry Dream Bars

MAKES 32

1 (18.25-ounce) box white or yellow cake mix

8 tablespoons (4 ounces) unsalted
    butter, room temperature

1¼ cups old-fashioned oats

1 large egg

1 (14-ounce) can cherry pie filling

½ cup toasted and finely chopped pecans

¼ cup firmly packed light brown sugar

1 Preheat the oven to 350°F and place a rack in the center. Line a 9 by 13-inch metal pan with nonstick foil, or line it with regular foil and spray the foil with nonstick baking spray.

JUNE 18

International Picnic Day

Grab your picnic basket and wash out the cooler, because today is International Picnic Day, a day to pack your food and eat it somewhere other than the kitchen. The origin of picnics dates back to medieval times when hunting parties would find a spot and stage an outdoor meal. Because hunting parties often included nobility, picnics were elegant affairs. Today's picnics are more casual, with coolers and buckets of chicken standing in for the fancy baskets of yore.

In honor of Picnic Day and the fact it's also Cherry Tart Day, here's a cherry tart in bar cookie form.

Other Events on This Day:
Juggling Day

2   In a large mixing bowl, stir together the cake mix, 6 tablespoons of the butter, and 1 cup of the oats until the mixture is moist and crumbly. Measure out 1 cup and set aside. Add the egg to the dough remaining in the bowl and stir until well mixed. Press the mixture into the bottom of the prepared pan. Spread the cherry pie filling over the top.

3   Place the reserved 1 cup of dough back in the mixing bowl. Stir in the remaining 2 tablespoons of butter, pecans, and brown sugar. Mix well. Sprinkle over the cherries.

4   Bake for 30 to 35 minutes, or until the edges are lightly browned and the top is hot and bubbly. Let cool completely in the pan. Cut into thirty-two bars.

JUNE 19

Juneteenth

The Emancipation Proclamation was issued on January 1863, but it wasn't until June 19, 1865, after an order from Union general Gordon Granger, that Texas freed its slaves. Today Juneteenth commemorates that day and focuses on more positive areas such as education, achievement, and self-improvement.

Central Texas hosts many Juneteenth festivities. Among them are the 2K Freedom Run, a parade, poetry readings, and various cookouts and

Pecan Pie Bars   MAKES 24

BASE

2 cups (9 ounces) all-purpose flour

½ cup granulated sugar

½ teaspoon salt

12 tablespoons (6 ounces) cold unsalted butter, cut up

FILLING

8 tablespoons (4 ounces) unsalted butter

1 cup firmly packed light brown sugar

1 cup light corn syrup

¼ teaspoon salt

4 large eggs

1 teaspoon vanilla extract

2 to 2½ cups toasted and chopped pecans

1. Preheat the oven to 350°F and place a rack in the center. Line a 9 by 13-inch metal pan with nonstick foil.

2. **Make the base:** Combine the flour, sugar, and salt in the bowl of a food processor or in a large bowl. If using the food processor, add the butter and pulse until the mixture is coarse and crumbly. If using a bowl, add the butter and cut it in with a pastry cutter or your fingers until coarse and crumbly. Press the mixture evenly into the prepared pan and bake for 18 minutes, or until it's just set and slightly brown around the edges.

3. **Make the filling:** In a large, microwave-safe mixing bowl, microwave the butter on high for 30 seconds, or until melted. Whisk in the sugar, corn syrup, and salt. Return the bowl to the microwave and heat for 40 to 60 seconds, or just until the mixture comes to a boil. Whisk again to dissolve the sugar. Let cool slightly, then whisk in the eggs, one at a time, and the vanilla. Stir in 2 cups of pecans (use more if desired) and pour the filling over the crust.

4. Bake for 32 to 35 minutes, or until set, and then let cool completely in the pan. For a clean cut, chill before slicing. Lift from the pan, set on a cutting board, and score into twenty-four bars.

Vanilla Bean Sugar Cookie Bars MAKES 32

BASE

8 tablespoons (4 ounces) unsalted
    butter, room temperature

1 cup granulated sugar

2 large eggs

1 teaspoon vanilla bean paste (see Baker's Notes)

1 teaspoon salt

¼ teaspoon baking soda

2½ cups (11.3 ounces) all-purpose flour

gatherings, featuring both Texas and soul food favorites, such as pecan pie.

Other Events on This Day:
National Martini Day

National Vanilla Milk Shake Day

It's National Vanilla Milk Shake Day, so make yourself a milkshake and be glad the drink has evolved, because the first milk shakes were alcoholic tonics made with whiskey and eggs. Yuck! Syrups were added in the early 1900s, ice cream came next, and by the 1930s, milk shakes as we know them today appeared at soda fountains across the country.

In honor of the vanilla milk shake, here's a cookie whose flavor might remind you of one.

Other Events on This Day:
National Ice-Cream Soda Day

FROSTING

8 tablespoons (4 ounces) unsalted butter, softened

1 teaspoon vanilla bean paste

¼ teaspoon salt

2 cups confectioners' sugar

2½ tablespoons milk

1 Preheat the oven to 350°F and place a rack in the center. Rub a 9 by 13-inch metal pan with butter or line the inside with nonstick foil.

2 **Make the base:** In the bowl of a stand mixer fitted with a paddle attachment, or in a large mixing bowl, using a handheld electric mixer, beat the butter and sugar gradually going from medium to high speed for about 3 minutes, or until light and creamy. Reduce the speed to medium-low and add the eggs, one at a time, scraping the sides of the bowl often. Continue beating on medium-low speed. Add the vanilla bean paste, salt, and baking soda. Reduce the mixer speed to low or, stirring by hand, gradually add the flour, stirring until incorporated.

3 Spread the batter in the prepared pan and bake for 10 to 15 minutes, until light golden brown or a toothpick comes out clean. If you've lined the pan with foil, you may lift the baked base out of the pan and transfer it to a flat surface before frosting. Let cool completely before frosting.

4 **Make the frosting:** In the bowl of a stand mixer fitted with a paddle attachment, or in a large mixing bowl, using a handheld electric mixer, beat the butter, vanilla bean paste, and salt together at low speed. Gradually add the confectioners' sugar and beat until combined. Add 1 tablespoon of the milk. Increase the mixer speed and continue adding the milk 1 tablespoon at a time, until the frosting is the consistency for spreading. Frost the cookie and cut into thirty-two bars.

Baker's Notes: If you're feeding a very large crowd, you may double this mixture and bake it in a 13 by 18-inch half sheet pan. The key ingredient is the Nielsen-Massey vanilla bean paste, which you can find at some nicer grocery stores and most gourmet stores.

Peaches and Cream Bars MAKES 24

CRUST

2 cups (9 ounces) all-purpose flour

¾ teaspoon baking powder

¼ teaspoon salt

**10 tablespoons (5 ounces)
    cold unsalted butter, cut up**

1 large egg, lightly beaten

FILLING

6 tablespoons granulated sugar

½ teaspoon vanilla extract

½ cup sour cream

2 tablespoons all-purpose flour

3 cups peeled and diced peaches

1 Preheat the oven to 350°F and place a rack in the center. Line a 9-inch square pan with nonstick foil, or line it with regular foil and spray the foil with flour-added baking spray.

2 **Make the crust:** In the bowl of a food processor, combine the flour, baking powder, and salt and pulse to mix. Add the butter and pulse until the mixture is coarse and crumbly. Add 2 tablespoons of the beaten egg, reserving what's left for the filling. Pat about two-thirds of the dough into the pan and bake for 20 minutes. Remove from the oven and set aside.

3 **Make the filling:** Combine the remaining 2 tablespoons of egg and the sugar, vanilla, and sour cream in a mixing bowl and stir well. Stir

Summer Solstice

Today is usually the summer solstice, which means it's the longest day of the year in the Northern Hemisphere and the shortest day in the Southern Hemisphere. It also happens to be Peaches and Cream Day, according to some calendars, so make a long day sweeter by creating a dessert with peaches and cream. I like these bars chilled, but my mom prefers them at room temperature.

Other Events on This Day:
Go Skateboarding Day

in the flour, and then stir in the peaches. Pour the peach filling over the baked crust and sprinkle with the reserved crust mixture.

4 Bake for 25 minutes, or until the filling starts to appear set around the edges. The top won't brown very much and the filling will not be completely set until it is cool. Let cool in the pan for about an hour, then chill for 2 or 3 hours, or until the bars are very cold. Grasp the foil, lift from the pan, and cut into twenty-four bars.

National Candy Month

June is National Candy Month, so to kick it off, here's a cookie that might remind you of a popular chocolate candy bar. These bar cookies are supposed to taste like Kit Kats. In my opinion, they don't, but they're unique in their own right, with a crumbly sugary paste sandwiched between light and flaky crackers. Plus, they're also a no-bake recipe, which is handy for the hot summer months.

Other Events on This Day:
Chocolate Éclair Day

Chocolate-Covered Wafer Cookies MAKES 32

84 round butter crackers, such as Ritz
12 tablespoons (6 ounces) unsalted butter
1½ cups graham cracker crumbs
¾ cup firmly packed light brown sugar
1 cup granulated sugar
⅓ cup whole or reduced-fat milk
1 cup butterscotch chips
1 cup semisweet chocolate chips
¾ cup creamy peanut butter

1 Line a 9 by 13-inch pan with nonstick foil. Spread a layer of crackers across the bottom and set aside.

2 In a small saucepan, melt the butter. Add the graham cracker crumbs, both sugars, and milk. Bring to a boil over medium heat. When the mixture begins to boil, set a timer and boil gently for 5 minutes, stirring occasionally. Pour half of this mixture over the crackers, then layer more crackers over the boiled mixture. Pour the remaining boiled mixture over the second layer of crackers, and then top with one last layer of crackers.

3 Combine the butterscotch chips, chocolate chips, and peanut butter in a microwave-safe bowl and microwave at 50 percent power, stirring every 60 seconds, until melted and smooth. Pour over the bars.

4 Let cool in the pan for 1 hour and then chill for about 30 minutes, or as long as it takes for the final topping to set. When it has set, remove from the refrigerator, lift from the pan, set on a cutting board, and score into thirty-two bars.

Baker's Note: This recipe halves well. Halve all the ingredients and use an 8-inch square pan.

Slice-and-Bake Pecan Sandies MAKES 36

1 cup (8 ounces) unsalted butter, room temperature
1⅓ cups confectioners' sugar, plus ¼ cup
    for grinding with the pecans
½ teaspoon baking powder
1 teaspoon salt
1 teaspoon vanilla extract
2 large egg yolks
2½ cups (11.25 ounces) all-purpose flour
1½ cups pecans, toasted and cooled
2 large egg whites, lightly beaten

1 In the bowl of a stand mixer fitted with a paddle attachment, or in a large mixing bowl, using a handheld electric mixer, beat the butter and 1⅓ cups of the confectioners' sugar on medium speed until creamy. Scrape the sides of the bowl and beat in the baking powder, salt, vanilla, and egg yolks. By hand or using the lowest speed of the mixer, stir in the flour.

2 In a food processor or coffee or nut grinder, coarsely grind the pecans with the remaining ¼ cup of confectioners' sugar. Stir the pecans into the batter. Divide the dough into two equal portions and shape each portion into a log about 2 inches in diameter. Wrap the logs tightly in waxed paper or plastic wrap and chill for at least 2 hours, or until the dough is very firm.

Pecan Sandies Day

I f your favorite pecan cookies are made by little elves that live in a tree, here's a scratch version you may want to try at home.

Other Events on This Day:
National Columnists Day (created by the National Society of News Columnists)

3 Preheat the oven to 325°F and place a rack in the center. Line two baking sheets with parchment paper or nonstick foil.

4 Using a serrated knife, slice the logs ½ inch thick and arrange the rounds about 2 inches apart on the prepared baking sheets. Brush the rounds with lightly beaten egg white. Bake for 15 minutes, or until lightly browned around edges. Transfer to a wire rack to cool completely.

Baker's Note: Brushing the cookies with egg white and topping with a pecan half (optional) before baking gives them a nice finish.

Swim a Lap Day

It's officially Swim a Lap Day, but as the origin is unknown and there are no clear-cut guidelines, it's safe to say taking a dip is fine, too. So swim a lap or take a dip. Just get wet, because chances are it's hot outside.

Other Events on This Day:
Creamy Praline Day

Chocolate-Dipped Cookies
MAKES 48

COOKIES
6 ounces semisweet chocolate, or 1 cup semisweet chocolate chips

2 cups (9 ounces) all-purpose flour

½ teaspoon salt

½ teaspoon baking soda

½ teaspoon baking powder

8 tablespoons (4 ounces) unsalted butter, room temperature

1 cup granulated sugar

2 large eggs

1 teaspoon vanilla extract

DIPPING CHOCOLATE
8 ounces white, dark, or milk chocolate dipping chocolate

2 teaspoons shortening (optional)

1 Preheat the oven to 350°F and place a rack in the center. Line two baking sheets with parchment paper or nonstick foil.

2 **Make the cookies:** Melt the chocolate in the top of a double boiler or in a medium-size microwave-safe bowl using 50 percent power and stirring every 30 seconds. Set aside to cool slightly.

3 Mix the flour, salt, baking soda, and baking powder together in a medium-size bowl; set aside.

4 In the bowl of a stand mixer fitted with a paddle attachment, or in a large mixing bowl, using a handheld electric mixer, beat the butter and sugar on medium speed until creamy. Reduce the mixer speed slightly and beat in the eggs, beating just until mixed. Beat in the vanilla and melted chocolate. By hand, stir in the flour mixture. Chill the dough for 30 minutes, or just until it is easy to handle.

5 With a measuring teaspoon, scoop up rounded teaspoonfuls of dough and shape into balls. Arrange the balls about 2½ inches apart on the prepared baking sheets. Bake one sheet at a time for 12 minutes, or until the cookies appear set. Let cool on the baking sheets for about 5 minutes, then transfer to a wire rack to cool completely.

6 **Make the dipping chocolate:** Melt the dipping chocolate as directed on the package. Line a baking sheet with parchment paper. Dunk the cookies, one at a time, into the chocolate so that half of each cookie is coated with chocolate, and place on the prepared pan. Leave at room temperature until the frosting sets.

S'mores Bars MAKES 16

1⅓ cups (6 ounces) all-purpose flour

¾ cup graham cracker crumbs

1 teaspoon baking powder

¼ teaspoon salt

8 tablespoons (4 ounces) unsalted
　　butter, room temperature

¼ teaspoon salt

¾ cup granulated sugar

1 large egg

1 teaspoon vanilla extract

6-ounces milk chocolate bars, chopped or
　　broken, or 1 cup milk chocolate chips

1 cup marshmallow crème, such as Marshmallow Fluff

JUNE 25

Great American Backyard Campout Night

Sleep under the stars tonight! The National Wildlife Federation has declared June 25 Great American Backyard Campout Night. Pitch a tent in the backyard, put a sleeping bag on the balcony, or head to the local campground. The point of this holiday is to connect with the nature in your own community, even if the neighbors are just squirrels and cicadas.

One of my daughter's favorites, this is a campfire treat in bar form.

Other Events on This Day:
Catfish Day

1 Preheat the oven to 350°F and place a rack in the center. Line an 8-inch square metal baking pan with nonstick foil.

2 Mix the flour, graham cracker crumbs, baking powder, and salt together in a bowl; set aside.

3 In the bowl of a stand mixer fitted with a paddle attachment, or in a large mixing bowl, using a handheld electric mixer, beat the butter, salt, and sugar on medium speed until creamy. Beat in the egg and vanilla. By hand or using the lowest speed of the mixer, add the flour mixture to the butter mixture until incorporated. Press half of the dough into the prepared pan.

4 Arrange the chocolate over the dough, pressing it down slightly so that you won't pull it up when you spread on the marshmallow crème. Spread the marshmallow crème over the chocolate. Scatter bits of the remaining dough over the marshmallow; carefully press to form a layer. Bake for 25 to 30 minutes, or until lightly browned. Let cool completely in the pan. Cut into sixteen bars when completely cool.

Baker's Notes: While it would be convenient to use regular marshmallows, it's best to use marshmallow crème in this recipe because marshmallows tend to dry out during long baking times. Omit the additional salt if using salted butter.

JUNE 26

Chocolate Pudding Day

My mom didn't bake, but she could make a mean batch of Jell-O pudding. Sometimes she'd even serve it as "pudding in a cloud," which was pudding in a wineglass lined with whipped cream. I liked getting pudding in my lunchbox, too, and have fond memories of it being in a can. Remember that? Remember when pudding was served in a little tin can? I feel like an old

Chocolate Pudding Cookies
MAKE 36

2 cups (9 ounces) all-purpose flour

1 teaspoon baking soda

¾ teaspoon salt

1 teaspoon instant espresso powder

1 (3.4-ounce) package instant chocolate
    fudge pudding mix

1 cup (8 ounces) unsalted butter, room temperature

¼ cup granulated sugar

¾ cup firmly packed light brown sugar

1 teaspoon vanilla extract

2 large eggs

2 cups semisweet chocolate chips

1 cup walnuts, toasted and chopped (optional)

1 Preheat the oven to 375°F and place a rack in the center. Have ready two ungreased baking sheets.

2 Mix the flour, baking soda, salt, espresso powder, and pudding mix in a bowl; set aside.

3 In the bowl of a stand mixer fitted with a paddle attachment, or in a large mixing bowl, using a handheld electric mixer, beat the butter and both sugars on medium speed until creamy. Reduce the mixer speed to medium-low and beat in the vanilla and eggs. By hand or using the lowest speed of the mixer, add the flour mixture and stir until incorporated. Stir in the chocolate chips and walnuts.

4 Drop heaping teaspoonfuls of dough about 2 inches apart onto the baking sheets. Bake for 10 to 12 minutes, or until set. Let cool on the baking sheet for about 2 minutes, then transfer to a wire rack to cool completely.

Orange Blossom Bars MAKES 32

BASE

1 (18.25-ounce) box orange cake mix

8 tablespoons (4 ounces) unsalted butter, melted

1 large egg

FILLING

1 (15- to 16-ounce) can vanilla frosting

1 (8-ounce) package cream cheese, softened

1 large egg

TOPPING

4 ounces cream cheese, softened

4 tablespoons (2 ounces) unsalted butter, room temperature

½ cup confectioners' sugar

½ teaspoon vanilla extract

1 teaspoon freshly squeezed orange juice

lady all of a sudden. Get off my lawn! I'm going to go make some pudding.

Other Events on This Day: **Beautician's Day, Log Cabin Day, National Forgiveness Day**

Birthday Song Melody Written

The melody for the world's most popular birthday song was written in 1859 by two Kentucky teachers, sisters Mildred J. Hill and Patty Smith Hill. First sung as "Good Morning to You," it's said to have evolved as children changed the words "Good Morning" to "Happy Birthday."

In light of the fact that today is also Orange Blossom Day, here's a cookie made with a strong orange flavor from orange cake mix. I got this recipe from my mom, who used to make it with lemon cake mix.

1 Preheat the oven to 350°F and place a rack in the center. Line a 9 by 13-inch metal pan with nonstick foil.

2 **Make the base:** In a mixing bowl, stir together the cake mix, melted butter, and egg. Press firmly into the prepared pan.

3 **Make the filling:** In a mixing bowl, stir together the frosting and softened cream cheese. Add the egg and stir, but do not beat, until smooth. Pour the cream cheese mixture over the cake mix mixture and spread to the edges.

4 Bake for 30 minutes, or until the edges are slightly browned and set. The middle should still be jiggly. Don't overbake. The filling will set as it cools and after it chills. Let the pan cool to room temperature.

5 **Make the topping:** Beat together the cream cheese, butter, confectioners' sugar, vanilla, and orange juice in a bowl. Carefully spread the topping over the cream cheese layer. Chill for about 2 hours. Grasp the edges of the foil and lift from the pan. Set on a cutting board and cut into thirty-two squares.

JUNE 28

Paul Bunyan Day

Originally created to promote the logging industry, Paul Bunyan was a mythical lumberjack who wandered the frontier with a big blue ox named Babe. Famous for his stature and skill with an ax, Paul's amazing feats included clearing North Dakota, creating the Grand Canyon, and digging the Great Lakes. While he is said to have originated in Bangor, Maine, his real birthplace was the minds of journalist James MacGillivray and ad copywriter W. B. Laughead. During the early 1900s, stories and illustrations featuring the

Paul Bunyan Cookie Pizza SERVES 12

2 cups plus 2 tablespoons (9.6 ounces) all-purpose flour

1 teaspoon baking soda

½ teaspoon salt

1 cup (8 ounces) unsalted butter, room temperature

1 cup firmly packed light brown sugar

½ cup granulated sugar

1 teaspoon vanilla extract

2 large eggs, room temperature

2 cups semisweet chocolate chips

½ cup candy-coated chocolates (optional)

1 Preheat the oven to 350°F and place a rack in the center. Line a 14-inch round pizza pan with nonstick foil or parchment paper.

2 Mix the flour, baking soda, and salt together in a medium-size bowl; set aside.

3 In the bowl of a stand mixer fitted with a paddle attachment, or in a large mixing bowl, using a handheld electric mixer, beat the butter and both sugars on medium speed until light and creamy. Reduce the mixer speed slightly and add the vanilla and eggs, one at a time, beating well after each addition.

4 By hand or using the lowest speed of the mixer, add the flour mixture. When the flour is absorbed, stir in the chocolate chips and candies (if using). Spread the batter across the bottom of the prepared pan to make a circle about 12 inches in diameter (the cookie will spread slightly as it bakes). Bake until the edges are golden and the cookie is set but the center is still slightly soft, 20 to 25 minutes. Let cool in the pan for 10 minutes, then transfer to a wire rack to cool completely.

Best-Ever Almond Butter Crunch

MAKES ABOUT 1¼ POUNDS

1½ cups sliced almonds

1 cup (8 ounces) unsalted butter

1 cup granulated sugar

½ cup warm water

½ teaspoon salt

½ teaspoon baking soda

8 ounces dark or milk chocolate, chopped

1 Preheat the oven to 350°F and place a rack in the center. Spread about ½ cup of the almonds on a rimmed baking sheet and bake for 6 to 8 minutes, or until toasted and aromatic. Set aside.

lumberjack as the spokesman for the Red River Lumber Company made Paul famous.

Other Events on This Day: **Tapioca Day, Treaty of Versailles signed in 1919**

JUNE 29

National Almond Butter Crunch Day

Almond butter crunch is a candy made with butter, sugar, and almonds. It's fairly easy to make, and perfect for bake sales, since it can be broken up and wrapped in cute little packages. This recipe, which I've been making since I was fourteen, is my family's favorite. Follow the directions carefully, and it may become your family's favorite, too.

2 Line a 9 by 13-inch or 10 by 15-inch pan with parchment paper or nonstick foil and set it next to the stove.

3 Place the butter in a heavy-bottomed, nonstick, 3-quart saucepan and melt over medium heat. When the butter is almost fully melted, stir in the sugar, warm water, and salt. Set a thermometer in the pan, being careful that the bulb is not touching the bottom of the pan. Cook the mixture over medium heat, stirring once in a while, until its temperature reaches 240°F on a candy or deep-frying thermometer.

4 At 240°F, add the remaining 1 cup of sliced almonds to the sugar mixture and stir constantly, keeping a close eye on the temperature and making sure it's rising at a slow and steady rate. If it's not, raise the heat a tiny bit. When the mixture reaches 290°F (make sure it's no less than 290°F and no more than 295°F), immediately remove from the heat and stir in the baking soda. It will bubble up and lighten a bit and seem almost fluffy. Quickly pour into the prepared pan. The mixture should be kind of a liquid blob at this point and if you are on track, the saucepan will be clean when you have turned the candy out onto the parchment. The mixture will begin to firm, and the butter may pool and separate. Do not pour off any excess butter. Do not panic, because if you cooked the toffee to between 290° and 295°F, your candy should set. Sometimes it just takes longer.

5 While the candy is still very hot and in the process of setting, scatter the chopped chocolate across the top and let the chocolate melt into and over the candy as the candy firms. Using the back of a spoon, spread the melted chocolate evenly over the candy. Crush your toasted almonds and sprinkle over the melted chocolate. Let the candy cool for 30 minutes or more at room temperature, then chill for about 1 hour to firm the chocolate.

6 When the chocolate is set, lift the candy from the pan by grasping the parchment. Break the candy into large chunks.

Baker's Note: Rather than a candy thermometer or even an instant-read digital, I like to use a long, skinny, deep-frying thermometer with a piece of metal that prevents the bulb from touching the bottom of the pan. Holding a spoon in one hand and the thermometer in the other, I stir with both the spoon and the thermometer.

Kryptonite Macarons MAKES 16
TO 30, DEPENDING ON HOW LARGE YOU PIPE THE CIRCLES

1 cup (3.9 ounces) confectioners' sugar

⅓ cup (1.5 ounces) raw, unsalted, shelled
　　pistachios (see Baker's Notes)

¼ cup plus 2 tablespoons (1.5 ounces) almond flour

2 large egg whites, room temperature

Pinch of cream of tartar

2 tablespoons granulated sugar

½ teaspoon almond extract

1 to 2 dabs green food coloring paste

Green sprinkles or sparkling sugar (optional)

⅓ cup heavy cream

3 ounces dark chocolate (50 to 70%
　　cacao), finely chopped

1　Fit a large pastry bag with a ½-inch tip. Take two sheets of parchment paper that are about as big as your baking sheets, and using the bottom of a spice jar or a 1½-inch round cookie cutter as a guide, draw about twenty circles with a pencil on each sheet of parchment, spacing 1-inch apart. Turn the parchment over and set it on the baking sheet so that you can see the circles through the paper.

2　In a small spice grinder, food processor, or old coffee grinder, combine ¼ cup of the confectioners' sugar and the pistachios and grind until very fine. Combine the pistachio mixture with the almond flour and the remaining confectioners' sugar, and then push through

JUNE 30

Superman's Birthday Celebration

Unleash your inner Lex Luther by celebrating with some Kryptonite-inspired macarons.

　You'll feel like a superhero when you make your first batch of French macarons. Although they appear complex, making them is fairly simple once you've gotten the hang of it. This is my favorite recipe.

Other Events on This Day:
Meteor Watch Day

205

a sieve set over a large bowl. Re-grind any large pieces of nuts, if possible, but if you end up tossing out a couple of teaspoons of nut remnants, that's okay.

3   In a large, metal mixing bowl using a handheld electric mixer, beat the egg whites and cream of tartar on high speed until soft peaks form. Beat in the granulated sugar 1 tablespoon at a time, then beat in the almond extract and food coloring.

4   With a scraper, gently fold the pistachio mixture into the egg mixture in three parts. The batter should not be runny at this point. Transfer to the piping bag and pipe circles of batter about 1 inch in diameter into the center of your 1½-inch circles. As the macarons sit, the batter should spread a little bit to fill the pattern. If it doesn't spread enough to fill the circle pattern, don't worry. The important thing is to try to keep them in a circular shape. Let the two baking sheets of circles sit at room temperature for 1 full hour, or until they lose their sheen. If you're using sprinkles, go ahead and sprinkle them on half the cookies at this point.

5   Preheat the oven to 375°F and place a rack in the center. Place one baking sheet in the oven, close the door, and immediately decrease the heat to 325°F. Bake for 10 to 12 minutes, or until the macarons appear set and small "feet" have developed. Let cool on the parchment paper. Meanwhile, raise the oven heat back up to 375°F and repeat the process of baking the macarons, lowering the oven to 325°F after you've put them in the oven. When cool, peel the macarons from the paper and pair them up according to size and shape.

6   Heat the cream in a microwave-safe, 2-cup Pyrex measuring cup on high for about 30 seconds or just until it begins to boil. Add the chocolate. Let sit for 5 minutes, then stir until the chocolate is melted and smooth. If the chocolate is too hot and runny, let it cool and thicken a bit or chill it for a few minutes to speed up the process. It should

be the about the consistency of sour cream. Gently spoon a little in the center of half of the macarons. Cap each with a second macaron. Chill until the chocolate is set.

Baker's Note: The pistachio flavor is fun, but if you'd prefer vanilla (and less work), just omit the pistachios and add an extra 6 tablespoons (1.5 ounces) of almond flour, use vanilla extract in place of the almond extract, and substitute yellow coloring for green. For the best results, make sure to let your piped macarons sit on the baking sheets for an hour before baking them. Because having the correct ratio of confectioners's sugar to nuts is crucial to macarons, I've included the weight of both the sugar and the pistachios.

Nanaimo Bars MAKES 32

BASE

8 tablespoons (4 ounces) unsalted butter

¼ cup granulated sugar

1 large pasteurized egg, lightly beaten

5 tablespoons unsweetened natural cocoa powder

2 cups graham cracker crumbs

½ cup chopped and toasted pecans

½ cup sweetened flaked coconut

FILLING

4 tablespoons (2 ounces) unsalted
    butter, room temperature

2 cups confectioners' sugar, lightly spooned

2 tablespoons instant vanilla pudding
    mix or custard powder

2 to 3 tablespoons milk

1 teaspoon vanilla extract

TOPPING

1½ tablespoons unsalted butter

6 ounces semisweet chocolate

Canada Day

Today marks the anniversary of the union of the British North American provinces. Canada Day celebrations include fireworks, parades, parties, and really good cookies.

My favorite Canadian cookie is the Nanaimo bar. Named after the city of its origin, it's a no-bake bar cookie with a crust of crumbs, butter, and nuts layered with pudding and topped with chocolate.

Other Events on This Day:
Wally Amos's birthday (b. 1936); Gingersnap Day; first US zoo, in Philadelphia

1 Line a 9 by 13-inch pan with nonstick foil.

2 **Make the base:** In the top of a double boiler or in a mixing bowl set over but not touching a pan of simmering water, melt the butter. Remove from the heat and whisk in the sugar, egg, and cocoa powder. Return the pan to the heat and whisk for about 3 minutes. Remove from the heat and stir in the graham cracker crumbs, pecans, and coconut. Spread in the prepared pan and press down tightly. Chill the pan while you make the second layer.

3 **Make the filling:** In a medium-size mixing bowl, stir together the butter and confectioners' sugar, then beat with a handheld electric mixer until fluffy. Beat in the pudding mix, milk, and vanilla. Spread the filling over the cooled crust, and then chill for about an hour.

4 **Make the topping:** In the top of a double boiler, or in the microwave using 50 percent power, melt the butter and the chocolate, stirring at 1-minute intervals. Spread the melted chocolate over the custard layer and chill until set. When ready to serve, lift from the pan, set the bars on a cutting board, and cut into thirty-two squares.

Baker's Notes: These are traditionally made with custard powder, a product found at many American grocery stores. If you can't find it, regular instant vanilla pudding mix also works. Because the egg isn't cooked very long, I've recommended using a pasteurized egg.

JULY 2

World UFO Day

World UFO day marks the day in 1947 when a man in Roswell, New Mexico, discovered the wreckage of what he thought to be a UFO on his ranch. Organized to raise awareness of the existence of UFOs and to encourage governments to declassify information collected throughout history, World

Flying Saucer Cookies
MAKES 12 LARGE COOKIES

1²/₃ cups (7.5 ounces) all-purpose flour

½ teaspoon baking soda

½ teaspoon salt

4 tablespoons (2 ounces) unsalted butter, room temperature

¼ cup (1.7 ounces) shortening

¾ cup firmly packed light brown sugar

⅓ cup granulated sugar

1 teaspoon mild molasses

2 tablespoons instant vanilla pudding mix

1 large egg, room temperature

1 large egg yolk, room temperature

1½ teaspoons vanilla extract

1 cup bittersweet chocolate chips

¾ cup canned coconut pecan frosting

1 Preheat the oven to 350°F and place a rack in the center. Have ready two ungreased baking sheets.

2 Mix the flour, baking soda, and salt together in a bowl; set aside.

3 In the bowl of a stand mixer fitted with a paddle attachment, or in a large mixing bowl, using a handheld electric mixer, beat the butter, shortening, and both sugars on medium speed until light and creamy. Beat in the molasses and pudding mix. Reduce the speed slightly and beat in the egg, egg yolk, and vanilla. By hand or using the lowest speed of the mixer, beat in the flour mixture. When the flour is incorporated, stir in the chocolate chunks.

4 Divide the batter into twelve large portions and shape each portion into a ball. Arrange about 4 inches apart on the baking sheets (six to a sheet) and press down the tops slightly so that you have thick disks instead of balls. Bake one sheet at a time for 10 to 14 minutes, or until the edges are browned and the centers are hot and bubbly, but still a little pale. The cookies will spread on the baking sheets. Remove from the oven and tap the edges inward with the tip of a spatula to give the cookies a rounded shape. Tap the center with the back of a spoon to make a shallow depression. Let cool on the baking sheets for about 5 minutes, then transfer to a wire rack to cool completely. Fill each depression with a tablespoon of frosting.

UFO Day devotees encourage you to get together with friends and have viewing parties. You never know what you might see, especially with a pitcher of margaritas on hand.

Created by my friend Janice, these cookies are as big as flying saucers.

Other Events on This Day:
I Forgot Day, Anisette Day

Known as the "Grande Dame of Food Writers," M. F. K. Fisher was born in 1908. Her first book, *Serve It Forth*, was published in 1937. She went on to write twenty-nine more, and in 1949 she translated Brillat-Savarin's *The Physiology of Taste*. M. F. K. Fisher's books contained essays rather than cookbooks, but she did include a few recipes. One of her most popular cookie recipes is Ginger Hottendots, which she claimed had three times as much ginger as other cookies and acted as a digestive. Make a batch and see if they're as good as Better Than Elevator Lady's Cookies (page 164).

Richard Sax adapted this recipe in his book *Classic Home Desserts*.

Other Events on This Day:
Compliment Your Mirror Day, Eat Beans Day

Mini Ginger Cookies MAKES 90

1¾ cups plus 2 tablespoons (8.5 ounces) all-purpose flour
¾ teaspoon baking soda
1 tablespoon ground ginger
½ teaspoon ground cinnamon
⅛ teaspoon ground cloves
6 tablespoons (3 ounces) unsalted butter, room temperature
1 cup granulated sugar
1 large egg, lightly beaten
¼ cup dark molasses (see Baker's Notes)
1 teaspoon apple cider vinegar
¼ cup finely chopped crystallized ginger

1   Preheat the oven to 325°F and place a rack in the center. Line two baking sheets with nonstick foil or parchment paper.

2   Mix the flour, baking soda, ground ginger, cinnamon, and cloves in a medium-size bowl; set aside.

3   In the bowl of a stand mixer fitted with a paddle attachment, or in a large mixing bowl, using a handheld electric mixer, beat the butter and sugar on medium speed for about 3 minutes, or until very light and creamy. Reduce the mixer speed to medium-low and beat in the egg, molasses, and vinegar. By hand or using the lowest speed of the mixer, beat in the flour mixture. Stir in the crystallized ginger.

4   Scoop up slightly rounded half-teaspoonfuls (these cookies are small) of dough and roll into little balls. Arrange about 1 inch apart on the prepared baking sheets. Bake one sheet at a time until set, 6 or 7 minutes. They will firm and crisp as they cool; mine are usually crisp on the edges and chewy in the center. Transfer to a wire rack to cool completely.

Baker's Notes: This calls for dark molasses, which is slightly more robust than mild, but definitely milder than blackstrap. If you can't find dark, mild will work just fine. I like to decorate these with colored sprinkles.

Red, White, and Blue Crispy Rice Treats

MAKES 12 TO 16

8 tablespoons (4 ounces) salted butter

8 cups miniature marshmallows

1 teaspoon vanilla extract

10 cups crispy rice cereal, such as Rice Krispies

2 ounces white dipping chocolate, such as almond bark

Red, white, and blue sprinkles

1 Line a 9 by 13-inch pan with nonstick foil.

2 Melt the butter in a large saucepan set over medium-low heat. When the butter is melted, add the marshmallows and stir until melted. Remove from the heat and stir in the vanilla and cereal. Stir until the cereal is coated with marshmallow. Pour the mixture into the prepared pan, and using a sheet of parchment or greased foil, press the mixture evenly and firmly into the pan. Let cool completely in the pan. When cool, lift from the pan, set on a cutting board, and cut into twelve to sixteen cubes.

3 Melt the white chocolate coating according to the directions on the package, or melt in the top of a double boiler. Have ready a cooling rack set on top of a paper towel or a sheet of waxed paper. Dip each treat in the melted white coating and set on the wire rack. When the white coating is tacky but not completely set, sprinkle with red, white, and blue sprinkles. Leave at room temperature to set completely.

Graham Crackers MAKES 40

2 cups (9 ounces) graham flour (whole wheat flour)

⅓ cup (1.5 ounces) all-purpose flour

½ teaspoon salt

¾ teaspoon baking powder

¼ teaspoon baking soda

1 teaspoon ground cinnamon

Created in 1829, the graham cracker was originally marketed as Dr. Graham's Honey Bisket, to be used as part of a diet he developed to "suppress carnal urges." Graham, who believed that the modern diet of refined wheat flour and chemical additives was the cause of many afflictions, made his crackers with a mixture of finely ground white flour, coarsely ground wheat bran, and wheat germ.

Based on a recipe from the show *Good Eats*, this is our family's favorite graham cracker. I use honey in place of the molasses, cream in place of milk, and, on occasion, coconut palm sugar in place of brown.

𝒪ther 𝒮vents on 𝒯his 𝒟ay:
National Workaholic Day, Dolly the cloned sheep born in 1996

¼ teaspoon ground ginger

6 tablespoons (3 ounces) unsalted butter, room
   temperature, cut into 1-inch chunks

6 tablespoons firmly packed dark brown
   sugar or coconut palm sugar

¼ cup honey

½ teaspoon vanilla extract

3 tablespoons heavy cream

1 to 3 tablespoons water

1 Mix the flours, salt, baking powder, baking soda, cinnamon, and ginger together in the bowl of a food processor. Add the butter and pulse until the mixture is crumbly. Add the brown sugar and pulse until mixed. Add the honey, vanilla, cream, and 1 tablespoon of the water and pulse until the dough is moist enough to form a ball. If the dough seems too dry to roll, add another tablespoon of water. Divide the dough into two equal portions, shape into ½-inch-thick rounds, and wrap in plastic wrap. Chill for 1 hour, or until ready to use.

2 Preheat the oven to 325°F and place a rack in the center.

3 Remove one portion of dough from the refrigerator. Place a large sheet of nonstick foil on your work surface and place the dough in the center. For easy rolling, lay a wide sheet of clear plastic wrap over the top of the dough. Roll the dough into a rectangle as large and thin as you can—at least 9 by 13 inches—trimming the edges as necessary. The thinner the dough, the crisper the cracker. If you have problems rolling the dough, roll small sections at a time. (Later, you can even cut out shapes with cookie cutters instead of scoring the dough.) Transfer the whole sheet of foil with the dough on it to a baking sheet, and with a pizza cutter, make five slices crosswise and 4 slices lengthwise so that you have twenty squares. Use a fork to poke holes in the dough. Repeat the process with the second portion of dough.

4 Bake one sheet at a time for 18 to 23 minutes, or until lightly browned around the edges. Let cool slightly on the baking sheet, then separate the squares and transfer to a wire rack to cool completely. If the cooled cookies are still not crisp enough for you, put them back in the oven and bake at 200°F for another 10 minutes.

Strawberry Malt–Topped Brownies MAKES 16

BROWNIES

¾ cup (3.4 ounces) all-purpose flour

¼ cup malted milk powder

½ teaspoon baking powder

½ teaspoon salt

12 tablespoons (6 ounces) unsalted butter

6 ounces dark or semisweet chocolate, chopped

2 large eggs

⅔ cup firmly packed light brown sugar

1 teaspoon vanilla extract

FROSTING

4 tablespoons (2 ounces) unsalted butter, softened

2 teaspoons malted milk powder

1 cup confectioners' sugar

1 tablespoon strawberry-flavored
    syrup, such as Hershey's

1 tablespoon whole milk, more as needed

¼ teaspoon vanilla extract

⅓ cup coarsely chopped malted milk balls,
    for garnishing (optional)

Malted Milk Goes on Sale in Wisconsin

Malted powder was developed by James Horlick, a British pharmacist who'd conceived it as a supplement for infants. After moving to Wisconsin to join his brother William in Racine, the two set up a company in 1873 and manufactured the supplement, eventually developing a new formula that in 1887 was patented as malted milk. It gained a new following. Explorers such as Admiral Richard Byrd appreciated its nonperishable qualities so much he named a mountain range after it.

If you're interested in trying a malted, look for Ovaltine, Horlick's, Carnation, or another brand of malted milk powder at your local grocery store.

Other Events on This Day:
Fried Chicken Day

1 Preheat the oven to 325°F and place a rack in the center. Line a 9-inch square metal pan with nonstick foil.

2 **Make the brownies:** Mix the flour, malted milk powder, baking powder, and salt together in a bowl; set aside.

3 In a microwave-safe bowl, microwave the butter on high for 30 seconds, or until melted. Add the chocolate to the melted butter and stir until the chocolate is fully or partially melted. If the chocolate hasn't completely melted, return the bowl to the microwave and heat on high, stirring every 20 seconds, until it's fully melted. Let cool slightly.

4 In a large mixing bowl, using a handheld electric mixer, beat the eggs and brown sugar. Stir in the slightly cooled chocolate mixture and vanilla. Add the flour mixture and stir just until the flour is incorporated. Pour the batter into the prepared pan and bake for 23 to 25 minutes, or until the brownies start to pull away from the pan. Let cool completely in the pan.

5 **Make the frosting:** Stir together the butter, malted milk powder, and confectioners' sugar. With a handheld electric mixer, beat until mixed. Beat in the syrup and milk and continue beating until creamy. Beat in the vanilla. Add more milk as needed until you get a spreading consistency. Frost the brownies and garnish with chopped malted milk balls, if desired.

Baker's Note: For the malted milk powder, I use the plain Carnation brand. Horlick's and plain Ovaltine Malted Milk Powder will also work.

Triple Chocolate Bites MAKES 64

8 tablespoons (4 ounces) unsalted
    butter, room temperature
⅓ cup confectioners' sugar
¼ cup plus 1 tablespoon unsweetened natural
    or Dutch-processed cocoa powder
⅛ teaspoon salt
¾ cup (3.4 ounces) all-purpose flour
4 ounces milk chocolate, chopped
2 ounces bittersweet chocolate, chopped
½ ounce unsweetened chocolate, chopped
1 (8-ounce) package cream cheese, softened
¼ cup granulated sugar
½ teaspoon vanilla extract
1 large egg, room temperature
Lightly sweetened whipped cream or topping (optional)

1 Preheat the oven to 350°F and place a rack in the center. Line an 8-inch square metal pan with nonstick foil.

2 In the bowl of a stand mixer fitted with a paddle attachment, or in a large mixing bowl, using a handheld electric mixer, beat the butter and confectioners' sugar on medium speed until creamy. Beat in the cocoa powder and salt, then add the flour and stir until mixed. Press into the bottom of the prepared pan and bake for 8 minutes.

3 Combine the milk, bittersweet, and unsweetened chocolate in a microwave-safe bowl. Microwave at 50 percent power, stirring at 1-minute intervals, until the chocolate is fully melted; set aside.

4 In the bowl of a stand mixer fitted with a paddle attachment, or in a large mixing bowl, using a handheld electric mixer, beat the cream cheese, sugar, and vanilla on medium speed until well mixed and smooth. Stir in the slightly cooled melted chocolate, then beat in the egg. Spread over the chocolate crust and bake for 20 to 22 minutes. Let cool in the pan

World Chocolate Day

World Chocolate Day commemorates the date in 1550 when the South American drink was introduced to Europe. Although cacao beans were introduced to Spain much earlier (Columbus and Cortés are both said to have brought the bean back from their voyages), it was in the 1550s that Dominican friars popularized chocolate as a beverage by introducing it to royalty and spreading the word from monastery to monastery. In 1657, London's first chocolate house opened and the British began drinking it as a cure-all; and in 1660, Maria Theresa of Spain made chocolate fashionable in France.

Other Events on This Day:
Tell the Truth Day

for 1 hour, then chill for 3 hours, or until very cold. When ready to serve, lift from the pan, set on a cutting board, and cut into sixty-four squares. Serve in mini cupcake liners with a dot of whipped cream if desired.

Wall Street Journal First Published

Founded by Charles Dow, Edward Jones, and Charles Bergstresser, the *Wall Street Journal* was first published in 1889 to give information regarding fluctuations in the prices of stocks, bonds, and some commodities. Prior to becoming the *Wall Street Journal*, it had been called the *Customers' Afternoon Letter*, which Dow and Jones had started in 1883.

Other Events on This Day: **The ice-cream sundae was invented in 1881. Also, today is Video Game Day, which means there are two, if you include the one that falls in September.**

Millionaire Bars MAKES 16

BASE

1 cup (4 ounces) cake flour

¼ teaspoon salt

¼ cup cornstarch

8 tablespoons (4 ounces) unsalted butter, room temperature

3½ tablespoons granulated sugar

FILLING

7 tablespoons (3.5 ounces) unsalted butter, room temperature

½ cup firmly packed dark brown sugar

1 cup sweetened condensed milk (do not use the full can)

Scant ¼ teaspoon salt

1 teaspoon vanilla extract

TOPPING

4 tablespoons (2 ounces) unsalted butter

3 ounces semisweet or dark chocolate, chopped

1 Preheat the oven to 350°F and place a rack in the center. Line an 8-inch square metal pan with nonstick foil.

2 **Make the base:** Combine the cake flour, salt, and cornstarch in a small bowl. In a mixing bowl, using a handheld electric mixer, or a stand mixer fitted with the paddle, beat the butter and sugar until creamy. Add the flour mixture and stir by hand until mixed. Transfer to the prepared pan and press tightly onto the bottom. Chill for 30 minutes or until the dough is very firm and cold, and then bake for 20 to 22 minutes, or until lightly browned around the edges. Remove from the oven and let cool in the pan.

3 **Make the filling:** Combine the room temperature butter and brown sugar in a 2- to 3-quart nonstick saucepan. Heat over medium-low, stirring often, until the butter is melted and the sugar has dissolved. Add the condensed milk and heat over medium-low to medium heat, stirring constantly, just until bubbles start to appear on the surface and the mixture begins to boil. Before the mixture reaches a full boil, remove from the heat and stir in the salt and vanilla; pour over the cooled shortbread. Let cool at room temperature for about 30 minutes, then chill for about 2 hours, or until the caramel is firm.

4 **Make the topping:** In a microwave-safe mixing bowl or 2-cup Pyrex measuring cup, microwave the butter on high for 30 seconds, or until melted. Add the chocolate and stir until melted. If the chocolate doesn't melt completely in the hot butter, heat for another 15 seconds and stir. Let cool slightly (it will thicken a bit as it cools), then pour over the caramel mixture and chill until set. Store leftovers in the refrigerator.

Baker's Note: Popular in the United Kingdom, these bars consist of a shortbread base topped with layers of caramel and chocolate. After trying at least ten different versions, this was my favorite.

Monster-Size Sugar Cookies
MAKES 8 GIANT COOKIES

2 cups (9 ounces) all-purpose flour

2 tablespoons cornstarch

1 teaspoon baking powder

½ teaspoon baking soda

½ teaspoon salt

8 tablespoons (4 ounces) unsalted
    butter, room temperature

2 tablespoons (0.8 ounces) butter-flavored
    or plain vegetable shortening

¾ cup granulated sugar

*National
Sugar Cookie Day*

Whether you prefer hard and crunchy, dense and chewy, or soft and cakey, sugar cookies fall into a category of foods I call "impossible not to like."

2 tablespoons light brown sugar

1 tablespoon maple syrup or pancake syrup

1 large egg

1 teaspoon vanilla extract

¼ teaspoon almond extract

Colored sprinkles or coarse sugar

1 Preheat the oven to 350°F and place a rack in the center. Line two baking sheets with parchment or nonstick foil.

2 Mix the flour, cornstarch, baking powder, baking soda, and salt together in a bowl; set aside.

3 In the bowl of a stand mixer fitted with a paddle attachment, or in a large mixing bowl, using a handheld electric mixer, beat the butter and shortening until creamy. Add both sugars slowly and beat for a full 5 minutes. Beat in the syrup. Reduce the speed to medium-low and beat in the egg, vanilla, and almond extract.

4 On the lowest speed of the mixer, add the flour mixture, stirring just until incorporated. Divide the dough into eight equal-size balls. Arrange four of the balls on the prepared baking sheet and press down the centers with a drinking glass. Sprinkle with colored sprinkles. Repeat with the remaining cookie dough.

5 Bake one sheet at a time until the edges are golden, 11 to 13 minutes. Let cool on the baking sheet for about 4 minutes, then transfer to a wire rack to cool completely.

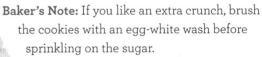

Baker's Note: If you like an extra crunch, brush the cookies with an egg-white wash before sprinkling on the sugar.

Piña Colada Cookies MAKES 32

1¼ cups (5.6 ounces) all-purpose flour

½ teaspoon baking soda

½ teaspoon salt

8 tablespoons (4 ounces) unsalted
    butter, room temperature

½ cup firmly packed light brown sugar

½ cup granulated sugar

1 large egg

½ teaspoon vanilla extract

1 teaspoon rum extract

1⅓ cups sweetened flaked coconut

⅔ cup toasted and chopped pecans

½ cup diced dried pineapple

½ cup white chips

1 Preheat the oven to 350°F and place a rack in the center. Line two baking sheets with parchment paper or nonstick foil.

2 Mix the flour, baking soda, and salt together in a bowl; set aside.

3 In the bowl of a stand mixer fitted with a paddle attachment, or in a large mixing bowl, using a handheld electric mixer, beat the butter and both sugars on medium speed until creamy. Reduce the mixer speed to low and add the egg, vanilla, and rum extract, scraping the sides of the bowl often; beat for about a minute on medium speed. By hand or using the lowest speed of the mixer, add the flour mixture gradually and stir until mixed, then mix in the coconut, pecans, pineapple, and white chips. The dough will be fairly thick and easy to shape.

4 At this point you can chill the dough until you are ready to use it (in which case the cookies will be slightly thicker) or just keep going.

5 Shape the dough into 1-inch balls (a little bigger if you like) and arrange about 2½ inches apart on the prepared baking sheets. Press down the tops slightly. Bake the

Piña Colada Day

Today we celebrate the piña colada, a frosty, creamy drink made with rum, pineapple juice, and cream of coconut. Preferably served on a beach, the deck of a yacht, or alongside a zero-edge infinity pool looking out over the ocean, a piña colada is the quintessential vacation food.

This cookie might not beat the real thing, but since you can't carry a box of piña coladas to the office or share them with the kids, it's an excellent stand-in.

Other Events on This Day:
Teddy Bear Picnic Day, Daniel Hess received a patent for a vacuum cleaner in 1960

cookies one sheet at a time for 10 to 13 minutes, or until lightly browned around the edges. Let cool on the baking sheets for about 5 minutes, then transfer to a wire rack to cool completely.

Cheer Up the Lonely Day

Created by Francis Pesek of Detroit, Michigan, the goal of Cheer Up the Lonely Day is simply to promote kindness. Think of it as an opportunity to reach out to a relative, friend, or acquaintance who you think may need some special cookie-shaped attention.

As it's also Blueberry Muffin Day, here's a cookie that's almost muffin or scone-like in texture. You can make these with fresh or dried blueberries.

Other Events on This Day:
World Population Day

Blueberry Muffin Cookies
MAKES 12 TO 18

1¾ cups (8 ounces) all-purpose flour
½ teaspoon baking powder
½ teaspoon baking soda
½ teaspoon salt
8 tablespoons (4 ounces) unsalted
    butter, room temperature
½ cup granulated sugar
2 tablespoons light brown sugar
1 teaspoon lemon zest
1 large egg
¾ cup fresh blueberries, or ½ cup dried
Coarse sugar

1 Preheat the oven to 350°F and place a rack in the center. Line two baking sheets with nonstick foil or parchment paper.

2 Mix the flour, baking powder, baking soda, and salt together in a medium-size bowl; set aside.

3 In the bowl of a stand mixer fitted with a paddle attachment, or in a large mixing bowl, using a handheld electric mixer, beat the butter and both sugars on medium speed until light and creamy. Beat in the lemon zest. Reduce the mixer speed and add the egg. Beat until the egg is blended in. By hand or using the lowest speed of the mixer, add the flour mixture and stir until it is mixed in. If using fresh berries, carefully fold the berries into the dough. If using dried, stir them in.

4 Scoop up tablespoonfuls of dough and shape into small balls. Arrange 2½ inches apart on the prepared baking sheets and sprinkle with coarse sugar. Bake one sheet at a

time for 12 minutes, or until lightly browned on the edges and top. Let cool on baking sheets for about 5 minutes, then transfer to a wire rack to cool completely.

Vanilla Pudding Chocolate Chip Cookies MAKES 36

2¼ cups (10.1 ounces) all-purpose flour

1 teaspoon baking soda

½ teaspoon salt

1 cup (8 ounces) unsalted butter,
    room temperature

¾ cup firmly packed light or dark brown sugar

¾ cup granulated sugar

1 (3.4-ounce) package instant vanilla pudding mix

2 large eggs

2 teaspoons vanilla extract

1 cup quick-cooking oats (not instant)

2 cups semisweet chocolate chips

½ cup toasted and chopped pecans

1 Preheat the oven to 350°F and place a rack in the center. Line two baking sheets with parchment paper or nonstick foil.

2 Mix the flour, baking soda, and salt together in a bowl; set aside.

3 In the bowl of a stand mixer fitted with a paddle attachment, or in a large mixing bowl, using a handheld electric mixer, beat the butter and both sugars on medium speed until creamy, scraping the sides of the bowl often. Beat in the vanilla pudding mix. When well mixed, add the eggs and vanilla and beat until the eggs are blended in.

4 Add the flour mixture and stir until it is almost fully incorporated. Add the oats and continue stirring until the flour disappears. Stir in the chocolate chips and pecans.

5 Drop tablespoonfuls of batter about 2½ inches apart onto the prepared baking sheets. Bake one sheet at a time for

Bill Cosby's Birthday

Hey, hey, hey! Bill Cosby was born today in 1937. He got his start in the 1960s doing stand-up comedy and producing award-winning albums, then made history by being the first African American to co-star in a TV drama, with *I Spy*. In the 1970s, Cosby became the creator of *Fat Albert and the Cosby Kids*, thus becoming very popular with kids such as myself. Thanks to syndicated TV, today's kids know him as Dr. Huxtable, the patriarch of *The Cosby Show* family.

Other Events on This Day:
Birthdays of George Washington Carver (b. 1861 or 1864), Henry David Thoreau (b. 1817), and Richard Simmons (b. 1948)

12 minutes, or until the edges are browned and the tops appear set. Let cool on the baking sheets for about 5 minutes, then transfer to a wire rack to cool completely.

National Pork and Beans Day

Made with navy beans and chunks of pork in a sugar sauce, pork and beans is a popular dish with kids who don't care for other types of beans. Or maybe that was just me. I loved the beans when I was young, but these days I find them so sweet I'd rather bake them into a cookie. Or in this case, a bar.

These cakey bar cookies have an intriguing smoky flavor. If you don't believe me, you can skip the recipe and buy a box of doughnuts. The first Krispy Kremes went on sale today in 1937.

Other Events on This Day: **National French Fry Day, anniversary of the Live Aid concert in 1985**

Pork and Beans Bars MAKES 24

1⅓ cups (6 ounces) all-purpose flour
¾ teaspoon ground cinnamon
¼ teaspoon baking powder
½ teaspoon baking soda
1¼ cups granulated sugar
⅔ cup vegetable oil
2 large eggs
¾ teaspoon vanilla extract
1 generous cup (10-ounce can) baked beans with pork
⅔ cup raisins (optional)
Confectioners' sugar, for dusting

1 Preheat the oven to 350°F and place a rack in the center. Line a 9 by 13-inch metal baking pan with nonstick foil or just spray it with flour-added baking spray.

2 Mix the flour, cinnamon, baking powder, baking soda, and granulated sugar together in a medium-size bowl; set aside.

3 In a large mixing bowl, using a handheld electric mixer, beat the sugar, oil, eggs, vanilla, and beans. As you beat, mash the beans up with the mixer—you'll have a few whole beans, but that's okay because they add character to the bars. Add the flour mixture gradually and stir until it is incorporated. Stir in the raisins (if using). Spread the mixture in the prepared pan and bake for 30 minutes, or until a toothpick inserted in the center comes out clean.

Let cool completely in the pan. Cut into twenty-four squares and dust with confectioners' sugar.

Cow Chip Cookies

MAKES 24 EXTRA-LARGE COOKIES

1 cup (4.5 ounces) all-purpose flour (see Baker's Note)

1 cup (4.5 ounces) white whole wheat flour

1 teaspoon salt

1 teaspoon baking powder

1 teaspoon baking soda

1 cup (8 ounces) unsalted butter, room temperature

1 cup granulated sugar

1 cup firmly packed light brown sugar

2 large eggs, room temperature

1 tablespoon vanilla extract

½ cup dried cranberries

1 cup quick-cooking or old-fashioned oats

1 cup not-too-sweet flaked cereal, such as Wheaties

½ cup toasted and chopped pecans

½ cup shredded or flaked coconut (optional)

1 cup semisweet chocolate chips

1 cup peanut butter chips

½ cup candy-coated chocolates

1 Preheat the oven to 350°F and place a rack in the center. Have ready two or more ungreased baking sheets.

2 Mix both flours and the salt, baking powder, and baking soda together in a large bowl; set aside.

3 In the bowl of a stand mixer fitted with a paddle attachment, or in a very large mixing bowl, using a handheld electric mixer, beat the butter on medium speed until creamy. Reduce the speed to low and add both sugars, then increase the speed to medium-high and beat for about 5 minutes, or until the mixture is very light, scraping the sides of the bowl often. Add the eggs, one at a time, and beat until they are well blended, scraping the bowl often. Beat in the vanilla. By hand or using the lowest speed of the mixer, gradually blend in the flour mixture. Stir in the cranberries, oats, cereal, pecans, coconut, chocolate chips, peanut butter chips, and candy.

Cow Appreciation Day

Have you hugged your cow today? I hope so, because it's Cow Appreciation Day. It must be a floating holiday, because I've seen it celebrated July 9, July 14, and as late as July 25. At any rate, we should appreciate cows every day, because not only are they cute, they supply the world with 90 percent of its dairy.

You can celebrate Cow Appreciation Day by learning some interesting facts such as these:

• Cows have an acute sense of smell and can smell something up to 6 miles away.

• Cows that are called individually by name and cows that are played classical music provide more milk.

This cookie doesn't contain milk, but you'll need a lot of it to wash one down. Each a quarter-pound, these are perfect for bake sales.

Other Events on This Day:
Pandemonium Day, Bastille Day, National Nude Day

4 With a ¼-cup measure, scoop out big hunks of dough. Arrange about 4 inches apart on the baking sheets (six to a sheet). Press down the tops slightly. Bake one sheet at a time for 14 to 18 minutes, stopping to turn the baking sheet halfway through the baking process. Let cool on the baking sheets for 4 minutes, then transfer to a wire rack to cool completely.

Baker's Note: I like to trick myself into believing they are healthier with half all-purpose and half whole wheat flour, but if you have a more realistic viewpoint, just use 4 cups of all-purpose.

JULY 15

Margarine Invented in France

Today in 1869, Hippolyte Mège-Mouriès of Provence, France, patented a butter substitute to be used by the French Navy. In 1871, he sold the patent.

According to Margarine. org, Americans eat twice as much "buttery spread" than they do butter. In my house, we keep pure unsalted butter on hand for baking, but there's generally a tub of spread in the refrigerator for using on rice, potatoes, and toast, and these cookies, a recipe based on one I learned while visiting the Unilever test kitchen.

Other Events on This Day:
Gummi Worm Day

Jumbo Hazelnut Chocolate Cookies   MAKES 16 BIG COOKIES

2¼ cups (10.1 ounces) all-purpose flour
½ teaspoon baking soda
1 cup (8-ounces) cold buttery spread, such as I Can't Believe It's Not Butter!
1 cup firmly packed light brown sugar
½ cup granulated sugar
1 large egg
1 teaspoon vanilla extract
½ cup unsweetened natural cocoa powder
6 ounces bittersweet chocolate with hazelnuts, chopped

1 Preheat the oven to 350°F and place a rack in the center. Line two baking sheets with parchment paper or nonstick foil.

2 Mix the flour and baking soda together in a bowl; set aside.

3 In the bowl of a stand mixer fitted with a paddle attachment, or in a large mixing bowl, using a handheld electric mixer, beat the spread and both sugars on medium speed until creamy. Reduce the mixer speed to low and beat in the egg and vanilla, then beat in the cocoa powder,

scraping the sides of the bowl as you go. By hand or using the lowest speed of the mixer, stir in the flour mixture. When fully blended, stir in the chocolate. At this point you can chill the dough until ready to use, or bake the cookies immediately.

4 Scoop up level ¼-cup portions of dough and drop about 3 inches apart onto the prepared baking sheets. Bake one sheet at a time for 10 to 13 minutes. Do not overbake. The cookies will firm as they cool. Let cool on the baking sheets for 2 minutes, then transfer to a wire rack to cool completely.

Baker's Notes: Make sure to weigh the tub-style buttery spread on your kitchen scale. It's easier and more accurate than trying to press it all into a measuring cup. Set the mixing bowl on the scale, set the tare to zero, then scoop buttery spread into the bowl.

Oat and Coconut White Chocolate Candy Cookies

MAKES ABOUT 60

2 cups (9 ounces) all-purpose flour
1 teaspoon baking soda
1 teaspoon salt
8 tablespoons (4 ounces) unsalted
    butter, room temperature
½ cup (3.4 ounces) shortening
1 cup granulated sugar
1 cup firmly packed light brown sugar
2 large eggs
1 teaspoon vanilla extract
2¼ cups quick-cooking oats (not instant)
⅔ cup toasted and very finely chopped pecans
⅔ cup flaked sweetened coconut
About 60 white chocolate drop candies,
    such as Hershey's Hugs

JULY 16

Kissing Banned in England

Note this for your next trivia game: On this day in 1439, King Henry VI banned kissing in an attempt to stop the spread of disease in England. I have yet to find the date the ban was lifted.

Other Events on This Day: **National Corn Fritter Day, Orville Redenbacher's birthday (b. 1907)**

1 Preheat the oven to 350°F and place a rack in the center. Have ready two ungreased baking sheets.

2 Mix the flour, baking soda, and salt together in a bowl; set aside.

3 In the bowl of a stand mixer fitted with a paddle attachment, or in a large mixing bowl, using a handheld electric mixer, beat the butter, shortening, and both sugars on medium speed until creamy. Reduce the speed to medium and beat in the eggs, one at a time. Beat in the vanilla. With the mixer on low, beat in the flour mixture, followed by the oats, pecans, and coconut.

4 Roll into 1-inch balls and arrange 2 inches apart on the baking sheets. Bake for 10 to 12 minutes, or until lightly browned. Remove from the oven and immediately press a candy into the center of each cookie. While the cookies are still hot, with the tip of a spatula, gently nudge the edge of the cookies inward to make wrinkles. Transfer to a wire rack to cool completely.

Disneyland Opens in Anaheim

I n 1955, Walt Disney's vision became a reality when Disneyland opened its doors to thousands of guests who had come to experience a special televised event. Given the larger than anticipated crowd, things didn't run smoothly—traffic backed up, rides broke down, a gas leak occurred, and the sun softened the asphalt on Main Street. Dubbed "Black Sunday," it might be viewed as Disney's first lesson in crowd control, an art they've since mastered. Disney now welcomes about 40,000 people

Snickerdoodles MAKES 24

COOKIES

2¾ cups (12.4 ounces) all-purpose flour

2 teaspoons cream of tartar

1 teaspoon baking soda

¾ teaspoon salt

1 cup (8 ounces) unsalted butter, room temperature

1½ cups granulated sugar

2 large eggs

2 teaspoons vanilla extract

TOPPING

¼ cup granulated sugar

2 tablespoons ground cinnamon

1. Preheat the oven to 375°F and place a rack in the center. Have ready two ungreased baking sheets.

2. **Make the cookies:** Mix the flour, cream of tartar, baking soda, and salt together in a medium-size bowl; set aside.

3. In the bowl of a stand mixer fitted with a paddle attachment, or in a large mixing bowl, using a handheld electric mixer, beat the butter on medium speed until creamy. Add the granulated sugar and beat until creamy, then add the eggs and vanilla, beating just until the eggs are mixed in. By hand or using the lowest speed of the mixer, gradually add the flour mixture.

4. Scoop up level tablespoonfuls of dough and shape into balls about 1 inch in diameter.

5. **Make the topping:** Combine the sugar and cinnamon on a small plate. Roll the balls in the cinnamon sugar mixture. Arrange about 2 inches apart on the baking sheets and press down slightly with the bottom of a drinking glass. Bake for 10 to 14 minutes, or until lightly browned around the edges. Transfer to a wire rack and let cool completely.

Baker's Note: For best results, beat the eggs just until they are blended into the butter mixture—do not beat until fluffy.

Malted Pretzel Peanut Butter Chip Cookies MAKES 32

1⅓ cups (6 ounces) all-purpose flour

¼ teaspoon baking soda

¼ teaspoon salt

8 tablespoons (4 ounces) unsalted
    butter, room temperature

¾ cup granulated sugar

¼ cup firmly packed brown sugar

¼ cup malted milk powder

½ teaspoon vanilla extract

1 large egg

per day and is known as the happiest place on earth. In honor of that, here's a crowd-pleasing cookie.

Other Events on This Day: National Ice Cream Day is the third Sunday in July, Polaroid camera patented in 1970

JULY 18

National Ice Cream Month

In light of the fact that it's National Ice Cream Month, here's a cookie based on Ben & Jerry's Chubby Hubby. To translate the ice cream to cookie form, I made a cookie with a light malt base and added pretzels, peanut butter chips, malt balls, and chocolate chips.

1 scant tablespoon chocolate syrup

½ cup semisweet chocolate chips

1 cup broken pretzels or whole goldfish pretzels (see Baker's Notes)

½ cup peanut butter chips

⅔ cup malt balls, coarsely chopped

Other Events on This Day:
Caviar Day, Nelson Mandela's birthday (b. 1918; Mandela Day), Sally Ride became the first American woman in outer space in 1983

1 Preheat the oven to 350°F and place a rack in the center. Line two baking sheets with parchment paper or nonstick foil.

2 In a medium-size bowl, mix together the flour, baking soda, and salt and set aside.

3 In the bowl of a stand mixer fitted with a paddle attachment, or in a large mixing bowl, using a handheld electric mixer, beat the butter and both sugars on medium speed for 3 minutes, or until creamy, scraping the sides of the bowl occasionally. Reduce the speed to medium-low and add the malt powder, vanilla extract, egg, and chocolate syrup; beat for another 30 seconds, or until mixed. By hand or using the lowest speed of the mixer, add the flour mixture and stir until it is incorporated. Stir in the chocolate chips, pretzels, peanut butter chips, and malt balls. The dough will be really packed with add-ins.

4 Scoop up tablespoonfuls of dough and shape into balls. Arrange about 2½ inches apart on the baking sheets and press down slightly. Bake one sheet at a time for 11 to 13 minutes, or until the cookies appear set and the edges are lightly browned. Let cool on the baking sheet for 2 minutes, then transfer to a wire rack to cool completely.

Baker's Notes: You can use any type of pretzels, but goldfish pretzels stay crisp in cookies and have a lighter texture. The ice cream uses peanut butter–filled pretzels coated with chocolate. I tried using peanut butter–filled pretzels, but just didn't get the same crispness as I did using a combo of pretzels and peanut butter–flavored chips.

Daiquiri Cookies MAKES 36

COOKIES

2½ cups (11.3 ounces) all-purpose flour

1 teaspoon baking powder

1 teaspoon salt

12 tablespoons (6 ounces) unsalted butter, room temperature

1 cup granulated sugar

½ teaspoon vanilla extract

1 teaspoon rum extract

1 tablespoon lime zest

2 large eggs

Green sprinkles (optional)

GLAZE

1 tablespoon (0.5 ounce) unsalted butter, melted

1½ cups confectioners' sugar

1½ tablespoons rum

1½ tablespoons freshly squeezed lime juice

1 Preheat the oven to 350°F and place a rack in the center. Have ready two ungreased baking sheets.

2 **Make the cookies:** Mix the flour, baking powder, and salt together in a medium-size bowl; set aside.

3 In the bowl of a stand mixer fitted with a paddle attachment, or in a large mixing bowl, using a handheld electric mixer, beat the butter and sugar on medium speed until light and creamy. Beat in the vanilla, rum extract, and lime zest, scraping the sides of the bowl often. Reduce the speed of the mixer and add the eggs, one at a time, mixing just until blended. By hand or using the lowest speed of the mixer, add the flour mixture and stir until it is absorbed and you have a soft but easy-to-handle dough.

4 Scoop up level tablespoonfuls of dough and roll into balls. Arrange about 2 inches apart on the baking sheets. Press down slightly. Bake one sheet at a time for 10 minutes, or until the edges are nicely browned. Transfer to a wire rack placed over a sheet of waxed paper to cool completely.

Daiquiri Day

The daiquiri was invented in 1898 by a US mining engineer named Jennings Cox, who was working in Cuba. A blend of rum, sugar, and freshly squeezed lime juice served over ice, the drink was a local favorite for some time, but Cox promoted it and introduced it to friends, eventually naming it Daiquiri after the mining town where he'd worked. In 1910, Cox shared the cocktail with US Navy officer Lucius W. Johnson. Johnson liked it so much he took the recipe ingredients on a voyage around the world and back home to America, where he introduced it to bartenders. The flavor of these cookies will remind you of a daiquiri.

Other Events on This Day:
First US parking meters installed in 1935

5 **Make the glaze:** In a small bowl, mix together the melted butter and the confectioners' sugar. Stir in the rum and lime juice. Spoon the glaze over the cool cookies.

Baker's Note: For more fun, you can tint the glaze green or just use a white glaze and add green sprinkles.

Man Walks on the Moon

*A*pollo 11 astronauts Neil Armstrong and Edwin "Buzz" Aldrin landed on the moon today in 1969. Famously named the Eagle, the lunar module touched down on a part of the moon's surface known as the Sea of Tranquility. It spent twenty-one hours and thirty-one minutes on the lunar surface, while Michael Collins orbited above in the Columbia command module. When Armstrong stepped on the surface, nearly 700 million television viewers heard him say, "That's one small step for man, one giant leap for mankind."

The astronauts returned to Earth with 47.5 pounds of moon rocks.

Other Events on This Day:
Ugly Truck Day

Moon Rock Cookies MAKES 24

2 cups (9 ounces) all-purpose flour
¾ teaspoon ground cloves
¾ teaspoon freshly grated nutmeg
2 teaspoons ground cinnamon
¾ teaspoon salt
2 large eggs, separated
11 tablespoons (5.5 ounces) unsalted
      butter, room temperature
1 cup granulated sugar
¾ teaspoon baking soda dissolved
      in 1½ tablespoons water
1½ cups pecans, toasted and chopped
¾ cup raisins
¾ cup semisweet chocolate chips
Confectioners' sugar, for dusting

1 Preheat the oven to 375°F and place a rack in the center. Line two baking sheets with parchment paper or nonstick foil.

2 Mix the flour, cloves, nutmeg, cinnamon, and salt together in a bowl; set aside.

3 In the bowl of a stand mixer fitted with a whisk attachment, or in a large mixing bowl, using a handheld electric mixer at high speed, beat the egg whites until stiff peaks form. Transfer the whipped whites to a separate bowl. Place the butter and granulated sugar in the original mixing bowl and beat until creamy. Beat in the egg yolks, scraping the sides of the bowl once or twice. Fold in the whipped egg whites. When the egg whites are mixed in, stir in the flour mixture and the baking soda

mixture. The dough will be thick. Stir in the pecans, raisins, and chocolate chips.

4 Drop rounded tablespoonfuls (about 1.4 ounces each) of dough about 2½ inches apart on the prepared baking sheets. Bake one sheet at a time for 10 minutes, or until the edges are nicely browned and the cookies appear set. Transfer to a wire rack to cool completely. Dust with confectioners' sugar when cool.

Double Trouble Chocolate and Potato Chip Cookies

MAKES ABOUT 22

1 cup (4.5 ounces) all-purpose flour

½ teaspoon baking soda

¼ teaspoon plus an extra pinch of salt

6 tablespoons (3 ounces) unsalted
    butter, room temperature

½ cup firmly packed light
    brown sugar

½ cup granulated sugar

1 large egg

½ teaspoon vanilla extract

1 cup crushed salted potato chips
    (about 2½ ounces by weight)

¾ cup semisweet chocolate mini chips

Fact:
The average American eats about 24.5 pounds of candy per year, 11.6 pounds of which is chocolate candy.

1 Preheat the oven to 350°F and place a rack in the center. Have ready two ungreased baking sheets.

2 In a medium-size bowl, mix together the flour, baking soda, and salt and set aside.

3 In the bowl of a stand mixer fitted with a paddle attachment, or in a large mixing bowl, using a handheld electric mixer, beat the butter and both sugars at medium-high speed speed until light and fluffy. Reduce the mixer speed to medium; add the egg and vanilla and beat for about 30 seconds, or until incorporated. By hand or with the lowest

National Junk Food Day

Today is National Junk Food Day, and you can celebrate it as you see fit. Suggestions include indulging in your favorite "junk," or taking the opposite approach and using the day to denounce junk food. I'll probably do both. Potato chips give these cookies a light texture. I use Lay's regular. Barbecue or Sour Cream flavor is not recommended.

Other Events on This Day:
Tug-of-War Day

speed of the mixer, add the flour mixture and stir until fully blended. Stir in the potato chips and chocolate chips.

4 Drop tablespoonfuls of dough about 2½ inches apart on the baking sheets. Bake one sheet at a time for 13 to 14 minutes, or until lightly browned. Let cool on the baking sheets for about 3 minutes, then transfer to a wire rack to cool completely.

National Penuche Day

So what is penuche and how is it pronounced? I always thought it was "peh-noo-kee" but in researching this important day, I've learned it has an Italian pronunciation of "puh-noo-chee." And as you may know, it's a fudgelike candy without any chocolate, but rather flavored with vanilla, brown sugar, and butter. In the South, they call it brown sugar fudge candy.

Penuche was once very popular in Hawaii, where the name was localized as *panocha* or *panuche*. As an icing, it was common as a topping for prune cake.

Other Events on This Day:
Gregor Mendel's birthday (b. 1822), National Baby Food Festival in Michigan (third week in July)

Spiced Prune Bars with Penuche Icing MAKES 18

BASE

1 cup (4.5 ounces) all-purpose flour

1 teaspoon baking soda

1 teaspoon ground cinnamon

¼ teaspoon ground allspice

¼ teaspoon ground cloves

½ teaspoon salt

1 cup granulated sugar

¾ cup vegetable oil

2 large eggs

¾ cup (6 ounces) prune baby food

ICING

8 tablespoons (4 ounces) unsalted butter

1 cup firmly packed light brown sugar

¼ scant teaspoon salt

¼ cup whole milk

¼ teaspoon vanilla extract

2 cups sifted confectioners' sugar

1 Preheat the oven to 350°F and place a rack in the center. Line a 9 by 13-inch metal pan with nonstick foil or spray with flour-added baking spray.

2 **Make the base:** Mix the flour, baking soda, cinnamon, allspice, cloves, and salt together in a small bowl; set aside.

3   In a large mixing bowl, using a handheld electric mixer on medium speed, beat the sugar, oil, and eggs. Beat in the baby food. By hand or using the lowest speed of the mixer, stir in the flour mixture. Pour the batter into the prepared pan and bake for 20 minutes, or until a toothpick inserted into the center comes out clean. Let cool completely in the pan.

4   **Make the icing:** In a medium-size saucepan over medium heat, melt the butter. Add the brown sugar and salt. Increase the heat slightly and bring to a gentle but steady boil, reducing the heat if necessary, and continue boiling for 2 minutes, stirring constantly. Add the milk and let the mixture return to a boil, stirring constantly; remove from the heat. Let cool to lukewarm. Stir in the vanilla. Gradually add the sifted confectioners' sugar, beating with a wooden spoon until the icing is smooth and pourable. Pour over the prune bars and allow the icing to set at room temperature before serving.

Baker's Note: Unlike prune bars with a shortbread crust and stewed prune filling, these are spice cake bars topped with a thick layer of penuche icing.

Almond Tuiles   MAKES ABOUT 10

5 tablespoons (2.5 ounces) unsalted butter,
      plus extra for rubbing the pan

2 large egg whites

6½ tablespoons granulated sugar

⅛ teaspoon salt

¼ teaspoon vanilla extract

¼ teaspoon almond extract

⅓ cup (1 ounce) all-purpose flour, sifted

⅓ cup sliced almonds, toasted and roughly chopped

1   Preheat the oven to 350°F and place a rack in the center. Rub a large rimmed baking sheet with butter so that it is thinly coated, and have ready two rolling pins or one rolling pin plus a couple of drinking glasses for cooling the cookies on.

Waffle Cone Debuts in St. Louis

Until 1904, Americans were happy to eat ice cream out of small glasses called "penny licks" or lick it off little papers called "hokey pokeys." Things changed in 1904, when a lady at the St. Louis World's Fair took a soft waffle and rolled it around her ice cream, giving the Menches brothers, ice-cream vendors, the idea for the cone. The cone was so popular that people began producing molds and machines to be used for baking ice-cream cones. Or at least that's how the story goes. It's a fact that in September 1903,

Italo Marchiony applied for a patent for ice-cream cone molds. It's also fact that books dating back to the thirteenth century describe twisting waffles into cones. It's probably safe to say the St. Louis World's Fair helped launch the cone's popularity.

Other Events on This Day:
Hot Dog Day, Vanilla Ice Cream Day

JULY 24

Cousin's Day

Whether you have a couple or a couple dozen, today's the day we're all supposed to reach out and say hello to our cousins.

In honor of Cousin's Day, here's a recipe dedicated to my daughter's little cousins who all approve heartily of M&M's in cookies.

Other Events on This Day:
Amelia Earhart Day

2 Melt the remaining 5 tablespoons of butter on high in a microwave-safe custard cup or small bowl, about 30 seconds, and let cool completely.

3 In a medium-size mixing bowl, whisk together the egg whites, sugar, salt, vanilla, and almond extract. Whisk in the cooled butter and flour, and stir in the almonds.

4 Drop tablespoonfuls of batter about 3½ inches apart on the buttered baking sheet. Using the back of a spoon, spread the batter evenly into rounds about 3 inches wide. Bake for 11 to 14 minutes, or until the edges are browned. The centers will remain fairly pale. While the cookies are hot, quickly scoop them up with a spatula and drape over the rolling pin (it's okay if they overlap a little bit) and drinking glasses. Leave on the rolling pin to cool and crisp. Repeat with the remaining batter, rubbing the pan with more butter as needed.

Malted Milk and Candy Cookies

MAKES ABOUT 48

2 cups plus 2 tablespoons (9.5 ounces) all-purpose flour

¼ cup malted milk powder

1 teaspoon baking soda

1 teaspoon salt

1 cup (8 ounces) unsalted butter, room temperature

¾ cup granulated sugar

¾ cup firmly packed light brown sugar

1 teaspoon vanilla extract

2 large eggs

1 cup semisweet chocolate chips

1 cup candy-covered chocolates

1 Preheat the oven to 350°F and place a rack in the center. Have ready two ungreased baking sheets.

2 Mix the flour, malted milk powder, baking soda, and salt together in a bowl; set aside.

3 In the bowl of a stand mixer fitted with a paddle attachment, or in a large mixing bowl, using a handheld electric mixer, beat the butter and both sugars on medium speed until creamy. Beat in the vanilla and eggs. Add the flour mixture gradually and stir until almost blended, then add the chocolate chips and candies and stir until all the flour is incorporated.

4 Scoop up slightly rounded tablespoonfuls of dough and arrange 2 inches apart on the baking sheets. Bake for 12 to 14 minutes, or until the edges are browned and the cookies look done. Let cool on the baking sheets for about 2 minutes, then transfer to a wire rack to cool completely.

Baker's Note: If your cookies spread too much while baking, immediately tap the edges inward with a spatula and nudge them into rounds.

Chocolate Sundae Cookies
MAKES 32 TO 36

COOKIES

1½ cups (6.8 ounces) all-purpose flour

½ teaspoon baking soda

½ teaspoon salt

²/₃ cup firmly packed light brown sugar

8 tablespoons (4 ounces) unsalted butter, room temperature, or ½ cup (3.4 ounces) shortening (see Baker's Note)

1 large egg

1 teaspoon vanilla extract

2 ounces unsweetened chocolate, melted and cooled

2 tablespoons milk

¼ cup maraschino cherry juice

¼ cup maraschino cherries, drained and chopped (optional)

½ cup walnuts, chopped (optional)

16 large marshmallows, cut in half

JULY 25

Culinarians Day

It's National Culinarians Day. Some say it's a day to celebrate chefs, while others have designated it as a day recognizing anyone with culinary skills. Either way, it's a good excuse to make any type of cookies you want or hone your culinary skills by making a more complicated or less familiar cookie. As today is also National Sundae Day, how about a batch of Chocolate Sundae Cookies? This is my take on an old recipe popularized at an early Pillsbury Bake-Off.

Other Events on This Day:
Hot Fudge Sundae Day

GLAZE
4 tablespoons (2 ounces) unsalted butter
6 ounces semisweet chocolate, chopped
4 teaspoons light corn syrup or golden syrup
¼ teaspoon vanilla extract

1 Preheat the oven to 350°F and place a rack in the center. Have ready two ungreased baking sheets.

2 **Make the cookies:** Mix the flour, baking soda, and salt together in a medium-size bowl; set aside. In the bowl of a stand mixer fitted with a paddle attachment, or in a large mixing bowl, using a handheld electric mixer, beat the brown sugar, butter, egg, and vanilla on medium speed until well blended. Add the melted unsweetened chocolate and mix well. Add the flour mixture and stir until mixed, then stir in the milk, cherry juice, cherries, and walnuts; mix until well blended.

3 Drop tablespoonfuls of batter about 2½ inches apart onto the baking sheets. Bake for 8 to 10 minutes, or until the cookies appear set. Remove from the oven and immediately press a marshmallow half in the center of each cookie. Let the cookies cool on the baking sheets for about 5 minutes, then transfer to a wire rack.

4 **Make the glaze:** In a small saucepan, melt the butter over medium heat. When the butter is melted, reduce the heat to low and stir in the chocolate and corn syrup. Stir until smooth. Remove from the heat and stir in the vanilla. You can also make the glaze in a microwave-safe 2-cup Pyrex measuring cup. Melt the chocolate and butter together on high, stirring every 30 seconds until melted, then stir in the corn syrup and vanilla. Spoon the glaze over each marshmallow, covering it completely. Cap with a stemmed cherry or cherry half, if desired.

> **Baker's Notes:** Shortening will give you a puffier cookie that stays fresher longer. I like to garnish these with stemmed cherries or cherry halves, but since my daughter has a strange aversion to them, I often leave them off.

Blackberry Bars MAKES 24

CRUST

1 cup (4.5 ounces) all-purpose flour

1 cup quick-cooking oats

⅛ teaspoon baking soda

¼ teaspoon salt

½ teaspoon ground cinnamon

½ cup firmly packed light brown sugar

8 tablespoons (4 ounces) unsalted butter,
   cut up and room temperature

FILLING

1 (1-pound) bag frozen blackberries, thawed

2½ tablespoons cornstarch

4½ tablespoons granulated sugar

1 tablespoon freshly squeezed lemon juice

1 tablespoon seedless berry preserves
   (blackberry, raspberry, or blueberry)

1 Preheat the oven to 350°F and place a rack in the center. Line a 9-inch square metal pan with nonstick foil, or line it with regular foil and spray the foil with flour-added baking spray.

2 **Make the crust:** Combine the flour, oats, baking soda, salt, cinnamon, and sugar in the bowl of a food processor. Add the butter and pulse until the mixture is dry and crumbly. Press about two-thirds of the mixture into the prepared pan and bake for 15 to 20 minutes, or until lightly browned.

3 **While the crust cools, make the filling:** Drain the thawed berries, reserving the juice; they should yield about ½ cup of juice. Add enough water to the juice to make 1 cup of liquid. In a medium-size saucepan, combine the berry juice mixture and cornstarch and stir until the cornstarch is dissolved. Cook over medium heat at a gentle boil, stirring constantly, until the mixture goes from cloudy to shiny. Stir in the lemon juice, drained berries, and preserves. Pour the berry mixture over the cooled crust. Crumble the remaining oatmeal mixture over the berries and bake for 25 to 30 minutes, or until the top is lightly browned. Let cool in the pan before cutting.

Aunt and Uncle Day

It may not be on every calendar, but many people call today Aunt and Uncle Day. And why shouldn't it be? Mothers, fathers, grandparents, and even cousins have their day, so it seems only natural that the siblings of our parents—especially the fun ones who babysit, dole out advice, or take their beloved nieces and nephews on outings to the zoo, roller rink, or mall—should be honored as well. Celebrate Aunt and Uncle Day by making a bar cookie featuring your aunt's or uncle's favorite treat.

Other Events on This Day:
Coffee Milkshake Day, New York became a state in 1788

Fact:
Coconut oil is a saturated fat, but some people believe that the lauric acid in coconut oil has health benefits. For these cookies, natural coconut oil or virgin is fine.

Peanut Butter, Coconut, and Pepita Cookies MAKES 24

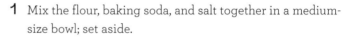

1 cup (4.5 ounces) white whole wheat flour

½ teaspoon baking soda

¼ teaspoon salt

½ cup coconut oil

½ cup creamy peanut butter

½ cup firmly packed light brown sugar

½ cup granulated sugar

1 large egg

¾ teaspoon vanilla extract

¼ cup salted or unsalted toasted pepitas (pumpkin seeds)

⅓ cup shredded sweetened coconut, for rolling

1 Mix the flour, baking soda, and salt together in a medium-size bowl; set aside.

2 In the bowl of a stand mixer fitted with a paddle attachment, or in a large mixing bowl, using a handheld electric mixer, beat the coconut oil, peanut butter, and both sugars on medium speed until well mixed. Beat in the egg and vanilla. By hand or using the lowest speed of the mixer, stir in the flour mixture. Stir in the pepitas. Cover the bowl and chill for about 1 hour, or until the dough is thick enough to handle.

3 Preheat the oven to 350°F and place a rack in the center. Line two baking sheets with parchment paper.

4 Scoop up rounded teaspoonfuls of dough and shape into balls about 1 inch in diameter. Sprinkle the coconut on a plate and dip the tops of the balls in the coconut. Arrange 2½ inches apart on the prepared baking sheets and press down the tops slightly. Bake one sheet at a time for 10 minutes, or until the edges are lightly browned. Let cool on baking sheets for 5 minutes, then transfer to a wire rack to cool completely.

Milk Chocolate Middle Cookies MAKES 24

1½ cups (6.8 ounces) all-purpose flour

½ teaspoon baking powder

⅜ teaspoon salt

10 tablespoons (5 ounces) unsalted
    butter, room temperature

¾ cup confectioners' sugar plus an extra cup for rolling

1 teaspoon vanilla extract

1 large egg yolk

½ cup toasted and finely chopped pecans

24 milk chocolate candies, such as Hershey's Kisses

4 teaspoons granulated sugar

¼ teaspoon cinnamon

1 Preheat the oven to 350°F and place a rack in the center. Have ready two ungreased baking sheets.

2 In a medium-size bowl, stir together the flour, baking powder, and salt; set aside.

3 In the bowl of a stand mixer fitted with a paddle attachment, or in a large mixing bowl, using a handheld electric mixer, beat the butter until creamy. Gradually add ¾ cup of the confectioners' sugar. Continue beating on medium speed until smooth, and then beat in the vanilla and egg yolk. By hand, stir in the flour mixture and the pecans.

4 Wrap about 1 tablespoon of dough around each chocolate candy, making sure to cover the candy completely. Mix the granulated sugar and cinnamon together and sprinkle over or dip the tops of the dough balls in cinnamon sugar. Arrange on the baking sheets about 2½ inches apart. Bake for 12 to 14 minutes or until the edges are lightly browned. Place a wire rack over foil or waxed paper and transfer the cookies to the rack. While the cookies are still warm, sprinkle the tops with the remaining confectioners' sugar and let the remaining fall on the paper, reserving it for later. When the cookies are cool, reroll the cookies in the reserved confectioners' sugar.

National Milk Chocolate Day

Chocolate came to Europe in the sixteenth century, but it wasn't until the late 1800s that milk chocolate was invented. For that, we can thank Daniel Peter of Vevey, Switzerland, who experimented for eight years. The date given for the invention of milk chocolate is generally 1876, but Peter continued to refine the product and in 1887 had the original formula for what was to become the first successful milk chocolate. He called his confection Gala, from the Greek word for "milk."

It didn't take long for milk chocolate to become popular in America, and for that, credit goes to Milton Hershey.

Other Events on This Day: **Sir Thomas Harriot introduced potatoes to Europe in 1586, Henry VIII married Catherine Howard, Beatrix Potter's birthday (b. 1866)**

Baker's Notes: These come out of the oven rather soft, but firm as they cool. For extra flavor, I sprinkle them with cinnamon sugar before baking and then roll in extra confectioners' sugar. And I have been known to swap out the chocolate for a peanut butter cup.

JULY 29

Feast of Saint Martha

Today marks the feast of Saint Martha, patron saint of hospitality and cooks, whose Bible story in Luke 10:38–42 might serve as a reminder that being present and attentive to guests rather than rushing around cleaning and obsessing over minor details is the most important element of entertaining. In that spirit, celebrate Saint Martha with a convenient cookie that can be kept on hand for many days and served to whomever drops by.

Other Events on This Day:
Talk in an Elevator Day

Easy Oatmeal Biscotti
MAKES ABOUT 30

5½ tablespoons (2.75 ounces)
   unsalted butter, softened
1 large egg
1 (17.5-ounce) pouch oatmeal cookie
   mix, such as Betty Crocker
¼ teaspoon ground cinnamon
¼ cup (1.1 ounces) all-purpose flour, plus a
   little more if the dough seems dry
½ cup pecans, toasted and chopped
⅓ cup dried cranberries (optional)

1 Preheat the oven to 350°F and place a rack in the center. Line a baking sheet with parchment paper or nonstick foil.

2 In a large bowl, using a handheld electric mixer on low, beat together the butter, egg, cookie mix, cinnamon, and flour until mixed yet still crumbly. Stir in the pecans and dried cranberries (if using). Using your hands, work the mixture until it comes together to form a dough. It should be fairly dry, but not so dry that you can't form logs. Divide the dough in half.

3 Dampen your hands with a little water and form each portion of dough into a log about 10 by 2 inches. Place the logs about 6 inches apart on the prepared baking sheet. Bake for 28 to 30 minutes. Let cool on the pan for at least 20 minutes, then using a serrated knife, slice the logs into ¾-inch-thick slices. Place cut side down on the prepared pan. Bake for another 15 minutes. Let cool completely on a wire rack.

New York Cheesecake Bars

MAKES 32

CRUST

1½ cups graham cracker crumbs

3 tablespoons granulated sugar

⅛ teaspoon salt

6 tablespoons (3 ounces) unsalted butter, melted

FILLING

2 (8-ounce) packages cream
cheese, softened

½ cup granulated sugar

2 large eggs, room
temperature

¼ cup whole milk

1½ tablespoons freshly
squeezed lemon juice

½ teaspoon vanilla extract

⅛ teaspoon orange extract

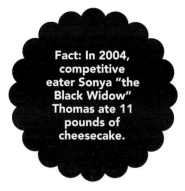

Fact: In 2004,
competitive
eater Sonya "the
Black Widow"
Thomas ate 11
pounds of
cheesecake.

1 Preheat the oven to 350°F and place a rack in the center. Line a 9 by 13-inch metal pan with nonstick foil.

2 **Make the crust:** In a large mixing bowl, stir together the graham cracker crumbs, sugar, and salt. Add the melted butter and stir until moist, then transfer the mixture to the prepared pan and press it down to make a crust.

3 **Make the filling:** Beat the cream cheese and sugar until well mixed. By hand or using the lowest speed of the mixer, stir in the eggs, milk, lemon juice, vanilla, and orange extract. Pour the filling over the crust and bake for 25 to 30 minutes. The cheesecake might puff up, but it should settle as it cools and chills. Let cool in the pan and then chill thoroughly—3 hours is okay, but overnight is better.

Baker's Notes: For these bars, follow the basic rules of cheesecake making, including using room-temperature ingredients, not overbeating the eggs, and taking the cheesecake out on time. It will set as it cools and firm as it chills.

National Cheesecake Day

Cheesecake has been on the menu since the domestication of animals, but the first printed recipe is credited to Athenaeus, who wrote about it in AD 230. Of course it took hundreds of years for it to evolve into the type we in America are used to, and much of that credit goes to William Lawrence of Chester, New York. While trying to reproduce a French cheese called Neufchâtel in 1872, Lawrence accidentally invented the cream cheese we know and love. He called it Philadelphia Brand and sold it in foil wrappers.

Other Events on This Day:
National Father-in-Law Day

Happy birthday, J. K. Rowling. Born in 1965 in England, Joanne Kathleen Rowling gained literary fame by writing about a young wizard named Harry Potter. Since then she has written at least ten books that have been translated into sixty-nine languages and sold in over two hundred territories.

Other Events on This Day: **Raspberry Cake Day, Mutt's Day**

Magic Wands MAKES 24

4 ounces semisweet or dark chocolate,
     or white dipping chocolate
24 pretzel rods
1 cup chopped peanuts or pecans or sprinkles
     or miniature chocolate-coated candies

1 In a microwave-safe bowl, melt the chocolate at 50 percent power, stirring every 60 seconds until melted and smooth. Alternatively, you may do this over a double boiler.

2 Have ready a sheet of parchment paper. Dip about a third of each pretzel rod in the chocolate, and then place on the parchment paper. Let the chocolate set just until it is tacky but not quite firm. Roll in nuts, candy, or sprinkles.

On this day in 1774, Joseph Priestly found that mice put in sealed containers with oxygen lived longer.

Oxygen, although not yet named, had already been discovered by a Swedish chemist, Carl Wilhelm Scheele, but Priestly published his findings earlier and is usually credited. Antoine Lavoisier, a French chemist, also discovered oxygen, in 1775, and was the first to recognize it as an element. Lavoisier coined the term *oxygen*, which means "acid producer."

Lighter-Than-Air Mini Chip Cookies MAKES ABOUT 30

2 large egg whites, room temperature
⅓ cup granulated sugar
¼ cup firmly packed brown sugar
⅛ teaspoon salt
1 teaspoon vanilla extract
1 cup semisweet chocolate mini chips

1 Preheat the oven to 350°F and place a rack in the center. Line two baking sheets with nonstick foil or parchment paper.

2 Using a handheld electric mixer on high speed, beat the egg whites until soft peaks just barely start to form, then gradually add both sugars; continue to beat until stiff peaks form. Add the salt and vanilla. Stir in the chocolate chips.

3 Drop teaspoonfuls of dough about 3 inches apart onto the prepared baking sheets. Bake one sheet at a time for 8 minutes. When all the cookies are baked, turn off the oven and leave the pans in the oven for a few hours, or until the cookies are dry.

Baker's Note: Also known as Forgotten Cookies, they are put in the oven and forgotten about for several hours. Since I never remember to bake them at night and put them in the oven before bed, I start them in the daytime, give them a short bake at 350°F, and let them sit in the oven for a couple of hours until they dry out. The cookies are light textured, sweet, and stay fresh for a week.

Crime-Fighting Ice-Cream Sandwich Cookies MAKES 24

2 cups (9 ounces) all-purpose flour

¾ cup unsweetened natural cocoa powder

1 teaspoon baking soda

¾ teaspoon salt

1¼ cups (10 ounces) unsalted butter,
    room temperature

2 cups granulated sugar

2 large eggs

2 teaspoons vanilla extract

1 cup semisweet chocolate chips (optional)

About 3 cups vanilla ice cream, softened

1 Preheat the oven to 350°F and place a rack in the center. Have ready two ungreased baking sheets.

2 Mix the flour, cocoa, baking soda, and salt together in a medium-size bowl; set aside.

Other Events on This Day:
Raspberry Cream Pie Day,
Colorado joined the Union in
1876

AUGUST 2

National Night Out

Created by the National Association of Town Watch, a nonprofit, crime-prevention organization, National Night Out encourages neighbors to socialize and have fun while also sending a message to potential vandals and burglars that the community members are watching out for one another. Since the first National Night Out in 1984, the event has gained the support of organizations across the country. In 2010, 37 million people participated.

Today is also National Ice-Cream Sandwich Day, so make some ice-cream sandwiches for the neighbors.

Other Events on This Day:
National Forgiveness Day

3 In the bowl of a stand mixer fitted with a paddle attachment, or in a large mixing bowl, using a handheld electric mixer, beat the butter and sugar on medium speed until light and fluffy. Add the eggs and vanilla; beat well.

4 With the mixer on low speed, add the flour mixture to the butter mixture. Stir in the chocolate chips, if using.

5 Scoop up generously rounded tablespoonfuls of dough, and shaping as neatly as you can into rounds, arrange about 2½ inches apart (six to a sheet). Bake one sheet at a time for 12 to 15 minutes, or until the cookies appear set—be careful not to overbake, because you want them soft and chewy to complement the ice cream. Let cool slightly on the baking sheets, then transfer to a wire rack to cool completely.

6 Spread vanilla ice cream on a cookie, sandwich it with another, wrap in plastic, and freeze until firm. Repeat with the remaining cookies and ice cream.

AUGUST 3

Simplify Your Life Week

The first week of August is Simplify Your Life Week, a week dedicated to raising awareness of cluttered e-mail boxes, messy closets, and the problem of not being able to say no. For bakers, this is a good week to find a tried-and-true recipe shortcut. This recipe is all about convenience, and whenever I make it I get asked for the recipe.

Other Events on This Day:
National Watermelon Day

White Chocolate Raspberry Cheesecake Bars MAKES 24

1 (18-ounce) package refrigerated
    macadamia and white chocolate chunk
    ready-to-bake cookie dough
1 (6-ounce) white chocolate baking
    bar, broken into chunks
2 (8-ounce) packages cream cheese, softened
½ cup granulated sugar
2 large eggs, room temperature
1 teaspoon vanilla extract
½ cup raspberry preserves

1 Preheat the oven to 325°F and place a rack in the center. Line a 9 by 13-inch metal pan with nonstick foil, or line it with regular foil and spray the foil with flour-added baking spray. Press the cookie dough evenly into the bottom of the prepared pan.

2 Place the white chocolate in a microwave-safe bowl and heat at 50 percent power for about 2 minutes, stopping every 30 seconds to stir, until the white chocolate is completely melted. In a large bowl, beat the cream cheese and sugar. Stir in the melted white chocolate. Add the eggs and vanilla, stirring just until combined—do not overbeat. Pour over the unbaked dough.

3 In a small, microwave-safe bowl or cup, microwave the raspberry preserves at 50 percent power for about 10 seconds to soften. With a spoon, carefully drizzle five lines of preserves lengthwise across the cheesecake batter. Place the pan so its lines of preserves are on the horizontal in front of you. Starting from the far edge of the pan, near its left corner, drag a clean knife crosswise (vertically) through the lines toward the edge of the pan nearest you. Move one inch to the right and repeat the motion, this time starting at the edge nearest you and dragging the knife across toward the far end. Repeat six to eight times at 1-inch increments and working crosswise alternately from the near and far edges, until you have reached the right edge of the pan. Bake for 37 minutes, or until the edges are slightly browned. The center area of the bars will be slightly wiggly. Let cool in the pan for 2 hours, then chill thoroughly.

"Big as a Boat" Oatmeal Cookies MAKES 12

1½ cups (6.8 ounces) all-purpose flour

1¼ cups old-fashioned oats

½ teaspoon salt

½ teaspoon baking soda

½ teaspoon ground cinnamon

½ cup (3.4 ounces) shortening

4 tablespoons (2 ounces) unsalted butter

½ cup granulated sugar

¾ cup firmly packed dark brown sugar

½ teaspoon vanilla extract

AUGUST 4

United States Coast Guard Day

Older than the nation's navy, the United States Coast Guard was established in 1790 when Congress authorized the construction of ten vessels to enforce tariff and trade laws. Since then, the Coast Guard has participated in every national conflict. During peace time, they operate as a part of the Department of Homeland Security, so next time you're sailing out to sea on a cruise ship, wave hello to the Coast Guard escort.

Other Events on This Day:
National Chocolate Chip Day

1½ tablespoons honey

1 large egg

⅓ cup pecans or walnuts, toasted and coarsely chopped

½ cup raisins or chocolate chips (optional)

1   Mix the flour, oats, salt, baking soda, and cinnamon together in a medium-size bowl; set aside.

2   Place the shortening and butter in a microwave-safe mixing bowl and melt for 1 minute on high. Using a wooden spoon, stir in both sugars and the vanilla, honey, and egg. Stir the flour mixture into the sugar mixture until thoroughly combined. Stir in the nuts and raisins.

3   Using a ¼-cup measure, scoop up the dough and arrange twelve mounds on a foil-lined plate. The dough should be a little sticky at this point, but chilling will fix that. Chill for an hour, or until the dough is firm.

4   Preheat the oven to 350°F and place a rack in the center. Line a baking sheet with parchment paper or nonstick foil.

5   Let the dough balls come to room temperature. Arrange the dough balls about 5 inches apart on the prepared baking sheet and press down slightly to make 2½-inch rounds. Bake for 10 to 15 minutes, or until the edges of the cookies are browned and the middles appear set. Let cool on the baking sheet for about 5 minutes, then transfer to a wire rack to cool completely.

Baker's Notes: Because these cookies are big and all ovens are different, you may have to adjust the time and temperature a bit. If your cookies brown too quickly around the edges and the dough in the middle seems raw, reduce the temperature by 25°F and bake for a longer time. To be safe, I recommend baking one cookie first, to nail down the proper time in your oven.

Colossal Ginger Cookies

MAKES 10

¾ cup (5.1 ounces) shortening

2 cups (9 ounces) all-purpose flour

½ teaspoon salt

½ teaspoon baking soda

2 teaspoons unsweetened natural cocoa powder

1 teaspoon ground cinnamon

½ teaspoon ground cloves

½ teaspoon ground ginger

¼ teaspoon ground mustard

1 large egg

1 cup granulated sugar

½ teaspoon vanilla extract

½ cup mild molasses

Crystal sugar (optional)

1 In a microwave-safe bowl, heat the shortening on high for 30 seconds, or until melted, and set it aside to cool.

2 While the shortening cools, mix the flour, salt, baking soda, cocoa, cinnamon, cloves, ginger, and mustard powder together in a medium-size bowl; set aside.

3 In the bowl of a stand mixer fitted with a paddle attachment, or in a large mixing bowl, using a handheld electric mixer, beat the egg on medium speed until light and fluffy. Add the sugar and beat for another minute, then beat in the melted shortening, vanilla, and molasses. By hand or using the lowest speed of the mixer, stir in the flour mixture.

4 Using a generous ¼-cup measure, scoop the dough and shape into mounds. Place on a foil-lined plate and chill thoroughly for at least 3 hours, or chill in the freezer for 1 hour.

5 Preheat the oven to 350°F and place a rack in the center. Line two baking sheets with parchment. Dip the dough mounds in crystal sugar (if using) and arrange half of the mounds 3½ inches apart on each prepared baking sheet, keeping the remaining mounds chilled until ready to bake.

National
Mustard Day

Mustard isn't just for hot dogs and pretzels. Try it in these bake-sale-worthy molasses cookies and see if people can detect its flavor.

Other Events on This Day: First traffic light installed at Euclid Avenue and East 105th Street in Cleveland, Ohio, in 1914

6 Bake one pan at a time for 15 to 20 minutes. If the cookies seem brown after the first 15 minutes, lay a sheet of foil loosely over the top. Let cool on the baking sheets for 2 to 3 minutes. The cookies will be large, thick, and crispy on the outside and soft on the inside.

Baker's Note: This big dense cookie gets its texture from melted shortening.

Root Beer Float Day

Root Beer with ice cream is so popular that not only do we have a National Black Cow Day, there's Root Beer Float Day. Celebrate by drinking a glass of root beer with ice cream in it, or by baking some flavored biscotti. These cookies are perfect with almonds, pecans, or chocolate chips. I like them with the chocolate chips, but my daughter prefers toasted almonds.

Other Events on This Day:
Birthdays of Lucille Ball (b. 1911) and Andy Warhol (b. 1928)

Root Beer Biscotti   MAKES 32 TO 36

1¾ cups (8 ounces) all-purpose flour
¼ teaspoon salt
1 teaspoon baking powder
¼ cup vegetable oil
½ cup granulated sugar
1½ teaspoons root beer extract, such as Watkins
2 large eggs
1½ cups toasted chopped almonds or pecans
⅓ cup semisweet chocolate chips (optional)

1 Preheat the oven to 300°F and place a rack in the center. Line a large baking sheet with nonstick foil or parchment paper.

2 Mix the flour, salt, and baking powder in a medium-size bowl; set aside.

3 In the bowl of a stand mixer fitted with a paddle attachment, or in a large mixing bowl, using a handheld electric mixer, beat the oil and sugar on medium speed until well blended. Beat in the extract, and then beat in the eggs. By hand or using the lowest speed of the mixer, add the flour mixture and stir to make a dough. Stir in the almonds and chocolate chips (if using).

4 Divide the dough in half. Form each portion into a log 12 by 2 inches directly on the prepared baking sheet, spacing the logs about 4½ inches apart. If the dough is sticky, wet your hands with cool water first.

5 Bake for 35 minutes at 300°F, or until the logs are light brown. Let cool on the pan for 10 to 15 minutes. Reduce the oven temperature to 275°F.

6 Cut crosswise slightly on the diagonal every ¾ inch. Place cut side down on the lined baking sheet. Bake for 8 to 10 minutes, or until the cookies appear dry. Let cool completely on a wire rack.

Raspberries and Cream Cookies MAKES 48

2¼ cups (10.1 ounces) all-purpose flour
1 teaspoon baking soda
1 scant teaspoon salt
1 cup (8 ounces) unsalted butter, room temperature
1 cup granulated sugar
½ cup firmly packed light brown sugar
1 teaspoon raspberry extract
¼ teaspoon vanilla extract
6 drops red food coloring, or as needed (optional)
2 large eggs
2 cups white chocolate chips

1 Preheat the oven to 350°F and place a rack in the center. Have ready two ungreased baking sheets.

2 Mix the flour, baking soda, and salt together in a medium-size bowl; set aside.

3 In the bowl of a stand mixer fitted with a paddle attachment, or in a large mixing bowl, using a handheld electric mixer, beat the butter and both sugars on medium speed until creamy. Scrape the sides of the bowl and beat in the raspberry extract, vanilla, and food coloring. Reduce the mixer speed and beat in the eggs, one at a time, until they are fully incorporated. With the mixer on low speed, add the flour mixture. Stir in the white chips.

4 Drop rounded teaspoonfuls of batter about 2 inches apart onto the baking sheets. Bake one sheet at a time for 10 to

AUGUST 7

National Raspberries and Cream Day

Treat yourself to a bowl of raspberries today and feel good about the fact that berries are rich in vitamin C, a good source of fiber, and a powerful source of anti-oxidants. Or celebrate with something sweeter. In the spirit of Raspberries and Cream Day, here's a cookie tribute to the flavor combo.

Other Events on This Day:
National Friendship Day

12 minutes, or until golden brown around the edges. Let cool on the baking sheets for 5 minutes, then transfer to a wire rack to cool completely.

National Zucchini Day

I n honor of National Zucchini Day, today's cookie is designed to make use of what I hope is a bumper crop of zucchini in your garden.

This recipe was inspired by an old zucchini bread recipe from Jane Brody's *Good Food Book*. As I made the bread, I noticed the batter was very thick and decided to see if it would hold up when baked as cookies. It did. These are tasty as-is, but for a richer cookie, top with cream cheese icing or your favorite lemon glaze.

Other Events on This Day:
National Dollar Day

Zucchini Bread Cookies

MAKES 20 LARGE COOKIES

1¼ cups (5 ounces) zucchini, grated

1½ cups (6.7 ounces) white whole wheat or all-purpose flour

½ cup coconut palm sugar or lightly packed light brown sugar

1 teaspoon baking powder

½ teaspoon baking soda

¼ teaspoon salt

1 teaspoon pumpkin pie spice

½ teaspoon ground cinnamon

1 large egg white

1 whole large egg

6 tablespoons vegetable oil

1 teaspoon vanilla extract

½ cup toasted and chopped pecans

½ cup golden raisins

1 Preheat the oven to 350°F and place a rack in the center. Line two baking sheets with nonstick foil or parchment paper.

2 Spread the grated zucchini on a stack of paper towels. Press the towels over the zucchini to soak up any extra moisture, then let stand for about 10 minutes.

3 Mix the flour, sugar, baking powder, baking soda, salt, pumpkin pie spice, and cinnamon together in a large mixing bowl. In a second bowl, mix the egg white, egg, oil, vanilla, and zucchini. Pour the zucchini mixture into the flour mixture and stir just until blended. Stir in the pecans and raisins.

4   Drop generously rounded tablespoonfuls of batter 2½ inches apart onto the baking sheets. Bake one sheet at a time for 10 to 12 minutes, or until the cookies appear set, then transfer to a wire rack to cool completely. These taste best when completely cooled and set.

Polish Kolaczki MAKES 30

8 tablespoons (4 ounces) unsalted butter,
    room temperature
3 ounces cream cheese, softened
¼ teaspoon salt
1 cup (4.5 ounces) all-purpose flour
Raspberry or your favorite flavor preserves or jam
Confectioners' sugar, for dusting (optional)

1   In a large mixing bowl, using a handheld electric mixer, beat the butter, cream cheese, and salt until creamy. By hand, stir in the flour. Shape the dough into two balls. Wrap tightly and chill for an hour, or until you can handle the dough.

2   Remove the dough from the refrigerator. If the dough has become very hard, allow it to come back to room temperature.

3   Preheat the oven to 350°F and place a rack in the center. Line a baking sheet with parchment paper or nonstick foil.

4   Break off pieces of dough and roll into ¾-inch balls. Place about 2 inches apart on the pan. With your finger, make a deep indentation in each ball and fill it with about ¼ teaspoon of preserves or jam. Bake for 15 to 18 minutes or until the cookies appear set. Let cool on the baking sheet for about 3 minutes, then transfer to a wire rack set over paper towels. Let the cookies cool completely, then dust with confectioner's sugar for extra sweetness.

Baker's Notes: Like the polka, the kolaczki or kolache is a pastry rooted in Czech and Polish heritage. In central Texas, the pastry is usually made Czech-style, with yeast dough filled with preserves, pie filling, or sausage. This soft and tender version contains no yeast and is somewhere between a cookie and a pastry.

AUGUST 9

National Polka Day

The polka originated in 1834 in Bohemia as an accompaniment to a local folk song. In less than a year it became popular in Prague, and shortly after that, Paris. By 1849 the polka was danced in England and the United States. Considered the national dance of Polish immigrants, it is now performed all over the United States at various festivals, including those held for Pulaski Day.

Other Events on This Day:
National Book Lover's Day

National Lazy Day

If today falls on a weekend, great! Sleep late, skip the gym, and spend the morning surfing the Internet or just lying around doing nothing. If Lazy Day falls on a workday, don't cut corners on the job; rather, make a mental note to schedule a Lazy Day in the near future. We all need one once in a while. Make the most of Lazy Day by buying a bag of your favorite packaged cookies, or making something extremely simple that doesn't require much effort or skill.

Other Events on This Day:
The Smithsonian established in 1846, National S'mores Day

Microwave S'mores   MAKES 1

2 rectangles from a bar of milk chocolate, such as Hershey's

2 graham cracker squares

1 large marshmallow

OPTIONAL EXTRAS

1 teaspoon chocolate hazelnut spread

1 teaspoon peanut butter

Sliced bananas

A small spoonful of caramel (the kind you dip apples in)

A spoonful of *dulce de leche* or *cajeta*

1 Lay two rectangles of milk chocolate on one graham cracker square. Top with one marshmallow and the second graham cracker square. Microwave on high for 20 to 45 seconds, just until the marshmallow puffs up. Press down slightly so that the hot marshmallow melts the chocolate.

2 If using an optional variation, such as a spread, incorporate it as you see fit. For instance, spread it on the top or lower cracker closer to the chocolate or closer to the marshmallow.

Baker's Note: If you're not too lazy and want to focus on the fact that it's National S'mores Day, other good recipes include S'mores Chocolate Chip Cookies (October 30) and S'mores Bars (June 25).

Cappuccino and Crème Cookies MAKES 26

2½ cups (11.3 ounces) all-purpose flour

½ cup unsweetened natural or Dutch-
  processed cocoa powder

2 teaspoons ground cinnamon

1 tablespoon instant coffee granules

1 teaspoon baking powder

1 teaspoon baking soda

¾ teaspoon salt

1 cup (8 ounces) unsalted
  butter, room temperature

1½ cups granulated sugar

1 cup firmly packed light
  brown sugar

1 teaspoon vanilla extract

2 large eggs

6 ounces bittersweet or semisweet
  chocolate, cut into chunks

6 chocolate sandwich cookies, such as
  Oreos, broken into pieces

1   Preheat the oven to 350°F and place a rack in the center. Have ready two ungreased baking sheets.

2   Mix the flour, cocoa powder, cinnamon, coffee granules, baking powder, baking soda, and salt together in a bowl; set aside.

3   In the bowl of a stand mixer fitted with a paddle attachment, or in a large mixing bowl, using a handheld electric mixer, cream the butter and both sugars on medium speed until light. Reduce the mixer speed slightly and beat in the vanilla and the eggs. When the eggs are incorporated, reduce the mixer speed to low and beat in the flour mixture. Stir in the chocolate and cookie chunks.

4   Scoop up generously heaping tablespoonfuls of dough and place about 3 inches apart on the baking sheets. Bake for 12 minutes, or until the cookies puff up and appear set

Patent for Instant Coffee

On this day in 1903, Satori Kato, a Japanese chemist living in Chicago, received a patent for his "Coffee Concentrate and Process of Making Same." He'd applied for the patent two years earlier in 1901 after introducing it at the Pan-American Exposition in Buffalo, New York. In the years that followed, other chemists would refine and perfect instant coffee.

Other Events on This Day:
Two moons of Mars, Phobos and Deimos, discovered in 1887

Fact: In 1938, Nescafé was introduced in Switzerland.

with a little moisture in the center. Let cool on the baking sheets for 5 minutes, then transfer to a wire rack to cool completely.

Middle Child Day

Being eldest of two and mom to one, I haven't had firsthand experience, but birth order researchers believe that children with two siblings, one older and one younger, are susceptible to "middle child syndrome," a situation where the middle child, wedged between the natural leader and the stereotypical carefree "baby of the family" doesn't get as much attention, resulting in introvert and loner traits. Whether or not you agree, it's fair to say middle children deserve a special day.

Other Events on This Day:
International Youth Day, Singer sewing machine patented in 1865

Oatmeal Sandwich Cookies   MAKES 18 SANDWICHES

COOKIES

1 cup plus 2 tablespoons (5 ounces) all-purpose flour

1 teaspoon ground cinnamon

¼ teaspoon freshly grated nutmeg

¾ teaspoon baking soda

½ teaspoon salt

12 tablespoons (6 ounces) unsalted butter, softened, or ¾ cup shortening

1⅓ cups firmly packed light brown sugar

2 large eggs

1¼ teaspoons vanilla extract

2 cups old-fashioned or quick-cooking oats (not instant)

FILLING

1 cup (8 ounces) unsalted butter, room temperature

2 cups confectioners' sugar

1 (7.5-ounce) jar marshmallow crème, such as Marshmallow Fluff

2 teaspoons vanilla extract

1   **Make the cookies:** Mix the flour, cinnamon, nutmeg, baking soda, and salt together in a bowl; set aside.

2   In the bowl of a stand mixer fitted with a paddle attachment, or in a large mixing bowl, using a handheld electric mixer, cream the butter and brown sugar on medium-high speed. Reduce the speed to medium and beat in the eggs, one at a time, beating well after each addition. Beat in the vanilla. Stir in the flour mixture, then stir in the oats. Chill the dough for 1 hour, or until firm enough for you to shape into balls.

3 Preheat the oven to 350°F and place a rack in the center. Line two baking sheets with nonstick foil or parchment paper.

4 Shape the dough into 1-inch balls and arrange about 2 inches apart on the prepared baking sheets. Press down the tops slightly. Bake one sheet at a time for 10 to 12 minutes, or until golden brown. Let cool on the baking sheets for 5 minutes, then carefully transfer to a wire rack to cool completely.

5 **Make the filling:** Beat the butter until smooth. Stir in the confectioners' sugar until incorporated. Beat until smooth, then beat in the marshmallow crème and vanilla until light and fluffy, 2 to 3 minutes.

6 Spread the underside of one cookie with a generous table-spoonful of the filling, then top base to base with another cookie. Repeat until all the cookies are sandwiched.

Left-Handed Chocolate Cookies MAKES 48

8 tablespoons (4 ounces) unsalted butter

2 cups (12 ounces) semisweet or
   extra-dark chocolate chips

¼ cup firmly packed light brown sugar

1 (14-ounce) can sweetened condensed milk

1¼ teaspoons vanilla extract

1 cup (4.5 ounces) all-purpose flour

1 cup toasted and coarsely chopped pecans or walnuts

1 Preheat the oven to 350°F and place a rack in the center. Line two baking sheets with parchment paper or nonstick foil.

2 Melt the butter in a 3-quart saucepan over medium heat. Reduce the heat to low and stir in the chocolate chips and brown sugar. Continue heating on low to medium-low, stirring constantly, until melted and smooth. Stir in the condensed milk. Remove from the heat and stir in the vanilla and flour. When the flour is incorporated, stir in the pecans or walnuts. Let the mixture stand for about 5 minutes or until it is thick enough to spoon.

AUGUST 13

International Left Handers Day

Launched in 1992 by the Left-Handers Club, here's a day that puts "sinistrality" in the spotlight. Celebrate with a recipe so easy you can make it with your left hand, even if you're right-handed. This recipe goes by many names, including "Fudgies," "Chocolate Nuggets," and my personal favorite, "Dulces," which was bestowed upon the cookie by the Austin Junior League in our city's official cookbook, *Austin Entertains*.

3 Drop rounded teaspoonfuls of dough about 2 inches apart onto the prepared baking sheets. Bake one sheet at a time for 10 minutes, taking care not to overbake them. Let cool on the baking sheet for 3 minutes, then transfer to a wire rack to cool completely.

AUGUST 14

Creamsicle Day

Those Popsicles with cream in the middle have their own day. Have you eaten one lately? If you're over the age of ten, probably not, but today's a good day to buy a box for nostalgia's sake and ponder the subtle differences in Creamsicles vs. Dreamsicles. Apparently Creamsicles are filled with ice cream, whereas Dreamsicles are filled with ice milk, but these days, both words are used interchangeably by people to describe foods with a combination of orange and vanilla flavors.

Other Events on This Day:
National Navajo Code Talkers' Day

Orange Dream Cookies

MAKES 36

2¼ cups (10.1 ounces) all-purpose flour
¾ teaspoon baking soda
¾ teaspoon salt
8 tablespoons (4 ounces) unsalted
    butter, room temperature
½ cup (3.4 ounces) shortening
⅔ cup firmly packed light brown sugar
½ cup granulated sugar
1 large egg
2 teaspoons orange zest
1 teaspoon orange extract
¾ teaspoon vanilla extract
1½ cups vanilla or white chips

1 Preheat the oven to 350°F and place a rack in the center. Have ready two ungreased baking sheets.

2 Mix the flour, baking soda, and salt together in a medium-size bowl; set aside.

3 In the bowl of a stand mixer fitted with a paddle attachment, or in a large mixing bowl, using a handheld electric mixer, beat the butter, shortening, and both sugars on medium speed until creamy. Add the egg, orange zest, orange extract, and vanilla, beating until blended.

4 By hand or using the lowest speed of the mixer, add the flour mixture to the butter mixture and stir until the flour is incorporated. Stir in the white chips.

5 Scoop up tablespoonfuls of dough and arrange about 2½ inches apart on the baking sheets. Bake one sheet at a time

for 12 minutes, or until the edges are lightly browned. Let cool on the baking sheets for 2 minutes, then transfer to a wire rack to cool completely.

Mango Cream Pie Bars

MAKES 16

CRUST

1½ cups graham cracker crumbs

½ cup sweetened flaked coconut

2 tablespoons granulated sugar

¼ scant teaspoon salt

6 tablespoons (3 ounces) unsalted butter, melted

TOPPING

12 ounces frozen mango chunks, thawed

½ cup freshly squeezed Persian lime or key lime juice

2 teaspoons unflavored gelatin

1 (14-ounce) can sweetened condensed milk

Lightly sweetened fresh whipped cream or
    whipped topping, for garnishing

16 stemmed maraschino cherries,
    for garnishing (optional)

1 Preheat the oven to 350°F and place a rack in the center. Line a 9-inch square metal pan with nonstick foil.

2 **Make the crust:** Mix the graham cracker crumbs, coconut, sugar, and salt. Add the melted butter and stir to coat the crumbs. Press the mixture into the prepared pan and bake for 8 to 10 minutes, or until set. Let cool in the pan.

3 **Make the topping:** In a food processor or blender puree the mangoes to make 1½ cups of puree. Set aside.

4 Pour the lime juice into a small saucepan; sprinkle the gelatin over it, and let stand until the gelatin softens, about 5 minutes. Cook over low heat, stirring, just until the gelatin dissolves, about 2 minutes. Remove from the heat. Stir in the sweetened condensed milk and mango puree. Pour the mixture over the baked crust. Chill for at

AUGUST 15

*National
Relaxation Day*

G rab a book, sit down, and kick off your shoes. Today is National Relaxation Day. Some tips for enjoying it include getting a massage, listening to classical music, taking a long walk, or baking some bar cookies whose flavor may remind you of relaxing on the beach in the Caribbean. They were inspired by mango cream pie I ate one night at a Cuban restaurant. It was good, but kind of chalky and overly sweet. I decided to try making a less chalky bar cookie version of the pie and came up with these.

Other Events on This Day:
**Julia Child's birthday
(b. 1912), Crisco patented
in 1911**

least 4 hours, or until the topping is nicely set. When firm, grasp the foil, lift from the pan, set on a cutting board, and cut into sixteen squares. Serve garnished with whipped cream and cherries, if using.

AUGUST 16

Tell a Joke Day

Spread some laughter today by telling a joke. If you don't know any, ask your friends to tell a joke in exchange for one of these nutty bar cookies. By the end of the day you should have sixteen new jokes and sixteen recipe requests.

Other Events on This Day:
Mrs. Fields opened her first store in 1977 in Palo Alto, California.

Nutty Shortbread Bars   MAKES 16

CRUST
1 cup (4.5 ounces) all-purpose flour
⅓ cup confectioners' sugar
¼ teaspoon salt
6 tablespoons (3 ounces) unsalted butter, room temperature

TOPPING
6 tablespoons (3 ounces) unsalted butter
⅛ teaspoon salt
¼ cup firmly packed light brown sugar
¼ cup honey
1½ tablespoons heavy whipping cream
⅛ teaspoon vanilla extract
1¼ cups mixed nuts, roughly chopped

1 Preheat the oven to 350°F and place a rack in the center. Line an 8-inch metal pan with nonstick foil, or line it with regular foil and spray the foil with flour-added baking spray.

2 **Make the crust:** Pulse the flour, confectioners' sugar, and salt in the bowl of a food processor once or twice to mix. Add the butter and process until crumbly. Press the mixture into the bottom of the prepared pan and bake for 20 minutes. Let cool in the pan for 20 minutes.

3 **Make the topping:** Melt the butter in a saucepan. Add the salt, brown sugar, and honey and bring to a boil over medium heat. Just as the mixture starts to boil, remove from the heat and stir in the whipping cream, followed by the vanilla and mixed nuts. Pour the mixture over the crust and bake for another 18 to 20 minutes, or until the bars look hot and bubbly and the edges are browned. Let the bars cool completely in the pan. Grasp the foil, lift from the pan, set on a cutting board, and cut into sixteen squares.

Thrifty Chocolate Chip Cookies MAKES 24

½ cup vegetable oil

1 large egg

¼ cup granulated sugar

½ cup firmly packed light brown sugar

1 teaspoon vanilla extract

½ teaspoon baking soda

¼ teaspoon salt

1½ cups (6.7 ounces) all-purpose flour

1½ cups semisweet chocolate chips

⅓ cup toasted and chopped walnuts

1 Preheat the oven to 350°F and place a rack in the center. Have ready two ungreased baking sheets.

2 Mix the oil, egg, both sugars, and vanilla together in a mixing bowl. Stir in the baking soda and salt, and then stir in the flour. When blended, add the chocolate chips and walnuts.

3 Scoop up tablespoonfuls of dough (it may be quite crumbly) and shape into tight rounds ¾ to 1 inch in diameter. Arrange about 2 inches apart on the baking sheets. The mounds should be bursting with chips. (Note: If the dough balls seem really dry, press them together a little bit.) Press down the mounds of dough a little to make ½-inch-thick circles. Bake one pan at a time for 8 to 10 minutes. Let cool on the baking sheets for 2 minutes, then transfer to a wire rack to cool completely.

Baker's Notes: This dough is very dry, but if you've used the right amount of oil and flour, you should be able to shape it into balls. Load the cookies with chips and you won't miss the butter.

National Thrift Shop Day

You know that big pile of clothes in the back of your closet? Today's the day to take them to your local thrift shop. While you're there, be sure to go through the array of kitchen items because you never know what you might find. Here's a chocolate chip cookie with a thrifty twist—oil stands in for the butter.

Other Events on This Day: **Vanilla Custard Day, prospectors in Alaska found gold in 1896, setting off the Klondike gold rush**

Almonds have been cultivated since 1400 BC. They're mentioned in the Bible, Ancient Romans used them as fertility charms, and explorers carried them on their journeys. A source of protein, fiber, and vitamins, almonds are a way to zap a few nutrients into just about any snack, which, in this case, means cookies!

Other Events on This Day:
National Bad Poetry Day, Soft Ice Cream Day

Chocolate Nut Toasts MAKES 24

½ ounce unsweetened chocolate

2 large egg whites, room temperature

¼ cup plus 2 teaspoons (2 ounces) granulated sugar

⅛ teaspoon salt

¼ teaspoon almond extract

½ teaspoon vanilla extract

½ cup minus 1 tablespoon (2 ounces) all-purpose flour

½ cup chopped almonds or a mix of almonds and other nuts

½ cup mixed dried fruit, such as apricots, raisins, and cranberries

1 Preheat the oven to 350°F and place a rack in the center. Line six muffin cups with paper liners and spray the liners with flour-added baking spray. Alternatively, you can skip the paper liners and just spray the muffin cups.

2 Melt the chocolate in a small, microwave-safe bowl, using 50 percent power and stirring at 30-second intervals.

3 In the bowl of a stand mixer fitted with a whisk attachment or in a large mixing bowl, using a handheld electric mixer on high speed, beat the egg whites until stiff peaks form. Gradually add the sugar, and then beat in the salt, almond extract, and vanilla. With a large scraper, fold in the flour. Fold in the melted chocolate, almonds, and fruit.

4 Spoon the mixture into the muffin cups, dividing equally among all six, and bake at 350°F for 20 to 25 minutes, or until the "muffins" appear dry and the edges are lightly browned (it's harder to tell with chocolate, but 20 minutes should do the trick). Remove from the oven and let cool slightly, then remove from the muffin cups and pull off the paper liners. Transfer to a wire rack to cool completely, then wrap loosely in foil and chill for about 4 hours, or until very cold. This makes the "muffins" much easier to slice.

5   Reduce the oven temperature to 200°F. Lay the cold
    "muffins" on their sides, and using a large serrated knife,
    slice them into thin rounds. You should get at least three
    rounds and one stubby-looking top per muffin. Arrange
    the rounds in one big layer on a baking sheet and bake
    at 200°F for 1 hour to 1 hour and 15 minutes, or until
    dried out. They'll dry out even more as they cool, so if the
    centers aren't completely firm after the full baking time,
    take them out anyway. Let cool completely on a wire rack.
    Store in a tightly covered container.

Baker's Notes: If you have a scale, I recommend making this
recipe using flour and sugar weights rather than volume. Muffin
paper liners are optional, but they give the cookies little ridges.

Salted Peanut Bars   MAKES 24

BASE
1½ cups (6.8 ounces) all-purpose flour
¾ cup firmly packed light brown sugar
½ teaspoon salt
8 tablespoons (4 ounces)
    unsalted butter, melted
2 cups lightly salted peanuts

TOPPING
½ cup light corn syrup
1 tablespoon water
2 tablespoons unsalted butter
1 cup butterscotch chips

1   Preheat the oven to 350°F and place a rack in the center.
    Line a 10 by 15-inch metal pan with nonstick foil, or line it
    with regular foil and spray the foil with flour-added bak-
    ing spray.

2   **Make the base:** Mix the flour, brown sugar, and salt
    together in a large mixing bowl. Stir in the melted butter.
    Press into the bottom of the prepared pan and bake for 10
    minutes. Remove from the oven and sprinkle the peanuts
    over the crust, pressing down slightly.

3   **Make the topping:** In a small saucepan, combine the corn syrup, water, and butter and heat over medium heat until very hot. Add the butterscotch chips and continue heating until the mixture boils. Boil gently for 2 minutes, stirring constantly. Pour the butterscotch mixture over the peanuts. Bake for 10 to 12 minutes. Let cool completely in the pan, then lift from the pan, set on a cutting board, and cut into twenty-four bars.

Chocolate Pecan Pie Day

Pecan pie is a big deal in our family, and everyone has an opinion on how it should be. My grandmother liked it with dark corn syrup, my mom prefers light; I like the pecans whole, my husband likes them chopped.

For the most part, we're pecan pie traditionalists, but we won't say no to a little added chocolate. Chocolate pecan pie is rich, but if made properly, not overly sweet. The bitterness in the chocolate tempers some of the sugar. Try it for yourself today. Here it is in bar form, which is perfectly acceptable for Chocolate Pecan Pie Day.

Other Events on This Day:
National Radio Day

Chocolate Pecan Pie Bars

MAKES 32

BASE

1½ cups (6.8 ounces) all-purpose flour

¼ scant teaspoon salt

¼ cup firmly packed light brown sugar

8 tablespoons (4 ounces) unsalted butter, softened

TOPPING

3 large eggs

¾ cup light or dark corn syrup

½ cup firmly packed light brown sugar

2 tablespoons (1 ounce) unsalted butter, melted and cooled

1 teaspoon vanilla extract

1½ cups semisweet chocolate chips

2 cups toasted and chopped pecans (see Baker's Note)

1   Preheat the oven to 350°F and place a rack in the center. Line a 9 by 13-inch metal pan with nonstick foil.

2   **Make the base:** Combine the flour, salt, and brown sugar in the bowl of a food processor. Add the butter and pulse until crumbly. Press firmly into the bottom of the prepared pan. Bake for 12 minutes, or until lightly browned.

3   **Make the topping:** In a large mixing bowl, whisk the eggs, corn syrup, brown sugar, butter, and vanilla together. Stir in the chocolate chips and pecans. Pour evenly over the baked crust. Bake for 25 to 30 minutes, or until set. Let cool completely in the pan. Grasp the foil, lift from the pan, set on a cutting board, and cut into thirty-two squares.

Baker's Note: For the pecans, consider the amount listed as a guideline and add more or less to taste.

Spiced Dried Plum Cookies

MAKES ABOUT 40

COOKIES

1¾ cups (8 ounces) whole wheat pastry
    flour or all-purpose flour

½ teaspoon baking soda

½ teaspoon salt

½ teaspoon freshly grated nutmeg

½ teaspoon ground cinnamon

⅛ teaspoon ground cloves

8 tablespoons (4 ounces) unsalted butter, softened

1 cup firmly packed light brown sugar

1 large egg

3 to 4 tablespoons whole or 2% milk

1 cup loosely packed chopped, pitted dried plums

ICING

1 tablespoon unsalted butter, melted

1 cup confectioners' sugar

4 teaspoons whole or 2% milk, plus more as needed

¼ teaspoon vanilla extract

1   Preheat the oven to 375°F and place a rack in the center. Line two baking sheets with parchment paper or nonstick foil

2   Mix the flour, baking soda, salt, nutmeg, cinnamon, and cloves together in a small bowl; set aside.

3   In the bowl of a stand mixer fitted with a paddle attachment, or in a large mixing bowl, using a handheld electric mixer, beat the butter and brown sugar on medium speed until light. Reduce the mixer speed slightly and beat in the egg. By hand or using the lowest speed of the mixer, stir in 3 tablespoons of the milk and the flour mixture, adding the last tablespoon of milk only if the dough seems too dry. Stir in the dried plums.

Senior Citizens Day

Declared by President Ronald Reagan in 1988, Senior Citizens Day recognizes the achievements, contributions, and wisdom of seniors in the community. Take a moment to recognize a senior—that is, if you can figure out who they are. Maybe it's because I'm getting older, but the over-sixty-five set seems more youthful than ever these days.

Prunes, now marketed as dried plums, were a more popular ingredient in the 1930s and '40s and tend to be associated with grandparents. As it happened, my ten-year-old loved these tender, spicy cookies.

Other Events on This Day:
Spumoni Day

4 Drop rounded teaspoonfuls of dough about 2 inches apart onto the baking sheets. Bake one sheet at a time for 10 minutes, or until the edges are light brown. Let cool on the baking sheets for about 2 minutes, then transfer to a wire rack, set over a paper towel or waxed paper, to cool completely. When completely cool, prepare the icing.

5 **Make the icing:** Mix together the melted butter and confectioners' sugar, then add milk 1 teaspoon at a time until you get the consistency of glue. Stir in the vanilla. Drizzle over the cookies.

AUGUST 22

National Tooth Fairy Day

No one knows the Tooth Fairy's real age, but parents have been telling their children about her since the early 1900s.

There are other ways of dealing with tooth loss. Vikings paid their kids for each tooth and put them on a string, whereas in medieval Europe, they buried teeth in the garden. Some Latin countries have the "tooth mouse," while in Asia it is customary to throw the lost tooth over the roof. You won't really lose a tooth on these cookies—or at least I hope not. But if you do, the cookies are worth it.

Other Events on This Day:
The schooner America won a yachting competition in 1851 in England. It was the namesake for the America's Cup.

Cornflake and Peanut Brittle Cookies MAKES 32

1 cup (4.5 ounces) all-purpose flour

½ teaspoon baking soda

½ teaspoon baking powder

⅜ teaspoon salt

8 tablespoons (4 ounces) unsalted butter, softened

¼ cup firmly packed light brown sugar

¼ cup granulated sugar

1 large egg

1 teaspoon vanilla extract

3 cups cornflakes, crushed

½ cup crushed peanut brittle

½ cup sweetened flaked coconut

1 Preheat the oven to 350°F and place a rack in the center. Line two baking sheets with nonstick foil or parchment paper.

2 Mix the flour, baking soda, baking powder, and salt together in a medium-size bowl; set aside.

3 In the bowl of a stand mixer fitted with a paddle attachment, or in a large mixing bowl, using a handheld electric mixer, beat the butter and both sugars on medium-high speed until light and creamy. Beat in the egg and vanilla

and continue mixing on medium-high speed for another minute. By hand, stir in the flour mixture until incorporated. Stir in the cereal, peanut brittle, and coconut.

4 Scoop up level tablespoonfuls of batter and shape into balls. Arrange the balls about 2½ inches apart on the prepared baking sheets. Bake for 10 to 12 minutes, or until the edges are lightly browned. Let cool on the baking sheet for about 3 minutes, then transfer to a wire rack to cool completely.

Madeleines MAKES 24 TO 26

1 cup (4 ounces) cake flour
½ teaspoon baking powder
⅛ teaspoon salt
3 large eggs, room temperature
¾ cup granulated sugar
½ teaspoon orange zest
1 teaspoon vanilla extract
8 tablespoons (4 ounces) unsalted butter
Confectioners' sugar, for dusting (optional)

1 Sift together the flour, baking powder, and salt; set aside.

2 In the bowl of a stand mixer fitted with a paddle attachment, or in a large mixing bowl, using a handheld electric mixer, whip the eggs and granulated sugar at high speed until thick and lemon colored, about 3 minutes. Stir in the orange zest and vanilla.

3 In a microwave-safe mixing bowl or Pyrex measuring cup, microwave the butter on high for 30 seconds, or until melted. Slowly pour the melted butter into the batter and beat lightly until it is mixed in. Fold in the flour mixture. Cover and refrigerate for 15 minutes.

AUGUST 23

National Sponge Cake Day

If the first thing that comes to your mind on National Sponge Cake Day is Twinkies, you're not alone. Don't worry, they have their day.

Today we pay tribute to homemade sponge cake, an airy and light-textured cake made from eggs, sugar, flour, and flavorings such as orange and vanilla. In some cases, a sponge cake can be a cookie. The madeleine, popularized in literature by Proust, is probably the most famous example.

Other Events on This Day: **Rudolph Valentino died in 1926, Galileo demonstrated the telescope**

4 Preheat the oven to 325°F and place a rack in the center.

5 Spray a madeleine pan with flour-added baking spray, or coat it with shortening or butter. Spoon about 1 tablespoon of batter into each cavity, being careful not to overfill. Bake for 14 to 16 minutes, until the madeleines are firm. Remove from the oven and immediately turn the pan upside down over a wire rack. Tap the back of the pan to help release the cakes. Let cool completely. Dust with confectioners' sugar before serving, if desired.

AUGUST 24

National Waffle Iron Day

Today we celebrate waffles and the apparatus used to make them. Waffle irons have been around since the fourteenth century and came to America in the early seventeenth century with Dutch pilgrims. They were made with two hinged iron plates imprinted with elaborate patterns and connected with a long wooden handle for setting over the stove. On this day in 1869, American inventor Cornelius Swarthout patented the first US waffle iron.

Other Events on This Day:
Johns Hopkins died in 1867 and left $7.5 million in his will for the founding of a medical school with his name on it.

Chocolate Waffle Cookies

MAKES ABOUT 24

8 tablespoons (4 ounces) unsalted butter

2 ounces unsweetened chocolate, chopped

2 large eggs

1 cup firmly packed light brown sugar

¾ teaspoon vanilla extract

¼ teaspoon almond extract

1 teaspoon baking powder

¾ teaspoon salt

1½ cups (6.7 ounces) all-purpose flour

Confectioners' sugar, for dusting

Fact: The first fully electric waffle iron was made July 26, 1911.

1 In a medium-size, microwave-safe bowl or a 2-cup Pyrex measuring cup, melt the butter on high for 30 seconds. Add the chopped chocolate and stir until melted; heat for another 20 seconds in the microwave if the chocolate does not fully melt. Let cool for about 5 minutes.

2 In a mixing bowl, whisk together the eggs, brown sugar, vanilla, and almond extract. Add the melted chocolate, and then stir in the baking powder, salt, and flour. Mix just until blended.

3 Preheat the waffle iron as directed by the manufacturer. Brush the hot waffle iron with oil or shortening (butter will burn, so avoid using that).

4 Drop tablespoonfuls of dough onto the waffle iron. Close the iron and bake for 1 to 1½ minutes, or until the cookies are set. Let cool on a wire rack or serve warm, dusted with confectioners' sugar. Continue making cookies until your batter is gone. The cookies come out of the iron kind of soft, but they firm up as they cool.

Baker's Note: If you're really in a rush, try this variation recommended by my sister: Grease your waffle iron with vegetable oil and place a section of canned biscuit or cinnamon roll dough on each burner. Cook for 1 to 2 minutes or until golden.

Banana Split Cups MAKES 12

CRUST

¾ cup graham cracker crumbs

1½ tablespoons granulated sugar

3 tablespoons (1.5 ounces) unsalted butter, melted

TOPPING

6 tablespoons (3 tablespoons) unsalted
    or salted butter, softened

²/₃ cup confectioners' sugar

1 large pasteurized egg

½ teaspoon vanilla extract

1 large banana, sliced

1 (8-ounce) can crushed pineapple in
    juice, drained, juice reserved

Sweetened whipped topping

½ cup toasted and chopped walnuts

12 maraschino cherries

1 Preheat the oven to 325°F and place a rack in the center. Line twelve muffin cups with paper liners.

2 **Make the crust:** In a mixing bowl, combine the graham cracker crumbs and sugar; add the melted butter and stir well. Divide evenly among the muffin cups and press down tightly. Bake for about 5 minutes, keeping a close eye on them to prevent burning. Let cool completely in the muffin cups.

National Banana
Split Day

Declared by the University of Pittsburgh, the inventor's alma mater, Banana Split Day honors pharmacy student David Evans Strickler who, in 1904, cut a banana in half and built a sundae over it.

In honor of this humble and innovative ice cream genius, treat yourself to an actual banana split, or carry a batch of these convenient "cups" to the office.

Other Events on This Day:
First CAT scan in 1973

3 **Make the topping:** In a medium-size mixing bowl, beat the butter and confectioners' sugar until creamy. Beat in the pasteurized egg and vanilla. Spoon the mixture into each cup, dividing evenly; you'll use about a tablespoon per muffin cup. Toss the banana slices in a little reserved pineapple juice to keep them from turning brown. Lay two banana slices over the mixture in each cup, and then spoon the crushed pineapple over the bananas, dividing the pineapple evenly among the cups. Top the pineapple with a very small spoonful of whipped cream. Chill for 2 hours, or until the banana splits are firm. When ready to serve, top with more sweetened whipped cream, chopped nuts, and maraschino cherries. Serve in the paper liners or peel them away.

AUGUST 26

𝒩ational 𝒟og 𝒟ay

Woof! It's National Dog Day! Created in 2004 by Colleen Paige, a celebrity animal behaviorist, lifestyle expert, and founder of the Animal Miracle Network, Dog Day salutes canines that have braved life in shelters, put their life on the line in rescue careers, and given us loyal companionship.

Our corgi, Lizzie, loves these meat-flavored dog biscuits. They're so easy to put together, my entrepreneurial daughter bakes them, puts them in cute sacks, and sells them to the neighbors.

𝒪ther 𝒮vents on 𝒯his 𝒟ay:
Women's Equality Day

Lizzie's Dog Biscuits
MAKES ABOUT 18, DEPENDING ON THE SIZE OF YOUR CUTTER

1 cup quick-cooking oats (not instant)
½ cup (2.8 ounces) rice flour
1 large egg
1 (2.5-ounce) jar meat-flavored baby food
2 ounces water

1 Preheat the oven to 350°F and place a rack in the center. Line a baking sheet with parchment paper or nonstick foil.

2 Mix the oats, rice flour, egg, baby food, and water together in a large mixing bowl. Press the dough about ¼ inch thick on a piece of parchment paper. Using a small cookie cutter, cut out your favorite shapes and transfer them to the prepared baking sheet. These don't spread, so you don't have to space them out very much. Bake for 20 minutes. Turn the cookies and bake for another 20 minutes. Let cool completely on the pan or on a wire rack.

Banana Bars with Amaretto Frosting MAKES 36

BARS
2 cups (9 ounces) all-purpose flour
1 teaspoon baking soda
½ teaspoon salt
½ teaspoon ground cinnamon
8 tablespoons (4 ounces) unsalted butter, room temperature
1½ cups granulated sugar
2 large eggs
1 cup regular or light sour cream
1 teaspoon vanilla extract
1 cup mashed banana

AMARETTO FROSTING
8 tablespoons (4 ounces) unsalted or salted butter, room temperature
2 cups confectioners' sugar, sifted
1 tablespoon whole or 2% milk
2 to 3 tablespoons amaretto liqueur (see Baker's Notes)

⅓ cup store-bought butterscotch sundae sauce, chilled

AUGUST 27

First Oil Well in America

O n this day in 1859, Colonel Edwin L. Drake drilled the first successful oil well in the United States. Known as Petroleum Day, it is a day to recognize achievements in the oil and gas industry or, depending on how you look at it, a day to reflect on ways to curb our petroleum usage. I'm not sure how eating a banana plays into this, but I couldn't let the fact that it's also Banana Lover's Day "slip" by, so here's my favorite banana bar recipe.

Other Events on This Day:
LBJ Day in Texas

1 Preheat the oven to 350°F and place a rack in the center. Spray a 10 by 15-inch jelly-roll pan with baking spray.

2 **Make the bars:** Mix the flour, baking soda, salt, and cinnamon together in a medium-size bowl; set aside.

3 In the bowl of a stand mixer fitted with a paddle attachment, or in a large mixing bowl, using a handheld electric mixer, beat the butter and sugar on medium speed until light and creamy. Add the eggs, one at a time, beating well after each addition. Stir in the sour cream, vanilla, and banana, until well mixed. By hand or using the lowest speed of the mixer, add the flour mixture and stir until incorporated. Spread evenly in the prepared pan and bake for 20 to 25 minutes, or until a toothpick inserted in the center comes out clean. Let cool completely in the pan.

4 **Make the frosting:** In a mixing bowl, combine the butter and 1 cup of the confectioners' sugar. Beat on the low

speed of a handheld electric mixer until combined, and then gradually add the remaining cup of confectioners' sugar and the tablespoon of milk. Increase the mixer speed to high. Add the amaretto until you've reached a level where you can taste it and the icing is still of a spreading consistency.

5 Frost with the amaretto frosting. Put the butterscotch topping in a zipper bag. Snip a tiny piece off the bottom corner of the bag and drizzle the topping over the frosting.

Baker's Notes: Amaretto-flavored liquid coffee creamer can be substituted for the amaretto. If you really like amaretto, brush about 2 tablespoons of straight amaretto over the cooled bars before frosting.

AUGUST 28

Tom Thumb Locomotive Invented

Today in 1830, Peter Cooper's newly designed Tom Thumb locomotive rolled along a track pulling a wagonload of people while a horse pulling a B&O Railroad car ran alongside it. While Cooper's intent was to prove that steam trains could do the job better than horses, the Tom Thumb threw a belt and the horse won. Still, the demonstration was deemed a great success, and it wasn't long before the B&O Railroad replaced horses with steam-powered trains.

Other Events on This Day: Martin Luther King Jr. gave his "I Have a Dream" speech.

Chocolate-Covered Cherry Thumbprints   MAKES ABOUT 27

1½ cups (6.8 ounces) all-purpose flour

½ cup unsweetened natural cocoa powder

½ teaspoon salt

¼ teaspoon baking powder

¼ teaspoon baking soda

8 tablespoons (4 ounces) unsalted butter, room temperature

1 cup granulated sugar

1 large egg

1½ teaspoons vanilla extract

About ⅔ cup sour cherry preserves or cherry jam

3 ounces semisweet chocolate, chopped

1 Preheat the oven to 350°F and place a rack in the center. Line two baking sheets with nonstick foil or parchment paper.

2 Mix the flour, cocoa powder, salt, baking powder, and baking soda together in a small bowl; set aside.

3 In the bowl of a stand mixer fitted with a paddle attachment, or in a large mixing bowl, using a handheld electric

mixer, beat the butter and sugar on medium speed until creamy. Reduce the mixer speed to low and beat in the egg and vanilla. By hand or using the lowest speed of the mixer, stir in the flour mixture, being careful not to overbeat.

4 Scoop up level tablespoonfuls of dough and shape into about twenty-seven balls. Arrange about 2 inches apart on the prepared baking sheets. Press down the center of each ball with your thumb. Place a rounded ½ teaspoon- ful of preserves in each thumbprint. Bake the cookies for about 10 minutes, or until they appear set, then transfer to a wire rack to cool completely.

5 When the cookies are cool, place the chocolate in a small, microwave-safe bowl and melt at 50 percent power or lower, stopping to stir every 30 seconds. Drizzle the melted chocolate decoratively over the cookies and leave at room temperature until the chocolate sets.

Alfajores MAKES ABOUT 32 SANDWICHES

2 cups (9 ounces) all-purpose flour

1 cup cornstarch

¼ teaspoon salt

1 teaspoon baking powder

1 cup (8 ounces) unsalted
    butter, softened

²/₃ cup granulated sugar

1 large egg

2 large egg yolks

3 tablespoons whiskey,
    brandy, or rum

¾ teaspoon vanilla extract

¼ teaspoon lemon zest (optional)

About 1 cup homemade or store-
    bought *dulce de leche*

²/₃ cup sweetened flaked or shredded coconut
    or finely chopped nuts, for rolling

AUGUST 29

Death of Atahualpa

In 1533, Atahualpa, the last Incan king of Peru, was murdered on orders from Spanish conqueror Francisco Pizarro. This is said to have been the end of the Incan Empire.

Mark the date with a cookie. This recipe was inspired by my friend Louise, who convinced me to try *alfajores*, a light cornstarch-based sandwich cookie filled with a popular South American spread called *dulce de leche*.

Other Events on This Day:
Lemon Juice Day

1 Preheat the oven to 325°F and place a rack in the center. Line two baking sheets with parchment paper or nonstick foil.

2 Mix the flour, cornstarch, salt, and baking powder together in a medium-size bowl; set aside.

3 In the bowl of a stand mixer fitted with a paddle attachment, or in a large mixing bowl, using a handheld electric mixer, beat the butter and sugar on medium speed until light and fluffy. Beat in the egg and egg yolks, one at a time. Beat in the whiskey, vanilla, and lemon zest (if using). By hand or using the lowest speed of the mixer, stir the flour mixture into the butter mixture to make a somewhat dry dough.

4 Working on a flat, floured or parchment-lined surface, scoop out portions of dough and press them to about ⅛-inch thickness. Using a round cutter between 1 and 2 inches in diameter, punch out circles and place them on the prepared baking sheets. Don't worry about spreading, because the shape of the dough rounds shouldn't change much. Bake the cookies one sheet at a time for 10 to 12 minutes, or until they appear dry—the cookies don't brown much. Let them cool on the baking sheets for about 4 minutes, then transfer to a wire rack to cool completely. Spread the underside of one cookie with the *dulce de leche*, then top base to base with another cookie. Repeat until all the cookies are sandwiched. Roll the edges in coconut or chopped nuts.

Houston Founded

On this day in 1836, Houston was founded along the banks of the Buffalo Bayou. The country's fourth largest city, culturally diverse Houston embraces science, arts, sports, business, and technology. It's the home of NASA, the world's largest medical center, the Energy Corridor, and several

Whole Wheat Fig Bars

MAKES 24

FILLING

6 ounces dried figs, chopped
  (1 very tightly packed heaping cup)
2 cups water
½ cup apple juice
¼ cup granulated sugar
½ teaspoon lemon zest

DOUGH

1 cup plus 2 tablespoons (5 ounces) white whole wheat or all-purpose flour

⅛ teaspoon baking soda

¼ teaspoon salt

4 tablespoons (2 ounces) unsalted butter, softened

¼ cup firmly packed dark brown sugar

¼ cup granulated sugar

1 large egg

1 large egg yolk

1 teaspoon vanilla extract

1 **Make the filling:** Combine the figs, water, juice, sugar, and lemon zest in a saucepan and bring to a boil over medium-high heat. Reduce the heat to a simmer and simmer uncovered for 35 to 45 minutes, stirring every so often, or until the figs start to fall apart and the mixture appears to have thickened somewhat. Remove from the heat. Let cool, then puree in a food processor or blender. Keep chilled until ready to use.

2 **Make the dough:** Mix the flour, baking soda, and salt together in a small bowl; set aside.

3 In the bowl of a stand mixer fitted with a paddle attachment, or in a large mixing bowl, using a handheld electric mixer, beat the butter and both sugars on medium speed until creamy. Beat in the egg, egg yolk, and vanilla. By hand, stir in the flour mixture to form a dough. Wrap in plastic wrap and chill for at least 3 hours, or until ready to use.

4 When ready to bake, take out the dough and let it come to room temperature. Preheat the oven to 375°F and place a rack in the center. Line a large baking sheet with parchment paper.

5 On a well-floured surface, roll the dough into a 10-inch square. Cut lengthwise into three strips. Spoon about one-third of the filling in a long, thin line down the center of the first strip. With a spatula, lift the dough on each side of that first strip of dough and gently fold over the fig filling,

public and private universities. Houston has its own fine arts museum, the Menil Collection, and the Mark Rothko Chapel, which was recognized as one of the greatest artistic achievements of the second half of the twentieth century. In honor of Houston, here's a cookie made with a fruit that grows particularly well in Houston's climate.

Other Events on This Day: **Toasted Marshmallow Day; Frankenstein Day (Mary Shelley's birthday [b. 1797]); Melbourne, Australia, founded in 1835**

pressing the seam together and covering the figs. Repeat with the remaining two strips of dough and figs. With your spatula, lift one strip of dough and invert seam side down onto the prepared baking sheet. Repeat with the other two strips, spacing the strips about 3 inches apart. Bake the fig strips for 15 to 17 minutes. Remove from the oven and let cool on the baking sheet for about 10 minutes. Score each strip into eight pieces, so that you have a total of twenty-four cookies.

Eat Outside Day

Cross your fingers and hope for good weather, because today is eat outside day.

Pack a lunch and brave the elements or go to your favorite restaurant with a patio.

Since it also happens to be National Trail Mix Day, here's a cookie you can make with your favorite flavor of trail mix.

Other Events on This Day:
Invent a New Sandwich Day

Crunchy Trail Mix Cookies
MAKES ABOUT 36

1 cup (4.5 ounces) all-purpose flour
1 teaspoon baking soda
1 teaspoon ground cinnamon
½ teaspoon salt
12 tablespoons (6 ounces) unsalted
    butter, room temperature
½ cup firmly packed dark brown sugar
½ cup firmly packed light brown sugar
½ cup granulated sugar
2 tablespoons honey
2 tablespoons pure maple syrup
1 large egg
1 teaspoon vanilla extract
3 cups old-fashioned oats
1½ cups nutty trail mix (see Baker's Note)

1 Preheat the oven to 350°F and place a rack in the center. Line two baking sheets with nonstick foil or parchment paper.

2 In a medium-size bowl, stir together the flour, baking soda, cinnamon, and salt; set aside.

3 In the bowl of a stand mixer fitted with a paddle attachment, or in a large mixing bowl, using a handheld electric mixer, beat the butter and all the sugars on medium speed until creamy. Beat in the honey and maple syrup. Reduce the mixer speed slightly and beat in the egg and

vanilla. By hand or using the lowest speed of the mixer, add the flour mixture, followed by the oats and trail mix.

4 Dampen your hands with a little water and form the mixture into 1-inch balls. Arrange about 2½ inches apart on the prepared baking sheets and press down slightly to make rounds. Bake one sheet at a time for 11 to 13 minutes, or until the edges are browned. Transfer to a wire rack to cool completely. They will crisp and firm up quite a bit as they cool.

Baker's Note: If the mix has whole almonds or large pieces in it, chop it up a little with a chef's knife before adding to the dough.

Floating Holiday: Grandparents Day was created by Marian McQuade, a housewife in Fayette County, West Virginia, who wanted to raise awareness of the elderly in the community and connect children to the wisdom only they can provide. Jimmy Carter endorsed that holiday and, in 1978, proclaimed it would be celebrated the Sunday after Labor Day. While today's too early to celebrate, it's a good day to mark your calendar and start thinking about special treats to bake the grandparents in your life.

Pat's Breakfast Cookies

MAKES ABOUT 32

½ pound thinly sliced bacon

1 cup (4.5 ounces) all-purpose flour

¼ teaspoon baking soda

¼ teaspoon salt

8 tablespoons (4 ounces) unsalted
    butter, room temperature

¾ cup granulated sugar

1 large egg

1 teaspoon vanilla extract

2 cups multigrain flakes cereal with bits of
    dried fruit, crushed after measuring

½ cup dried cranberries, chopped

Better Breakfast Month and International Bacon Day

September is Better Breakfast Month, which means you have thirty days to either upgrade your breakfast or just try something different. Because many people take comfort in eating the same breakfast every day, this could be challenging. So rather than tamper with your breakfast, why not serve these cookies as a morning snack? Better yet, serve them at a party and see if people can guess the secret ingredient, which honors International Bacon Day. My stepmother, Pat, came up with this recipe.

Other Events on This Day:
Telephone Operator Day in honor of Emma M. Nutt, who became the first woman telephone operator in 1878

Back to School!

If you've been known to throw a cookie or two in the old lunchbox, I've got just the recipe for you. Made with a full 2 cups of granola, this cookie has some nutritional value, tastes great, and is the best way to use that last bit of granola in the bottom of the box. In this case, that box would be Cascadian Farms Granola, which is where I found the original version of this recipe.

1 Preheat the oven to 350°F and place a rack in the center. Have ready two ungreased baking sheets.

2 Cook the bacon until crisp. Let it cool, and then chop it into very small pieces.

3 Mix the flour, baking soda, and salt together in a bowl; set aside.

4 In the bowl of a stand mixer fitted with a paddle attachment, or in a large mixing bowl, using a handheld electric mixer, beat the butter and sugar on medium speed until creamy. Reduce the mixer speed slightly and beat in the egg and vanilla. By hand or using the lowest speed of the mixer, stir in the flour mixture, followed by the cereal, cranberries, and bacon.

5 Drop rounded teaspoonfuls of batter 2 inches apart onto the baking sheets. Bake one sheet at a time for 10 to 12 minutes, or until the cookies are browned around the edges. Let cool on the baking sheets for about 4 minutes, then transfer to a wire rack to cool completely.

Granola Chocolate Chip Cookies MAKES 36

1 cup plus 2 tablespoons (5 ounces)
    all-purpose or white whole wheat flour

½ teaspoon baking soda

⅜ teaspoon salt

8 tablespoons (4 ounces) unsalted
    butter, room temperature

6 tablespoons granulated sugar

6 tablespoons firmly packed dark
    or light brown sugar

1 teaspoon vanilla extract

1 large egg

2 cups granola, lightly crushed
    after measuring

½ cup extra-dark chocolate chips

1. Preheat the oven to 350°F and place a rack in the center. Line two baking sheets with nonstick foil or parchment paper.

2. Mix the flour, baking soda, and salt together in a bowl; set aside.

3. In the bowl of a stand mixer fitted with a paddle attachment, or in a large mixing bowl, using a handheld electric mixer, beat the butter and both sugars on medium speed until fluffy. Beat in the vanilla and egg and continue beating for another 30 seconds. Add the flour and stir on the lowest speed of the mixer until the flour is almost fully absorbed, then add the granola and chocolate chips. Stir well.

4. Shape the dough into 1-inch balls and arrange about 2 inches apart on the prepared baking sheets. Press down to make rounds about ½ inch thick. Bake one sheet at a time for 11 to 13 minutes. Transfer to a wire rack to cool completely.

Double Chocolate Almond Biscotti

MAKES 24 LARGE, PLUS SOME SMALL ONES FROM THE END

2¼ cups (11.25 ounces) all-purpose flour

¼ cup unsweetened cocoa powder

1 teaspoon baking powder

¼ teaspoon salt

8 tablespoons (4 ounces) unsalted butter, softened

1¼ cups plus 2 teaspoons granulated sugar

1 teaspoon almond extract

2 large eggs

1 cup whole almonds, toasted and roughly chopped

½ cup semisweet chocolate chips

¾ teaspoon ground cinnamon

Fact: Sullivan coined the phrase, "Form ever follows function."

Other Events on This Day: George Gershwin's Porgy and Bess opened on Broadway in 1935. In 1969, the first automatic teller machine opened at the Chemical Bank in Rockville Centre, New York.

SEPTEMBER 3

Skyscraper Day

Skyscraper Day celebrates the birthday of American architect Louis Sullivan, who was born in 1856. Known as "the Father of Modern Architecture," Sullivan took advantage of the mass production of steel by designing tall buildings with steel frameworks. He is also known for replacing classical elements of the day with his own flora designs and using vertical bands to draw the eye upward and emphasize height. His most famous buildings include the Wainwright Building in St. Louis and the Carson, Pirie, Scott, and Company Building (now the Sullivan Center) in Chicago.

1 Preheat the oven to 350°F and place a rack in the center. Line a baking sheet with parchment paper or nonstick foil.

2 Mix the flour, cocoa powder, baking powder, and salt together in a medium-size bowl; set aside.

3 In the bowl of a stand mixer fitted with a paddle attachment, or in a large mixing bowl, using a hand-held electric mixer, beat the butter and 1¼ cups of the sugar on medium speed until creamy. Beat in the extract, and then beat in the eggs. Reduce the speed to low and add the flour mixture. When the flour mixture is fully blended, stir in the almonds and chocolate chips.

4 On the prepared baking sheet, shape the dough into a rectangle about 12 inches long and 4 inches wide. Mix the remaining 2 teaspoons of sugar with the cinnamon and sprinkle over the top of the rectangle. Bake for 35 minutes, or until slightly firm to the touch. Let cool on the baking sheet for 35 minutes. When cool, set on a cutting board, and using a large chef's knife, slice crosswise slightly on the diagonal to create, long, thin slices. Place cut side down on the baking sheet. Bake for 18 to 20 minutes, turning halfway through. Let cool completely on a wire rack.

SEPTEMBER 4

National Newspaper Carrier Day

Not to be confused with the October News-paper Carriers Day declared by Ronald Reagan, this day commemorates the first paper boy hired in 1833 to deliver the *New York Sun*. His name was Barney Flaherty, and he was ten years old.

This cookie is a tribute to an old riddle my grandfather used to tell me. Like the riddle, this recipe is a good one for

Black and White and Red All Over Cookies

MAKES ABOUT 36

1 (18.25-ounce) box red velvet cake mix

2 large eggs

8 tablespoons (4 ounces) unsalted butter, room temperature

½ cup white chips

½ cup semisweet chocolate chips

½ cup roughly chopped toasted macadamia nuts (optional, but it is National Macadamia Day)

1. Preheat the oven to 350°F and place a rack in the center. Line two baking sheets with nonstick foil or parchment paper.

2. In the bowl of a stand mixer fitted with a paddle attachment, or in a large mixing bowl, using a handheld electric mixer, beat the cake mix, eggs, and butter on medium speed to form a smooth dough. Stir in the chips and macadamias.

3. Scoop up tablespoonfuls of dough and shape into 1-inch balls. Place the balls 1 inch apart on the prepared baking sheets and flatten slightly with the palm of your hand.

4. Bake one sheet at a time for 10 to 12 minutes, or until done. Transfer to a wire rack to cool completely.

Chocolate Cookie Truffles

MAKES 48

1 package (14 to 16 ounces) chocolate
    sandwich cookies, such as Oreos
1 (8-ounce) package cream cheese, softened
1 pound semisweet chocolate, for dipping

1. In a food processor, process the cookies into crumbs—you should get about 4¼ cups. Transfer the crumbs to a large mixing bowl. Add the cream cheese and stir until you have a big, gloppy mass of black goo. At this point, it's hard to believe this mixture transforms into a tasty treat, but forge ahead! It will all work out. Shape into small balls (about 1 inch) and place in the refrigerator to chill.

2. Have ready a sheet of parchment paper. Melt the chocolate in the top of a double boiler or in a chocolate warmer. Alternatively, you may melt it in the microwave. Heat on 50 percent power for 1 minute. Stir and repeat, stirring at 30-second intervals until the chocolate is melted and smooth. To keep it warm, set the bowl of chocolate on a heating pad—the kind you'd use for sore muscles. Skewer the truffles on toothpicks, dunk in the warm chocolate, and place on the parchment paper. Leave at room temperature to set.

kids. Of course, if you ask them the old riddle, they may give you a different answer involving penguins.

Other Events on This Day: **National Macadamia Day, Box camera patented in 1888**

Labor Day

Since Labor Day was declared a federal holiday in 1894, Americans have been honoring the work force by taking the day off and relaxing alone or with friends. Celebrated on the first Monday of September, Labor Day is a weekend for traveling, barbecues, or just sitting back and enjoying the (hopefully!) cooler weather. Cousin to cake balls, these truffles are popular with the kids in our neighborhood.

Other Events on This Day: **Be Late for Something Day**

Pamper a payroll specialist this week! Founded by the American Payroll Association in 1996, this week recognizes staff working in corporate payroll and government withholding programs such as Social Security, Medicare, fair labor standards, and child support, which, according to the American Payroll Association, contribute 71.9 percent of US Treasury revenue. As for cookies, this is a perfect day to try an old recipe inspired by a candy bar.

Other Events on This Day:
Coffee Ice Cream Day

Payroll Bars MAKES 24

CRUST

6 tablespoons (3 ounces) unsalted butter

1 (18.25-ounce) box yellow cake mix

1 large egg

FILLING

3 cups miniature marshmallows

4 tablespoons (2 ounces) unsalted butter

2 cups peanut butter chips

²/₃ cup light corn syrup

2 teaspoons vanilla extract

2 cups salted peanuts

2 cups crispy rice cereal, such as Rice Krispies

1 Preheat the oven to 350°F and place a rack in the center. Line a 9 by 13-inch metal pan with nonstick foil, or line it with regular foil and spray the foil with flour-added baking spray.

2 **Make the crust:** In a small microwave-safe bowl, microwave the butter on high for 30 seconds, or until melted. In the bowl of a stand mixer fitted with a paddle attachment, or in a large mixing bowl, using a handheld electric mixer, mix the cake mix, melted butter, and egg at medium speed to make a dough. Press the dough into the prepared pan and bake for 12 to 18 minutes.

3 **Make the filling:** Sprinkle the marshmallows evenly over the baked dough and return the pan to the oven for 5 minutes to melt the marshmallows. In a large (3-quart) saucepan, melt the butter over medium heat. Reduce the heat to low and add the peanut butter chips and corn syrup. Stir until melted. Remove from the heat and stir in the vanilla, peanuts, and cereal. Drop blobs of the cereal mixture over the marshmallows, spreading gently to cover. Let cool completely, then chill until very cold so the bars will be easier to slice. Grasp the foil, lift from the pan, set on a cutting board, and use a chef's knife trim the edges. Cut the bars into squares.

Chocolate Salami

MAKES ABOUT 30 SLICES

8 ounces dark or semisweet chocolate, chopped

4 tablespoons (2 ounces) unsalted butter

¼ cup heavy cream

1 cup hazelnuts, skins removed, or almonds,
   toasted and roughly chopped

1 cup broken graham crackers or firm
   cookies, such as digestive biscuits

Handful of miniature marshmallows (optional)

¾ cup of your choice of dried fruit, such
   as golden raisins or cranberries

Confectioners' sugar, for rolling

1 Combine the chocolate, butter, and cream in a microwave-safe mixing bowl and heat on 50 percent power, stirring every 60 seconds, until smooth and melted. Alternatively, you may do this in a large saucepan set over low to medium-low heat.

2 Add the nuts, cookies, marshmallows (if using), and fruit to the melted chocolate. At this point it will be fairly soupy. Chill the mixture for about an hour, or until cool enough to transfer to a piece of plastic wrap. With a scraper, scrape the chocolate mixture onto a big sheet of plastic wrap and push it into a blob. Alternatively, you can divide it in half and make two blobs on two sheets of plastic. It's a little easier to work with if you make your rolls smaller. Cover the blobs loosely with the plastic wrap and continue to chill for another hour, or until firm enough to shape into sausage(s). When firm, shape each blob to resemble a sausage. Chill for another 2 hours, or until firm enough to slice.

3 When chilled, roll your sausage(s) in confectioners' sugar. Slice with a serrated knife. If the salami is too firm to slice, let it sit at room temperature for a few minutes.

Salami Day

Founded by salami lovers in 2007, this charcuterie lover's holiday recognizes everything from cotto to sopressatta. To celebrate, buy yourself a salami sandwich and reflect on salami's rich cultural history. While its origin is unknown, the dried and fermented sausage is believed to hail from the early Greeks and Romans, who used it as a way of preserving meat.

If you like chocolate better than salami and still want to participate in salami day, today's recipe should come in handy. Chocolate salami is a mass of firm ganache stuffed with nuts, candy, and dried fruit and rolled into the shape of a sausage.

Other Events on This Day:
Henry David Thoreau left Walden Pond in 1847.

In November 1965, UNES-CO proclaimed September 8 International Literacy Day, the goal of which was to raise awareness of the 780 million adults who do not know how to read or write and the 94 to 115 million children without access to education. Sponsored annually by the International Reading Association, the day is marked by many events throughout the world.

To celebrate, bake something with the kids and teach them the importance of following written directions.

Other Events on This Day: **Founding of Saint Augustine, Florida, in 1565; Scotch tape invented in 1930**

Flourless Peanut Butter Cookies MAKES ABOUT 40

1 large egg
1 cup granulated sugar, plus
    2 tablespoons for topping
1 teaspoon baking soda
½ teaspoon Mexican
    vanilla extract
1 cup creamy peanut butter
1 teaspoon ground cinnamon

1 Preheat the oven to 350°F and place a rack in the center. Have ready two ungreased baking sheets.

2 In a mixing bowl, using a wooden spoon, beat the egg, 1 cup of the sugar, baking soda, and vanilla. Next, beat in the peanut butter.

3 Drop teaspoonfuls of batter onto about 2 inches apart on the baking sheets, or if you want, shape into little balls. The dough will be slightly sticky, but it's usually fairly easy to shape into balls. In a small bowl, mix the remaining 2 tablespoons of sugar with the cinnamon. Sprinkle the tops or roll the balls in the cinnamon sugar. Bake one sheet at a time for 10 minutes, or just until the edges barely start to brown. Let cool on the baking sheet for about 5 minutes, then transfer to a wire rack to cool completely.

On this day in 1850, California joined the Union as a non-slave state. Celebrate "the Golden State" by baking a cookie featuring some of California's finest—apricots, walnuts, oranges, and bears!

California Cookies MAKES ABOUT 28

½ cup honey-flavored teddy bear–shaped
    cookies, such as Teddy Grahams
¾ cup (3.4 ounces) all-purpose flour
½ teaspoon baking soda
⅛ teaspoon ground cinnamon
½ teaspoon salt
9 tablespoons (4.5 ounces) cold or
    very cool unsalted butter

¾ cup firmly packed light brown sugar

¼ cup granulated sugar

1 large egg

½ teaspoon orange zest

½ teaspoon vanilla extract

1 slightly rounded cup old-fashioned oats

½ cup toasted chopped walnuts

1 cup dried apricots, chopped

2 ounces white chocolate, chopped

Resist the temptation to eat all the teddy bear crackers as you bake!

Other Events on This Day:
Weinerschnitzel Day

1 Preheat the oven to 350°F and place a rack in the center. Line two baking sheets with parchment paper or nonstick foil.

2 Grind the cookies in a food processor or blender and set aside. You should have a little less than ½ cup of crumbs.

3 Mix the flour, baking soda, cinnamon, and salt together in a medium-size bowl; set aside.

4 In the bowl of a stand mixer fitted with a paddle attachment, or in a large mixing bowl, using a handheld electric mixer, beat the butter and both sugars on medium speed until light and creamy. Add the egg, orange zest, and vanilla and continue beating on high speed for 1 minute, or until the batter is very light. Stir in the cookie crumbs, followed by the flour mixture, oats, walnuts, apricots, and white chocolate.

5 Scoop up tablespoonfuls of dough and shape into balls a little less than 1 inch in diameter. Arrange 2½ inches apart on the prepared baking sheets and press down slightly. Bake one sheet at a time for 8 to 11 minutes, or until the cookies have spread and appear golden brown and set. Let cool on the baking sheets for 1 to 2 minutes, then transfer to a wire rack to cool completely.

DNA fingerprinting was discovered in London by English geneticist Sir Alec Jeffries in 1984.

While studying the genetic patterns of inheritance of illness in families, Jeffries noticed that all fingerprints were unique and could be traced back to one core individual.

I tried a lot of different thumbprint recipes, and the winner was this one, adapted from an old issue of *Cooking Light*. The original cookies were rolled in hazelnuts and filled with Nutella, but I used pecans and a rich filling that is a cross between ganache and fudge.

Other Events on This Day:
National Chewing Gum Day

Double Chocolate Thumbprints MAKES 24

COOKIES

1 cup (4.5 ounces) all-purpose flour

1 cup confectioners' sugar

⅓ cup unsweetened natural cocoa powder

¼ teaspoon salt

8 tablespoons (4 ounces) unsalted butter, room temperature

2 large egg yolks

1 teaspoon vanilla extract

FILLING

1 tablespoon (0.5 ounce) unsalted butter

4 ounces semisweet chocolate

2 tablespoons golden syrup or light corn syrup

1 tablespoon water

1 teaspoon vanilla extract

1 Preheat the oven to 350°F and place a rack in the center. Have ready two ungreased baking sheets.

2 **Make the cookies:** Mix the flour, confectioners' sugar, cocoa powder, and salt together in a small bowl; set aside.

3 In the bowl of a stand mixer fitted with a paddle attachment, or in a large mixing bowl, using a handheld electric mixer, beat the butter on medium speed until creamy. Beat in the egg yolks and vanilla. By hand or using the lowest speed of the mixer, stir in the flour mixture.

4 Shape the dough into balls just about 1 inch in diameter. Arrange 2 inches apart on the baking sheets, and with your thumb, make an indentation in the center of each ball. Bake one sheet at a time for 10 to 12 minutes. While the cookies bake, prepare the filling.

5 **Make the filling:** In a small, microwave-safe bowl, melt the butter and chocolate together, using 50 percent power, and stirring every 30 seconds. When completely melted, stir in the syrup, water, and vanilla. Let cool slightly—the mixture will thicken as it cools.

6   Remove the cookies from the oven and immediately press
    the little indentations back down with the tip of a wooden
    spoon. Let cool slightly on the baking sheet, then, with a
    small spoon, fill the little indentations with the chocolate
    filling. Let the filling set.

Janet's One-Bowl Honey Cookies   MAKES 30

²/₃ cup vegetable oil
1 cup granulated sugar
1 large egg
¼ cup honey
2 teaspoons baking soda
½ teaspoon salt
1 teaspoon vanilla extract
2 cups (9 ounces) all-purpose flour
Sparkling sugar, for rolling

Fact: Honey is sweeter than sugar and has several B vitamins.

1   Preheat the oven to 375°F and place a rack in the center.
    Have ready two ungreased baking sheets.

2   Stir the oil, granulated sugar, egg, honey, baking soda,
    salt, and vanilla together in a large mixing bowl. Add the
    flour and stir until fully blended.

3   Shape the cookies into balls about ¾ to 1 inch in diameter
    and roll them in sparkling sugar. Arrange 2½ inches apart
    on the baking sheets. Bake one sheet at a time for 10 to
    12 minutes. They should be nicely
    browned around the edges,
    crackly and golden. Let cool
    on a baking sheet for about
    2 minutes, then transfer
    to a wire rack to cool
    completely.

Fact: An average honeybee makes only about ¹/₁₂ teaspoon of honey in its lifetime.

September Is Honey Month

Whether you stir it into tea, drizzle it over biscuits, or pour it into cookie batter, honey is one of the world's favorite sweeteners and has been for thousands of years. Honey's flavor depends on where it comes from. In the United States alone, there are more than three hundred unique varieties of honey, whose flavors depend on their floral source. Popular American flavors include clover and orange blossom.

This recipe was given to me by my friend Janet.

Other Events on This Day: Blueberry Popsicle Day, *Titanic* wreckage located in 1985, US Department of Treasury established in 1789

Video Games Day

Wwhile hours of sitting still playing games doesn't offer any fitness benefits, some studies show that gaming increases various cognitive skills, improves certain reflexes, and may possibly improve vision.

Wakka, wakka, wakka. Celebrate Video Games Day with a batch of these Pac Man–inspired no-bake cookies.

Other Events on This Day:
Chocolate Milk Shake Day

Power Pellets MAKES 36

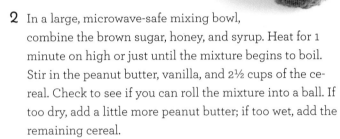

¼ cup firmly packed light brown sugar
2 tablespoons honey
2 tablespoons golden syrup or light corn syrup
1 cup creamy peanut butter
1 teaspoon vanilla extract
2½ to 3 cups cornflakes, lightly
   crushed after measuring
½ cup finely chopped peanuts (optional)
¼ cup toasted wheat germ (optional)

1 Line a baking sheet or two large plates with parchment paper or nonstick foil.

2 In a large, microwave-safe mixing bowl, combine the brown sugar, honey, and syrup. Heat for 1 minute on high or just until the mixture begins to boil. Stir in the peanut butter, vanilla, and 2½ cups of the cereal. Check to see if you can roll the mixture into a ball. If too dry, add a little more peanut butter; if too wet, add the remaining cereal.

3 Scoop up heaping teaspoonfuls of dough, and with buttered hands, shape into balls. Place the balls on the prepared baking sheet. Chill for about 10 minutes, or until the balls are slightly firm. Roll the balls in the chopped peanuts, toasted wheat germ, or a mixture of both. Return the pan to the refrigerator and chill for another hour, or until very firm.

Celiac Awareness Day

The cause of celiac disease is unknown and its symptoms vary from person to person, but the primary reason for the symptoms is a reaction to the gluten in wheat.

Even if you don't have wheat intolerance, it's fun to

Chocolate Truffle Cookies
MAKES 16

6½ ounces good quality dark chocolate, chopped
2 large egg whites, room temperature
⅛ teaspoon cream of tartar
¼ teaspoon vanilla extract
¼ cup granulated sugar

1 Preheat the oven to 350°F and place a rack in the center. Line two baking sheets with parchment paper or nonstick foil.

2 **Melt the chocolate:** Put the chocolate in a microwave-safe bowl and heat on 50 percent power for 1 minute. Stir well. Repeat, heating at 50 percent power and stirring at 30-second intervals until smooth. Set aside.

3 In the bowl of a stand mixer fitted with a whisk attachment or in a large, preferably metal, mixing bowl using an electric mixer on high speed, beat the egg whites and cream of tartar until stiff peaks just start to form. Beat in the vanilla. Add the sugar 1 tablespoon at a time, beating on high, until glossy. With a rubber scraper, fold in the melted chocolate. Using a heaping teaspoon, drop batter 2½ inches apart on one of the prepared baking sheets. Bake one sheet at a time for 8 to 10 minutes or until the cookies appear set. Let cool on the baking sheet for about 2 minutes, then carefully transfer to a wire rack to cool completely.

master a few recipes that are gluten free. This one is fairly simple and doesn't require any special gums or expensive wheat-free baking mix.

𝒪ther 𝒺vents on 𝒯his 𝒟ay: **Positive Thinking Day, Defy Superstition Day, Milton Hershey's birthday (b. 1857)**

ℛed, 𝒲hite, and 𝓑lue 𝓑ars   MAKES 24 SMALL BARS

8 tablespoons (4 ounces) unsalted butter

2 cups white chocolate chips

2 large eggs

½ cup granulated sugar

1 cup (4.5 ounces) all-purpose flour

½ teaspoon salt

½ teaspoon almond extract

¼ cup seedless raspberry preserves or pie filling

¼ cup blueberry preserves or pie filling

¼ cup sliced almonds

1 Preheat the oven to 325°F and place a rack in the center. Line a 9-inch square metal pan with nonstick foil.

2 Melt the butter in a medium-size, microwave-safe bowl on high for 1 minute; stir. Add 1 cup of the chips; let stand. Do not stir.

"𝒯he 𝒮tar-𝒮pangled 𝓑anner" 𝒲ritten

𝒪n this day in 1814, after witnessing the Battle at Fort McHenry from a British ship on which he was being detained, Francis Scott Key wrote a poem on the back of an envelope. It was called "Defense of Fort McHenry." Key gave it to his brother-in-law, who had it printed and distributed. The poem was eventually put to the music of a drinking song and became quite popular, but it wasn't until March 3, 1931, that it was made our national anthem.

Other Events on This Day:
**Cream-Filled Doughnut Day;
the first American lighthouse,
Boston Light, was lit in 1716**

3 With a handheld electric mixer on medium-high speed, beat the eggs in a large mixer bowl until foamy. Add the sugar; beat until light and lemon colored, about 3 minutes. Stir in the white chip mixture and then stir in the flour, salt, and almond extract.

4 Spread about two-thirds of the batter into the prepared pan and bake for 15 to 17 minutes, or until lightly browned around the edges. Let cool slightly in the pan. Soften the preserves in separate small, microwave-safe bowls or cups at 50 percent power for 5 to 10 seconds, then spread over the baked crust, spreading half of the crust with raspberry and the other half with blueberry.

5 Stir the remaining white chips into the reserved batter and drop spoonfuls of batter over the jam, spreading gently to cover it. The jam will still show through a bit. Sprinkle the almonds over the top. Return the pan to the oven and bake for 25 to 30 minutes, or until the edges are browned. Let cool completely in the pan, and then chill briefly (for about an hour) so that you can make a cleaner cut when slicing. Lift the bars from the pan and set on a cutting board. Carefully cut along the center seam where the berry toppings meet, then cut each half into twelve bars.

SEPTEMBER 15

Make a Hat Day

Tip your hat to the art of millinery by celebrating Make a Hat Day. Its origin is unknown, but most sources seem to think the idea came from preschool and elementary teachers who observed that children loved making paper hats (it's true, right?). So make a hat today using butter, sugar, and flour. Modeled after the three-cornered hat worn by the evil Haman, hamantaschen are Jewish cookies eaten throughout the year, but primarily on Purim.

Hamantaschen MAKES ABOUT 30

DOUGH

2 cups (9 ounces) all-purpose flour

1 teaspoon baking powder

1 teaspoon salt

**8 tablespoons (4 ounces) unsalted
    butter, room temperature**

1 (8-ounce) package cream cheese, softened

½ cup granulated sugar

1 large egg, room temperature

1 teaspoon vanilla extract

FILLING

2 cups (12 ounces) pitted prunes

½ cup chopped and toasted walnuts

2 tablespoons granulated sugar

½ teaspoon orange zest

1 large egg yolk mixed with 1 tablespoon water

Other Events on This Day:
International Day of Democracy

1 Preheat the oven to 350°F and place a rack in the center. Line two baking sheets with parchment paper or non-stick foil.

2 **Make the dough:** Mix the flour, baking powder, and salt together in a medium-size bowl; set aside.

3 In the bowl of a stand mixer fitted with a paddle attachment, or in a large mixing bowl, using a handheld electric mixer, beat the butter, cream cheese, and sugar on medium speed until light and creamy. Beat in the egg and vanilla. By hand or using the lowest speed of the mixer, add the flour mixture, ½ cup at a time, to form a soft dough. Wrap the dough tightly and chill while you make the filling.

4 **Make the filling:** Put the prunes in a food processor and process. Add the nuts, sugar, and orange zest and pulse to mix.

5 On a floured surface, roll out the dough to ¼-inch thickness. With a 3-inch round cookie cutter or the rim of a glass, cut out circles and arrange 2½ inches apart on the prepared baking sheets. Place a heaping teaspoon of filling in the center of each circle. With a pastry brush or your fingers, brush the egg mixture around the edge of each circle. Gently fold three sides of the each dough circle over the filling to form a triangle and pinch the corners together, leaving the center of the triangle open to show the filling. Bake one sheet at a time for 13 to 16 minutes, or until the cookies are slightly browned around the edges. Let cool on the baking sheets for a few minutes, then transfer to a wire rack to cool completely.

Mayflower Day

Today in 1620, the Mayflower set sail from Plymouth, England, on a journey that would take the Pilgrims to Provincetown, Massachusetts. Its provisions included oatmeal, peas, vinegar, butter, water, and spices such as sugar, pepper, cloves, cinnamon, mace, nutmegs, and "fruit," which might have referred to currants or raisins. As for livestock, it's said there were a goat, a pig, and some chickens, so it's likely the voyagers had eggs. In honor of the Mayflower, here's a cookie made with ingredients that might have been on the ship.

Other Events on This Day:
Mexican Independence Day, Stepfamily Day, National Cinnamon Raisin Bread Day, aluminum foil went on sale in 1947

Spiced Oatmeal and Currant Cookies   MAKES ABOUT 42

1 cup (4.5 ounces) unbleached all-purpose flour

¾ teaspoon baking soda

½ teaspoon baking powder

1 teaspoon salt

1 teaspoon ground cinnamon

½ teaspoon freshly grated nutmeg

½ teaspoon ground ginger

¼ teaspoon ground pepper

14 tablespoons (7 ounces) unsalted butter, room temperature

1 cup granulated sugar

¼ cup firmly packed light brown sugar

1 large egg

1 teaspoon vanilla extract

½ teaspoon almond extract

2½ cups quick-cooking oats (not instant)

1 cup almonds, toasted and finely chopped

½ cup dried currants

1   Preheat the oven to 375°F and place a rack in the center. Line two baking sheets with nonstick foil or parchment paper.

2   Mix the flour, baking soda, baking powder, salt, cinnamon, nutmeg, ginger, and pepper together in a medium-size bowl; set aside.

3   In the bowl of a stand mixer fitted with a paddle attachment, or in a large mixing bowl, using a handheld electric mixer, beat the butter and both sugars on medium speed until creamy. Beat in the egg, vanilla, and almond extract. Add the flour mixture gradually and stir until combined. Stir in the oats, almonds, and currants.

4   Drop rounded teaspoonfuls of batter 2½ inches apart onto the prepared baking sheets. Bake one sheet at a time for 10 to 12 minutes, or until the cookies appear set and the edges are browned. Let cool on the baking sheets for about 2 minutes, then transfer to a wire rack to cool completely.

1787 Date Bars   MAKES 18

FILLING

¾ **pound dates, pitted and finely chopped**

½ **cup granulated sugar**

¾ **cup water**

1 **tablespoon unsalted butter**

¾ **teaspoon vanilla extract**

²⁄₃ **cup toasted and finely chopped walnuts**

CRUST

1 **cup old-fashioned oats**

1 **cup (4.5 ounces) white whole wheat flour**

¼ **teaspoon baking powder**

¾ **teaspoon baking soda**

²⁄₃ **cup firmly packed light brown sugar**

¼ **teaspoon salt**

6 **tablespoons (3 ounces) unsalted butter, melted**

1 Preheat the oven to 350°F and place a rack in the center. Line a 9-inch square metal pan with nonstick foil, or line it with regular foil and spray the foil with flour-added baking spray.

2 **Make the filling:** Combine the dates, sugar, and water in a small saucepan. Bring to a boil and simmer uncovered for about 10 minutes, or until the mixture is thick. Remove from the heat. Mash slightly with a fork and stir in the butter, vanilla, and walnuts. At this point, you can set it aside and use it whenever you're ready.

3 **Make the crust:** In a large mixing bowl, combine the oats, flour, baking powder, baking soda, brown sugar, and salt. Pour in the melted butter and stir until mixed. Press about two-thirds of this mixture into the prepared pan to make the crust. Spread the filling over the crust; if the filling has become very thick, drop it out in little blobs and nudge them together with your spoon. Sprinkle the remaining oat mixture over the top. Bake for 20 to 24 minutes, or until the filling is hot and bubbly. Let cool completely in the pan. Lift from the pan, set on a cutting board, and score into 18 bars.

Constitution Day

This day used to be called Citizenship Day, but in 2004 Congress passed a law establishing Constitution Day and Citizenship Day, in observance of both the signing of the Constitution in 1787 and those who have become citizens. Along with the name change, Congress enacted a law saying that on this day public institutions that receive federal funding must teach a history of the Constitution. In honor of Constitution Day, here's a bar cookie to help you remember the year it was signed.

Other Events on This Day:
National Apple Dumpling Day, Boston founded in 1630

Today is National Cheese-
burger Day, so dessert
should be something light.

Rice Krispies were intro-
duced in February of 1928,
but the real fun started in the
1940s when the recipe for
these marshmallow- and cereal-
based treats appeared on the
box. Attributed to two Kellogg's employees, Mildred Day
and Malitta Jensen, the recipe
has been revised over the
years by home cooks who have
added everything from peanut
butter and candy, to you name
it. My friend David makes a
fiery version with chipotle powder and smoked paprika.

Other Events on This Day:
Play-Doh Invented

Marshmallow and Peanut Butter Crispy Rice Treats MAKES 9 OR 18

4 tablespoons (2 ounces) unsalted butter

Tiny pinch of salt

4 cups miniature marshmallows
(or about 32 large marshmallows)

⅓ cup creamy peanut butter

¼ teaspoon vanilla extract

5 cups crispy rice cereal,
such as Rice Krispies

1 Line an 8-inch square pan with nonstick foil, or line it with
regular foil and spray the foil with cooking or baking spray.

2 Melt the butter in a 3-quart, nonstick saucepan set over
medium-low heat. Add the salt. When the butter is
melted, add the marshmallows and stir until melted. Stir
the mixture for about 1 minute after it is fully melted.
Don't let it burn.

3 Remove from the heat and stir in the peanut butter,
vanilla, and cereal. Stir until the cereal is coated with the
marshmallow mixture. With a sheet of parchment paper
or greased or nonstick foil, press the mixture evenly and
firmly into the prepared pan. Let cool completely in the
pan. When fully set, grasp the foil and lift from the pan.
Set on a cutting board and cut into nine large squares or
eighteen small bars, using a large chef's knife.

Argh! It's Talk Like a Pirate
Day, and every bilge
rat in the pub be talkin' like
a pirate. I'm going to go to
the galley and make me some
cookies. Argh!

Chocolate Rum Balls MAKES 48

10 ounces vanilla wafer cookies (about
64 cookies or 2½ cups crumbs)

1 cup pecans, toasted

1 cup (about 6 ounces) semisweet chocolate chips

½ cup confectioners' sugar, plus more for rolling

3 tablespoons golden syrup or light corn syrup

½ cup vanilla rum, such as Whaler's (see Baker's Notes)

1. In the bowl of a food processor, process the wafers into fine crumbs. Add the pecans and process the mixture until finely ground. Melt the chocolate in a large, microwave-safe bowl, using 50 percent power and stirring every 60 seconds. Stir in the confectioners' sugar, syrup, and rum. Stir in the crumb mixture.

2. Roll scant tablespoonfuls of the mixture into generous 1-inch balls. Roll the balls in extra confectioners' sugar to coat evenly. Cover and refrigerate overnight or up to 5 days.

Baker's Notes: These are also good made with chocolate Teddy Grahams instead of vanilla wafers. For less vanilla flavor, use regular rum in place of vanilla rum.

Big-as-a-Fist Breakfast Cookies MAKES 8

¼ cup melted virgin coconut oil, slightly cooled

1 cup plain Greek yogurt, room temperature

2 tablespoons pure maple syrup, room temperature

1 teaspoon vanilla extract

2 cups (9 ounces) whole wheat pastry flour

2 teaspoons baking powder

½ teaspoon baking soda

¾ teaspoon salt

1 cup extra-dark or semisweet chocolate chips

½ cup toasted and chopped walnuts or pecans

1 tablespoon turbinado, raw, or coarse sugar

½ teaspoon cinnamon

1. Preheat the oven to 425°F and place a rack in the center. Line a large baking sheet with nonstick foil or parchment paper.

2. In a large mixing bowl, whisk together the melted coconut oil, yogurt, maple syrup, and vanilla.

3. In a second mixing bowl, stir together the pastry flour, baking powder, baking soda, and salt.

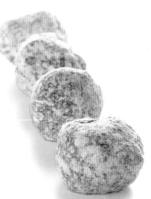

Other Events on This Day:
Butterscotch Pudding Day

SEPTEMBER 20

Happy National Punch Day

It's National Punch Day, a day to celebrate the fruity beverage served at preschools, church socials, and the blood donation center. So drink some punch with your cookies, and be glad the day celebrates the beverage rather than a fist punch. Speaking of which, here's a semi-wholesome cookie that's about the size of a fist, and if you try to eat the whole thing all in one sitting, you'll need a gallon of punch (though milk would be my first choice) to wash it down.

Other Events on This Day:
First Whole Foods Market opened in 1980

4 Add the flour mixture to the yogurt mixture and stir until halfway mixed, then stir in the chocolate chips and walnuts. Stir until the mixture comes together.

5 Divide and shape the mixture into 8 balls. Arrange the balls about 3 inches apart on the baking sheet and press the tops down slightly to make mounds. Mix together the turbinado sugar and the cinnamon and sprinkle generously over the tops.

6 Bake for 12 to 14 minutes or until the outsides are browned and the insides are no longer doughy. Let cool on a wire rack for about 15 minutes before serving.

Baker's Notes: Because the coconut oil may solidify when exposed to cold ingredients, make sure your maple syrup and yogurt are at room temperature. If you're in a rush, bring them to room temperature by combining them in a small bowl, microwaving on high for 5 seconds, stirring and repeating if necessary.

First Day of Fall

The sky is cloudy, and chimneys fill the air with the smell of burning wood. Inside, the house is fragrant with cinnamon and spice, sweaters have been pulled out of the closet, and everyone's drinking hot cocoa. This is the idyllic first day of fall.

Interestingly, it's also International Peace Day and World Gratitude Day, so theoretically this should be a day of warm, fuzzy, comforting flavors. Given that, here's a homey oatmeal cookie with browned butter and a touch of maple flavoring.

Other Events on This Day:
World Alzheimer's Day

Maple-Glazed Brown Butter Oat Cookies MAKES 36

COOKIES

1 cup (8 ounces) unsalted butter, room temperature

1½ cups (6.8 ounces) all-purpose flour

1 teaspoon baking soda

½ teaspoon salt

1 teaspoon ground cinnamon

⅔ cup firmly packed light or dark brown sugar

⅔ cup granulated sugar

2 large eggs

½ teaspoon vanilla extract

½ teaspoon maple flavoring

2½ cups old-fashioned oats

1 cup toasted and chopped pecans

GLAZE

6 tablespoons (3 ounces) unsalted butter

6 tablespoons firmly packed light brown sugar

¼ cup whole or 2% milk

1 cup confectioners' sugar

½ teaspoon vanilla extract

¼ teaspoon maple flavoring

1   Preheat the oven to 350°F and place a rack in the center. Line two baking sheets with parchment paper or nonstick foil.

2   **Make the cookies:** Place the butter in a heavy saucepan and melt over medium heat. Keep over the heat until the butter starts to bubble and turn brown. Turn off the heat and swirl the browned butter. Set aside to cool for 10 minutes.

3   Meanwhile, in medium-size bowl, stir together flour, baking soda, salt, and cinnamon.

4   In a large bowl, stir together both sugars. Add the browned butter and stir until thoroughly mixed. Stir in the eggs, vanilla, and maple flavoring, followed by the flour mixture, oats, and pecans. Spoon rounded tablespoonfuls of dough onto the prepared baking sheets. Bake one sheet at a time for 10 to 12 minutes. Let cool on the baking sheets for 1 minute, then transfer to a wire rack set over paper towels.

5   **Make the glaze:** In a small saucepan, melt the butter over medium heat. Stir in the brown sugar and milk. Bring to a boil and boil for 30 seconds, stirring constantly. Turn off the heat and stir in the confectioners' sugar, vanilla, and maple flavoring. Drizzle over the cookies and allow the glaze to set before serving.

Apple Chunk with White Chocolate Cookies

MAKES ABOUT 24

1 cup (4.5 ounces) all-purpose flour

¼ teaspoon baking soda

¼ teaspoon salt

¼ teaspoon ground cinnamon

8 tablespoons (4 ounces) unsalted butter, room temperature

¼ cup granulated sugar

Elephant Appreciation Day

Inspired by an elephant paperweight given to him by his daughter, Wayne Hepburn came up with the idea for Elephant Day in 1996. His goal was to raise awareness of elephants as the noble, intelligent, loyal beasts they are. Recognized by circuses, zoos, magazines, and several online calendars, Elephant Day is not only a great excuse to bake cookies, but also to head to your local zoo.

Other Events on This Day:
National White Chocolate Day

½ cup firmly packed light brown sugar

2 tablespoons unsweetened applesauce

1 large egg

2 teaspoons pure maple syrup

½ teaspoon vanilla extract

¼ teaspoon maple flavoring

¾ cup quick-cooking or old-fashioned oats (not instant)

½ cup finely chopped green apple, such as Granny Smith

¼ cup walnuts, toasted and chopped

¼ cup raisins

2 ounces white chocolate

Fact: Elephants are herbivores that eat mostly grass, hay, and plant matter.

Fact: While peanuts are said to be the creatures' favorite food, most sources say that what elephants really like are sweets such as watermelons, pumpkin, bananas, and apples.

1 Preheat the oven to 350°F and place a rack in the center. Line two baking sheets with nonstick foil or parchment paper.

2 Mix the flour, baking soda, salt, and cinnamon together in a small bowl; set aside.

3 In the bowl of a stand mixer fitted with a paddle attachment, or in a large mixing bowl, using a handheld electric mixer, beat the butter and both sugars on medium speed until creamy. Beat in the applesauce. Continue beating on medium speed, scraping the bowl often. Add the egg, maple syrup, vanilla, and maple flavoring; continue beating until well mixed. By hand, stir in the flour mixture until incorporated. Stir in the oats, apple, walnuts, and raisins.

4 Drop rounded teaspoonfuls of dough 2 inches apart onto the prepared baking sheets. Bake one sheet at a time for 10 to 13 minutes, or until the edges are lightly browned. Let cool completely on a wire rack set over some paper towels. In a microwave-safe bowl, melt the white chocolate at 50 percent power, stirring every 30 seconds. Drizzle the white chocolate over the cookies.

Checkerboard Cookies

MAKES ABOUT 48

1 cup (8 ounces) unsalted butter, room temperature

1½ cups confectioners' sugar

1 teaspoon vanilla extract

1 large egg

¾ teaspoon salt

2⅔ cups (12 ounces) all-purpose flour

¼ cup unsweetened natural cocoa powder

1 tablespoon whole or 2% milk

1 Line a large baking sheet with parchment paper.

2 In the bowl of a stand mixer fitted with a paddle attachment, or in a large mixing bowl, using a handheld electric mixer, beat the butter and confectioners' sugar on medium speed until creamy. Beat in the vanilla extract, egg, and salt. By hand or using the lowest speed of the mixer, stir in the flour. Divide the dough in half and remove half from the mixing bowl. To the remaining dough, add the cocoa powder and milk and knead gently until you have an evenly colored chocolate dough.

3 Set the chocolate and plain doughs side by side on the prepared baking sheet and pat each portion of dough into a 6½-inch square. The doughs should still be a little sticky at this point, so do the best you can to shape the squares. Place the baking sheet in the refrigerator and chill the dough until firm.

4 When the dough is very cold, transfer the dough squares to a floured work surface, and using a sharp knife, cut each square lengthwise into nine equal strips. On your work surface, arrange three strips—a white, a chocolate, and a white, next to each other so that the sides are snugly touching each other. Stack on a second layer of strips, alternating colors. Top with a final layer of chocolate and white to make a rectangular log. Wrap in plastic wrap. Repeat with the remaining dough so you have two rectangular logs each made with nine

Checkers Day

Today, also known as "Dogs in Politics Day," marks the anniversary of the date in 1952 when Richard Nixon gave his famous "Checkers" speech. Celebrate Checkers Day by making checkerboard cookies.

Other Events on This Day:
Restless Leg Syndrome Awareness

alternating strips of brown and plain dough. Chill the logs for about 2 hours, or until very firm and easy to slice.

5 Preheat the oven to 375°F and place a rack in the center. Have ready two ungreased baking sheets. Cut the rectangles crosswise into ¼-inch slices. Arrange about 1 inch apart on the baking sheets. Bake one sheet at a time for 8 to 10 minutes, or until set, then transfer immediately to a wire rack to cool completely.

Baker's Note: The yield may vary slightly depending on how thick you cut the cookie dough.

SEPTEMBER 24

Cherries Jubilee Day

*C*reated by the legendary chef and writer Auguste Escoffier, Cherries Jubilee is composed of cherries and Kirschwasser flambéed and served over vanilla ice cream. The name is a reference to Queen Victoria's Golden Jubilee, the event at which it was first served. This recipe is adapted from an old one called "Cherry Chewbilees," a cleverly titled cookie recipe put out years ago by the Cherry Marketing Institute.

Other Events on This Day:
Jim Henson's birthday (b. 1936)

Cherry Cashew Cookies
MAKES ABOUT 48

2¼ cups (10.1 ounces) all-purpose flour
1 teaspoon baking soda
¾ teaspoon salt
1 cup (8 ounces) unsalted butter, room temperature
¾ cup granulated sugar
¾ cup firmly packed light brown sugar
2 large eggs
¾ teaspoon vanilla extract
¾ teaspoon almond extract
6 ounces white chocolate, chopped, or 1 cup white chips
1½ cups dried tart cherries, roughly chopped
1 cup cashews, coarsely chopped

1 Preheat the oven to 350°F and place a rack in the center. Line two baking sheets with nonstick foil or parchment paper.

2 Mix the flour, baking soda, and salt together in a medium-size bowl; set aside.

3 In the bowl of a stand mixer fitted with a paddle attachment, or in a large mixing bowl, using a handheld electric mixer, beat the butter and both sugars on medium speed

until creamy. Reduce the mixer speed slightly and beat in the eggs, vanilla, and almond extract.

4 By hand or using the lowest speed of the mixer, stir in the flour mixture. Stir in the white chocolate, cherries, and cashews.

5 Drop rounded tablespoonfuls of batter about 2½ inches apart onto the prepared baking sheets. Bake one sheet at a time for 10 to 12 minutes, or until light golden brown. Do not overbake. Transfer to a wire rack to cool completely.

Sunflower Seed Butter Monsters MAKES 10

3 tablespoons (1.5 ounces) unsalted
    butter, room temperature

⅓ cup firmly packed light brown sugar

⅓ cup granulated sugar

⅔ cup (6 ounces) sunflower seed butter, such as SunButter

¼ teaspoon salt

1 large egg

1 teaspoon vanilla extract

¾ teaspoon baking soda

1½ cups quick-cooking oats (not instant)

¾ cup bittersweet or semisweet chocolate
    chips or chunks of chocolate

½ cup pecans, walnuts, or any other nut,
    toasted and roughly chopped

1 Preheat the oven to 350°F and place a rack in the center. Line two baking sheets with parchment paper.

2 In the bowl of a stand mixer fitted with a paddle attachment, or in a large mixing bowl, using a handheld electric mixer, cream the butter and both sugars on medium speed. Reduce the speed to medium-low and beat in the sunflower seed butter, salt, egg, and vanilla. Beat in the baking soda, making sure it's evenly distributed, then add the oats and stir until mixed. Stir in the chocolate chips and nuts.

Celebrate Banned Books Week

What do *Where the Sidewalk Ends*, *Superfudge*, and *Harriet the Spy* have in common? They're just a few of the books that have been challenged, pulled from shelves, or deemed "dangerous" by school libraries in the United States.

The idea of banned books is scary, and the first thing that came to mind for this day was "monsters."

Other Events on This Day:
World Ataxia Day

3 Shape the dough into ten equal-size balls and arrange 4 inches apart (five to a sheet) on the prepared baking sheets. Press down the tops to make rounds a little over 2 inches in diameter. Bake one sheet at a time for 11 to 13 minutes, or until the cookies are browned and appear set. Oven times may vary, so keep a close eye on your first batch. Let cool on the baking sheets for 5 to 8 minutes, then transfer to a wire rack to cool completely.

Baker's Note: Earthy, toasty, and full-flavored, sunflower seed butter, sold under the brand name SunButter, is an interesting alternative to peanut butter and a good option if you're baking for a school where peanuts have been banned.

SEPTEMBER 26

Sugar Rationing Ended in Great Britain

During World War II, sweets and chocolate were rationed in Great Britain. This rationing went on for eleven years, until September 1953, when the food minister derationed sugar. In the years that followed, sales of confectionary treats skyrocketed.

Mark that great day in the United Kingdom by baking a bar version of a popular British treat, the Bakewell tart.

Other Events on This Day:
Johnny Appleseed Day, National Pancake Day

Bakewell Bars MAKES 16

BASE

6 tablespoons (3 ounces) unsalted butter, room temperature

¼ teaspoon salt

¼ cup granulated sugar

1 large egg yolk

½ teaspoon vanilla extract

½ teaspoon baking powder

1 cup (4.5 ounces) all-purpose flour

1 tablespoon milk

⅔ cup raspberry preserves

TOPPING

4 tablespoons (2 ounces) unsalted butter, room temperature

¼ cup granulated sugar

⅛ teaspoon salt

1 large egg

½ teaspoon vanilla extract

½ teaspoon almond extract

1 cup ground almonds

3 tablespoons all-purpose flour

¼ teaspoon baking powder

ICING

1 teaspoon melted unsalted butter

½ cup confectioners' sugar

2 to 4 teaspoons water, or as needed

¼ teaspoon vanilla extract

1 Preheat the oven to 350°F and place a rack in the center. Line an 8-inch square pan with nonstick foil.

2 **Make the base:** Beat the butter, salt, and sugar together in a large mixing bowl using a handheld electric mixer on medium-high speed. Add the egg yolk and vanilla and beat until mixed. By hand, stir in the baking powder, then add the flour and stir until mixed. Add the milk to soften the dough. Press the dough into the bottom of the prepared pan and bake for 15 minutes. Let cool in the pan. Spread the preserves over the cooled crust.

3 **Make the topping:** In a medium mixing bowl, beat together the butter, sugar, and salt. Beat in the egg, vanilla, and almond extract, then stir in the ground almonds, flour, and baking powder. Drop spoonfuls of the almond mixture over the jam and gently spread to cover the preserves.

4 Bake for 25 to 30 minutes, or until the top is browned and appears set. Let cool completely in the pan.

5 **Make the icing:** In a small bowl, combine the melted butter and confectioners' sugar and stir well. Add water 1 teaspoon at a time until the mixture is the right consistency for drizzling. Stir in the vanilla. Drizzle over the bars and allow to set. Lift from the pan, set on a cutting board, and cut into sixteen squares. For firmer, easier-to-slice squares, chill before cutting.

*Ancestor
Appreciation Day*

Genealogy enthusiasts will be happy to know that today is Ancestor Appreciation Day, a day to think about our grandparents' grandparents and the legacies they left behind. To celebrate, talk to your oldest living family members and gather as much information as possible about names, dates, and memories.

This recipe is in honor of my great-grandmother from Louisiana, an amateur genealogist who loved both cookies and pecans.

Other Events on This Day:
National Chocolate Milk Day

Chocolate Pecan Chewies
MAKES 10 LARGE COOKIES

1¾ cups confectioners' sugar

⅓ cup (1 ounce) unsweetened natural cocoa powder

¼ scant teaspoon salt

½ teaspoon vanilla extract

2 large egg whites, room temperature

1⅓ cups (4.5 ounces) finely chopped pecans

1 Preheat the oven to 400°F and place a rack in the center. Line two large baking sheets with parchment paper or nonstick foil. In the bowl of a stand mixer fitted with the paddle attachment or in a large mixing bowl, gently mix together the confectioners' sugar, cocoa powder, salt, vanilla, and egg whites. When the ingredients come together, raise the mixing speed to medium-high and beat for exactly 2 minutes, scraping the sides of the bowl occasionally. The mixture should be glossy. Add the pecans and stir just until they're mixed in.

2 Spoon heaping tablespoonfuls of the mixture about 3 inches apart onto the prepared baking sheets. Bake one sheet at a time for 10 to 12 minutes, or until the cookies appear set. Let cool completely on the baking sheets. When cool, peel away from the liner.

*Happy Birthday
Confucius*

On this day in 551 BC, Chinese thinker and philosopher Confucius was born. Naturally, today's cookie is a fortune cookie.

There are multiple theories as to the origin of fortune cookies, but many believe they date back to ancient Japan,

Fortune Cookies
MAKES ABOUT 45, PLUS A FEW PRACTICE COOKIES

3 large egg whites

¾ cup granulated sugar

8 tablespoons (4 ounces) unsalted butter, melted and cooled

¼ teaspoon salt

½ teaspoon vanilla extract

¼ teaspoon almond extract

1 cup (4.5 ounces) all-purpose flour

3 to 4 tablespoons water

1. Type fortunes onto paper and cut into long strips. Have them ready to go before you begin the cookies.

2. Preheat the oven to 375°F and place a rack in the center. Line two rimless baking sheets with nonstick foil.

3. With a handheld electric mixer, beat the egg whites and sugar on high speed for about 2 minutes, or until light. Reduce the speed to low and add the melted butter, salt, vanilla, almond extract, and flour. Add 2 to 3 tablespoons of water and stir well, then add more water until you get a very soft dough—not quite a batter, but close to it. You don't want the dough to flow too quickly from the spoon.

4. Scoop up heaping teaspoonfuls of batter and form six paper-thin circles about 3 inches in diameter on one of the prepared baking sheets. Bake the cookies for 5 to 7 minutes, or until your circles have brown edges. Remove from the oven, and working quickly, with one circle at a time, put a fortune in the center of the circle, fold the cookie over once to make a rounded half-moon, then fold the far edges toward each other. Set in a muffin tin and let cool. Repeat with the remaining hot circles, doing your best to keep the folded fortune cookies closed as they set and cool. Start another sheet. While one batch of cookies bakes, spoon out the batter for the next batch.

where the cookies, then savory, were made in small irons called *kata*, then stuffed with a paper fortune and rolled. Credit for introducing the fortune cookie to America goes to a Japanese immigrant named Makoto Hagiwara.

Other Events on This Day: **National Strawberry Cream Pie Day, Drink a Beer Day**

You are a good athlete despite what people say.

Java Crunch Cookies
MAKES 36 TO 42

1 tablespoon instant coffee granules

2 tablespoons hot water

1½ cups (6.8 ounces) all-purpose flour

1 teaspoon baking powder

½ teaspoon salt

6 tablespoons (3 ounces) unsalted
    butter, room temperature

6 tablespoons (2.6 ounces) shortening

½ cup granulated sugar

¼ cup firmly packed light brown sugar

1 large egg

1½ cups sweetened flaked coconut

National Coffee Day

Today's perfect for recognizing that moderate consumption of coffee may have some positive effects on health. Along with the obvious alertness-enhancing and energy level-raising properties, the caffeine in coffee has also been suggested to reduce the risk of Parkinson's disease and type 2 diabetes. It helps relieve headaches, and new studies show it may help reduce the risk of strokes in women. That, plus coffee itself is loaded with antioxidants.

The original version of this recipe, an old contest winner created by Joann Gambaro of St. Louis, called for shortening. I use a combination of shortening and butter for a little extra flavor.

Other Events on This Day:
Poisoned Blackberries Day

1 Preheat the oven to 350°F and place a rack in the center. Have ready two ungreased baking sheets.

2 Dissolve the coffee in the hot water and set aside.

3 Mix the flour, baking powder, and salt together in a bowl; set aside.

4 In the bowl of a stand mixer fitted with a paddle attachment, or in a large mixing bowl, using a handheld electric mixer, beat the butter, shortening, and both sugars on medium speed until light and creamy. Reduce the mixer speed to low and beat in the egg until mixed. By hand or using the lowest speed of the mixer, add the flour mixture. Stir in the dissolved coffee and the coconut. Drop rounded teaspoonfuls of batter about 2½ inches apart onto the baking sheets. Bake one sheet at a time for 10 to 12 minutes, or until the edges are lightly browned. Let cool on the baking sheets for about 5 minutes, then transfer to a wire rack to cool completely.

Fact: Dark roasted coffee has less caffeine than medium roast because caffeine burns off during the roasting process.

Mulled Cider Day

*F*all is barely here, but some eager beaver decided to declare today mulled cider day. And why not? It makes the whole house feel like a chilly day in New England even if you're in Texas and it's still 80°F outside.

Other Events on This Day:
National Chewing Gum Day, National Mudpack Day

Mulled Apple Cider Cookies MAKES 20 LARGE COOKIES

COOKIES

2¼ cups (10.1 ounces) all-purpose flour

1 teaspoon ground cinnamon

½ teaspoon baking soda

¼ teaspoon salt

½ teaspoon freshly grated nutmeg

¼ teaspoon ground cloves

8 tablespoons (4 ounces) unsalted butter, room temperature

⅔ cup granulated sugar

⅓ cup firmly packed light brown sugar

1 large egg

¼ cup apple cider or juice

1 cup finely chopped or shredded
   apple, peeled if desired
1 cup chopped walnuts or pecans, toasted

ICING
1½ cups confectioners' sugar
2½ tablespoons (1.25 ounces) unsalted
   butter, room temperature
½ teaspoon vanilla extract
4 to 5 tablespoons apple cider or juice

1 Preheat the oven to 375°F and place a rack in the center.
Line two baking sheets with nonstick foil or parchment
paper.

2 **Make the cookies:** Mix the flour, cinnamon, baking soda,
salt, nutmeg, and cloves together in a bowl; set aside.

3 In the bowl of a stand mixer fitted with a paddle attachment, or in a large mixing bowl, using a handheld electric
mixer, beat the butter and both sugars on medium speed
until creamy. Reduce the mixer speed slightly and beat
in the egg and apple cider. By hand or using the lowest
speed of the mixer, stir in the flour mixture, followed by
the apple and nuts.

4 Drop generously rounded teaspoonfuls or level
tablespoonfuls of dough about 2 inches apart onto the
prepared baking sheets. Bake one sheet at a time for
10 to 12 minutes, or until the edges are lightly browned.
Transfer to a wire rack to cool completely.

5 **Make the icing:** In a medium-size mixing bowl, beat the
confectioners' sugar, butter, vanilla, and 4 tablespoons of
apple juice until smooth, adding more apple juice based
on the desired consistency of your icing. Drizzle the icing
over the cooled cookies.

National Homemade Cookie Day is an unofficial US holiday observed on October 1. Cookies made with store-bought cookie dough are perfectly acceptable, but scratch cookies are even better. Celebrate October 1 by going all out and making the homiest homemade cookies of all—spiced molasses. This recipe was adapted from the wickedly funny children's book author Ann Hodgman, who challenged readers to try to find a better cookie in her cookbook *Beat That!*.

Other Events on This Day:
World Vegetarian Day
(So make sure you let the vegetarians know, should you decide to use that lard.)

Crackly Top Spiced Molasses Cookies   MAKES ABOUT 30

2 cups (9 ounces) all-purpose flour

2 teaspoons baking soda

¼ teaspoon salt

¼ teaspoon cayenne

1 tablespoon ground cinnamon

1 tablespoon ground ginger

½ tablespoon ground cloves

¼ teaspoon freshly grated nutmeg

½ cup plus 2 tablespoons (4.2 ounces) shortening or lard (see Baker's Notes)

1 cup granulated sugar

1 large egg

¼ cup mild molasses

Coarse or sparkling sugar, for rolling

1   Mix the flour, baking soda, salt, cayenne, cinnamon, ginger, cloves, and nutmeg together in a medium-size bowl; set aside.

2   In the bowl of a stand mixer fitted with a paddle attachment, or in a large mixing bowl, using a handheld electric mixer, beat the shortening and sugar on medium speed for 2 minutes. Reduce the mixer speed slightly and beat in the egg and molasses. With a spoon, stir (do not beat) the flour mixture into the sugar mixture. Cover the dough and chill for at least an hour.

3   Preheat the oven to 375°F and place a rack in the center. Line a baking sheet with nonstick foil or parchment paper.

4   Shape the dough into 1-inch balls and roll in coarse sugar. Arrange 2½ inches apart on the prepared baking sheet. Bake for 10 to 12 minutes, or until the cookies are crackly and appear crispy around the edges. Let cool on the baking sheet for about 5 minutes, then transfer to a wire rack to cool and crisp.

Baker's Notes: There are plenty of great spice cookie recipes with butter, but this is one where shortening or lard makes a tremendous difference in texture. Lard, found in most grocery stores, is usually hydrogenated, but nonhydrogenated leaf lard can be ordered on the Internet from sources such as Prairie Pride Farm in Minnesota.

Super Pumpkin Chocolate Chip Cookies MAKES 36

1 cup canned pumpkin (not pumpkin pie mix)

1 large egg

1 scant cup granulated sugar

6 tablespoons vegetable oil

1 teaspoon vanilla extract

1 teaspoon ground cinnamon

½ teaspoon salt

½ teaspoon baking soda

1½ teaspoons baking powder

2 cups (9 ounces) all-purpose flour or
    white whole wheat flour

1 cup semisweet chocolate chips

1 Preheat the oven to 375°F and place a rack in the center. Line two baking sheets with nonstick foil or parchment.

2 Beat the pumpkin, egg, sugar, oil, vanilla, cinnamon, salt, baking soda, and baking powder together in a mixing bowl. Make sure all the leavenings are dissolved (no lumps). Add the flour and stir just until it is mixed in, then stir in the chocolate chips.

Fact: Charles Schulz's first dog, Spike, was the inspiration for Snoopy.

3 Drop generously rounded tablespoonfuls of dough about 2 inches apart onto the prepared baking sheets (the cookies shouldn't spread much). Bake one sheet at a time for 13 to 15 minutes. Transfer to a wire rack to cool completely.

OCTOBER 2

Launch of Peanuts Comic Strip

Originally titled *Li'l Folks* and changed by King Features to *Peanuts* (a name Charles M. Schulz didn't care for), this comic strip debuted in eight newspapers in 1950. Progressive for its time, with an athletic female, coed baseball team, and an African American character named Franklin, *Peanuts* went on to become one of the most popular comics of all time, making Charles Schulz a billionaire.

Other Events on This Day: National Custodial Workers' Day

Fact: There's a Charles M. Schulz Museum and Research Center in Santa Rosa, California.

Surprise Mint Cookies MAKES 20

In 1955, *The Mickey Mouse Club* began broadcasting on ABC. Some of my happiest memories were coming home from school, grabbing a snack, and watching the not-quite-as-well-known 1970s remake *The New Mickey Mouse Club.* My favorite sketch from the show was "Surprise Day, Surprise Day," and thirty years later the song still gets stuck in my head. If you like the Mouseketeers or just surprises in general, here's your cookie for today.

Other Events on This Day:
Virus Appreciation Day, German Unity Day

1½ cups (6.8 ounces) all-purpose flour

½ teaspoon baking powder

¼ teaspoon plus an extra pinch of salt

8 tablespoons (4 ounces) unsalted
    butter, room temperature

½ cup granulated sugar

¼ cup firmly packed light brown sugar

1 large egg

½ teaspoon vanilla extract

32 chocolate mint candies, such as Andes

1   Preheat the oven to 375°F and place a rack in the center. Line two baking sheets with nonstick foil or parchment paper.

2   Mix the flour, baking powder, and salt together in a bowl; set aside.

3   In the bowl of a stand mixer fitted with a paddle attachment, or in a large mixing bowl, using a handheld electric mixer, beat the butter and both sugars on medium speed until creamy; add the egg and vanilla and beat for 30 seconds. Beat in the flour mixture. If the dough seems too wet to handle, cover and chill for 30 minutes. You probably won't have to.

4   With floured hands, shape a tablespoon of dough around each candy, forming twenty rectangular cookies. Reserve the remaining mints. Place the rectangles 2 inches apart on the prepared baking sheets. Bake one sheet at a time for 10 to 12 minutes, or until the edges are golden brown. Transfer to a wire rack to cool completely. Using a very low microwave setting (I use the defrost setting), melt the remaining mint candies and then drizzle over the cookies.

Outrageous Southern Comfort Brownies   MAKES 12

12 tablespoons (6 ounces) unsalted butter

3½ ounces unsweetened chocolate, chopped

1 ounce bittersweet chocolate, chopped

1 cup granulated sugar

3 large eggs, room temperature

½ cup firmly packed light brown sugar

1 teaspoon vanilla extract

2 tablespoons Southern Comfort, plus 2 to
    3 tablespoons for brushing

½ teaspoon salt

1 cup (4.5 ounces) all-purpose flour

⅓ cup pecans, toasted and finely chopped,
    or 12 pecan halves

1   Preheat the oven to 350°F and place a rack in the center. Line
    an 8-inch metal baking pan with nonstick foil, or line it with
    regular foil and spray the foil with flour-added baking spray.

2   Melt the butter in a saucepan set over medium heat. Re-
    duce the heat to low and add both types of chocolate; stir
    constantly until the chocolate is melted. Add the granu-
    lated sugar to the melted chocolate and stir over low heat
    for 1 minute. Cool for about 5 minutes.

3   In a large mixing bowl, using a handheld electric mixer
    on high speed, beat the eggs until very light. Add the
    brown sugar and continue beating for 2 minutes. Add the
    melted chocolate to the egg mixture. Scrape the sides of
    the bowl and beat in the vanilla, 2 tablespoons of South-
    ern Comfort, and the salt. Stir in the flour.

4   Pour into the prepared pan and sprinkle or arrange the
    pecans over the top. Bake for 28 minutes, or until set. Let
    cool in the pan for 20 minutes, then brush the top with the
    remaining 2 to 3 tablespoons of bourbon. Let cool to room
    temperature, then transfer to the refrigerator to chill for
    a few hours or overnight (see Baker's Note). Lift from the
    pan, set on a cutting board, and cut into twelve squares.

Janis Joplin Died

Known for her raspy voice
and perfect pitch, singer
and songwriter Janis Joplin
died today in 1970.

Born in 1943, Janice
grew up in Port Arthur, Texas.
She was a good student with
natural singing talent, and she
was quite popular up until her
teen years, when she became
somewhat of a rebel. At age
seventeen, Janice left home to
perform in Austin and Houston, eventually landing in San
Francisco, where she played
with a band called Big Brother
and the Holding Company. After years of playing at smaller
venues, she was finally noticed
at The Monterey Pop Festival.

Other Events on This Day:
**The Brooklyn Dodgers Won
the World Series in 1955**

Texas is OK if you want
to settle down and do
your own thing quietly,
but it's not for outrageous
people, and I was
always outrageous.

—Janis Joplin

Baker's Note: The chilling/sitting time is important. The texture changes as the brownies chill. This also gives the bourbon flavor some time to develop, though it is quite mild.

World Teacher Day

It's World Teacher Day! Different from National Teacher's Day (May 3), which was started by the National Association for Education and the PTA, World Teacher Day was initiated by UNESCO and recognizes teachers around the world. The date of October 5 was chosen in 1993 to commemorate the day in 1966 when UNESCO and the International Labor Organization signed the Recommendation Concerning the Status of Teachers.

Other Events on This Day:
Apple Betty Day; Founder of McDonald's Corporation, Ray Kroc's birthday (b. 1902)

Pumpkin Pie Spiced Biscotti
MAKES ABOUT 24 PIECES AND SOME NUBS

2 cups (9 ounces) all-purpose flour
2 teaspoons baking powder
2 teaspoons pumpkin pie spice
½ teaspoon ground cinnamon
½ teaspoon salt
2 large eggs
¼ cup vegetable oil
¾ cup granulated sugar
2 tablespoons mild molasses
1 tablespoon honey
⅓ cup canned pumpkin (not pumpkin pie mix)

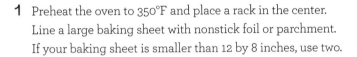

1 Preheat the oven to 350°F and place a rack in the center. Line a large baking sheet with nonstick foil or parchment. If your baking sheet is smaller than 12 by 8 inches, use two.

2 Mix the flour, baking powder, pumpkin pie spice, cinnamon, and salt together in a medium-size bowl; set aside.

3 In the bowl of a stand mixer fitted with a paddle attachment, or in a large mixing bowl, using a handheld electric mixer, beat the eggs, oil, sugar, molasses, honey, and pumpkin on medium speed. By hand or using the lowest speed of the mixer, beat in the flour mixture. The dough will be very sticky.

4 Divide the dough in half and form each portion into a log about 2½ inches by 10 inches. Place the logs at least 6 inches apart on the baking sheet. If the dough seems too sticky to handle, wet your hands to help you shape it. Bake the logs at 350°F for 30 minutes. Let cool on the pan for at least 20 minutes. Transfer to a cutting board.

5 Reduce the oven temperature to 325°F. Using a serrated knife, slice each log crosswise into ¾-inch slices. Place

cut side down on the baking sheet. Return the pan to the oven and bake at 325°F for about 25 minutes, or until the cookies are dry and firm. They might be slightly soft in some spots, but should firm as they cool. Transfer to a wire rack to cool completely.

Noodle Cookies   MAKES ABOUT 20

2 cups chow mein noodles

½ cup miniature marshmallows

½ cup unsalted or lightly salted peanuts

⅔ cup butterscotch chips

4 ounces dark chocolate, or about
    16 Dove or Hershey's Bliss squares

1   Line a baking sheet with nonstick foil or parchment paper. Make sure it's one that's small enough to fit in the refrigerator.

2   In a large mixing bowl, stir together the noodles, marshmallows, and peanuts. Set aside.

3   In a small, microwave-safe bowl, combine the butterscotch chips and chocolate; heat at 50 percent power, stirring every 60 seconds, until melted and smooth. With a rubber scraper, scrape the chocolate into the noodle mixture and stir to coat the mixture. Drop by tablespoonfuls onto the prepared baking sheet. Chill until firm.

Peanut Butter Haystacks
MAKES ABOUT 20

1 cup (6 ounces) butterscotch chips

½ cup creamy peanut butter

½ cup unsalted or lightly salted peanuts

2 cups chow mein noodles

1   Line a baking sheet with parchment paper or nonstick foil. Mix the butterscotch chips and peanut butter together in a medium-size, microwave-safe bowl. Microwave at 50 percent power for 30 seconds; stir and repeat, microwaving for another 30 seconds, or until the

National Noodle Day

Known as Haystacks, Chinese New Year Cookies, or Tingalings, there's no better way to celebrate this brilliant excuse for eating starch than with crunchy chow mein noodles mixed with peanuts and held together by a matrix of chocolate and butterscotch.

Other Events on This Day:
**Come and Take It! Day,
German American Day,
Physician's Assistant Day**

If you are more of a peanut butter fan, try this version.

chips are melted and smooth. Stir in the peanuts and chow mein noodles. Drop by tablespoonfuls onto the prepared baking sheet. Chill until firm.

OCTOBER 7

World Showcase Food and Wine Fest at Epcot

Epcot's annual Food and Wine Fest takes place this month! Celebrated every October, when the weather is brisk and the crowds are moderate, The World Showcase features authentic street food, book signings by famous chefs, and special concerts so you can listen to music as you sample goodies from all over the globe.

Because my favorite treat at the World Showcase is the Black Forest Cake in Germany, here is a recipe for Black Forest Cookies.

Other Events on This Day:
Bathtub Day, Frappé Day, East Germany created in 1949

Black Forest Cookies MAKES 12

1 teaspoon instant coffee granules
2 tablespoons very hot water
¾ cup (3.4 ounces) all-purpose flour
¾ teaspoon baking powder
¼ teaspoon plus an extra pinch of salt
¾ cup granulated sugar
4 tablespoons (2 ounces) unsalted butter
⅓ cup unsweetened natural cocoa
   powder (see Baker's Note)
1 large egg
½ teaspoon vanilla extract
½ cup semisweet chocolate chips
½ cup dried tart cherries
¾ cup confectioners' sugar, for rolling

1 Preheat the oven to 350°F and place a rack in the center. Line two baking sheets with parchment paper or nonstick foil.

2 Dissolve the coffee in the hot water and set it aside to cool completely.

3 Mix the flour, baking powder, salt, and sugar together in a small bowl; set aside.

4 In a microwave-safe mixing bowl, microwave the butter on high for 30 seconds, or until melted. Add the cocoa powder and stir until smooth. Stir in the egg, cooled coffee mixture, and vanilla. Stir the flour mixture into the chocolate mixture just until combined. Fold the chocolate chips and cherries into the dough until evenly distributed.

5 Scoop up by generous tablespoonfuls and shape into twelve large balls. Roll the balls in the confectioners' sugar, then arrange 2 inches apart on the prepared baking sheets. Bake one sheet at a time for 12 to 14 minutes, or

until the cookies are cracked yet still soft; do not over-bake. Let cool on the baking sheet for about 2 minutes, then transfer to a wire rack to cool completely.

Baker's Note: Make sure you use natural cocoa powder rather than Dutch-processed. The natural style has a little more acid to it, so the cookies seem to rise a little higher. These cookies should be fat, slightly cakey, and rich, as opposed to very fudgy, and not too sweet.

Fluffernutter Cookies MAKES 24

1 cup peanut butter, preferably creamy

½ cup lightly packed light brown sugar

½ cup granulated sugar

1 large egg

1 teaspoon vanilla extract

¼ teaspoon salt

1 teaspoon baking soda

1 (7.5-ounce) jar marshmallow crème,
    such as Marshmallow Fluff

1 Preheat the oven to 350°F and place a rack in the center. Line a baking sheet with nonstick foil or parchment paper.

2 Mix the peanut butter and both sugars together in a large mixing bowl. Beat in the egg and vanilla. Add the salt and baking soda and stir until they are thoroughly mixed in.

3 Scoop up tablespoonfuls of dough and shape into balls. Arrange about 2 inches apart onto the prepared baking sheets. With your thumb, press an indentation into the middle of each dough ball. Bake for 10 to 12 minutes. Remove the baking sheet from the oven and press down the indentation once more (working quickly; the cookies will be hot), then let cool on the baking sheet for 2 minutes.

OCTOBER 8

National Fluffernutter Day

Marshmallow lovers around the United States, especially in our northeastern states, have declared October 8 National Fluffernutter Day. A registered trademark of the Durkee Company, a Fluffernutter is a sandwich made with white bread, peanut butter, and Marshmallow Fluff. A bill to make the Fluffernutter the official sandwich of Massachusetts has been introduced twice in the state legislature. Whether it passes remains to be seen, as the state already has five official state foods: the baked navy bean, corn muffin, chocolate chip cookie, Boston cream pie, and Boston cream doughnut.

Other Events on This Day:
Touch Tag Day, Children's Day

4   Transfer the cookies to a wire rack to cool completely. Once they are cool, fill the center of each cookie with a spoonful of marshmallow crème.

John Lennon's Birthday

*Y*ou may know the lyrics to dozens of his songs, but did you know that John Lennon was a fan of cornflakes? It's cited in dozens of sources as his favorite food, but given Lennon's dry sense of humor, it's questionable. What is most likely true is that he wrote the lyrics to "Good Morning Good Morning" after hearing a cornflakes commercial.

My friend Cheri gave me this recipe. She makes it with Grape-Nuts flakes.

Other Events on This Day:
Leif Erikson Day

Good Morning Butterscotch Cookies   MAKES 48

1 cup (8 ounces) unsalted butter, room temperature

1 cup granulated sugar

1 cup firmly packed light brown sugar

2 large eggs

2 teaspoons vanilla extract

1 tablespoon water

2 cups (9 ounces) all-purpose flour

1 teaspoon baking soda

½ teaspoon baking powder

½ teaspoon salt

2 cups quick-cooking oats (not instant)

2 cups butterscotch chips

1 cup cornflakes or other flaked cereal

½ cup walnuts or pecans, toasted and chopped (optional)

1   Preheat the oven to 350°F and place a rack in the center. Line two baking sheets with nonstick foil or parchment.

2   Beat the butter until creamy. Add both sugars and continue beating for about 5 minutes. Beat in the eggs, one at a time, and beat for another minute, then beat in the vanilla and water.

3   Mix together the flour, baking soda, baking powder, and salt in a second bowl. Add the flour mixture to the butter mixture and stir well. Add the oats, butterscotch chips, cornflakes, and nuts and mix until well incorporated.

4   Drop heaping teaspoonfuls of dough about 2 inches apart on the prepared baking sheets or shape into 1-inch balls and arrange 2½ inches apart on the sheets. With moistened fingertips, gently press each cookie to flatten it slightly. Bake one sheet at a time until lightly browned, about 12 minutes. Transfer to a wire rack to cool completely.

Hunter's Moon Cookies

MAKES 26

1¼ cups (5.5 ounces) all-purpose flour

½ cup unsweetened natural cocoa powder

1 teaspoon baking soda

½ teaspoon salt

3 ounces chopped bittersweet (70% cacao) chocolate

2 teaspoons instant espresso powder

8 tablespoons (4 ounces) unsalted
    butter, room temperature

¼ cup granulated sugar

⅓ cup firmly packed light brown sugar

1 teaspoon vanilla extract

1 large egg

1½ cups semisweet or extra-dark chocolate chips

26 white chocolate candies, such as Hershey's Hugs

1 Preheat the oven to 350°F and place a rack in the center. Have ready two ungreased baking sheets.

2 Mix the flour, cocoa powder, baking soda, and salt together in a small bowl; set aside.

3 In a small, microwave-safe bowl, microwave the chocolate at 50 percent power, stirring at 30-second intervals until melted. When fully melted, stir in the espresso powder. Set aside and let it cool slightly.

4 In the bowl of a stand mixer fitted with a paddle attachment, or in a large mixing bowl, using a handheld electric mixer, beat the butter and both sugars on medium speed until light and fluffy. Add the melted chocolate to the butter mixture and stir well. Add the vanilla and egg to the chocolate mixture. Stir in the flour mixture. Make sure the batter is cool, and then fold in the chocolate chips.

5 Scoop up tablespoonfuls of dough and shape into twenty-six balls. Place about 3 inches apart on the baking sheets, but don't flatten. Bake for 8 minutes, or just until the cookies look set—do not overbake. As soon as the cookies come out of the oven, place a white chocolate candy in

Hunter's Moon

October's full Moon is called the Hunter's Moon. It gets its name from the hunters who used moonlight to help them track prey. The Hunter's Moon appears on a different night every year, so check your almanac.

These cookies were inspired by a recipe from King Arthur Flour called Midnights, a cookie dark as night. My friend Kristen came up with the idea of sticking an upside-down white chocolate in the center, so that the dark night has a full moon.

Other Events on This Day:
World Mental Health Day, Columbus Day, Angel Food Cake Day

the center, point side down, so that the bottom looks like a full moon. Let cool on the baking sheet for 5 minutes, then transfer to a wire rack to cool completely.

Henry Heinz's Birthday

Born on this day in 1844, Henry Heinz grew up in a household of German immigrants and was guided by the principles of thrift and resourcefulness.

If you pride yourself on being thrifty, here's a recipe for when you feel like baking cookies and are down to the last few household staples. It is adapted from a Heinz Ketchup recipe, and you have to try this to believe it. They do have kind of a reddish hue, and you will taste the ketchup slightly, but it works.

Other Events on This Day:
Take Your Teddy Bear to Work Day

Ketchup Cookies MAKES 36

1½ cups (6.8 ounces) all-purpose or
 white whole wheat flour
½ teaspoon baking soda
½ teaspoon salt
¾ cup creamy or crunchy peanut butter
8 tablespoons (4 ounces) unsalted
 butter, room temperature
½ cup granulated sugar
½ cup firmly packed brown sugar
¼ cup ketchup
1 large egg

1 Preheat the oven to 350°F and place a rack in the center. Line two baking sheets with parchment paper or nonstick foil

2 Mix the flour, baking soda, and salt together in a bowl; set aside.

3 In the bowl of a stand mixer fitted with a paddle attachment, or in a large mixing bowl, using a handheld electric mixer, beat the peanut butter, butter, and both sugars on medium speed until creamy. Add the ketchup and egg and beat on low speed until mixed. Mix the flour mixture into the peanut butter mixture until thoroughly blended.

4 Drop tablespoonfuls of dough about 2½ inches apart onto the baking sheets. Press each mound flat with a fork in both directions, if you wish to make the crisscross design. Bake one sheet at a time for 8 to 10 minutes, or until the edges are nicely browned. Let cool on the baking sheets for about 5 minutes, then transfer to a wire rack to cool completely.

Aztec Chocolate Cookies

MAKES 52

1¾ cups (8 ounces) all-purpose flour

½ teaspoon salt

1¼ cups unsweetened natural cocoa powder

2½ teaspoons ground cinnamon

2 teaspoons baking soda

¼ teaspoon freshly ground black pepper

⅛ teaspoon cayenne

¾ cup (5.1 ounces) vegetable shortening

8 tablespoons (4 ounces) unsalted butter, room temperature

¾ cup plus ⅓ cup granulated sugar

¾ cup firmly packed light brown sugar

1 teaspoon vanilla extract

2 large eggs

1 cup semisweet chocolate chips

1 Preheat the oven to 350°F and place a rack in the center. Line two baking sheets with parchment paper or nonstick foil.

2 Mix the flour, salt, cocoa powder, 1½ teaspoons of the cinnamon, and the baking soda, ground pepper, and cayenne together in a medium-size bowl; set aside.

3 In the bowl of a stand mixer fitted with a paddle attachment, or in a large mixing bowl, using a handheld electric mixer, beat the shortening, butter, ¾ cup of the granulated sugar, and the brown sugar on medium speed until creamy. Beat in the vanilla and eggs, only until the eggs are blended. Add the flour mixture to the butter mixture and stir until incorporated. Add the chocolate chips. Chill the dough for 1 hour, or until easy to handle.

4 Stir together the remaining ⅓ cup of granulated sugar and remaining teaspoon of cinnamon. Shape the dough into 1-inch balls and roll in the cinnamon sugar. Arrange on the prepared baking sheets about 2½ inches apart. Bake one sheet at a time for 8 to 10 minutes. Let cool on the baking sheets for about 5 minutes, then transfer to a wire rack to cool completely.

El Día de la Raza

On this day in 1492, Columbus landed in the New World. While viewed as a celebratory and historical milestone by many, the holiday is controversial. Some have cited Columbus's treatment of the indigenous peoples as brutal and inhuman. El Día de la Raza (Day of the Race) was not meant to replace Columbus Day, but commemorates the fact that October 12 marks the arrival of a new race in the Americas and a reminder to celebrate our ancestors.

Other Events on This Day:
Farmer's Day

Molly Katzen's Birthday

Until Molly Katzen led me through the Enchanted Broccoli Forest, vegetarianism was a bit intimidating. And while I never did give up meat completely, with her cute illustrations and approachable prose, Katzen introduced many of us to a whole new world of vegetables. So, happy birthday to Molly Katzen.

This is similar to a recipe I entered in a contest sponsored by *Eating Well* magazine.

Other Events on This Day: Although it's also celebrated on January 13, Skeptics Day is celebrated today. Hmm, I don't know . . .

Blueberry, Oatmeal, White Chocolate Chunk Ginger Cookies MAKES 24

1 cup (4.5 ounces) all-purpose flour

¼ cup regular or toasted wheat germ

½ teaspoon baking soda

½ teaspoon salt

¼ teaspoon ground ginger

1 large egg

¾ cup firmly packed dark brown sugar

⅓ cup vegetable oil

1¼ teaspoons vanilla extract

½ cup quick-cooking or old-fashioned oats (not instant)

2 ounces white chocolate, chopped

⅓ cup dried blueberries

¼ cup crystallized ginger, chopped

1 Preheat the oven to 375°F and place a rack in the center. Line two cookies sheets with parchment paper or non-stick foil.

2 Mix the flour, wheat germ, baking soda, salt, and ground ginger together in a bowl; set aside.

3 In a mixing bowl, whisk the egg, brown sugar, oil, and vanilla. Add the dry ingredients to the wet ingredients and stir just until combined. Add the oats, white chocolate, blueberries, and crystallized ginger; stir just to combine.

4 Drop tablespoonfuls of batter 2 inches apart onto the prepared baking sheets. Bake one sheet at a time until puffed and barely golden around the edges, switching the pans back to front halfway through, 8 to 10 minutes. Let cool on the baking sheets for about 5 minutes, then transfer to a wire rack to cool completely.

Flapjacks MAKES 9 BARS

2 cups old-fashioned or quick-cooking oats (not instant)

2 teaspoons golden flaxseeds

⅛ teaspoon salt

¾ cup pecans, toasted and chopped

⅓ cup firmly packed chopped dried apricots

9 tablespoons (4.5 ounces) unsalted butter

⅔ cup firmly packed light or dark brown sugar

2 tablespoons honey

¼ teaspoon vanilla extract

1 Preheat the oven to 350°F and place a rack in the center. Line an 8-inch square metal pan with nonstick foil, or line it with regular foil and spray the foil with flour-added baking spray.

2 In a large mixing bowl, toss the oats and flaxseeds with the salt. Stir in the pecans and apricots. Melt the butter in a saucepan set over medium-low heat. Add the brown sugar and honey and heat just until the butter is hot and the brown sugar is melted. Remove from the heat and pour over the oat mixture. Stir well, then stir in the vanilla.

3 Pour the mixture into the prepared pan and press down firmly. Bake for 20 minutes, or until golden brown and bubbly. Let cool in the pan until warm, then grasp the foil and lift from the pan. Set on a cutting board and score into nine bars, but do not separate. Chill the bars for an hour, then carefully separate into bars and serve cold or at room temperature.

OCTOBER 14

Winnie-the-Pooh Published

A. A. Milne published *Winnie-the-Pooh* on October 14, 1926. The characters in the story are based on members of his son Christopher Robin's stuffed animal collection. Christopher Robin's stuffed bear was originally named Edward, but after a trip to the London Zoo, where he met a black bear named Winnie, Christopher Robin renamed his bear. He later added "Pooh," the name of a swan they had met on vacation.

A simple cookie for a simple bear, this English cookie is a mixture of dried fruit and oats held together with butter, sugar, and of course, honey.

Other Events on This Day: **National Dessert Day, Chuck Yeager broke the sound barrier in 1947**

Shredded Wheat Patented

Things don't always go as planned, and sometimes that's for the best. Take the inventor Henry Perky. He had digestive problems, so he took boiled wheat to his friend William Ford, and together they developed a machine to make "little whole wheat mattresses." They intended to sell the machine, but the biscuits were more popular, so Perky moved to Massachusetts and started some bakeries, eventually adding the name "The Shredded Wheat Company." Shredded Wheat went on to be mass-produced in different countries.

This no-bake recipe is adapted from Post Cereal Company.

Other Events on This Day:
Grouch Day, National Mushroom Day

No-Bake Wheat and Peanut Butter Bars   MAKES 24

½ cup firmly packed light brown sugar

½ cup light corn syrup or honey

½ cup creamy peanut butter

½ teaspoon vanilla extract

½ cup chopped, lightly salted peanuts

3 cups spoon-size Shredded Wheat cereal, coarsely crushed (see Baker's Note)

1 Line an 8-inch square pan with nonstick foil.

2 Mix the sugar, corn syrup, and peanut butter in a large, microwave-safe mixing bowl; microwave on high for about 1 minute, or until hot and bubbly. Stir in the vanilla, peanuts, and cereal. Mix well and transfer to the prepared pan. Press down tightly and chill until firm. Lift from the pan, set on a cutting board, and cut into twenty-four bars.

Baker's Note: To crush the cereal, put it in a resealable heavy-duty plastic bag and mash it with a rolling pin.

Boss's Day

Boss's Day is a holiday officially proclaimed by the governor of Illinois. You can thank Patricia Bays Haroski. She forgot it was her boss's birthday; to make matters worse, her beloved boss was her father. To ensure that it would never happen again, she registered October 16 as a holiday with the Chamber of Commerce. Four years later, in

Raspberry Crumb Bars
MAKES 32

1 cup (8 ounces) unsalted butter, room temperature

½ scant teaspoon salt

½ cup firmly packed light brown sugar

2 cups (9 ounces) all-purpose flour

2 cups semisweet chocolate chips

1 (14-ounce) can sweetened condensed milk

½ teaspoon vanilla extract

½ cup chopped, toasted pecans

⅓ cup seedless raspberry preserves

1. Preheat the oven to 350°F and place a rack in the center. Line a 9 by 13-inch metal pan with nonstick foil.

2. In the bowl of a stand mixer fitted with a paddle attachment, or in a large mixing bowl, using a handheld electric mixer, beat the butter, salt, and brown sugar on medium speed until creamy. Add the flour and stir until crumbly. With floured fingers, press about 1¾ cups of the crumb mixture onto the bottom of the prepared pan; reserve the remaining crumb mixture. Bake for 10 to 12 minutes, or until the edges are golden brown.

3. When the crust has baked, combine 1 cup of the chocolate chips and the sweetened condensed milk in a small, heavy-duty saucepan, or alternatively, in a microwave-safe bowl. Warm over low heat, stirring until smooth, or if using the microwave, heat at 50 percent power for 30 seconds and stir. Repeat until the chips are melted. Remove from the heat (or microwave) and add the vanilla; carefully spread over the baked crust.

4. Stir the nuts into the reserved crumb mixture; sprinkle over the chocolate filling. Drop teaspoons of raspberry jam over the crumb mixture and then sprinkle with the remaining cup of chocolate chips. Return the pan to the oven and bake for 25 to 30 minutes, or until the center is set. Let cool in the pan until room temperature and then chill for about an hour. Lift from the pan, set on a cutting board, and cut into thirty-two bars.

Colorful Confetti Cookies

MAKES 36

COOKIES

1 (18.9-ounce) box cake mix with colorful sprinkles, such as Pillsbury Funfetti

⅓ cup vegetable oil

2 large eggs

1962, Governor Otto Kerner formally declared the holiday and it has been celebrated ever since.

These cookies are dedicated to all bosses, but especially my former boss, Wade, who enthusiastically endorsed bringing homemade goodies to work. I saw a version of these at a bake sale where they were hot sellers. After mentioning them to a friend, she sent me the recipe and I've been making them at home ever since.

Other Events on This Day: **Dictionary Day, World Food Day**

Wear Something Gaudy Day

Today's holiday comes courtesy of my old favorite TV show, *Three's Company*. Remember Jack's sleazy, womanizing friend, Larry? It was Larry Dallas (played by Richard Kline) who declared today as Wear Something Gaudy Day. So wear something colorful, loud, and out of style and complement your outfit with a quick batch of colorful, fun cookies.

Like *Three's Company*, cookies made with cake mix hold a special place in my heart. They were the first cookies I ever baked by myself. Back in the early 1970s we didn't have Funfetti cake mix so I used yellow cake mix and just added sprinkles to the batter.

Other Events on This Day:
Pasta Day

OCTOBER 18

Alaska Day

Alaska Day is an official state holiday marking the transfer of the territory from Russia to the United States in 1867. It is celebrated all over the state, but the place to be is in Sitka, where they hold a festival that goes on for three days. To celebrate the icy great state, why not make Bear Paw Cookies? They're cuter

FROSTING

8 tablespoons (4 ounces) unsalted butter, room temperature

3¾ cups confectioners' sugar

1 teaspoon vanilla extract

1 to 2 tablespoons whole or 2% milk

Sprinkles, for decorating

1 Preheat the oven to 375°F and place a rack in the center. Line two baking sheets with nonstick foil or parchment paper.

2 **Make the cookies:** Combine the cake mix, oil, and eggs in a large mixing bowl and stir until well mixed. Shape the dough into 1-inch balls and arrange 2 inches apart on the prepared baking sheets. Dip the bottom of a glass in a little flour and flatten the cookies to ¼-inch thickness.

3 Bake one sheet at a time for 6 to 8 minutes, or until the edges are light golden brown. Let cool for 1 minute on the baking sheets, then transfer to a wire rack to cool completely.

4 **Make the frosting:** In a medium-size to large mixing bowl, using a handheld electric mixer starting at a low speed and moving slowly toward medium-high, beat the butter and confectioners' sugar together until well mixed. Beat in the vanilla and 1 tablespoon of the milk. Continue adding more milk until the icing reaches a smooth, spreadable consistency. Spread on the cookies and sprinkle with sprinkles.

Bear Paw Cookies MAKES 36

2⅓ cups (10.5 ounces) all-purpose flour

2 teaspoons baking powder

1 teaspoon salt

1 cup (8 ounces) unsalted butter, room temperature

⅔ cup granulated sugar

½ cup chocolate syrup

2 large eggs

1 teaspoon vanilla extract

¼ cup whole or 2% milk

Peanut or cashew halves (see Baker's Note)

1. Preheat the oven to 375°F and place a rack in the center. Line two baking sheets with nonstick foil or parchment paper.

2. Mix the flour, baking powder, and salt together in a medium-size bowl; set aside.

3. In the bowl of a stand mixer fitted with a paddle attachment, or in a large mixing bowl, using a handheld electric mixer, beat the butter and sugar on medium speed until light and fluffy. Blend in the chocolate syrup. Add the eggs, one at a time, beating well after each addition. Blend in the vanilla.

4. Add the flour mixture alternately with the milk, beating well after each addition. Cover and chill for 1 hour.

5. Drop by heaping teaspoonfuls of batter about 3 inches apart onto the prepared baking sheets. Press four peanut halves along the edge of each cookie. Bake one sheet at a time for 10 to 12 minutes, or until the centers spring back when lightly touched. Let cool on the baking sheets for 2 minutes, then transfer to a wire rack to cool completely.

Baker's Note: You can use whatever type of nuts you want for the claws. I almost always use peanuts.

Bring in the Chips Cookies MAKES ABOUT 48

1¼ cups (5.6 ounces) all-purpose flour

½ teaspoon baking powder

¼ teaspoon baking soda

½ teaspoon salt

8 tablespoons (4 ounces) unsalted butter, room temperature

½ cup firmly packed brown sugar

½ cup granulated sugar

1 teaspoon vanilla extract

1 large egg

1 cup white chips

1 cup semisweet chips

1 cup butterscotch chips

1 cup crispy rice cereal, such as Rice Krispies

than Baked Alaska, and they won't melt.

This recipe was adapted from a website called Welcome to Alaska. The mildly chocolate dough bakes up into a slightly cakey, dense, perfectly paw-shaped cookie.

Other Events on This Day:
No-Beard Day

OCTOBER 19

National Cookie Month

October is National Cookie Month. I'm not sure who declared it, but if Mrs. Fields celebrates it (in the past, that company has given away cookies), then it must be so. Celebrate by buying cookies, baking cookies, and eating cookies—preferably with a big glass of milk, because tomorrow is World Osteoporosis Day.

I wasn't sure what to think about this recipe when I spotted it on the back of an Imperial Sugar box. Was it really worth buying all those chips? Wouldn't the hodgepodge of flavors just cancel each other out? No! They're delicious, and better still, they keep well. If you are looking for a cookie to pack in tins and give out at Christmas, look no further.

Other Events on This Day:
Rainforest Day

═══════════════════

Vegetarian Awareness Month

We're twenty days into Vegetarian Awareness Month. Have you hugged a vegetarian today?

This cookie is for the vegetarian in your life, and because many vegetarians have chosen to avoid animal products altogether, I've made it vegan.

Other Events on This Day:
Brandied Fruit Day, Home Movie Day, the US Senate ratifies the Louisiana Purchase in 1803

═══════════════════

1 Preheat the oven to 350°F and place a rack in the center. Have ready two ungreased baking sheets.

2 Mix the flour, baking powder, baking soda, and salt together in a medium-size bowl; set aside.

3 In the bowl of a stand mixer fitted with a paddle attachment, or in a large mixing bowl, using a handheld electric mixer, beat the butter and both sugars on medium speed until creamy. Beat in the vanilla and egg, beating just until mixed. Add the flour mixture to the sugar mixture and stir until almost blended. Add all the chips and the cereal; stir until well mixed and all the flour is absorbed.

4 Drop rounded teaspoonfuls of batter about 2½ inches apart onto the baking sheets. Bake one sheet at a time for 10 to 15 minutes, or until golden brown around the edges. Let cool on the baking sheets for 3 to 4 minutes, then transfer to a wire rack to cool completely.

Small-Batch Vegan Molasses Cookies MAKES 16

1 cup plus 2 tablespoons (5 ounces) all-purpose flour

1 teaspoon baking soda

½ teaspoon ground cinnamon

½ teaspoon ground ginger

¼ teaspoon ground cloves

⅛ teaspoon salt

½ cup firmly packed light brown sugar

6 tablespoons vegetable or melted coconut oil

2 tablespoons mild molasses

½ teaspoon vanilla extract

2 tablespoons drained unsweetened applesauce (see Baker's Note)

Sparkling sugar, for sprinkling

1 Preheat the oven to 325°F and place a rack in the center. Line two baking sheets with parchment paper or nonstick foil.

2 Mix the flour, baking soda, cinnamon, ginger, cloves, and salt together in a small bowl.

3 Mix the brown sugar, vegetable oil, molasses, vanilla, and applesauce together in a medium-size mixing bowl. Add the flour mixture to the brown sugar mixture and stir until blended.

4 Scoop up tablespoonfuls of dough and shape into ¾-inch balls. Arrange about 2½ inches apart on the prepared baking sheets and press down to about ½ inch thick. Sprinkle the tops with sparkling sugar. Bake one sheet at a time for 13 to 15 minutes. Let cool on the baking sheets for 2 minutes, then transfer to a wire rack to cool completely.

Baker's Note: Drain the applesauce on a paper towel before measuring it.

Pumpkin Cheesecake Cookies MAKES ABOUT 48

COOKIES

2½ cups (11.25 ounces) all-purpose flour

1 teaspoon baking powder

1 teaspoon baking soda

½ teaspoon salt

2 teaspoons pumpkin pie spice

1 teaspoon ground cinnamon

8 tablespoons (4 ounces) unsalted butter, room temperature

1½ cups granulated sugar

1 cup canned pumpkin (not pumpkin pie mix)

1 large egg

1 teaspoon vanilla extract

FILLING AND TOPPING

1 (8-ounce) package cream cheese, softened

¼ cup granulated sugar

Tiny pinch of salt

1 large egg

¼ teaspoon vanilla extract

3 ounces white chocolate, chopped

Reptile Awareness Day

If there's anything you want to be aware of, it's reptiles—especially snakes, which seem to appear out of nowhere even when they're just hanging out in their usual favorite places.

What do reptiles have to do with pumpkin cheesecake cookies? They serve as a reminder to watch out for snakes when you're in the pumpkin patch. Rodents just love pumpkin, and snakes go where the rodents are.

Other Events on This Day: **Apple Day (in the United Kingdom), National White Chocolate Day**

1 Preheat the oven to 350°F and place a rack in the center. Line two baking sheets with parchment paper or nonstick foil.

2 **Make the cookies:** Mix the flour, baking powder, baking soda, salt, pumpkin pie spice, and cinnamon together in a bowl; set aside.

3 In the bowl of a stand mixer fitted with a paddle attachment, or in a large mixing bowl, using a handheld electric mixer, beat the butter and sugar on medium speed until creamy. Beat in the pumpkin, egg, and vanilla and beat until smooth. By hand or using the lowest speed of the mixer, stir in the flour mixture. Cover the bowl with plastic wrap and keep chilled while you prepare the filling.

4 **Make the filling and topping:** Beat the cream cheese, sugar, and salt together in a medium-size bowl, using a handheld electric mixer. When smooth, beat in the egg and vanilla.

5 Remove the batter from the refrigerator. It will be slightly sticky, but you should be able to shape it if you put a little bit of water on your fingers to keep it from sticking.

6 Drop by rounded teaspoonfuls of batter about 3 inches apart onto the baking sheets. Wet your thumb and make a deep well in the center of each cookie. Spoon about ½ teaspoon of the cream cheese mixture into the well. Bake the cookies one sheet at a time for 12 minutes, or until the cookies appear set. Let cool on the baking sheets for about 5 minutes, then transfer to a wire rack to cool completely. When cool, melt the white chocolate in a microwave-safe bowl, using 50 percent power and stirring at 30-second intervals, or melt in the top of a double-boiler. Drizzle the melted white chocolate over the cookies.

No-Bake Honey Bars MAKES 9

2 cups crispy rice cereal, such as Rice Krispies

1 cup quick-cooking oats (not instant)

¼ cup shredded sweetened coconut

¼ cup peanuts, coarsely chopped

2½ tablespoons (1.25 ounces) unsalted butter

¼ cup honey

¼ cup creamy peanut butter

⅛ teaspoon salt

1½ cups miniature marshmallows

½ teaspoon vanilla extract

1 Line an 8-inch square pan with nonstick foil, or line it with regular foil and spray the foil with flour-added baking spray.

2 Mix the cereal, oats, coconut, and peanuts together in a mixing bowl. In a saucepan set over medium-low heat, combine the butter, honey, peanut butter, and salt. Add the marshmallows and stir until they are melted. Stir in the vanilla. Pour the peanut butter mixture over the cereal mixture and stir to coat. Press firmly into the pan and let cool slightly, then chill for about 30 minutes. Remove from the pan by lifting the foil, set on a cutting board, and score into nine squares.

Blue Sky Sugar Cookies
MAKES ABOUT 30

COOKIES

1 cup (8 ounces) unsalted butter

1½ cups sifted confectioners' sugar

½ scant teaspoon salt

1 large egg

1 teaspoon vanilla extract

½ teaspoon almond extract

Annette Funicello's Birthday

Here's a cookie tribute to a Hollywood legend. Before becoming one of the most popular Mouseketeers, Annette Funicello took singing and dancing lessons to overcome shyness. She went on to costar in movies with Frankie Avalon. As an adult, Annette did commercials for Skippy peanut butter, putting her trusted face behind the slogan, "It's Hard to Beat Skippy."

Other Events on This Day:
Stuttering Awareness Day

The Smurfs' First Appearance

On October 23, 1958, the Smurfs made their first appearance in a comic strip by Belgian cartoonist Peyo (Pierre Culliford). It was originally a story about a young page recovering a magic flute, but the

Smurfs eventually went from being secondary characters to stars of their own adventures. But music is what made them big. In 1977, Dutch musician Pierre Kartner wrote "The Smurf Song" (different from the one you're probably thinking of) to promote a Smurfs movie. The song was a hit all over the world, and plush toys, figurines, and merchandise followed.

Other Events on This Day:
National Mole Day (the mathematical mole, not the rodent) created to spark interest in chemistry and commemorate Avogadro's Number

1 teaspoon baking soda

1 teaspoon cream of tartar

2½ cups (11.25 ounces) all-purpose
   flour, plus more if needed

FROSTING

4 tablespoons (2 ounces) unsalted butter

1¾ cups confectioners' sugar

½ teaspoon vanilla extract, plus any other flavorings
   you like (such as almond or orange)

1 to 3 tablespoons whole milk

Pinch of salt

Blue sprinkles or blue sparkling sugar

1 **Make the cookies:** In a microwave-safe mixing bowl, microwave the butter on high for 30 seconds, or until melted. Let cool for 5 minutes, then add the confectioners' sugar and stir until smooth. Stir in the salt, egg, vanilla, and almond extract. Next, add the baking soda and cream of tartar. Stir well with a mixing spoon, making sure there are no clumps of baking soda or cream of tartar. Scrape the sides of the bowl and stir a little more. Add the flour and stir until blended. Do not beat it. The dough will be more like batter, so don't even think about rolling it.

2 Divide the dough into four portions and set each portion on a separate sheet of parchment paper or nonstick foil. Press down each portion of dough into a ⅓-inch-thick mass. Stack the portions of pressed dough on top of each other, using the parchment paper as dividers, and chill for 1 hour, or until firm.

3 Preheat the oven to 350°F and place a rack in the center. Line two baking sheets with nonstick foil or parchment paper.

4 Remove one portion of dough from the refrigerator. No need to roll, because you've already pressed it. Now, quickly cut some shapes. The dough gets soft as it sits, so you have to work fairly quickly. Lift the shapes from the dough and place on the prepared baking sheets. Lift up the scraps, press, and cut. Repeat with another portion of dough.

5   Bake the cutouts one sheet at a time for 8 to 10 minutes, or until they appear nicely set and the edges are browned. Let cool on the baking sheets for a few minutes, then transfer to a rack to cool completely.

6   **Make the frosting:** Mix together the butter, confectioners' sugar, vanilla, 1 tablespoon of milk, and salt, and beat until smooth. Add the remaining milk if the icing is still too thick to spread. Ice the cookies when they are cool, and then sprinkle with blue sprinkles or sparkling sugar.

Brunsli MAKES ABOUT 30,
DEPENDING ON THE SIZE OF YOUR CUTTER

9 ounces finely ground almonds or almond flour

2/3 cup plus 1 teaspoon granulated sugar

1/8 teaspoon salt

1/4 teaspoon ground cinnamon

1/8 teaspoon ground cloves

1/8 teaspoon cayenne

2 tablespoons natural or Dutch-processed cocoa powder

2 tablespoons all-purpose flour

2 large egg whites

3.5 ounces dark or semisweet chocolate, melted

2 teaspoons vanilla extract

Whole or 2% milk, optional

1   Line a large baking sheet with parchment paper.

2   Mix the almonds, sugar, salt, cinnamon, cloves, cayenne, cocoa powder, and flour together in a large mixing bowl. Add the egg whites and stir until the ingredients are evenly distributed. Add the melted chocolate and vanilla and knead to form a soft dough. If the dough is too dry, add milk 1 tablespoon at a time until the dough comes together. Transfer the dough to the prepared baking sheet and flatten it to a little less than 1/4 inch thick. At this point, it should be firm enough to cut with cutters, but still slightly sticky. If you're using simple cutters such as

United Nations Day

Today is United Nations Day, so make 192 cookies, each representing a different country, put them all on a tray together, and serve. That, or pick one country (preferably a member of the UN) and make one delicious cookie to promote peace in your little corner of the world.

In honor of my Swiss relatives who settled in Texas, here's a Swiss version of brownies which I've cut into the shape of the Lone Star State. The dough is easy to cut, so make yours any shape you'd like.

Other Events on This Day: **Bologna Day, Take Back Your Time Day**

rounds or hearts, you can cut it from this stage. Otherwise, put the baking sheet with the flattened dough in the refrigerator to chill for about 10 minutes, or until it's slightly firmer. Cut the dough into shapes, set about 1½ inches apart on the prepared baking sheet, and let them rest at room temperature for about 5 hours.

3 Preheat the oven to 450°F and place a rack in the center. Bake the shapes for about 5 minutes. Transfer to a wire rack to cool completely and serve.

Baker's Notes: This Swiss version of brownies is more like a rich, chewy, spicy, chocolate cookie. The process of drying them out before baking results in a cookie that's moist on the inside with a very firm and chewy shell. For the proper texture, let the cut cookie dough sit at room temperature for about 5 hours.

OCTOBER 25

Oregon's Hazelnut Harvest

Hazelnuts have been cultivated in different parts of the world for thousands of years, but America gets 99 percent of its hazelnuts from the rich and fertile soils of Oregon. Harvest season starts near the end of September or in early October, when the hazelnuts (also known as filberts) fall naturally to the ground. At that point, they are swept up by machines and picked up by harvesters who separate the nuts from the twigs.

Other Events on This Day:
Sourest Day (opposite of Sweetest Day)

Hazelnut Shortbread
MAKES ABOUT 24

½ cup hazelnuts, toasted, skins removed (see Baker's Note)
1 cup (8 ounces) unsalted butter, room temperature
½ teaspoon salt
½ cup confectioners' sugar
¾ teaspoon vanilla extract
½ cup cornstarch
1½ cups (6.8 ounces) all-purpose flour
2 ounces semisweet chocolate, finely chopped (optional)

1 Line a large baking sheet with parchment paper or non-stick foil.

2 In the bowl of a food processor, chop the hazelnuts so that they are very fine, being careful not to grind them into a meal. Remove the hazelnuts from the processor and add the butter; process the butter until it's creamy. Add the salt, sugar, and vanilla and pulse to mix, then add the cornstarch and flour and pulse until the mixture starts

to clump together. Add the hazelnuts and chocolate and pulse once or twice to mix. Transfer the mixture to the prepared baking sheet and press into a slab about ⅓ inch thick. Chill until very firm.

3 Preheat the oven to 350°F and place a rack in the center. Lift the liner from the pan and set the firm dough on a flat surface. Using a 1¾-inch round cutter or another one about the same size, cut circles and lay them 2 inches apart on an ungreased baking sheet. Bake for 12 to 15 minutes, or until the cookies appear set and the edges show a tiny bit of brown—they won't brown very much because of the cornstarch. Let cool on the baking sheet for about 4 minutes, then transfer to a wire rack to cool completely.

Baker's Note: Toast the hazelnuts on a rimmed baking sheet at 350°F for 7 to 9 minutes, or until aromatic. Transfer the hot nuts to a kitchen towel, then fold the sides of the towel up over the nuts. Press down on the towel and rub back and forth to rub off the skins.

Crunchy Nugget Chocolate Chip Cookies MAKES 28 LARGE COOKIES

8 tablespoons (4 ounces) unsalted
    butter, room temperature
½ cup firmly packed dark brown sugar
½ cup granulated sugar
3 scant tablespoons honey
2 large eggs
2 teaspoons vanilla extract
1 teaspoon baking soda
½ teaspoon salt
2 cups old-fashioned or quick-
    cooking oats (not instant)
1 cup (4.5 ounces) white whole wheat
    or all-purpose flour
1 cup barley nuggets cereal, such as Grape-Nuts
1 cup semisweet chocolate chips

Fact: Post named the cereal Grape-Nuts because it smelled like grapes as it baked.

1 Preheat the oven to 350°F and place a rack in the center. Line two baking sheets with nonstick foil or parchment paper.

2 In the bowl of a stand mixer fitted with a paddle attachment, or in a large mixing bowl, using a handheld electric mixer, beat the butter and both sugars on medium speed until creamy and smooth. Add the honey, eggs, and vanilla; mix well. Add the baking soda, salt, oats, flour, and cereal and stir until mixed. Stir in the chips.

3 Drop rounded tablespoons of dough 2 inches apart onto the prepared baking sheets. Bake one sheet at a time for 10 to 14 minutes, or until golden brown. Let cool on the baking sheets for 2 to 3 minutes, then transfer to a wire rack to cool completely.

OCTOBER 27

The New York Subway First Opens

On this day in 1904, the New York subway opened for business. Planned by the city's sharpest minds, the subway was built to meet the demands of that period and the future. An important element was the four-track design that made it possible to run trains as express and local. Today, with a ridership of well over 4 million people per day, it is the busiest rapid transit system in the entire Western Hemisphere.

In recognition of the subway system, these brownies have a tunnel of pumpkin cheesecake running beneath a delicious brownie.

Other Events on This Day:
Navy Day

Layered Pumpkin Cheesecake Brownies MAKES 16

FILLING

12 ounces cream cheese, softened

6 tablespoons firmly packed light brown sugar

2 tablespoons granulated sugar

¾ cup canned pumpkin (not pumpkin pie mix)

1 large egg plus 2 tablespoons beaten egg

½ teaspoon vanilla extract

¾ teaspoon pumpkin pie spice (see Baker's Note)

1½ tablespoons (0.4 ounce) all-purpose flour

BATTER

1 cup (8 ounces) unsalted butter, room temperature

¼ teaspoon plus a tiny pinch of salt

1½ cups granulated sugar

3 large eggs

1 teaspoon vanilla extract

9 ounces (1½ cups) bittersweet chocolate chips, melted and cooled

1 cup (4.5 ounces) all-purpose flour

1 Preheat the oven to 350°F and place a rack in the center. Line a 9-inch square metal pan with foil and spray the foil with flour-added baking spray.

2 **Make the filling:** Beat the cream cheese and both sugars together at medium-high speed with an electric mixer, then reduce the mixer speed to medium-low and beat in the pumpkin, egg, vanilla, and pumpkin pie spice. Stir in the flour. Set aside.

3 **Make the batter:** In a second bowl, beat the butter, salt, and sugar with an electric mixer on medium speed until creamy. Beat in the eggs and vanilla. Stir in the melted chocolate chips, then stir in the flour. Pour all but about ¾ cup of the chocolate mixture into the prepared pan.

4 Spoon the pumpkin mixture evenly over the brownie batter in the pan.

5 Drop the reserved brownie batter over the pumpkin to give the brownies a splotched, marbled look. Bake for 45 to 50 minutes, or until the brownies pull away from the edges and appear set. Let cool in the pan for about 2 hours and then chill for a few hours or overnight. Lift from the pan, set on a cutting board, and cut into sixteen squares.

Baker's Note: If you don't have pumpkin pie spice, substitute with a mixture of ½ teaspoon of ground cinnamon, ¼ teaspoon of ground ginger, ¼ teaspoon of freshly grated nutmeg, and a very tiny pinch of ground cloves.

Death by Giant Chocolate Cookies MAKES 18

2 (8-ounce) packages semisweet chocolate

4 tablespoons (2 ounces) unsalted butter

¼ teaspoon salt

¾ cup firmly packed light brown sugar

2 large eggs

National Chocolate Day

Not to be confused with International Chocolate Day in September, October 28 is a day we celebrate chocolate from America.

The first chocolate mill in America was founded in 1765 by Dr. James Baker and John Hannon. It was built along the banks of the Neponset River in Dorchester, Massachusetts, so that the flow of the river powered the stones that ground chocolate beans into syrup. The syrup was poured into molds and cooled to form chocolate bricks.

Adapted from a Baker's Chocolate ad, this recipe is my version of an old favorite from Baker's Chocolate Company. In fact, it may have bridged my transition from box mixes to scratch, as it's one of those recipes that proves scratch baking can be easy, not too messy, and extraordinarily delicious.

Other Events on This Day:
Statue of Liberty Dedication Day

---

1 teaspoon vanilla extract
¼ teaspoon baking powder
½ cup (2.3 ounces) all-purpose flour
1 cup walnuts, toasted and chopped

1 Preheat the oven to 350°F and place a rack in the center. Line two large baking sheets with parchment paper or nonstick foil.

2 Coarsely chop eight squares (one package) of the chocolate; set aside.

3 Microwave the butter and the remaining eight squares of chocolate in a large, microwave-safe bowl at 50 percent power for 1 to 2 minutes, stirring every 60 seconds. Beat in the salt, brown sugar, eggs, and vanilla extract, followed by the baking powder. When the baking powder is thoroughly mixed in, add the flour and stir just until blended, then stir in the nuts. If the mixture is still hot, let it cool slightly. When cool, stir in the reserved chopped chocolate and the walnuts. At this point, you can bake the cookies, or if the batter seems too wet to scoop, just chill it for about 20 minutes.

4 Scoop up generously heaping tablespoonfuls of dough and make 1½ inch mounds about 2½ inches apart on the prepared baking sheets. Bake one sheet at a time for 12 minutes, or until the cookies appear set. Let cool on the baking sheets for about 2 minutes, then transfer to a wire rack to cool completely.

Baker's Notes: For fatter cookies, chill the dough before shaping and baking. If using salted butter, omit the salt. I've also found that bleached flour produces a somewhat thicker cookie, but since I keep unbleached flour in the pantry, I usually just use that.

Hermit Bars MAKES 8 LARGE BARS

1½ cups (6.8 ounces) all-purpose flour

½ teaspoon baking soda

¾ teaspoon ground cinnamon

¼ teaspoon freshly grated nutmeg

¼ teaspoon ground cloves

¼ teaspoon salt

½ cup granulated sugar

¼ cup vegetable oil

¼ cup mild molasses

⅓ cup whole or 2% milk

½ cup raisins, regular or golden

½ cup walnuts, toasted and chopped

2 tablespoons shredded or sweetened
   coconut flakes or oats, for garnishing

1 Preheat the oven to 350°F and place a rack in the center. Line a 9-inch square metal pan with nonstick foil.

2 Mix the flour, baking soda, cinnamon, nutmeg, cloves, salt, and sugar together in a large mixing bowl. Make a little well in the center of the flour mixture. Into the well, pour the oil, molasses, and milk. Stir them together in the well. Add the rasins and walnuts, then mix everything together. Spread the mixture over the bottom of the prepared pan and sprinkle with coconut or oats. Bake for 25 minutes. Let cool completely in the pan, and then lift from the pan, set on a cutting board, and score into eight bars.

S'mores Chocolate Chip Cookies MAKES 32

1¼ cups (5.6 ounces) all-purpose flour

1 cup graham cracker crumbs

½ teaspoon baking soda

½ teaspoon salt

12 tablespoons (6 ounces) unsalted
   butter, room temperature

½ cup granulated sugar

National Hermit Day

If you enjoy being alone, today is your day. No one really knows the origin because it was probably thought up by tight-lipped hermits, but the Internet has declared it National Hermit Day and that's a good enough excuse to make some hermit cookies.

Hermit cookies are made as bars or cookies and use ingredients with preservative qualities, such as molasses and spices. Perhaps that's why they're called hermits: A hermit could take them to the woods and keep them for a long time before having to return to civilization to buy more cookies.

This particular hermit is the bar form. It has no eggs or butter.

Other Events on This Day:
Oatmeal Day

Juliette Gordon Low's Birthday

Her birthday isn't until tomorrow, but I couldn't let it get overshadowed by ghouls and goblins.

Juliette Magill Kinzie Gordon was born on October 31, 1860, in Savannah, Georgia. Known as "Daisy," Juliette grew up in a privileged household where she developed a lifelong appreciation for the arts and athletics. After meeting Sir Robert Baden-Powell, founder of the Boy Scouts and Girl Guides in England, Juliette returned to America and founded the Girl Scouts, an organization that brought girls from all walks of life to come together and learn about the arts, sciences, and business.

The best way to honor Juliette Low is to buy Girl Scout cookies, but until they go on sale, here's a recipe inspired by a Girl Scout favorite.

Other Events on This Day:
National Candy Corn Day, Mischief Night

½ cup firmly packed light brown sugar

1 teaspoon vanilla extract

1 large egg

1½ cups semisweet chocolate chips

1 cup miniature marshmallows

2 (1.45-ounce) milk chocolate bars, such as Hershey's, broken into small pieces

1 Preheat the oven to 375°F and place a rack in the center. Line two baking sheets with parchment paper or nonstick foil.

2 Mix the flour, graham cracker crumbs, baking soda, and salt together in a medium-size bowl; set aside.

3 In the bowl of a stand mixer fitted with a paddle attachment, or in a large mixing bowl, using a handheld electric mixer, beat the butter and both sugars on medium speed until creamy; add the vanilla and egg and beat for another 30 seconds. Scrape the sides of the bowl.

4 By hand or using the lowest speed of the mixer, stir in the flour mixture. When the flour mixture is incorporated, stir in the chocolate chips.

5 Drop rounded tablespoonfuls of dough about 2½ inches apart onto the prepared baking sheets. Bake one sheet at a time for 8 minutes or until the cookies appear almost set. Remove from the oven and quickly press a couple of marshmallows and a few small pieces of milk chocolate into the cookies. Return the pan to the oven and bake for about 3 more minutes or until the marshmallows have puffed up and the cookies appear set. If you are concerned about timing it just right, bake one cookie as a tester and repeat.

6 Let cool on the baking sheets for 3 minutes, then transfer to a wire rack to cool completely.

Darkest Hour Absinthe Brownies MAKES 24

12 tablespoons (6 ounces) unsalted butter

1²/₃ cups granulated sugar

1 cup unsweetened Dutch-processed cocoa powder,
    such as Hershey's Special Dark (see Baker's Note)

¾ scant teaspoon salt

¾ teaspoon baking powder

¾ teaspoon vanilla extract

1 tablespoon absinthe, plus more for brushing

3 large eggs

1 cup plus 2 tablespoon (5 ounces) all-purpose flour

1 cup semisweet or dark chocolate chips

1 Preheat the oven to 350°F and place a rack in the center. Line a 9-inch square metal pan with nonstick foil, or line it with regular foil and spray the foil with flour-added baking spray.

2 In a large microwave-safe mixing bowl, microwave the butter on high for 30 seconds, or until melted. Add the sugar and whisk to combine. Return the mixture to the microwave and heat for about 30 seconds. Stir well.

3 Stir in the cocoa powder, salt, baking powder, vanilla, and absinthe. Add the eggs, whisking until smooth. Add the flour and stir until combined, then let the batter cool for about 10 minutes so that you won't accidentally melt the chocolate chips. When the batter is cool, add the chocolate chips.

4 Spoon the batter into the prepared pan. Bake for 26 to 28 minutes, until a toothpick inserted in the center comes out clean. Let cool completely in the pan. If desired, brush the top with absinthe. When the brownies are cool, place the pan in the refrigerator and chill. When cold, lift from the pan, set on a cutting board, and cut into four squares. Cut each square in six pieces, to make twenty-four small, rich brownies.

Baker's Note: While any brand Dutch-processed cocoa will work, I recommend Hershey's Dark because it makes the brownies nice and dark for Halloween.

Halloween

Originally from Switzerland and dubbed "the green fairy" for its deep green color, absinthe gained a reputation among artists and intellectuals as a creativity-enhancing elixir and aphrodisiac. Based on the alleged harmful effects of a chemical in wormwood called thujone, and vilified by the temperance movement, absinthe was banned in 1915 in several countries.

In the 1990s, absinthe made a comeback and is now being produced in over a dozen countries. It's an acquired taste, with a slightly bitter flavor of licorice or anise. The traditional serving method is to pour ice-cold water over a cube of sugar that is resting on a slotted spoon suspended over a glass with the portion of absinthe, but there's also my method, which is to mix it into brownie batter and then brush a little over the top.

Other Events on This Day:
Increase Your Psychic Powers Day

Diwali

Diwali is a five-day-long Hindu festival celebrating good over evil and light over darkness. Commemorating Rama's return from a perilous journey to save his wife, Sita, Diwali is known as the Festival of Lights, with candle lightings, *diyas* (oil lamps), and firecrackers of different colors.

Sweets are an important part of Diwali, and candies made with cardamom, semolina, cashews, raisins, sesame, and coconut are kept on hand for guests who drop by.

This cookie is a very Americanized tribute to the flavors of Indian candies.

Other Events on This Day:
In 1873, Joseph Glidden began manufacturing barbed wire, closing the open range and ending the era of the cowboy.

Sesame, White Chip, and Oat Cookies MAKES ABOUT 48

1½ cups (6.8 ounces) white whole wheat or all-purpose flour

1 teaspoon ground cinnamon

¾ teaspoon baking soda

½ teaspoon salt

¼ teaspoon freshly grated nutmeg

12 tablespoons (6 ounces) unsalted butter, room temperature

1⅓ cups firmly packed light brown sugar

2 large eggs

1 teaspoon vanilla extract

1 cup sesame seeds, lightly toasted and
    cooled (see Baker's Note)

1 cup white chocolate chips or white chips

1 cup old-fashioned or quick-cooking oats (not instant)

⅓ cup sweetened flaked, or sweetened or
    unsweetened shredded coconut (optional)

1 Preheat the oven to 350°F and place a rack in the center. Have ready two ungreased baking sheets.

2 Mix the flour, cinnamon, baking soda, salt, and nutmeg together in a medium-size bowl; set aside.

3 In the bowl of a stand mixer fitted with a paddle attachment, or in a large mixing bowl, using a handheld electric mixer, beat the butter on medium-high speed until creamy. Beat in the brown sugar and continue beating for about 2 minutes, or until the mixture is smooth. Reduce the speed of the mixer to medium and beat in the eggs and vanilla. Reduce the mixer speed to low and gradually add the flour mixture. Stir in the cooled toasted sesame seeds, white chips, oats, and coconut, if using.

4 Scoop up rounded teaspoonfuls of dough and shape into ¾-inch balls. Arrange about 2 inches apart on the baking sheets and press down the tops slightly. Bake one sheet at a time for 11 to 13 minutes, or until golden brown. Let cool on the baking sheets for about 5 minutes, then transfer to a wire rack to cool completely.

Baker's Note: Make sure to toast the sesame seeds to bring out their flavor. I toast them by pouring them in a dry skillet and heating over medium, stirring often, until they become fragrant.

Bones of the Dead Cookies MAKES ABOUT 45

3 large egg whites

¼ teaspoon cream of tartar

⅛ teaspoon salt

⅔ cup granulated sugar

¾ teaspoon vanilla extract

¼ teaspoon almond extract

1 Preheat the oven to 200°F and place a rack in the center. Line a large baking sheet with nonstick foil.

2 In the bowl of a stand mixer fitted with a whisk or in a large mixing bowl, using a handheld electric mixer, beat the egg whites, cream of tartar, and salt at high speed until stiff peaks start to form. Beat in the sugar a few tablespoons at a time, and then beat in the vanilla and almond extract.

3 Transfer the mixture to a resealable heavy-duty freezer bag and snip about ¼ inch from the bottom corner. Pipe bone shapes about 2 inches apart onto the prepared baking sheet. Bake for 1 hour. Turn off the oven and let the cookies dry on the baking sheet in the oven for 1 hour.

Lisa's Coconut Chocolate Sandwich Cookies MAKES ABOUT 36

COOKIES

¾ cup (3.4 ounces) all-purpose flour

1 (7-ounce) bag shredded sweetened coconut

½ cup whole unsalted almonds, toasted

¼ teaspoon salt

NOVEMBER 2

All Souls' Day

Unless it falls on a Sunday, in which case it is moved up to Monday, All Souls' Day is always celebrated on November 2. Like its Mexican counterpart Day of the Dead, it is a day of remembrance of loved ones who have passed. In Mexico's Day of the Dead celebration, it's customary to visit graveyards and make sugar skulls and treats.

Other Events on This Day:
Deviled Egg Day

NOVEMBER 3

Sandwich Day

According to legend, the sandwich was invented in 1718 when the 4th Earl of Sandwich, not wanting to interrupt his gambling session, put some meat between two slices of bread and ate it while he played.

This recipe is from my friend Lisa, an expert baker who writes a blog called *The Snappy Gourmet*. It's a coconut rich cookie with a filling made of chocolate chips, coffee liqueur, and butter. I use Kahlúa; Lisa makes these with amaretto.

Other Events on This Day:
National Housewives' Day

8 tablespoons (4 ounces) unsalted butter, softened

½ cup granulated sugar

1 large egg

2 teaspoons coffee liqueur, such as Kahlúa

FILLING

2 cups semisweet or extra-dark chocolate chips

¼ cup coffee liqueur, such as Kahlúa

2 tablespoons (1 ounce) unsalted
    butter, room temperature

1   Preheat the oven to 350°F and place a rack in the center. Line two baking sheets with nonstick foil or parchment paper.

2   **Make the cookies:** Place the flour, coconut, almonds, and salt in food processor and process until the coconut and almonds are finely chopped.

3   In a large mixing bowl, beat the butter and sugar with an electric mixer on medium speed until creamy. Beat in the egg and the coffee liqueur until well blended. Stir in the flour mixture.

4   Drop teaspoonfuls of dough about 2 inches apart onto the prepared baking sheets. Gently flatten the cookies with your fingers to make small rounds. Bake one sheet at a time for 10 to 14 minutes, or until lightly browned underneath; watch carefully after the first 8 minutes, because the cookies start to brown rapidly. Let cool on the baking sheets for about 5 minutes, then transfer to a wire rack to cool completely.

5   **Make the filling:** Place the chocolate chips, liqueur, and butter in a microwave-safe bowl. Microwave on 50 percent power, stirring at 30-second intervals, until melted and smooth, 3 to 5 minutes. If the mixture is thin, let it cool slightly until it's spreadable.

6   Spread the underside of one cookie with the filling, then top base to base with another cookie. Repeat until all the cookies are sandwiched. Let cool completely on a wire rack.

Slice-and-Bake Oatmeal-Date-Nut Cookies

MAKES ABOUT 30 LARGE COOKIES

2½ cups (11.3 ounces) all-purpose flour

1 teaspoon salt

2 teaspoons baking soda

1¼ teaspoons ground cinnamon

½ cup (3.4 ounces) shortening

8 tablespoons (4 ounces) unsalted butter

1 cup firmly packed light brown sugar

1 cup granulated sugar

3 large eggs

1 teaspoon vanilla extract

2 cups old-fashioned or quick-cooking oats (not instant)

½ cup chopped dates

½ cup raisins

¾ cup coarsely chopped, toasted pecans

1 Mix the flour, salt, baking soda, and cinnamon together in a medium-size bowl; set aside.

2 In the bowl of a stand mixer fitted with a paddle attachment, or in a large mixing bowl, using a handheld electric mixer, beat the shortening, butter, and both sugars on medium speed until light and creamy. Reduce the mixer speed slightly and beat in the eggs and vanilla. Stir in the oats, dates, raisins, and pecans.

3 Divide the mixture in half. Form each portion into a log about 2 inches in diameter. Chill the dough for at least 1 hour.

4 When ready to bake, preheat the oven to 350°F and place a rack in the center. Line two large baking sheets with parchment paper.

5 Cut the logs into slices ½ inch thick and place 2½ inches apart on the prepared baking sheets. Bake for 10 to 12 minutes. Let cool on the baking sheets for about 5 minutes, then transfer to a wire rack to cool completely.

King Tut Day

On this day in 1922, Howard Carter discovered the first step leading to King Tut's Tomb in Egypt's Valley of the Kings. While the tomb was not opened until February 16, today has been deemed King Tut Day. Known as "the Teen King," Tutankhamen began his rule in 1333 BC, when he was nine years old. His reign ended with his death in 1324 BC.

This recipe is from my friend Holly, mom of three and a small business owner who likes cookies that are simple and delicious. Holly makes her cookies with shortening in place of butter and leaves out the raisins and dates.

Other Events on This Day: **Election Day; African American inventor Thomas Elkins patented an improved refrigerating apparatus in 1879. While he acknowledged that refrigeration itself was "an old and well-known process," his design cycled a coolant liquid through a large container. Elkins also held patents for a table and a type of commode.**

Guy Fawkes Day

It's Guy Fawkes Day in the United Kingdom. Commemorating the Gunpowder Plot of 1605 in which Guy Fawkes and co-conspirators attempted to blow up the House of Lords in London, Guy Fawkes Day is celebrated with bonfires, fireworks, and burning effigies of Guy called "guys." Have your own little Guy Fawkes celebration with some hot and spicy gingerbread "guys."

Other Events on This Day:
(another) National Doughnut Day

Spicy Chocolate Ginger Guys   MAKES ABOUT 30

1 teaspoon baking soda

¼ cup hot coffee

8 tablespoons (4 ounces) unsalted butter

½ cup granulated sugar

½ teaspoon salt

1 large egg

1 cup mild molasses

1 teaspoon vanilla extract

½ cup unsweetened natural cocoa powder

1 teaspoon ground ginger

1 teaspoon ground cinnamon

¼ teaspoon ground cloves

¼ teaspoon freshly grated nutmeg

3¾ cups (17 ounces) all-purpose flour

1   Preheat the oven to 350°F and place a rack in the center. Line two baking sheets with nonstick foil or parchment paper.

2   Dissolve the baking soda in the coffee and set aside.

3   In the bowl of a stand mixer fitted with a paddle attachment, or in a large mixing bowl, using a handheld electric mixer, beat the butter and sugar on medium speed until creamy. Beat in the salt, egg, molasses, and vanilla. Add the cocoa powder, ginger, cinnamon, cloves, and nutmeg and stir until mixed. By hand or using the lowest speed of the mixer, stir in the flour alternately with the coffee mixture.

4   Roll out the dough about ⅜ inch thick on a floured surface. Cut out gingerbread men and arrange them 2 inches apart on the prepared baking sheets. Bake for 8 to 10 minutes, or until the guys appear set. Transfer to a wire rack and let cool completely.

Jalapeño and Cranberry Biscotti MAKES ABOUT 20

2 large eggs

½ cup granulated sugar

¼ cup vegetable oil

1 teaspoon orange zest, or about
    ¼ teaspoon orange extract

¼ teaspoon vanilla extract

2 teaspoons picante sauce

1⅓ cups (6 ounces) all-purpose flour

½ cup (2 ounces) cornmeal

½ scant teaspoon salt

1 teaspoon baking powder

½ teaspoon ground black pepper

⅛ teaspoon ground cumin

2 teaspoons very finely chopped medium-
    hot canned jalapeños

⅔ cup (more or less) pecans, toasted
    and finely chopped

½ cup dried cranberries

National Saxophone Day

What do Charlie Parker, John Coltrane, "Cannon-ball" Adderly, and Zoot from the Muppets have in common? They're all famous saxophone players, and today's their day. Sadly, they have to share it with National Nachos Day.

This unusual biscotti evolved from a quick bread my stepmother and I like to make around the holidays. Thinking we could turn it into a cookie, we went back and forth with measurements and ended up with jalapeño-flavored biscotti.

Other Events on This Day: Composer John Philip Sousa, the March King, was born in Washington DC in 1854.

1 Preheat the oven to 300°F and place a rack in the center. Line two baking sheets with nonstick foil or parchment paper.

2 In a large bowl, using a handheld electric mixer, beat the eggs for about a minute on high speed or until pale and light. Beat in the sugar. Continue beating for another 30 seconds, and then gradually beat in the oil. Mix in the zest, vanilla, and picante sauce. In a separate bowl, combine the flour, cornmeal, salt, baking powder, pepper, and cumin; with a mixing spoon or using the lowest speed of the mixer, gradually add the flour mixture to the batter. Stir in the jalapeños, pecans, and cranberries.

3 At this point, the dough will seem slightly wet, but you should still be able to shape it. Lightly dampen your hands to keep it from sticking, and mold the dough into

two logs about 3 inches wide and 7 inches long directly on the prepared baking sheet, spacing them at least 4½ inches apart.

4 Bake for 35 minutes at 300°F, or until the logs are lightly browned. Let cool on the baking sheet for about 20 minutes. Reduce the oven heat to 275°F.

5 Using a large knife, cut crosswise slightly on the diagonal every ¾ inch. Place cut side down on the lined baking sheet. Bake at 275°F for about 20 minutes, or until the edges are very dry. Let the biscotti cool and crisp on a wire rack.

NOVEMBER 7

Bittersweet Chocolate with Almonds Day

According to the National Confectionary Association, today's the day we celebrate the combination of almonds and bittersweet chocolate. Almonds are nutrient dense and contain plant sterols, which may help lower cholesterol, while bittersweet and dark chocolate have flavonols, chemicals known to increase blood flow. Given the health benefits of today's featured ingredients, I thought I'd try to stick with the theme and create a slightly more heart-healthy cookie.

Other Events on This Day:
International Tongue Twister Day

Vegan Almond and Bittersweet Chocolate Cookies MAKES 24

1 cup (4.5 ounces) white whole wheat or all-purpose flour

½ teaspoon baking soda

½ teaspoon salt

2 generous tablespoons almond butter

⅓ cup vegetable oil

2½ tablespoons water

2 tablespoons ground flaxseeds

½ teaspoon vanilla extract

⅓ cup firmly packed light brown sugar

⅓ cup granulated sugar

½ cup quick-cooking oats (not instant)

⅔ cup extra-dark or bittersweet chocolate chips

⅓ cup almonds, toasted and chopped

½ cup regular or pomegranate juice–infused dried cranberries

1 Preheat the oven to 350°F and place a rack in the center. Have ready two ungreased baking sheets.

2 Mix the flour, baking soda, and salt together in a medium-size bowl; set aside.

3 In a large mixing bowl, stir together the almond butter, vegetable oil, water, flaxseeds, vanilla, and both sugars. Add the flour mixture to the almond butter mixture and stir until blended. Stir in the oats, chocolate chips, almonds, and cranberries. The mixture will be somewhat dry and crumbly.

4 Scoop up firmly packed tablespoonfuls of dough and shape into tightly packed balls about 1 inch in diameter. If the dough is too crumbly to shape, add ½ tablespoon of water at a time until you can shape it. Arrange about 2 inches apart on the baking sheets and press down slightly. Bake for about 12 minutes. Let cool on the baking sheets for about 5 minutes, then transfer to a wire rack to cool completely.

Peach Bars MAKES 24

3.5 ounces almond paste, such as Odense

1 (17.5-ounce) pouch oatmeal cookie
   mix, such as Betty Crocker

8 tablespoons (4 ounces) salted or unsalted
   butter, room temperature

1 cup peach preserves

½ cup chopped almonds

1 Preheat the oven to 350°F and place a rack in the center. Line a 9 by 13-inch metal pan with nonstick foil or spray with flour-added baking spray.

2 In a large mixing bowl, using your fingers, break up the almond paste or shred with a grater. Stir in the cookie mix, mashing it around with the almond paste, then add the butter and mix it all together so it's crumbly. Set aside about one-third of the mixture (doesn't have to be exact, just eyeball it) to use as the topping. Press the remaining crumb mixture onto the bottom of the prepared pan and bake for 15 minutes.

NOVEMBER 8

Margaret Mitchell's Birthday

Margaret Mitchell, author of *Gone with the Wind*, was born in 1900 in Atlanta today. Fascinated by the Civil War stories told by Confederate veterans, Mitchell based her novel around Scarlett O'Hara, a Southern Belle trying to save her plantation after Sherman's March. Mitchell's saga of the South was published in June 1936. Shortly thereafter, she won the Pulitzer Prize.

Other Events on This Day:
National Dunce Day

345

3 Remove from the oven. In the microwave, heat the preserves for 5 to 10 seconds, or just until soft. Spread the preserves over the baked cookie crust. Sprinkle the remaining crumb mixture and almonds over the top and return the pan to the oven for 18 to 20 minutes. Let cool completely in the pan; for a cleaner cut, chill slightly after cooling. Lift the foil from the pan, set on a cutting board, and cut into twenty-four bars.

Gail Borden's Birthday

Born on this day in 1801, Gail Borden is best known as the name behind Elsie the Cow. He's also credited with inventing condensed milk.

The idea came to him during a voyage when rough seas inhibited the onboard cows' ability to produce milk, which led to the death of several infant passengers. Borden began experimenting with a vacuum pan he'd seen Shakers use to make condensed juice. He eventually obtained a sweet, condensed milk that did not need refrigeration. Because it was calorically rich, the government ordered vats of it for Union soldiers during the Civil War. When the soldiers came home, they spread the word, and by the late 1860s, condensed milk became a popular canned product.

Other Events on This Day:
Chaos Never Dies Day

Creamy Lemon Bars   MAKES 36

1½ cups (6.8 ounces) all-purpose
   flour, sifted or weighed
1 teaspoon baking powder
½ teaspoon salt
6 tablespoons (3 ounces)
   unsalted butter,
   room temperature
1 cup firmly packed dark brown sugar
1 cup old-fashioned or quick-cooking oats (not instant)
1 (14-ounce) can sweetened condensed milk
½ cup freshly squeezed lemon juice
1½ teaspoons lemon zest
⅓ cup pecans, lightly toasted and finely chopped

1 Preheat the oven to 350°F and place a rack in the center. Line a 9 by 13-inch metal pan with nonstick foil.

2 Mix the flour, baking powder, and salt together in a small bowl; set aside.

3 In the bowl of a stand mixer fitted with a paddle attachment, or in a large mixing bowl, using a handheld electric mixer, beat the butter and brown sugar on medium speed until creamy. By hand, stir in the flour mixture and then stir in the oats. Press about two-thirds of this mixture over the bottom of the pan, covering it the best you can. It might be a little thin around the edges. It's more important to have enough to cover the bottom of the pan rather than the top, so borrow a little from your reserved topping if you need to.

4 Mix together the sweetened condensed milk, lemon juice, and lemon zest. Pour over the unbaked crust. Crumble the remaining topping and sprinkle over the top. Sprinkle with the pecans. Bake for 25 minutes, or until the edges are lightly browned. Let cool completely in the pan. Chill for a couple of hours before slicing and serving.

Chipotle Beer Brittle
MAKES ABOUT 1 POUND

½ teaspoon salt

1½ teaspoons baking soda

⅛ teaspoon chipotle powder

1½ teaspoons unsalted butter

½ teaspoon vanilla extract

1½ cups granulated sugar

½ cup light corn syrup

¼ cup ale, such as Shiner, or water

1½ cups raw peanuts (see Baker's Note)

1 Line a large rimmed baking sheet with nonstick foil or parchment paper and have ready a candy thermometer.

2 Mix together the salt, baking soda, and chipotle powder and set next to the stove. Measure out the butter and vanilla and have them ready, too.

3 In a 3-quart nonstick saucepan, combine the sugar, corn syrup, and beer. Bring to a boil over medium heat. Add the peanuts and continue to cook, stirring, until the temperature of the mixture reaches about 250°F, at which point you want to stir constantly to keep the peanuts from burning. Continue to cook, stirring, until the temperature reaches exactly 300°F. Remove from the heat and quickly stir in the butter, vanilla, and chipotle mixture.

4 Pour onto the prepared baking sheet. If you want to make the brittle a little thinner, tilt the baking sheet slightly so it spreads, but don't tilt it so much you burst all the nice air bubbles. Let the mixture stand at room temperature until it hardens, then break into pieces.

Baker's Note: If you can't find raw peanuts, use unsalted dry roasted peanuts and add them when the temperature is between 240° and 250°F on the candy thermometer.

NOVEMBER 11

Veterans Day

Veterans Day is a federal holiday honoring those who have served in the armed forces. It is also celebrated as Armistice Day, which was declared on November 11, 1918, with the German signing of the Armistice. Because rosemary is the herb of remembrance, here's a cookie featuring the classic combination of rosemary and lemon.

Other Events on This Day:
Sundae Day, the Mayflower landed at Cape Cod in 1620

Lemon Rosemary Shortbread   MAKES ABOUT 12 PIECES

¾ cup (3.4 ounces) all-purpose flour

⅓ cup granulated sugar

2 tablespoons rice flour (see Baker's Note)

½ tablespoon lemon zest

1 teaspoon chopped fresh rosemary

¼ teaspoon salt

6 tablespoons (3 ounces) butter, cut up and room temperature

½ teaspoon vanilla extract

Fact: The United States government has declared that Veterans Day is spelled as such, without the apostrophe.

1 Grease an 8-inch round metal cake pan and set aside.

2 Combine the flour, sugar, rice flour, lemon zest, rosemary, and salt in a food processor and pulse to mix. Add the butter and pulse until the mixture is coarse. Add the vanilla and pulse to mix. Place the dough on a flat surface and shape into a ball. Press into the prepared cake pan and poke holes in the top with the tines of a fork. Chill the dough in the pan for 1 hour or until ready to bake.

3 Preheat the oven to 300°F and place a rack in the center.

4 Bake for 38 to 42 minutes, or until set. Let cool in the pan for 5 minutes. Cut into twelve wedges while still warm, then let cool completely in the pan.

Baker's Note: Rice flour gives shortbread a light and crunchy texture. I use Bob's Red Mill brand.

White Chocolate Lemon Raspberry Dessert Pizza

MAKES 12 SERVINGS

1 pound refrigerated sugar cookie dough

6 ounces white chocolate, chopped

1 cup prepared lemon curd

2 cups whipped topping

Fresh raspberries, for garnishing

1 Preheat the oven to 325°F and place a rack in the center. Spray an approximately 11-inch tart pan or a 10- to 12-inch pizza pan with flour-added baking spray.

2 Press the cookie dough into the prepared pan and bake for 22 to 25 minutes, or until the edges are golden brown. Times may vary between cookie dough brands, so watch carefully. Let cool completely in the pan.

3 In a microwave-safe bowl, microwave the white chocolate, using 50 percent power and stirring at 30-second intervals until melted and smooth. Spread the melted white chocolate over the cooled cookie, leaving bare about a ½- to 1-inch rim. Let the white chocolate set at room temperature or chill to set quickly. When ready to serve, spoon the lemon curd over the white chocolate. Cover the topping-free rim with the whipped cream and arrange the raspberries decoratively over the top.

Baker's Note: This recipe calls for premade, ready-to-bake sugar cookie dough, but if you prefer scratch you may substitute that.

Lime Sugar Cookies MAKES 24

2¾ cups (12.4 ounces) all-purpose flour

1 teaspoon baking soda

2 teaspoons cream of tartar

¾ teaspoon salt

12 tablespoons (6 ounces) unsalted butter, room temperature

NOVEMBER 12

National Pizza with the Works Except Anchovies Day

The Anchovy Council can't be too happy with this "holiday." Why exclude anchovies? Anchovies have been eaten for centuries and are beloved by chefs across the world for their umami, or "the fifth taste." Still, omitting anchovies is part of this holiday's ritual, so here's a pizza where you won't have to think twice about leaving them off.

Other Events on This Day:
Origami Day

NOVEMBER 13

World Kindness Day

Launched in Singapore in November 2000, the goal of World Kindness Day is to inspire people to do something kind and overlook prejudices.

In the spirit of kindness, why not bake some bright and cheerful cookies?

Other Events on This Day:
National Indian Pudding Day

¼ cup light olive oil (not extra-virgin), such as Crisco Light Tasting

1½ cups granulated sugar

4 teaspoons lime zest

1 tablespoon freshly squeezed lime juice (see Baker's Note)

¼ teaspoon vanilla extract

2 large eggs

Green sparkling sugar or green sanding sugar

1 Mix together the flour, baking soda, cream of tartar, and salt in a small bowl; set aside.

2 In the bowl of a stand mixer fitted with a paddle attachment, or in a large mixing bowl using a handheld electric mixer, beat the butter, olive oil, and sugar on medium speed until light and creamy. Add the lime zest, lime juice, and vanilla; beat for another minute, then scrape the sides of the bowl and add the eggs, one at a time, beating for another minute after each addition. By hand, or using the lowest speed of the mixer, add the flour mixture and stir until blended. Chill for about 1 hour.

3 Preheat the oven to 350°F and place a rack in the center. Line two baking sheets with parchment paper or nonstick foil.

4 Scoop up heaping tablespoons of dough and shape into balls about 1 inch in diameter. Arrange 2½ inches apart on each prepared baking sheet and press down to make ¼-inch-thick rounds. Sprinkle with the green sugar. Bake one sheet at a time for 12 to14 minutes, or until the edges are browned. Transfer to a wire rack to cool and crisp.

Baker's Note: With 4 teaspoons of lime zest, you'll taste the fresh lime, but for a little extra punch, add a tiny drop of lime or lemon oil. You can order it online or pick some up at a gourmet market.

White Chocolate Cherry Energy Bars MAKES 12 OR 16

¼ cup granulated sugar

¼ cup pure maple syrup

¼ cup golden syrup (see Baker's Notes)

2 tablespoons almond butter or sunflower
seed butter, such as SunButter

1 large egg

1 teaspoon vanilla extract

½ teaspoon baking soda

¼ teaspoon salt

¾ teaspoon ground cinnamon

1 cup (4.5 ounces) white whole wheat flour

2 cups old-fashioned or quick-cooking oats (not instant)

1½ cups crispy rice cereal, such as Rice Krispies

½ cup white chips

⅓ cup dried cherries or cherry-
flavored dried cranberries

½ cup pecans, toasted and finely chopped

1 Preheat the oven to 350°F and place a rack in the center. Line a 9 by 13-inch metal pan with nonstick foil.

2 Combine the sugar, maple syrup, golden syrup, almond butter, egg, and vanilla in a large bowl and whisk until thoroughly blended. Whisk in the baking soda, salt, and cinnamon, and then stir in the flour and oats. Add the cereal, chips, cherries, and pecans and stir until well blended.

3 Press the mixture into the prepared pan and bake for 18 to 20 minutes, or until golden brown. Lift from the pan and score into twelve or sixteen bars while warm; do not separate. Let cool completely in the pan, and then cut along the scored areas to make bars.

Baker's Notes: A portable bar cookie, this recipe has ingredients you can easily mix and match. This version uses sunflower seed butter (the SunButter brand), but you may swap that out for almond butter or peanut butter. The syrup is interchangeable as well.

Operating Room Nurse Day

Established by Iowa governor Terry Branstad in 1989, today recognizes the caring people who keep operating rooms sterile; monitor patients before, after, and during surgery; and ensure that patients understand how to take care of themselves before and after procedures.

Because OR nurses are always on their feet, here's a cookie that can be eaten on the go.

Other Events on This Day:
National Pickle Day, National Guacamole Day, in 1922 the British Broadcasting Corporation (BBC) began domestic radio service

Established in 1997, today is America Recycles Day, a nationally recognized day dedicated to the promotion of recycling programs in the United States. To celebrate, try putting an old cookie in a new cookie. This is a take on a cookie I saw for sale at the gas station—a peanut butter cookie that was half peanut butter, half brownie. This one is part peanut butter cookie and part sandwich cookie.

Other Events on This Day: In 1492, Christopher Columbus documented how tobacco was used by Native Americans (smoked by Arawak and Taino)

Peanut Butter Sandwich Cookie Cups MAKES 12

8 tablespoons (4 ounces) unsalted butter
½ cup firmly packed light brown sugar
½ cup granulated sugar
1 cup creamy or crunchy peanut butter
1 large egg
½ teaspoon salt
½ teaspoon baking soda
½ teaspoon vanilla extract
1 cup (4.5 ounces) all-purpose flour
16 (1-inch) chunks of fudge brownie, frozen
12 chocolate sandwich cookies, such as Oreos
⅓ cup semisweet chocolate chips
1 teaspoon shortening
Candy-coated chocolates (optional)

1 In a large, microwave-safe mixing bowl, microwave the butter on high for 30 seconds, or until melted. Whisk in both sugars, then whisk in the peanut butter, egg, salt, baking soda, and vanilla. With a spoon or a heavy-duty spatula, mix in the flour to make a soft dough. At this point, the dough should be a little too soft to work with, so cover with plastic wrap and chill for 1 hour, or until you can easily shape the dough into balls.

2 Preheat the oven to 350°F and set a rack in the center. Line twelve standard muffin cups with foil liners.

3 Divide the dough into twelve equal-size balls. Wrap each ball of dough around a cookie, covering it completely. Set the dough covered cookies in foil liners. Bake for 18 to 20 minutes, or until lightly browned around the edges. Let cool completely on a wire rack. Carefully remove the foil liners from the cookies.

4 Stir the chocolate chips and shortening together in a microwave-safe bowl. Microwave at 50 percent power, stirring every 30 seconds, until the chocolate is of drizzling consistency. Drizzle the melted chocolate over the cooled cookies. Garnish with candy-coated chocolates if desired.

Baker's Note: Foil liners prevent the cookies from sticking to the cups, but paper liners coated with flour-added baking spray may also be used.

Cranberry Cornmeal Biscotti MAKES ABOUT 36

1¾ cups (8 ounces) all-purpose flour

1 cup fine yellow cornmeal

1½ teaspoons baking powder

¾ teaspoon salt

8 tablespoons (4 ounces) unsalted butter, room temperature

¾ cup granulated sugar

1 tablespoon freshly squeezed lemon juice

1 teaspoon vanilla extract

3 large eggs

¾ cup toasted and chopped pecans

½ cup dried cranberries

1 Preheat the oven to 350°F and place a rack in the center. Line a large baking sheet with parchment paper or non-stick foil.

2 Mix the flour, cornmeal, baking powder, and salt together in a medium-size bowl; set aside.

3 In the bowl of a stand mixer fitted with a paddle attachment, or in a large mixing bowl, using a handheld electric mixer, beat the butter and sugar on medium speed until creamy. Beat in the vanilla and eggs until well blended, scraping down the sides of the bowl as needed. Gradually add the flour mixture to the egg mixture. Stir in the pecans and cranberries.

4 Divide the dough in half. Form each portion of the dough into a log about 13 inches long and 2 inches wide, spacing the logs about 5 inches apart lengthwise down the baking sheet. Bake for 20 minutes. Leave the oven on. Let cool on the baking sheet for about 20 minutes, or until easy to handle.

NOVEMBER 16

Corn First Discovered in America

On this day in 1620, hungry Pilgrims discovered a basket of corn (maize) buried in the side of a hill in Provincetown, Massachusetts. It had been stashed by local Native Americans. The Pilgrims named the hill Corn Hill and took the corn, vowing to make restitution. The following spring, the corn they had taken was used for seed and produced a huge, flourishing crop. Today, there's a plaque on Corn Hill commemorating the date the Pilgrims found the corn.

Other Events on This Day:
National Fast Food Day, Saint Gertrude Day (patron saint of travelers)

353

5 Transfer to a cutting board, and with a sharp knife, cut crosswise slightly on the diagonal every ½ to ¾ inch. Carefully separate the slices and arrange cut side down on the baking sheet; don't worry about spacing. Return the pan to the oven and bake for 15 to 20 minutes. Gently slide the biscotti onto a wire rack to cool completely.

Baker's Notes: This dough is rather sticky, so you'll need to shape it with dampened hands. When cutting, use a straight up-and-down motion, as the baked dough tends to break.

National Baklava Day

P opular in Greece and Turkey, baklava is a bar cookie made with layers of phyllo dough, chopped nuts, honey, lemon, and butter. You can make it as bars and cut it into triangles or you can make it in individual phyllo cups. This recipe is very simple, yet elegant.

Other Events on This Day:
US patent issued for the computer mouse in 1970

Easy Baklava Cups   MAKES 30

FILLED SHELLS
2 boxes frozen mini phyllo pastry shells (30 total)
6 tablespoons (3 ounces) unsalted butter, melted
1½ cups toasted and chopped walnuts or pecans
¼ cup granulated sugar
¾ teaspoon ground cinnamon

SYRUP
½ cup granulated sugar
½ cup water
¼ cup honey
1½ tablespoons freshly squeezed lemon juice

1 Preheat the oven to 375°F and place a rack in the center. Line a baking sheet with nonstick foil or parchment paper.

2 **Make the filled shells:** Arrange the phyllo shells on the tray, spacing evenly, and brush them generously, inside and out, with the melted butter. Mix together the nuts, sugar, and cinnamon and divide equally among the shells. Bake for 8 to 10 minutes, or until the shells are golden brown.

3 **Meanwhile, make the syrup:** Bring the sugar, water, honey, and lemon juice to a boil in a small saucepan. Reduce the heat and simmer for about 10 minutes. Spoon a teaspoon of the sugar mixture over each baked shell. Serve warm or at room temperature.

Pumpkin Bars with Cream Cheese Frosting MAKES 24

BASE

1 cup (4.5 ounces) all-purpose flour

½ teaspoon salt

¾ teaspoon baking soda

½ teaspoon ground cinnamon

1 teaspoon pumpkin pie spice

8 tablespoons (4 ounces) unsalted
  butter, room temperature

1 cup firmly packed light brown sugar

1 teaspoon vanilla extract

½ teaspoon orange zest

2 large eggs

1 cup canned pumpkin (not pumpkin pie mix)

½ cup toasted and chopped pecans

FROSTING

3 ounces cream cheese, softened

6 tablespoons (3 ounces) unsalted
  butter, room temperature

½ teaspoon vanilla extract

¼ teaspoon orange zest

2 cups confectioners' sugar, sifted

1 Preheat the oven to 350°F and place a rack in the center. Line a 9 by 13-inch metal pan with nonstick foil or just spray the pan with flour-added baking spray.

2 **Make the base:** Mix the flour, salt, baking soda, cinnamon and pumpkin pie spice in a medium-size bowl; set aside.

3 In a mixing bowl, using a handheld electric mixer on medium-high speed, beat the butter and brown sugar until well mixed. Add the vanilla and orange zest. Beat in the eggs, one at a time. Stir in the flour mixture and mix just until blended. Stir in the pumpkin, followed by the pecans. Pour into the prepared pan and bake for 30 minutes, or until set. Let cool completely in the pan.

Benefits of Vitamin C Discovered

On this day in 1970, Nobel Prize–winning genius chemist Linus Pauling announced that large doses of vitamin C could shorten the duration of colds and help prevent them. Although there was opposition to the idea, many people believed Pauling and began taking vitamin C. Today it is widely believed that taking vitamin C won't prevent a cold, but that people who supplement with vitamin C before a cold starts may have colds with milder symptoms and shorter durations.

Pumpkin is a source of vitamin C. You won't meet your daily requirement with a pumpkin bar, but it's the thought that counts, no? This recipe is from my grandmother, but I'm pretty sure she got it from a pumpkin company.

Other Events on This Day:
National Vichyssoise Day

Fact: Most animals produce their own vitamin C, but humans cannot. Good sources include oranges, grapefruits, lemons, limes, strawberries, peppers, broccoli, and even pumpkins!

4 **Make the frosting:** Beat the cream cheese and butter in a medium-size bowl, using a handheld electric mixer. When smooth and creamy, beat in the vanilla and the orange zest. Add the confectioners' sugar ½ cup at a time, beating and scraping the sides of the bowl, until you get the consistency you like. Spread on the cooled bars. Using the foil (if you've lined the pan), lift the bars from the pan, set on a cutting board, and cut into twenty-four bars.

Gettysburg Address

Lincoln delivered the Gettysburg Address today in 1863, dedicating the Soldiers' National Cemetery in Gettysburg, Pennsylvania. Lincoln's speech lasted two minutes and eloquently expressed the idea that the ground had already been dedicated by the men who fought there and that it was up to us to dedicate ourselves to government of the people, by the people, and for the people.

Like the Gettysburg Address, this recipe is short, sweet, and memorable.

Other Events on This Day:
In 1959, Ford announced it would no longer be making the Edsel

Two-Ingredient Peanut Butter Cup Cookies MAKES 24

1 (18-ounce) package refrigerated peanut butter cookie dough
24 miniature peanut butter cups, unwrapped and frozen

1 Preheat the oven to 350°F and place a rack in the center. Spray twenty-four cups of a mini muffin tin with flour-added baking spray or line with mini muffin liners.

2 Unwrap the dough and shape into 1-inch balls. Place one ball in each prepared cup.

3 Bake for 5 to 7 minutes, or until the dough is set—this should be about 5 minutes less than the cookies' package directions instruct. Remove from the oven and carefully press one miniature peanut butter cup into each cookie. Remove from the tins when almost cool, then transfer to a wire rack to cool completely.

Peanut Butter Chip Chocolate Cookies MAKES ABOUT 60

2 cups (9 ounces) all-purpose flour

⅔ cup unsweetened natural cocoa powder

¾ teaspoon baking soda

½ teaspoon salt

1 cup (8 ounces) unsalted butter, room temperature

1½ cups granulated sugar

2 large eggs

2 teaspoons vanilla extract

1½ cups peanut butter chips

½ cup extra-dark chocolate chips

1 Preheat the oven to 350°F and place a rack in the center. Have ready two ungreased baking sheets.

2 Mix the flour, cocoa powder, baking soda, and salt together in a medium-size bowl; set aside.

3 In the bowl of a stand mixer fitted with a paddle attachment, or in a large mixing bowl, using a handheld electric mixer, beat the butter and sugar on medium speed until light and creamy. Reduce the mixer speed slightly and beat in the eggs and vanilla. By hand or using the lowest speed of the mixer, stir in the flour mixture until incorporated. Stir in the peanut butter chips and chocolate chips.

4 Drop rounded teaspoonfuls of batter 2½ inches apart onto the baking sheets. Bake one sheet at a time for 8 to 10 minutes, or until the cookies appear set. Let cool on the baking sheets for about 4 minutes, then transfer to a wire rack to cool completely.

Hello Dollies MAKES 16

8 tablespoons (4 ounces) unsalted butter

⅛ teaspoon salt

1½ cups graham cracker crumbs

1 (14-ounce) can sweetened condensed milk

1 cup semisweet chocolate chips

Universal Children's Day

Not to be confused with International Children's Day on June 1, Universal Children's Day is a result of the UN's recommendation that all countries establish a day recognizing children across the world in need of food, education, and health care. In the US, November 20 has become a fund-raising day for many children's charities.

Popular with the children who run through this house, these soft, dense, and fat chocolate cookies are the perfect vehicle for peanut butter and chocolate chips.

Other Events on This Day:
National Peanut Butter Fudge Day

World Hello Day

World Hello Day started in the fall of 1973 in response to conflict between Israel and Egypt. It was founded on the belief that the act of saying hello shows concern for your fellow man and opens a line of peaceful communication. Its founders encouraged others to say hello to ten different people. Since 1973, the holiday has gained a large following, as evidenced by letters from world leaders and public figures on the holiday's website. Show your support by saying hello to ten people and baking some Hello Dollies.

Other Events on This Day:
World Television Day, World Fisheries Day

---

1 cup butterscotch chips

²/₃ cup shredded sweetened
    coconut (optional)

1 cup chopped walnuts
    or pecans, toasted

1 Preheat the oven to
   350°F and place a rack in the center.
   Line an 8-inch square metal pan with nonstick foil or line
   with regular foil and spray with flour-added baking spray.

2 In a microwave-safe mixing bowl, microwave the butter
   on high for 30 seconds, or until melted. Stir in the salt
   and the graham cracker crumbs.

3 Pat the crumb mixture into the prepared pan. Drizzle the
   sweetened condensed milk over the crumbs. Sprinkle the
   chocolate and butterscotch chips, coconut, and nuts over
   the milk in the order given, then press down firmly. Bake
   for about 25 minutes. Let cool completely in the pan, then
   chill for a few hours before slicing. Lift from the pan, set
   on a cutting board, and cut into sixteen squares.

NOVEMBER 22

Start Your Own Country Day

The idea for Start Your Own Country Day is said to have come from the 1939 World's Fair, where it was conceived in jest as a way to honor those free-spirited enough to believe they could do a good job of it. While I've yet to find the person who declared it as November 22, plenty of folks have latched on to the date.

This cookie should appeal to both your inner anarchist and dictator alike. The cookies are baked free form and broken into randomly sized pieces, yet for flavor, you call

Cranberry, White Chip, and Ginger Cookie Bark
MAKES 20 PIECES

Approximately 1 tablespoon of shortening
    for greasing the pan

1 cup (4.2 ounces) sifted all-purpose
    flour (see Baker's Notes)

¼ teaspoon baking soda

¼ teaspoon salt

8 tablespoons (4 ounces) unsalted butter, room
    temperature, or ½ cup (3.4 ounces) shortening

½ cup firmly packed light brown sugar

1 teaspoon vanilla extract

¼ teaspoon ground ginger

1 lightly beaten large egg

1 cup toasted macadamia nuts or walnuts, chopped

½ cup white chocolate chips

3 tablespoons chopped candied
 ginger (or more if desired)

½ cup chopped dried cranberries

1 Preheat the oven to 325°F and place a rack in the center.
   Rub a 13 by 18-inch or 12 by 17-inch rimmed baking sheet
   evenly with shortening. Mix the flour, baking soda, and
   salt together in a small bowl; set aside.

2 In a mixing bowl, using a handheld electric mixer, beat
   the butter (or shortening) and brown sugar until light and
   creamy. Beat in the vanilla, ginger, and just 2 tablespoons
   of the egg. By hand, stir in the flour mixture and ½ cup of
   the nuts.

3 Spread the batter on the prepared baking sheet, pressing and
   shaping with dampened fingers to form a "highly imperfect"
   rectangle about 10 by 14 inches. For crispier bark, shape into
   4 rectangles, each about 5 by 7, spaced about an inch apart
   or whatever your baking sheet will allow. The dough doesn't
   spread much. It should be very thin and it's okay to have a few
   gaps here and there. With a pastry brush, gently brush a very
   thin coating of beaten egg over the top. You will not use it all.
   Mix together the remaining nuts, white chips, candied ginger,
   and cranberries and sprinkle evenly over the top.

4 Bake for 15 to 18 minutes or until the edges are browned
   and the center is golden. At this point, it may seem a little
   soft, but it should firm as it cools. Let cool for 3 minutes
   on the baking sheet. With a knife or pizza cutter, and
   while the cookie is still warm, cut out some fairly large
   sections about the size of or a little bigger than your
   spatula. Carefully run your spatula underneath the cookie
   parts and transfer the pieces to a wire rack to cool and
   crisp. When the bark has cooled and crisped, you can
   break it up some more if needed.

Baker's Notes: To get the brittle or barklike texture, it's
important to weigh the flour or sift it before measuring. The
dough shouldn't be too dry, and the cookies should bake up

all the shots. Given the season
and the fact that today is also
Cranberry Relish Day, I used
a combination of candied
ginger, macadamia nuts, dried
cranberries, and white chips.

Other Events on This Day:
**The SOS radio distress signal
adopted at the International
Radio Telegraphic Convention
in Berlin in 1906**

crisp, but slightly less so in the center. If you bake a batch and find you like the crispy edges best, shape your dough into four smaller rectangles so that you'll get more edge pieces. I usually recommend lining baking sheets, but in this case it's better to just rub shortening all over a nice clean baking sheet and bake the dough directly on the sheet. Butter is not recommended, as it may burn.

NOVEMBER 23

Thanksgiving

T hanksgiving's coming! Here's a cookie the kids can make while you focus on more complicated aspects of the meal.

Other Events on This Day:
National Cashew Day

Pilgrim Hat Cookies MAKES 20

20 fudge stripe cookies
20 miniature chocolate-covered caramel or peanut butter candies
Tube of yellow frosting fitted with the writing tip (see Baker's Note)

1   Turn the cookies fudge side up. Squeeze a small bit of frosting in the center of each cookie. Using the frosting as glue, stick the peanut butter cup in the center. Use the frosting to pipe a hatband around the peanut butter cup and to add a square buckle. Leave at room temperature to let the frosting set.

Baker's Note: For the frosting, I use Wilton decorator frosting, sold in the baking aisle of most grocery stores.

NOVEMBER 24

Start Planning a Cookie Exchange Day

I t seems like cookie exchanges are more popular than ever, so why not organize one yourself? They're a lot of fun, and exchanging cookies is a great icebreaker.

   If you've never heard the term, a cookie exchange is a

Candied Fruit and Bourbon Cookies MAKES 60

1 pound chopped candied fruit, such as cherries, pineapples, oranges, or citron mix (see Baker's Notes)
1¼ cups golden raisins
⅔ cup bourbon
2 cups (9 ounces) unbleached all-purpose flour
¼ teaspoon salt

½ teaspoon ground cinnamon

¼ teaspoon ground cloves

⅓ cup firmly packed dark brown sugar

⅓ cup granulated sugar

7 tablespoons (3.5 ounces) melted
   unsalted butter, cooled

2 large eggs, lightly beaten

¾ teaspoon baking soda dissolved
   in 2 teaspoons water

2½ cups chopped walnuts and pecans,
   or all pecans or walnuts

1 Mix the candied fruit and raisins in a bowl. Pour in the bourbon and stir to coat the fruit. Cover and let sit at room temperature overnight.

2 Preheat the oven to 325°F and place a rack in the center. Line two baking sheets with parchment paper or nonstick foil.

3 Mix the flour, salt, cinnamon, cloves, and both sugars together in a large mixing bowl.

4 Add the cooled melted butter, beaten eggs, and baking soda mixture to the flour mixture and stir until the ingredients are mixed. Add the soaked fruit and the nuts and stir until blended.

5 Scoop up generously heaping teaspoonfuls of batter and arrange 2½ inches apart on the prepared baking sheets. Bake for 15 to 18 minutes. Transfer to a wire rack to cool completely. Store covered and let the bourbon flavor mellow.

Baker's Notes: Grocery stores usually sell plenty of candied fruit this time of year, but if you're making these out of season, you can order candied fruit on the Internet. Also, note that although the batter does not look very appetizing, the cookies themselves are delicious and are much prettier when baked.

party where everyone brings a set number of cookies and leaves with a variety of cookies in that same amount. The participants walk around with empty cookie tins and take one or two of each cookie, depending on the number of participants and the set number of cookies.

Other Events on This Day: **Tie One On! Day (the tie being an apron; however, you are baking with bourbon, so it's your call)**

In 1884, John Meyenberg of St. Louis received a patent for evaporated milk. Not to be confused with its thick and sweet counterpart, condensed milk, evaporated milk is a shelf-stable, unsweetened milk with 30 percent less water than whole milk. It's a common ingredient in macaroni and cheese and gives thickness and body to sauces.

These bars have a big, thick, flavorful oatmeal short-bread crust. As for the topping, it's creamy but firm. The secret is the small amount of cream, which I discovered by accident one day when I ran out of evaporated milk and had to use a little cream in its place.

Other Events on This Day:
National Parfait Day

Pumpkin Pie Bars
MAKES 24

CRUST

12 tablespoons (6 ounces) unsalted butter, room temperature

¼ teaspoon salt

¾ cup firmly packed light brown sugar

1½ cups (6.8 ounces) all-purpose flour

¾ cup old-fashioned or quick-cooking oats (not instant)

FILLING

2 large eggs

¾ cup granulated sugar

1 (15-ounce) can pumpkin (not pumpkin pie mix)

1⅓ cups (11 ounces) evaporated milk

3 tablespoons heavy cream

½ teaspoon salt

1 teaspoon ground cinnamon

1½ teaspoons pumpkin pie spice

Sweetened whipped cream, for topping (optional)

1 Preheat the oven to 350°F and place a rack in the center. Line a 9 by 13-inch metal pan with nonstick foil or just spray with flour-added baking spray.

2 **Make the crust:** In the bowl of a stand mixer fitted with a paddle attachment, or in a large mixing bowl, using a handheld electric mixer, beat the butter, salt, and brown sugar on medium speed until creamy. By hand, stir in the flour and oats. Press into the bottom of the pan and bake for 13 to 15 minutes or until set.

3 **Make the filling:** In a large mixing bowl, whisk together the eggs, sugar, pumpkin, evaporated milk, cream, salt, cinnamon, and pumpkin pie spice. Pour over the baked crust and bake for 20 to 25 minutes, or until the edges seem set and the center still seems a little wobbly. Let cool completely in the pan. The wobbly center should firm as it cools. Chill the bars for about 2 hours before cutting. Cut into twenty-four bars. Top with whipped cream, if desired.

Glazed Lemon Poppy Seed Cookies MAKES 32

COOKIES

1⅓ cups (6 ounces) all-purpose flour

½ teaspoon baking soda

½ teaspoon salt

1 tablespoon poppy seeds

8 tablespoons (4 ounces) unsalted
butter, room temperature

⅔ cup granulated sugar

1 large egg

1 tablespoon lemon zest

GLAZE

1 cup confectioners' sugar

2 tablespoons freshly squeezed lemon juice

1 Preheat the oven to 350°F and place a rack in the center. Line two baking sheets with nonstick foil or parchment paper.

2 **Make the cookies:** Mix the flour, baking soda, salt, and poppy seeds together in a bowl; set aside

3 In the bowl of a stand mixer fitted with a paddle attachment, or in a large mixing bowl, using a handheld electric mixer, beat the butter and sugar on medium speed until creamy. Beat in the egg and lemon zest. By hand or using the lowest speed of the mixer, add the flour mixture.

4 Drop rounded teaspoonfuls of dough 2 inches apart on the prepared baking sheets. Bake for 11 to 12 minutes, or until the edges are lightly golden.

5 Let cool on the sheets for about a minute, then transfer to a wire rack to cool completely.

6 **Make the glaze:** Whisk the confectioners' sugar and lemon juice together in a bowl until smooth. Spoon the clear glaze over the cooled cookies.

W. Atlee Burpee Died

Today marks the death of W. Atlee Burpee, who founded the Burpee Seed Company in 1876. Burpee was only eighteen years old when he started the company with a $1,000 loan from his mother. He died in 1915.

Other Events on This Day: Charles M. Schulz's birthday (b. 1922), National Cake Day

Pear Season

While their Bartlett cousins arrived in late summer, late fall and winter is the time for Bosc, Comice, and Anjou pears. Bartlett and Comice pears are sweet, juicy, and perfect for eating straight. The Anjou is good for eating and baking, whereas the Bosc is best for baking and cooking. To get them at their best, buy pears when they're hard and not fully ripe. Leave on the counter to ripen.

Other Events on This Day:
Bavarian Cream Pie Day, Jimi Hendrix born in 1942

Mini Phyllo Pear Pies   MAKES 15

1 box mini phyllo shells (15 shells; see Baker's Note)
1½ tablespoons granulated sugar
Tiny pinch of salt
2 teaspoons all-purpose flour
¼ teaspoon ground cinnamon
¼ teaspoon lemon zest
1 cup peeled, diced pears
2 tablespoons pecans, toasted and chopped
2 tablespoons raisins
3 tablespoons (1.5 ounces) unsalted butter, melted
1 to 2 teaspoons freshly squeezed lemon juice

1 Preheat the oven to 350°F and place a rack in the center. Place the mini phyllo shells on a baking sheet lined with nonstick foil or parchment paper.

2 Combine the sugar, salt, flour, cinnamon, and lemon zest in a mixing bowl. Stir in the diced pears, pecans, and raisins. Add the butter and toss to coat.

3 Divide the pear mixture evenly among the shells. Drizzle the lemon juice lightly over the tops. Bake for 10 to 12 minutes. Transfer to a wire rack and cool completely.

Baker's Note: These cookies look and taste complicated, but in actuality they're something you can throw together in minutes. I use the mini phyllo shells made by Athens Foods. You can usually find them in the freezer aisle with the frozen pies and whipped topping.

Red Planet Day

Today is Red Planet Day, a day to think about the planet Mars or educate yourself about its geography, weather, and potential for sustaining any form of life. The date commemorates the 1964 launch of *Mariner 4*, the first

Big Red Velvet Cookies
MAKES 24

COOKIES

10 tablespoons unsweetened applesauce
1 cup plus 2 tablespoons (5 ounces) all-purpose flour
½ teaspoon baking soda
½ teaspoon salt
2 tablespoons unsweetened natural cocoa powder

6 tablespoons (3 ounces) unsalted
    butter, room temperature

¾ cup granulated sugar

1 large egg

1 teaspoon vanilla extract

1 teaspoon white vinegar

½ cup sour cream, room temperature

½ teaspoon red food coloring paste

FROSTING

3 ounces cream cheese, softened

3 tablespoons (1.5 ounces) unsalted or
    salted butter, room temperature

1¼ cups sifted confectioners' sugar

¾ teaspoon vanilla extract

1 tablespoon sour cream

1 Preheat the oven to 375°F and place a rack in the center. Have ready two ungreased baking sheets.

2 **Make the cookies:** Spoon the applesauce onto a stack of paper towels and spread into a 5- to 6-inch-diameter circle. Let stand on the towels for 5 to 10 minutes while you proceed with the recipe. The goal here is to drain as much liquid as possible from the applesauce, and in the end you should have 6 tablespoons.

3 Mix the flour, baking soda, salt, and cocoa powder together in a small bowl; set aside.

4 In a large mixing bowl, using a handheld electric mixer, beat the butter and sugar on medium speed until light and creamy. Add the egg and continue beating for about 1 minute. Using a tablespoon, scrape the 6 tablespoons of applesauce off the paper towel and add to the batter. Beat in the vanilla, vinegar, and sour cream. Add the red food gel and beat until the color is uniform.

spacecraft to return images of the Martian surface.

This is pretty much what you'd expect—red velvet cake in the form of a big, soft, cream cheese–frosted cookie. It's like eating the top of a cupcake!

Other Events on This Day: French Toast Day, the first instant camera went on sale for $89.75 in a Boston department store in 1948

Fact: Named after the Roman god of war, Mars gets its reddish hue from iron oxide–rich soil.

Add the flour mixture and stir with a mixing spoon until blended. The dough should be very soft—somewhere between a batter and a drop cookie.

5 Drop rounded tablespoonfuls of dough a little over 2½ inches apart onto the baking sheets. Bake for 10 minutes, or until the cookies appear set. Let cool on the baking sheets for about 3 minutes, then transfer to a wire rack to cool completely.

6 **Make the frosting:** In a medium-size mixing bowl, using a handheld electric mixer, beat the cream cheese and butter until smooth. Gradually add the confectioners' sugar and continue beating until creamy. Beat in the vanilla and sour cream. Spread the tops of the cooled cookies with the frosting.

Baker's Note: For this recipe, it's important to have your ingredients at room temperature.

NOVEMBER 29

National Square Dance Day

Square dancing evolved from early European folk dances. However, modern square dancing as we know it is based on the western square of the 1930s. Unlike traditional square, western square has a caller who calls out dance moves such as "allemande left" and "do-si-do."

Not to be confused with Ranger Cookies, which are usually made with cereal, Cowboys are loaded with oatmeal, chocolate chips, and coconut.

Other Events on This Day:
Iodine discovered in 1830

Cowboy Cookies
MAKES ABOUT 24 LARGE COOKIES

2 cups (9 ounces) all-purpose flour

1 teaspoon baking soda

½ teaspoon baking powder

½ teaspoon salt

1 cup (8 ounces) cold unsalted butter, cut into chunks

¾ cup granulated sugar

¾ cup plus 2 tablespoons firmly packed dark brown sugar

2 large eggs

2 teaspoons vanilla extract

2 cups old-fashioned or quick-cooking oats (not instant)

1 cup toasted and chopped pecans

½ cup sweetened flaked coconut

1⅔ cups semisweet chocolate chips

1 Preheat the oven to 350°F and place a rack in the center. Have ready two ungreased baking sheets.

2 Mix the flour, baking soda, baking powder, and salt together in a bowl; set aside.

3 In the bowl of a stand mixer fitted with a paddle attachment, or in a large mixing bowl, using a handheld electric mixer, beat the butter on medium speed until it is creamy. Add both sugars and continue beating for about 2 minutes, or until very light and creamy. Reduce the mixer speed to low and beat in the eggs and vanilla, scraping the sides of the bowl often. By hand or continuing on the lowest speed, gradually add the flour mixture, and then stir in the oats, pecans, coconut, and chocolate chips.

4 Using a ¼-cup measure, scoop up the dough and shape into large balls. Arrange about 3 inches apart on the baking sheets and press down to make ½-inch-thick rounds. Bake one sheet at a time for 12 to 14 minutes, or until the cookies are browned around the edges and set in the center. Let cool on the baking sheets for 5 minutes, then transfer to a wire rack to cool completely.

Baker's Note: For these cookies, using very cool or even cold butter and beating it into submission with a stand mixer makes for nicely rounded edges. If you don't have a stand mixer, just use slightly softened yet still cool butter.

Cookie Jar Cookie Mix
FILLS A 1-QUART JAR

1⅓ cups (6 ounces) all-purpose flour
1 teaspoon baking powder
1 teaspoon baking soda
½ teaspoon salt
1⅓ cups old-fashioned oats
½ cup granulated sugar
½ cup firmly packed light brown sugar
½ cup chopped pecans
½ cup of your favorite flavor chips
    (such as dark, white, or butterscotch)
⅓ cup candy-coated chocolates

NOVEMBER 30

Mason Jar Patented

On this day in 1858, a Philadelphia tinsmith named John Landis Mason patented the mason jar. Luckily, you won't need any canning skills to make this cookie mix. Some crafty skills would be nice, should you wish to make a fancy top and cute labels, but the process of making the mix itself is just measuring and layering ingredients.

A jar of cookie mix makes a great hostess gift. Or consider buying the jars and ingredients in bulk and making them for fundraisers. I've seen them at bazaars marked at $7.00 per jar.

Other Events on This Day:
Computer Security Day

1 Using a funnel or a piece of folded paper, add the flour, baking powder, baking soda, and salt to the jar. Mix the oats and both sugars together in a bowl, then add the oat mixture to the jar. Press it down as tightly as you can. Add the pecans, flavored chips, and candies.

2 If you want to decorate the top, pick a fabric of your choice and cut a circle with a diameter about 2 inches more than that of the jar. Lay the circle of fabric over the jar, set the flat metal lid piece over the fabric, then screw the ring around the top of the jar to hold the fabric and flat lid in place.

3 Include a card with the following instructions:

Preheat the oven to 375°F and place a rack in the center. In a large mixing bowl, combine ½ cup of melted unsalted butter, 1 large egg, and 1 teaspoon of vanilla extract. Pour everything from the jar into the bowl and stir until it all comes together. Shape into 1-inch balls. Place 2 inches apart on greased baking sheets. Bake for 11 to 13 minutes. Transfer from the baking sheets to cool on wire racks.

DECEMBER 1

Eat a Red Apple Day

Today is Eat a Red Apple Day, and with cold and flu germs around, that's not a bad idea. Apples have been keeping the doctor away for three thousand years. They're a good source of dietary fiber, and research has shown that the phytonutrients and antioxidants in apples may reduce the risk of certain types of cancers and lung problems.

Apple Butter Bars MAKES 36

1½ cups (6.8 ounces) all-purpose flour
1 teaspoon baking soda
1 teaspoon salt
2½ cups quick-cooking oats (not instant)
1 cup granulated sugar
⅓ cup firmly packed light brown sugar
1 cup (8 ounces) unsalted butter, melted
1 teaspoon vanilla extract
1½ cups Slow Cooker Apple Butter (recipe follows)
⅓ cup pecans, toasted and finely chopped

1. Preheat the oven to 350°F and place a rack in the center. Line a 9 by 13-inch metal pan with nonstick foil or spray with flour-added baking spray.

2. Mix the flour, baking soda, and salt together in a large mixing bowl and stir well. Add the oats and both sugars. Make a well in the center and add the butter and vanilla, then mix well with a wooden spoon until well blended. The mixture should be moist but still kind of crumbly.

3. Press half of the mixture into your prepared baking pan, pressing down tightly. Spread the apple butter over the top. Sprinkle with the remaining crumb mixture, pressing down slightly. Sprinkle the pecans over the top. Bake for 40 to 50 minutes, or until golden brown. Let cool completely in the pan and cut into thirty-six bars.

Baker's Notes: The recipe halves easily. If you halve it, check it at 5 or 6 hours. For the bars, check them at 40 minutes. A half-batch made in an 8-inch square pan should be done in about 40 minutes, but always go by whether the edges are browned.

Slow Cooker Apple Butter MAKES ABOUT 5½ CUPS

5 pounds Gala apples, peeled, cored, and finely chopped
1 cup granulated sugar
1 cup firmly packed brown sugar
1 tablespoon ground cinnamon
⅛ teaspoon ground cloves
¼ teaspoon ground allspice
¼ teaspoon salt

1. Put the apples, both sugars, all the spices, and the salt in a slow cooker and cover. Cook on high for 1 hour, then reduce the heat and cook for 6 to 8 hours, or until the mixture is dark and thick. Cook uncovered for about 1 hour. Remove from the heat and, with an immersion (stick) blender, beat the mixture until smooth. If you don't have an immersion blender, you can puree the mixture in a blender.

Health benefits aside, the smell of apples will enhance the holiday spirit. Start your apple butter in the morning and by midafternoon, the house will smell like Santa's workshop.

Other Events on This Day:
Dr Pepper sold for the first time in 1885

First Girl Scout Cookie Sale

In 1917, the Mistletoe Troop of Muskogee, Oklahoma, baked cookies and sold them as a service project. In 1922 the Girl Scout magazine, *The American Girl,* encouraged girls to have cookie sales as fund-raisers and published recipes, suggesting the girls price them at twenty-five to thirty cents per dozen. In the early years, Girl Scout cookies were homemade. According to the Girl Scouts website, the early recipe was a simple sugar cookie similar to this one.

Other Events on This Day:
National Fritters Day

Basic Sugar Cookies MAKES 32

2 cups (9 ounces) all-purpose flour
1 teaspoon salt
2 teaspoons baking powder
1 cup (8 ounces) unsalted butter, room temperature
1 cup granulated sugar
2 large eggs, well beaten
2 tablespoons whole or 2% milk
1 teaspoon vanilla extract
1 teaspoon lemon zest
1 teaspoon orange zest
Coarse sugar for sprinkling on top (optional)

1 Sift the flour, salt, and baking powder together into a medium-size bowl; set aside.

2 In the bowl of a stand mixer fitted with a paddle attachment, or in a large mixing bowl, using a handheld electric mixer, beat the butter and sugar on medium speed for about 2 minutes, or until very light and fluffy. Reduce the mixer speed and add the eggs, milk, vanilla, and lemon and orange zest. Using the lowest speed of the stand mixer, gradually stir in the flour mixture (if using a handheld mixer, add the flour mixture by hand). Chill the dough for an hour, or until it is less sticky and easy to handle.

3 Preheat the oven to 375°F and place a rack in the center. Line two baking sheets with nonstick foil or parchment paper.

4 Scoop up rounded tablespoonfuls of dough and shape into ¾- to 1-inch balls. Place the balls on the baking sheets about 2 inches apart and press down slightly with the palm of your hand so that they are about ½ inch thick. Sprinkle the tops with a little coarse sugar. Bake one sheet at a time for 8 to 10 minutes, or until the edges begin to brown. Let cool on the baking sheets for about 4 minutes, then transfer to a wire rack to cool and crisp.

Rugelach MAKES 16

DOUGH

4 ounces cream cheese, softened

8 tablespoons (4 ounces) unsalted
   butter, room temperature

Scant ¼ teaspoon salt

1 cup (4.5 ounces) all-purpose flour

FILLING

3 tablespoons granulated sugar

¾ teaspoon ground cinnamon

⅓ cup raisins or currants

⅓ cup pecans or walnuts, toasted and finely chopped

2 to 3 tablespoons apricot preserves

1 large egg, lightly beaten, for brushing

1 **Make the dough:** In the bowl of a stand mixer fitted with
   a paddle attachment, or in a large mixing bowl, using a
   handheld electric mixer, beat the cream cheese and butter
   on medium speed until light and creamy. Stir in the salt
   and flour. Shape the dough into a ball. Wrap in plastic
   wrap and chill the dough for a few hours or overnight.

2 When ready to bake, remove the dough from the refrigerator and let it come to room temperature. Preheat the
   oven to 350°F and place a rack in the center. Line a large
   baking sheet with nonstick foil.

3 **Make the filling:** Mix together the sugar, cinnamon,
   raisins, and nuts and set aside.

4 On a floured surface, roll the dough ball into a large circle
   about 12 inches in diameter. Lightly brush the circle
   with preserves. Sprinkle the filling mixture
   over the dough circle, and with a piece
   of nonstick foil or parchment paper,
   press it down lightly so that the filling
   sticks to the dough. With a pizza cutter, slice the circle into sixteen wedges.
   Working one wedge at a time, roll each into a
   tight crescent. Place the crescents on the prepared baking

Hanukkah Begins

Hanukkah begins on the
twenty-fifth eve of the
Jewish month of Kislev, so the
eight-day celebration starts
on a different date every year.
Given that, any time in early
December is a good time to
start planning the menu for the
Festival of Light. Traditional
Hanukkah fare includes fried
foods such as doughnuts and
potato pancakes, but it's also
a custom to eat dairy, which
means rugelach is perfect for
the holiday as well.

Other Events on This Day:

**The first Alka-Seltzer sold
in 1931. I suspect there was
a huge demand for it after
National Fritters Day (see
December 2)**

sheet. Brush lightly with the beaten egg. Bake for 20 to 25 minutes, or until golden brown. Transfer to a wire rack and let cool.

Baker's Note: This is a small batch geared for beginners. Once you've mastered the first batch, make another.

National Cookie Day

Today is National Cookie Day, proclaimed by Cookie Monster himself in the 1980 *Sesame Street Dictionary*. So why not make snowballs?

Snowballs require a conscientious baker committed to measuring the flour and toasting the nuts. The same goes for chocolate snowballs, in which case the baker must keep the delicate texture while incorporating the chocolate. Or maybe it's just a matter of having a good recipe. This is one I've used for years. The malt idea is new, and in an informal taste test done with a random sampling of ten-year-olds, the malt version beat out the regular version.

Other Events on This Day:
Santa's List Day

Chocolate Malt Snowballs MAKES ABOUT 50

1¼ cups (10 ounces) unsalted butter,
　　room temperature
⅔ cup granulated sugar
1½ teaspoons vanilla extract
½ cup unsweetened natural cocoa powder
½ teaspoon salt
3 tablespoons malted milk powder,
　　plus more for rolling
2 cups (9 ounces) all-purpose flour
⅓ cup semisweet chocolate mini chips
Sifted confectioners' sugar, for rolling

1　Preheat the oven to 350°F and place a rack in the center. Have ready two ungreased baking sheets.

2　In the bowl of a stand mixer fitted with a paddle attachment, or in a large mixing bowl, using a handheld electric mixer, beat the butter on medium speed until creamy. Add the granulated sugar and beat until well blended, then beat in the vanilla, cocoa powder, salt, and malted milk powder. By hand or using the lowest speed of the mixer (if using a handheld mixer, it's best to add the flour with a spoon), add the flour and stir until blended. Stir in the mini chocolate chips. The dough should not be dry, but slightly moist and malleable. If the dough seems too moist to shape, cover the bowl and put it in the refrigerator to chill for 10 minutes.

3 Scoop up small bits of dough and shape into balls a little over ½ inch in diameter. Arrange 1½ inches apart on the prepared baking sheets. Bake one sheet at a time for 8 minutes, or until the cookies appear set. Let cool slightly on the baking sheets. Roll the warm, set cookies in the confectioners' sugar. Sprinkle with extra malted milk powder and roll again in the sugar.

Chocolate Ninjabread Cookies (a.k.a. Chocolate Roll-out Dough) MAKES ABOUT 24

3 (1-ounce) squares unsweetened chocolate, chopped

12 tablespoons (6 ounces) unsalted butter, room temperature

1 cup granulated sugar

2 large eggs

1 teaspoon vanilla extract

½ teaspoon salt

1 teaspoon baking powder

3 cups (13.5 ounces) all-purpose flour

1 Preheat the oven to 375°F and place a rack in the center. Line two large baking sheets with nonstick foil or parchment paper.

2 In a small, microwave-safe bowl, melt the chocolate, using 50 percent power and stirring every 60 seconds. Set the melted chocolate aside to come to room temperature.

3 In the bowl of a stand mixer fitted with a paddle attachment, or in a large mixing bowl, using a handheld electric mixer, beat the butter on medium speed until creamy. Add the sugar and beat for another minute, or until very light and fluffy. Beat in the eggs and vanilla, just until mixed, and then stir in the melted chocolate, followed by the salt and baking powder. By hand or using the lowest speed of a stand mixer (do not beat the flour in with a handheld mixer), add the flour and stir just until it is

DECEMBER 5

Day of the Ninja

Today is a celebration of ninjas and their role in pop culture. Promoted by a website at dayoftheninja.com, this holiday was created to counter September's truly annoying Talk Like a Pirate Day. One way to celebrate is with ninja-shaped cookies made with "Ninjabread" cookie cutters.

Other Events on This Day: (another) National Doughnut Day; the undergraduate honor society, Phi Beta Kappa, was founded in 1776

mixed in. Divide the dough into two equal portions. Roll out right away or wrap tightly in plastic wrap and chill until ready to use.

4 To make the cookies, roll out the dough on a lightly floured surface to about ¼ inch thick. Cut out your ninja guys and arrange them about 1½ inches apart on the prepared baking sheets. Bake one sheet at a time for 8 to 10 minutes, or until they appear set. Let cool on the pan for a few minutes, then transfer to a wire rack to cool completely.

Baker's Notes: You can make ninja guys with just about any good cutout recipe. The dough for Smiley Face Cookies works well (June 15), as does the dough for Spicy Chocolate Ginger Guys (November 5). You can't have too many options, though, so here's a good chocolate roll-out dough. I discovered the cutters at the CakeSpy store in Seattle, but if you can't make it to Seattle, check the website of the manufacturer Fred & Friends.

Saint Nicholas Day

Saint Nicholas, a.k.a. Santa Claus, was known for his kind acts—in particular, saving girls from prostitution by giving them dowries, raising three boys from the dead, and helping sailors navigate stormy seas. For this, he was named patron saint of unmarried girls, children, and sailors. In some countries, especially in Northern Europe, people honor Saint Nicholas in early December. Saint Nicholas Day traditions include leaving gifts in children's shoes, dressing up as Saint Nicholas himself, and baking thin, spicy brown cookies called speculoos.

Speculoos MAKES 36

2 cups (9 ounces) all-purpose flour

½ teaspoon salt

1 teaspoon baking soda

2 teaspoons ground cinnamon

½ teaspoon freshly grated nutmeg

½ teaspoon ground ginger

¼ teaspoon ground allspice

¼ teaspoon ground cloves

¼ teaspoon ground cardamom

8 tablespoons (4 ounces) unsalted
    butter, room temperature

⅓ cup plus 1 tablespoon granulated sugar

½ cup firmly packed dark brown sugar

¼ teaspoon almond extract

1 large egg

2 tablespoons water

Coarse or sparkling sugar, for sprinkling

1 Mix the flour, salt, baking soda, cinnamon, nutmeg, ginger, allspice, cloves, and cardamom together in a medium-size bowl; set aside.

2 In the bowl of a stand mixer fitted with a paddle attachment, or in a large mixing bowl, using a handheld electric mixer, beat the butter and both sugars on medium speed until light and creamy. Add the almond extract and the egg and continue beating on medium until the egg is mixed in. By hand or using the lowest speed of the mixer, blend the flour mixture into the butter mixture until well combined, then stir in the water to make a soft dough.

3 Divide the dough in half and shape each portion into a ball. Place each ball on a piece of plastic wrap, then wrap tightly and chill until ready to use. When ready to use, bring to room temperature if the dough is too stiff to roll.

4 Preheat the oven to 350°F and place a rack in the center. Have ready two ungreased baking sheets.

5 Take about one-quarter of a dough ball and roll out to about ⅜ inch thick on a floured surface. Using 2-inch cookie cutters, cut out circles or flowers. Continue with all the remaining dough until you have about thirty-six cookies. Arrange 2 inches apart on the baking sheets and sprinkle the tops with coarse or sparkling sugar. Bake one sheet at a time for 12 minutes, or until the cookies appear set. Transfer to a wire rack to cool completely.

Other Events on This Day: The Thirteenth Amendment to abolish slavery in the United States was ratified in 1865.

Citrus and Rosemary Biscotti MAKES ABOUT 30

2 cups (9 ounces) all-purpose flour

1½ teaspoons baking powder

¼ teaspoon salt

1 teaspoon chopped fresh rosemary

8 tablespoons (4 ounces) unsalted butter

⅔ cup granulated sugar

2 teaspoons lemon zest

1 teaspoon grated orange zest

DECEMBER 7

Pearl Harbor Day

It's Pearl Harbor Day, so here's a cookie featuring rosemary, the herb of remembrance. Mourners tossed sprigs into graves so that the dead would not be forgotten, whereas students in ancient Rome wore garlands of it around their heads during exams. Inhalation of the essential oil has been attributed to improvement of mental clarity. Used in massage oil or added to a bath, rosemary is thought to help clear congestion, ease pain, and loosen joints. Of course, all of that applies to rosemary in the medicinal sense; using small amounts as a seasoning is known mainly for improving deliciousness.

Other Events on This Day:
National Cotton Candy Day

½ teaspoon vanilla extract

2 large eggs

½ cup walnuts, toasted and chopped

1 Preheat the oven to 350°F and place a rack in the center. Line a large baking sheet with nonstick foil or parchment paper.

2 Mix the flour, baking powder, salt, and rosemary together in a medium-size bowl; set aside.

3 In the bowl of a stand mixer fitted with a paddle attachment, or in a large mixing bowl, using a handheld electric mixer, beat the butter and sugar on medium speed until creamy. Add the lemon and orange zest, vanilla, and eggs. Reduce the mixer speed to low and gradually add the flour mixture. Stir in the walnuts.

4 Divide the dough in half. Shape each portion into a log about 10 by 2½ inches. Arrange 4 inches apart on the prepared baking sheet. Flatten each log to 1½ inches in width. Bake for 20 to 22 minutes, or until the bottom edges are light golden brown and set. Transfer to a wire rack and let cool for at least 15 minutes. Using a serrated knife, cut crosswise slightly on the diagonal every ½ inch. Place cut side down on an ungreased baking sheet and bake at 350°F for 10 to 12 minutes, turning once, until golden brown and crisp around the edges. Transfer to a wire rack to cool completely.

DECEMBER 8

National Brownie Day

A very special baked good made its debut in October 1893 at the World's Columbian Exposition in Chicago. As the story goes, Bertha Palmer, president of the Board of Lady Managers for the fair and wife of Palmer House Hotel owner Potter Palmer, asked the hotel chef to come up with a dessert for the Women's Pavilion. The

Spiked Brownies MAKES 16

8 tablespoons (4 ounces) unsalted butter

3 ounces unsweetened chocolate

1½ cups granulated sugar

3 large eggs

5 tablespoons coffee liqueur, such as Kahlúa

½ teaspoon baking powder

½ teaspoon salt

1½ cups (6.7 ounces) all-purpose flour

¾ cup walnuts or pecans, toasted and coarsely chopped

1 Preheat the oven to 350°F and place a rack in the center. Line an 8-inch square metal pan with nonstick foil.

2 In a microwave-safe mixing bowl, microwave the butter on high for 30 seconds, or until melted. Add the chocolate to the melted butter and stir until the chocolate is melted. If the chocolate isn't fully melted, microwave on high for another 20 seconds, then stir until fully melted. Whisk in the sugar, then whisk in the eggs, one at a time. Whisk in the coffee liqueur, then whisk in the baking powder and salt, making sure there are no stray lumps of baking powder. Add the flour and stir just until blended. Stir in the nuts.

3 Pour into the prepared pan and bake for 30 to 35 minutes, or until the top springs back in the center and the edges begin to pull away from the pan. Let cool completely in the pan. Lift from the pan, set on a cutting board, and cut into sixteen squares.

Butterfly Wings MAKES 18 TO 20

1 cup granulated sugar
1½ tablespoons ground cinnamon
1 sheet frozen puff pastry, thawed (see Baker's Notes)

1 Mix together the sugar and cinnamon and sprinkle about one-quarter of the mixture over a clean surface—I like to use a large melamine cutting board. Unroll the puff pastry and set it on the sugared surface so that you have a horizontal rectangle. Sprinkle more cinnamon sugar over the rectangle—you don't have to be precise; just cover the surface. Fold the left and right sides inward so they meet in the

Fact: Grace Murray Hopper invented a computer language that was later used to create the language COBOL.

She is credited with the quote, "It is often easier to ask for forgiveness than to ask for permission."

chef prepared the brownie, a dessert the women could eat with their hands, and thus the treat became quite popular. It's hard to say if the Palmer House brownie was truly the first, but most sources cite the earliest published chocolate brownies as appearing in early 1904 and 1907.

Other Events on This Day: **Louisiana moved its capital from New Orleans to Baton Rouge in 1879.**

Grace Murray Hopper's Birthday

A distinguished teacher, consultant, and recipient of many honors, including the National Medal of Technology, Grace Murray Hopper was born today in 1906. Despite her many accomplishments, her most well-known claim to fame was popularizing the term "computer bug."

Hopper joined the Navy in 1943. Her first assignment was programming Harvard's Mark 1, a computer used to calculate aiming angles in varying weather conditions. When her team found a moth in a relay system, Hopper commented that it needed "debugging." Although the word "bug" already existed, her comment made it famous, and that bug is now in the Smithsonian.

center. Sprinkle more sugar over the top; repeat, folding the left and right sides together a second time to meet in the middle. Make one last fold so that the two sides come together and you have a thick, U-shaped roll. Turn it seam side down and chill for about an hour, or until very firm.

And in 1969, she won the first computer science "Man of the Year" award.

4 Preheat the oven to 400°F and place a rack in the center. Have ready two ungreased baking sheets.

5 Remove the rolled dough from the refrigerator and place on a cutting board. With a serrated knife, cut the roll into ½-inch slices—you should get eighteen to twenty, depending on what your idea of ½ inch is. Again, you don't have to be precise. Arrange the slices about 2 inches apart on the baking sheets. Sprinkle with more sugar if you like. Bake one sheet at a time for 12 minutes, or until the butterfly wings are golden brown. Transfer to a wire rack and let cool completely.

Baker's Notes: I use Pepperidge Farm puff pastry. Each pack includes two rolls of pastry that unfold to make 10 by 14-inch rectangles. Consider the amount of sugar used a suggestion and use however much you want.

DECEMBER 10

Mississippi Joins the Union

On this day in 1817, Mississippi joined the Union and became the twentieth state. It is nicknamed the Magnolia State for its state flower and state tree. The Mississippi state dance is the square dance, the state bird is the mockingbird, the state insect is the bee, and the state beverage is milk. As

Mississippi Mud Cups MAKES 20

1 cup (4.5 ounces) all-purpose flour

½ teaspoon baking soda

½ teaspoon salt

8 tablespoons (4 ounces) unsalted butter

¾ cup firmly packed light brown sugar

1 large egg

1½ teaspoons vanilla extract

8 ounces dark chocolate, chopped

4 ounces white baking chocolate, chopped

1 cup pecans, toasted and chopped

20 large marshmallows, halved

1   Preheat the oven to 350°F and place a rack in the center. Line twenty muffin cups with paper liners.

2   Mix the flour, baking soda, and salt together in a medium-size bowl; set aside.

3   In the bowl of a stand mixer fitted with a paddle attachment, or in a large mixing bowl, using a handheld electric mixer, beat the butter and brown sugar on medium speed until creamy. Reduce the mixer speed slightly and beat in the egg and vanilla. By hand or using the lowest speed of the mixer, stir in the flour mixture. Stir in half of the dark chocolate, half of the white chocolate, and half of the pecans.

4   Spoon a slightly heaping tablespoonful of batter into each prepared muffin cup, dividing evenly among all twenty cups. Bake for 15 minutes, or until the cakes are browned and a toothpick comes out clean. Remove from the oven and immediately stick a marshmallow half, cut side down, in the center of each cake. Mix together the remaining chocolate and white chocolate and scatter around each marshmallow. Cover the pans fairly tightly (just enough to lock in some heat) with a sheet of non-stick foil and let sit for 5 to 10 minutes. Remove the foil. With the tip of a knife, swirl the softened chocolate and marshmallow around a little to make kind of a marbled pattern. Alternatively, you can skip the swirling and just leave it as is. Sprinkle the remaining pecans over the top. Let cool and set completely before serving. I like to chill mine a bit to speed up the chocolate setting process, but this is not necessary.

Baker's Note: You may substitute 1⅓ cups dark chocolate chips and ⅔ cup white chocolate chips for the chopped dark and white chocolate.

for the state cookie, it would have to be Mississippi Mud.

Traditional Mississippi mud bars are loaded with chocolate, nuts, and marshmallows. This recipe puts those things in a bake-sale and party-perfect cup form.

Other Events on This Day:
Human Rights Day

Boll Weevil Monument Erected

On this day in 1919, the citizens of Enterprise, Alabama, built a monument dedicated to a real pest. A small beetle native to Central America, the boll weevil came over from Mexico during the early 1900s and wrought havoc on the cotton crop, killing whole fields at a time. Call it fortuitous devastation, though, because the impact of the boll weevil prompted farmers to diversify their crop and grow peanuts. Today, Alabama harvests an average of more than 400,000 pounds of peanuts per year.

Other Events on This Day:
James Lewis Kraft's birthday (b. 1874)

Peanut Butter Oat Chocolate Chunk Cookies   MAKES ABOUT 48

1 cup (4.5 ounces) all-purpose flour

1 cup (4.5 ounces) white whole wheat flour

2 teaspoons baking soda

1 teaspoon salt

1 cup (8 ounces) unsalted butter, cold

²/₃ cup granulated sugar

1 cup firmly packed light brown sugar

1 cup extra-crunchy peanut butter

2 teaspoons vanilla extract

2 large eggs

1 cup old-fashioned or quick-cooking oats (not instant)

7 ounces semisweet chocolate, cut into small chunks

1 Preheat the oven to 325°F and place a rack in the center. Have ready two ungreased baking sheets.

2 Mix both flours, the baking soda, and the salt together in a medium-size bowl; set aside.

3 In the bowl of a stand mixer fitted with a paddle attachment, or in a large mixing bowl, using a handheld electric mixer, beat the butter on medium speed until creamy. Gradually add both sugars and beat for about 3 minutes, or until light. Beat in the peanut butter and vanilla. Reduce the mixer speed to medium-low and beat in the eggs, beating just until mixed. By hand or using the lowest speed of the mixer, beat in the flour mixture. When the flour is incorporated, stir in the oats and chocolate.

4 Drop generously rounded tablespoonfuls of dough about 2½ inches apart onto the baking sheets. Bake one sheet at a time for 13 to 15 minutes, or until the edges start to brown and the cookies appear set. Let cool on the baking sheets for about 5 minutes, then transfer to a wire rack to cool completely.

Ambrosia Cookies   MAKES 60

2 cups (9 ounces) all-purpose flour

1 teaspoon baking powder

½ teaspoon baking soda

¾ teaspoon salt

1 cup (8 ounces) unsalted butter, room temperature

1 cup minus 1 tablespoon granulated sugar

1 cup firmly packed light brown sugar

2 large eggs

1½ teaspoons vanilla extract

1½ cups quick-cooking oats (not instant)

1 teaspoon lemon zest

¾ cup chopped dried pineapple

1 cup sweetened flaked coconut

1 cup pecans, toasted and finely chopped

1 Preheat the oven to 350°F and place a rack in the center. Have ready two ungreased baking sheets.

2 Mix the flour, baking powder, baking soda, and salt together in a medium-size bowl; set aside.

3 In the bowl of a stand mixer fitted with a paddle attachment, or in a large mixing bowl, using a handheld electric mixer, beat the butter on medium speed until creamy. Add both sugars and beat for about a minute, then add the eggs, one at a time, beating well after each addition. Beat in the vanilla. Reduce the mixer speed to low and gradually add the flour mixture. Stir in the oats, lemon zest, pineapple, coconut, and pecans.

4 Drop rounded teaspoonfuls of batter 2½ inches apart onto the baking sheets. Bake one sheet at a time for 8 to 10 minutes, or until the edges are nicely browned. Transfer to a wire rack to cool completely.

Ambrosia Day

Ambrosia—food of the gods, and food of the southern United States. My grandmother used to serve it at every meal except breakfast. Typically, it consists of coconut, mandarin oranges, marshmallows, pineapple, nuts, and whipping cream, but she made it with whipped topping, fruit cocktail, coconut, and pineapple. She never used oranges and only added nuts during pecan season. In honor of Ambrosia Day and my grandma, here's a cookie modeled after her famous salad.

Other Events on This Day:
National Poinsettia Day

National Cocoa Day

Today we celebrate cocoa powder of all varieties. Cocoa comes from the bean of the cacao tree. The trees grow in many parts of the world, but the earliest known cultivation of cocoa was in the Amazon, where archaeologists have found evidence of its use dating back to 1900 BC. More famously, the Maya were known to have used the cocoa bean as food, and currency in fertility rites, while the Aztecs ground it into a bitter drink. Both cultures believed cocoa to be linked to the gods, but it wasn't until the 1700s that the taxonomer Linnaeus aptly named the source of cocoa beans Theabroma Cacao, meaning "gift of the gods."

Less sweet than some, these crinkle cookies are absolutely loaded with cocoa and just a hint of rum flavor. Because the cookies are made with baking powder, I make these with Dutch-processed cocoa and get fat, fudgy cookies every time.

Other Events on This Day:
National Violins Day

Chocolate Rum Crinkle Cookies MAKES 24

2 cups (9 ounces) all-purpose flour

2 teaspoons baking powder

½ teaspoon salt

1 cup Dutch-processed cocoa powder

4 large eggs

1 cup granulated sugar

½ cup vegetable oil

1 teaspoon rum extract

¾ teaspoon vanilla extract

3.5 ounces dark chocolate, finely chopped,
    or ⅔ cup dark chocolate chips

1 cup (more or less) confectioners' sugar

1 Mix the flour, baking powder, salt, and cocoa together in a small bowl; set aside.

2 In the bowl of a stand mixer fitted with a paddle attachment, or in a large mixing bowl using a handheld electric mixer, beat the eggs on medium-high speed for about 2 minutes or until light. Reduce the speed to medium and gradually add the granulated sugar. Using the lowest speed of a stand mixer, or with a mixing spoon, stir in the oil and extracts. Add the flour mixture and stir until incorporated, then remove from the mixer stand (if using) and stir in the chocolate. Cover the bowl with plastic wrap and place in the freezer for 40 minutes, or until firm enough to handle.

3 Preheat the oven to 350°F and place a rack in the upper third of the oven. Line two baking sheets with nonstick foil or parchment paper.

4 Pour or sift the confectioners' sugar onto a plate. Scoop up heaping tablespoons of cold dough and shape into 1½ inch balls. Roll the balls in the sugar to coat generously. Arrange the balls 2½ inches apart on the prepared baking sheets. Bake one sheet at a time for 10 minutes or just until they appear puffy and set. Immediately transfer to a wire rack to cool completely.

Baker's Notes: For the prettiest cookies, be very generous with the confectioners' sugar and bake the cookies in the upper third of the oven until they are just cooked through.

Mandel Bread MAKES ABOUT 48

BASE

1¾ cups (8 ounces) all-purpose flour

½ teaspoon baking powder

¼ teaspoon salt

2 large eggs

½ cup granulated sugar

1½ teaspoons vanilla extract

½ cup vegetable oil

½ cup toasted and finely chopped pecans

2 ounces semisweet chocolate, chopped

TOPPING

1 tablespoon granulated sugar

1½ teaspoons ground cinnamon

1 Preheat the oven to 350°F and place a rack in the center. Line a large baking sheet with parchment paper.

2 **Make the base:** Mix the flour, baking powder, and salt together in a medium-size bowl; set aside.

3 In the bowl of a stand mixer fitted with a paddle attachment, or in a large mixing bowl, using a handheld electric mixer, beat the eggs and sugar on medium speed for about 2 minutes, or until light and foamy. Beat in the vanilla extract. Reduce the mixer speed and add the oil. By hand or using the lowest speed of the mixer, stir in the flour mixture. When the flour is incorporated, stir in the pecans and chocolate.

4 Divide the batter into four equal-size portions. On the prepared baking sheet, shape each portion into a log about 5½ by 2½ inches, spacing the logs about 3½ inches apart to allow for spreading. The dough should be slightly sticky but not unmanageable. If the dough seems very sticky, place it in the refrigerator to chill for about 30 minutes.

Hanukkah Ends

Given Hanukkah's shifting schedule, this date may or may not match up to the Festival of Light. However, I wanted to share this Jewish cookie recipe because it's one of my favorites and the double bake time makes it perfect for baking on a cold December day. Mandel bread is similar to biscotti but easier on the teeth, as it has some oil to keep it from being too hard. And even though *Mandelbrodt* translates to "almond bread," it may be baked with different types of nuts. This one is made with toasted pecans and chopped chocolate.

Other Events on This Day:
Famous prophet and astrologer Nostradamus's birthday (b. 1503)

5 **Make the topping:** Stir together the cinnamon and sugar. Sprinkle the topping over the logs. Bake at 350°F for 25 minutes. Let the logs cool on the pan for 30 minutes, or until you are ready for round two of baking.

6 When ready to bake, preheat the oven to 350°F. Using a serrated knife, cut crosswise slightly on the diagonal every ½ inch. Place cut side down on an ungreased baking sheet. Bake for 12 to 15 minutes, or until the edges are dry. Transfer to a wire rack to cool completely.

Baker's Note: Because the dough is often looser, it may be baked in a loaf pan.

DECEMBER 15

Bill of Rights Day

On this day in 1791, ten amendments were added to the Constitution of the United States. Those amendments are the Bill of Rights and today we pay tribute to them. Do you know them by heart? If not, try to memorize them and reward yourself with a tiny cookie every time you get one right.

Other Events on This Day:
National Cupcake Day

Ten-at-a-Time Cookies

MAKES ABOUT 100 TINY COOKIES

½ cup (2.25 ounces) white whole wheat flour

¼ cup plus 2 teaspoons (1.1 ounces) barley flour

1 tablespoon cornstarch

¼ teaspoon baking soda

¼ teaspoon salt

4 tablespoons (2 ounces) unsalted butter, room temperature

¼ cup granulated sugar

¼ cup firmly packed light brown sugar

2 tablespoons lightly beaten egg

¾ teaspoon vanilla extract

2 teaspoons heavy cream

1 tablespoon whole milk

⅔ cup extra-dark chocolate chips

1 Mix the flour, barley flour, cornstarch, baking soda, and salt together in a medium-size bowl; set aside.

2 In a mixing bowl, using a handheld electric mixer, beat the butter and both sugars on medium speed until light and creamy; beat in the egg and vanilla, then beat in the cream and milk. Using a mixing spoon, stir in the flour mixture, followed by the chocolate chips. Chill the dough for 1 hour.

3 Preheat the oven to 375°F and place a rack in the center. Line two large baking sheets with nonstick foil or parchment paper.

4 Scoop rounded ¼ teaspoons of cold dough and shape into tiny balls no more than ½ inch in diameter. Place the balls onto the prepared baking sheets. Bake one sheet at a time for 6 to 9 minutes, or until the edges are browned and the cookies appear set. Let cool on the baking sheets for about 3 minutes, then transfer to a wire rack to cool completely. The cookies will crisp as they cool.

Baker's Notes: The mixture of white whole wheat and barley flour makes this cookie a little more wholesome, though most of it is comprised of chocolate chips. The cookies are tiny. I use ¼ teaspoon of dough per cookie, each having about three regular size (not miniature) chocolate chips and just enough dough to bind them. We enjoy the nutty flavor of barley flour, but if you can't find barley flour, substitute ¼ cup (1.1 ounce) all-purpose flour. For thicker cookies, shape the dough into tiny balls, put them in a sealable plastic bag, and chill them overnight. If you prefer thin cookies, subtract 2 teaspoons of barley flour and watch the cookies closely as they bake.

Chai-Chocolate Banana Tea Bars MAKES 16

1 cup (4.5 ounces) white whole wheat or all-purpose flour

½ teaspoon salt

½ teaspoon baking powder

⅛ teaspoon ground cardamom

¼ teaspoon ground ginger

¼ teaspoon ground cinnamon

⅛ teaspoon ground cloves

⅛ teaspoon freshly grated nutmeg

4 tablespoons (2 ounces) unsalted butter, room temperature

¾ cup minus 2 teaspoons granulated sugar

1 teaspoon vanilla extract

½ cup sour cream

1 large egg

DECEMBER 16

Boston Tea Party

On this day in 1773, infuriated colonists calling themselves "the sons of liberty" boarded ships and threw 342 chests of tea into the Boston Harbor. Known as the party that sparked a revolution, the tea party was an act of resistance against the Tea Act that the British Parliament had passed earlier, and a monopoly called the East India Tea Company that was underselling local merchants.

Other Events on This Day:
National Re-Gifting Day

¾ cup mashed bananas

⅔ cup semisweet chocolate chips

½ cup toasted and chopped walnuts (optional)

1 Preheat the oven to 350°F and place a rack in the center. Spray a 9-inch square metal pan with flour-added baking spray or line the inside with nonstick foil.

2 Mix the flour, salt, baking powder, cardamom, ginger, cinnamon, cloves, and nutmeg together in a small bowl; set aside.

3 In the bowl of a stand mixer fitted with a paddle attachment, or in a large mixing bowl, using a handheld electric mixer, beat the butter and sugar on medium speed until creamy. Beat in the vanilla and sour cream. Reduce the mixer speed and beat in the egg and banana until creamy. Scrape the sides of the bowl. With the mixer on low, gradually add the flour mixture. When the flour is absorbed, mix in the chocolate chips and walnuts.

4 Spread in the prepared pan and bake for 28 to 30 minutes, or until the bars are browned around the edges and appear set. Let cool completely in the pan. Cut into sixteen squares.

DECEMBER 17

National Maple Syrup Day

Move over, honey, today is Maple Syrup Day—a day to recognize the sweet sap of the maple tree, and partner to pancakes, waffles, and French toast. Can you imagine life without it? On Maple Syrup Day, pass on the imposters and treat yourself to the real thing. Grade B is the more robust type, while Grade A is perfect for adding very subtle flavor to baked goods.

Maple Oat Bars MAKES 16

8 tablespoons (4 ounces) unsalted
  butter, room temperature

½ cup granulated sugar

½ cup pure maple syrup

1 teaspoon vanilla extract

1 large egg

⅔ cup (3 ounces) all-purpose
  or white whole wheat flour

½ teaspoon baking powder

¼ teaspoon salt

1 cup pecans, toasted and chopped

1 cup quick-cooking or old-fashioned oats (not instant)

1 Preheat the oven to 350°F and place a rack in the center. Line an 8-inch metal pan with nonstick foil, or line it with regular foil and spray the foil with flour-added baking spray.

2 In a large mixing bowl, using a handheld electric mixer, beat the butter and sugar on medium-high speed until creamy. Beat in the maple syrup and vanilla. When light and creamy, reduce the speed to medium and beat in the egg. In a small bowl, thoroughly mix together the flour, baking powder, and salt. Add to the batter and stir until mixed. Stir in the pecans and oats.

3 Spread in the prepared pan. Bake for 30 minutes, or until lightly browned and set. Let cool completely in the pan. Lift from the pan, set on a cutting board, and cut into sixteen squares

Wine Cookies

MAKES 4 TO 6 DOZEN, DEPENDING ON SIZE

COOKIES

2¼ cups (10.1 ounces) all-purpose flour,
   plus more as needed
2 teaspoons baking powder
¼ teaspoon salt
½ teaspoon ground cinnamon
¼ teaspoon freshly grated nutmeg
⅛ teaspoon ground black pepper
½ cup chardonnay (or any other wine)
½ cup olive or vegetable oil
½ cup granulated sugar

TOPPING

2 tablespoons granulated sugar
1 teaspoon ground cinnamon

1 Preheat the oven to 350°F and place a rack in the center. Line two baking sheets with parchment paper.

2 **Make the cookies:** In a large mixing bowl, combine the flour, baking powder, salt, spices, pepper, wine, oil, and

Other Events on This Day:
First episode of the Simpsons aired in 1989

DECEMBER 18

Another Bake Cookies Day

You've been baking cookies all year, but now it's time to step up the game and make double, triple, or quadruple batches of all the family favorites. At some point, you may even find yourself in sugar overload. If that's the case, bake a batch of these not-too-sweet Italian style cookies for yourself and relax with a cup of coffee.

My friend Cecilia made a version of these cookies for a food blogger cookie exchange. Hers were a lovely shade of brown. I made them with red zinfandel and they were a dark purple. They still tasted good, but I think I prefer them with white wine.

sugar and mix with a spoon until blended. Finish mixing with your hands, kneading a little bit so that you have a thick dough. If the dough seems too dry, add a little water or milk; if it's too loose, add a little more flour.

3 Break off little pieces of dough and shape into small S shapes. Arrange them about 2 inches apart on the prepared baking sheets.

4 **Make the topping:** Mix the sugar and cinnamon together and sprinkle on top of the dough. Bake for 20 minutes, or until they appear dry. Let cool completely on a wire rack.

DECEMBER 19

Benjamin Franklin Published Poor Richard's Almanac

Writing under the pseudonym Richard Saunders, Benjamin Franklin published *Poor Richard's Almanac* today in 1732. A best seller in its time, the almanac contained information covering the weather, astronomy and astrology, a calendar, and humorous proverbs. Franklin was known to enjoy food, including cranberries, which he mentioned several times in his writings.

Other Events on This Day:
Oatmeal Muffin Day

Cranberry Streusel Bars MAKES 16

1 cup (4.5 ounces) all-purpose flour
¾ cup old-fashioned oats
⅔ cup firmly packed dark brown sugar
¼ scant teaspoon baking soda
¼ teaspoon salt
6 tablespoons (3 ounces) unsalted
    butter, melted and cooled
1 (8-ounce) package cream cheese, softened
⅓ cup granulated sugar
¼ teaspoon vanilla extract
2 teaspoons freshly squeezed lemon juice
2 large egg whites, room temperature
¼ cup whole-berry cranberry sauce
2 tablespoons pecans, toasted and finely chopped

1 Preheat the oven to 350°F and place a rack in the center. Line an 8-inch metal baking pan with nonstick foil.

2 In a large mixing bowl, thoroughly stir together the flour, oats, brown sugar, baking soda, and salt. Pour the butter over the flour mixture and stir with a wooden spoon until moist and crumbly. Set aside about 1 cup of the crumb mixture to use as a topping, then press the remaining crumb mixture into the bottom of the prepared pan.

3 In a medium-size mixing bowl, beat together the cream cheese, sugar, vanilla, and lemon juice. Stir in the egg whites just until mixed—do not overbeat. Pour into the pan over the crust. Drop spoonfuls of cranberry sauce over the cheese and then sprinkle the reserved crumb mixture and the pecans over the cream cheese and cranberries.

4 Bake for 22 to 25 minutes, or until the cheese mixture is set and the topping is cooked through. Let cool completely in the pan, then chill for at least 2 hours, or until ready to serve. Using the foil, lift from the pan and set on a cutting board. Cut into sixteen bars.

Bachelor's Buttons MAKES ABOUT 32

1 cup (8 ounces) unsalted butter, room temperature
¾ teaspoon salt
1 cup confectioners' sugar
1 large egg
1 teaspoon vanilla extract
2 cups (9 ounces) all-purpose flour
¼ cup of your favorite preserves (see Baker's Note)

1 Preheat the oven to 350°F and place a rack in the center. Line two baking sheets with parchment paper or nonstick foil.

2 In the bowl of a stand mixer fitted with a paddle attachment, or in a large mixing bowl, using a handheld electric mixer, beat the butter, salt, and confectioners' sugar on medium speed until creamy. Reduce the mixer speed slightly and beat in the egg and vanilla. By hand or using the lowest speed of the mixer, stir in the flour.

3 Shape the dough into ¾-inch balls and arrange 2½ inches apart on the prepared baking sheets. Use your finger to make an indentation in the center of each dough ball, then fill with preserves. Bake one sheet at a time for 10 to 12 minutes, or until the cookies are lightly browned around the edges. Let cool on the baking sheets for about 3 minutes, then transfer to a wire rack to cool completely.

DECEMBER 20

Bachelor Tax Enacted in Missouri

In 1820, Missouri enacted legislation to tax bachelors between twenty-one and fifty years of age one dollar per year for being unmarried.

Mark the date with some cookies that look like buttons. Or are they flowers? Either way, they're easy, and cute enough to serve at a party.

Other Events on This Day: National Sangria Day, winter solstice (falls on the 20th, 21st, or 22nd)

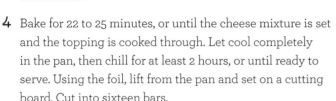

Baker's Note: Use the best preserves you can find. I like Smucker's Orchard's Finest and Dickinson's.

DECEMBER 21

Pilgrims Land on Plymouth Rock

In honor of the day the Pilgrims landed on Plymouth Rock, here's a rock-shaped cookie stuffed with cranberries, walnuts, and white chips. The fun part is cramming the "rocks" with add-ins, so consider my combination a suggestion and use your favorite nuts, dried fruit, and chips.

Other Events on This Day:
Disney's *Snow White* premiered in 1937

Colonial Rock Cookies MAKES 24

2 large eggs, separated

11 tablespoons (5.5 ounces) unsalted butter, room temperature

1 cup granulated sugar

¾ teaspoon salt

1 teaspoon vanilla extract

¾ teaspoon baking soda

1½ tablespoons water

2 cups (9 ounces) all-purpose flour

1½ cups walnuts, toasted and chopped

¾ cup dried cranberries

½ cup white chocolate chips

1 Preheat the oven to 375°F and place a rack in the center. Line two baking sheets with parchment paper or nonstick foil.

2 In the bowl of a stand mixer fitted with a whisk attachment or in a large mixing bowl, using a handheld electric mixer, beat the egg whites on high speed until stiff peaks form. Transfer the whipped whites to a separate bowl to wait. Add the butter, sugar, salt, and vanilla to the mixing bowl and beat on medium-high until creamy. Beat in the egg yolks, scraping the sides of the bowl once or twice. Mix the baking soda and water together to dissolve the baking soda, then add to the batter. Fold in the whipped egg whites, then stir in the flour. The dough will be thick. Stir in the walnuts, cranberries, and white chips.

3 Drop rounded tablespoonfuls of dough into large rounds about 1½ inches in diameter, about 2½ inches apart, on the prepared baking sheets. Bake one sheet at a time for 10 minutes, or until the edges are browned and the cookies appear set. Transfer to a wire rack and let cool completely.

Baker's Notes: The method of folding egg whites into cookie dough is one you don't see very often these days, but it gives the cookies an interesting sturdy-yet-somehow-light (despite the name) texture.

Lemon Bars MAKES 32

CRUST

2 cups (9 ounces) all-purpose flour

¼ cup granulated sugar

½ teaspoon salt

1 cup (8 ounces) unsalted butter, cut into small chunks, room temperature

FILLING

2 cups granulated sugar

1 teaspoon baking powder

3 large eggs

⅓ cup freshly squeezed lemon juice

2 packed teaspoons lemon zest

1½ tablespoons heavy cream

¼ cup confectioners' sugar, for dusting

1 Preheat the oven to 350°F and place a rack in the center. Spray a 9 by 13-inch metal baking pan with flour-added baking spray or line it with nonstick foil.

2 **Make the crust:** In the bowl of a food processor, mix the flour, sugar, and the salt; add the butter and pulse until the mixture is coarse and crumbly. Transfer the mixture to the prepared pan and press down to make a crust. Bake the crust for 15 minutes, or until the edges are lightly browned. Let the crust cool slightly in the pan while you prepare the filling.

3 **Make the filling:** In a mixing bowl, whisk together the sugar, baking powder, eggs, lemon juice, and zest. Stir in the cream. Spoon over the crust. Bake for 15 to 20 minutes, or until the edges are lightly browned. Let cool completely in the pan. Dust with confectioners' sugar. Grasp the foil, lift from the pan, set on a cutting board, and cut into thirty-two squares.

Lady Bird Johnson's Birthday

Happy birthday, Lady Bird Johnson. A gracious and intelligent first lady, she helped make the Johnson administration environmentally active by championing multiple legislation initiatives. After leaving Washington, she continued to devote herself to the land through various endeavors, including the founding of the National Wildflower Research Center and the beautification of Austin's Town Lake, both of which were renamed in her honor.

Lady Bird was a good hostess and had a number of recipes, including the Texas favorite, lemon squares. My version is similar to hers. She didn't add cream, but I've found that a little cream tones down the acid of the lemon without diminishing its flavor.

Other Events on This Day:
Date Nut Bread Day, Edward H. Johnson created Christmas tree lights in 1882

Pfeffernüsse Day

Today is Pfeffernüsse Day, and we all have an excuse to make the little German cookies so popular during the holiday season. As much as I love homemade cookies, this is one I like packaged, but I did manage to find one recipe that made me just as happy as the crunchy, confectioners' sugar ones I buy in late November.

Pfeffernüsse (pepper nuts) don't always have actual pepper in them, but this recipe does. It also has anise, which, like the pepper, is pretty much optional these days.

Other Events on This Day: **Fans of *Seinfeld* might tell you today is Festivus, a celebration of the airing of grievances and the feats of strength.**

Pfeffernüsse MAKES 48

6 tablespoons (3 ounces) unsalted butter, room temperature
½ cup granulated sugar
½ cup dark corn syrup
1½ tablespoons hot water
¼ teaspoon anise or vanilla extract
½ teaspoon black pepper
½ teaspoon baking soda
⅛ teaspoon ground cloves
⅛ teaspoon ground allspice
2¼ cups (10.1 ounces) all-purpose flour
Confectioners' sugar, for rolling

1 In the bowl of a stand mixer fitted with a paddle attachment, or in a large mixing bowl, using a handheld electric mixer, beat the butter and granulated sugar on medium speed until creamy. Beat in the corn syrup and hot water, then beat in the anise extract, pepper, baking soda, cloves, and allspice. By hand or using the lowest speed of the mixer, add the flour and stir to make a fairly firm dough. Wrap tightly in plastic wrap and chill for 2 hours.

2 Preheat the oven to 350°F and have ready an ungreased baking sheet.

3 Divide the dough into quarters and roll each portion into a ¾-inch-thick rope. Cut the ropes on the diagonal, spacing the cuts about 1 inch apart. Arrange the cookies 2 inches apart on the baking sheet. Bake for 10 to 13 minutes, or until golden brown. Let cool completely on a wire rack. When completely cool, roll in confectioners' sugar.

Eggnog Sandwich Cookies MAKES 20

National Eggnog Day

Excitement is in the air and the eggnog is flowing. If you'd rather eat it than drink it, here's eggnog in cookie form.

Other Events on This Day: **Christmas Eve**

COOKIES

1⅓ cups (6 ounces) all-purpose flour

3 tablespoons cornstarch

2 tablespoons instant vanilla pudding mix

½ teaspoon baking powder

½ teaspoon salt

½ teaspoon loosely packed freshly grated nutmeg

10 tablespoons (5 ounces) unsalted
     butter, room temperature

⅔ cup confectioners' sugar

1 large egg yolk

¾ teaspoon rum extract

¼ teaspoon vanilla extract

FILLING

6 tablespoons (3 ounces) unsalted
     butter, room temperature

2 teaspoons instant vanilla pudding mix

1⅔ cups confectioners' sugar

½ teaspoon vanilla extract

1 to 2 tablespoons whole milk, or as needed

1 Preheat the oven to 350°F and place a rack in the center. Line two baking sheets with parchment paper or nonstick foil.

2 **Make the cookies:** Mix the flour, cornstarch, pudding mix, baking powder, salt, and nutmeg together in a medium-size bowl; set aside.

3 In the bowl of a stand mixer fitted with a paddle attachment, or in a large mixing bowl, using a handheld electric mixer, beat the butter and confectioners' sugar on medium speed until creamy. Reduce the mixer speed to low and add the egg yolk; beat in the rum extract and vanilla. By hand or using the lowest speed of the mixer, add the flour mixture.

4 When fully mixed, transfer the dough to a floured surface and pat or roll out to about ⅛-inch thickness. Using a 1¾-inch round cookie cutter, cut out as many rounds as you can. Gather up the scraps and gently pat them down. Continue cutting out as many circles as you can. Arrange the rounds about 1½ inches apart on the prepared baking sheets. Bake one sheet at a time for 8 to 10 minutes, or until the edges are lightly browned. Let cool on the baking sheets for about 4 minutes, then transfer to a wire rack to cool completely.

5 **Make the filling:** In a medium-size mixing bowl, beat the butter, pudding mix, and confectioners' sugar until light and creamy. Beat in the vanilla. Add enough milk to get a spreading consistency. Spread the underside of one cookie with about 2 teaspoons of the filling, then top base to base with another cookie. Repeat until all the cookies are sandwiched.

Almond Ginger Toasts MAKES 24

2 large egg whites, room temperature

¼ cup granulated sugar

½ tablespoon mild molasses

⅛ teaspoon salt

½ teaspoon ground ginger

¼ teaspoon ground cinnamon

¼ teaspoon vanilla extract

½ cup minus 1 tablespoon (2 ounces) all-purpose flour

⅓ to ½ cup mixed nuts, mostly
    almonds, pecans, hazelnuts

½ cup mixed dried fruit, such as apricots,
    raisins, and cranberries

½ to 1 tablespoon chopped candied ginger (optional)

1 Preheat the oven to 350°F and place a rack in the center. Line six muffin cups with paper liners and spray the paper liners with flour-added baking spray.

2   In the bowl of a stand mixer fitted with a whisk attachment, or in a large mixing bowl, using a handheld electric mixer, beat the egg whites on high speed until stiff peaks form. Slowly add the sugar and continue beating until the sugar dissolves and the mixture is glossy. Beat in the molasses, salt, ginger, cinnamon, and vanilla. With a large scraper or mixing spoon, fold in the flour. Fold in the mixed nuts, fruit, and candied ginger.

3   Spoon the mixture into the muffin cups about three-quarters of the way full. Bake for 20 to 25 minutes, or until the tops are browned. Let cool slightly in the pan, then remove from the muffin cups and pull off the paper liners. Transfer to a wire rack to cool completely, then wrap loosely in foil and chill for about 4 hours or overnight, or until very cold. This makes them much easier to slice.

4   Preheat the oven to 200°F and have ready an ungreased baking sheet.

5   Lay the cold "muffins" on their sides, and using a large serrated knife, slice them into thin rounds. You should get at least three rounds and one stubby-looking top per muffin. Arrange the rounds in one big layer on the baking sheet and bake for 1 hour to 1 hour and 15 minutes, or until dried out. They'll dry out even more as they cool, so if the centers aren't completely firm after the full baking time, take them out anyway. Let cool completely on a wire rack. Store in a tightly covered container.

Peppermint Cookie Bark
MAKES ABOUT 1½ POUNDS

32 small, round chocolate mint cookies, such as
    Keebler Grasshoppers or Girl Scout Thin Mints
12 ounces dark chocolate, chopped
5 regular-size peppermint candy canes, crushed
3 ounces white chocolate

1   Line a 9 by 13-inch pan with nonstick foil or parchment paper. Lay the cookies flat across the bottom of the pan.

Boxing Day and Candy Cane Day

Boxing Day goes back to a tradition in which members of the upper class would give boxes of food and gifts to the lower classes. There are various explanations of its origin, but I think goodwill toward others sums it up.

It's also Candy Cane Day, so why not make something with some candy canes picked fresh off the old Christmas tree? You can box this bark up and give it to people during that period between Christmas and New Year's when you exchange presents with neighbors and people who drop by.

Other Events on This Day: **First Kwanzaa, a weeklong celebration with shifting dates, in 1966**

Howdy Doody Show Debuts

The Howdy Doody Show premiered on this day in 1947. Starring Buffalo Bob Smith and a redheaded marionette named Howdy Doody, the show had a live studio audience called the "Peanut Gallery." It consisted of about forty kids who helped open every show by singing "It's Howdy Doody Time."

In honor of all the kids who wished they could have been in the Peanut Gallery, here's a peanut butter cookie. I created the recipe for a contest. It didn't win, but someone with a similar idea of using refrigerated cookie dough and a cinnamon topping later won a big prize.

2 In a microwave-safe bowl, microwave the chocolate on 50 percent power, stirring every 60 seconds, or until completely melted. Alternatively, you may melt it in the top of a double boiler. Spread the chocolate over the cookies, covering them completely. Sprinkle the crushed candy canes over the chocolate-covered cookies and chill until the chocolate is set. In a microwave-safe bowl, melt the white chocolate, using 50 percent power or another low setting. With a spoon, drizzle or gently fling the white chocolate over the crushed candy. Return the pan to the refrigerator to set the white chocolate. When ready to serve, break apart.

Double Peanut Butter Truffle Cookies MAKES 22

FILLING

⅓ cup creamy peanut butter

¼ cup confectioners' sugar

COOKIES

1 (17.5-ounce) pouch peanut butter cookie mix

3 tablespoons unsalted or salted butter, softened

1 large egg

1 tablespoon water

Coarse or sparkling sugar, for sprinkling

1 Preheat the oven to 375°F and place a rack in the center. Have ready two ungreased baking sheets.

2 **Make the filling:** Beat together the peanut butter and confectioners' sugar. Place in the refrigerator and chill until ready to use.

3 **Make the cookies:** In a large mixing bowl, stir together the cookie mix and butter. Add the egg and water and stir with a spoon until the mixture comes together.

4 Scoop up tablespoonfuls and shape into twenty-two balls. Remove the filling from the refrigerator. Divide a dough ball in half and flatten the halves slightly. Scoop up a heaping ½ teaspoonful of the peanut butter mixture and place between the dough halves. Mold the dough around the peanut butter filling, rolling gently between your palms to make a ball. Set on a baking sheet and repeat until all the dough balls are filled with the peanut butter mixture. Sprinkle the balls with coarse or sparkling sugar. Bake one sheet at a time for 10 to 12 minutes, or until lightly browned around the edges. Let cool on the baking sheet for about 3 minutes, then transfer to a wire rack to cool completely.

One-Bowl White Chocolate Macadamia Cookies MAKES 32

8 tablespoons (4 ounces) unsalted
    butter, room temperature
½ cup (3.4 ounces) regular vegetable shortening
    or coconut oil (see Baker's Note)
¾ cup granulated sugar
½ cup firmly packed light brown sugar
1 large egg
2 teaspoons vanilla extract
¾ scant teaspoon salt
1 teaspoon baking soda
1¾ cups (8 ounces) all-purpose flour
½ cup roughly chopped, roasted (salted
    or unsalted) macadamia nuts
5 ounces white chocolate, chopped,
    or 1 cup white chips

1 Preheat the oven to 350°F and place a rack in the center. Have ready two ungreased baking sheets.

2 In the bowl of a stand mixer fitted with a paddle attachment, or in a large mixing bowl, using a handheld electric mixer, beat the butter, shortening, and both

Other Events on This Day:
National Fruitcake Day

DECEMBER 28

Dishwashing Machine Patented

On this day in 1886, Josephine Garis Cochran patented the first commercially successful dishwashing machine. Seven years later, it won an award at the Chicago's World's Columbian Exposition and gained attention, but for the most part, the washers were being sold only to restaurants and hotels. In the 1920s, Josephine's company changed hands and eventually became known as KitchenAid. It wasn't until the 1950s that dishwashers became popular in American homes.

Other Events on This Day:
Iowa joined the Union in 1846, chewing gum patented in 1869

sugars on medium speed until light and creamy—about 2 minutes. Add the egg and vanilla and beat for about 30 seconds. Scrape the sides of the bowl and beat in the salt and baking soda. Scrape the sides of the bowl again. Add the flour and stir until almost incorporated, then stir in the macadamia nuts and white chocolate.

3 Drop tablespoonfuls of dough about 2½ inches apart onto the baking sheets. Bake one sheet at a time for 12 to 14 minutes, or until the edges are golden brown. Let cool on the baking sheets for about 5 minutes, then transfer to a wire rack to cool completely.

Baker's Note: Shortening really enhances the texture, giving the cookies crispier, "snappier" edges. If you'd prefer not to use shortening, you can swap it out for more butter or try coconut oil.

National Chocolate Day (again)

It's another National Chocolate Day, as if we need an excuse to eat all the leftover candy from Christmas. At any rate, here's a fun chocolate cookie that uses those white swirled morsels you see in the baking aisle. If you can't find the swirled morsels, use white chocolate chips.

Other Events on This Day: **Pepper Pot Day, YMCA organized in Boston in 1851, Texas joined the Union in 1845**

Hazelnut Mocha Cookies MAKES ABOUT 48

2¼ cups (10.1 ounces) all-purpose flour

1 teaspoon baking soda

½ teaspoon salt

½ cup unsweetened natural cocoa powder

1 cup (8 ounces) unsalted butter, room temperature

2 teaspoons instant coffee

¾ cup firmly packed light brown sugar

⅔ cup granulated sugar

1½ teaspoons hazelnut extract

2 large eggs

1 cup white swirled morsels, such as Nestlé

1 cup semisweet chocolate chips

1 Preheat the oven to 350°F and place a rack in the center. Have ready two ungreased baking sheets.

2 Mix the flour, baking soda, salt, and cocoa powder together in a small bowl; set aside.

3   In the bowl of a stand mixer fitted with a paddle attach-
    ment, or in a large mixing bowl, using a handheld electric
    mixer, beat the butter on medium speed until creamy.
    Beat in the coffee and both sugars and continue to beat
    for about 2 minutes, or until light and creamy. Reduce the
    mixer speed slightly and add the hazelnut extract and the
    eggs, one at a time, beating until they are blended in. By
    hand or using the lowest speed of the mixer, gradually
    add the flour mixture. When the flour is blended in, stir in
    the swirled morsels.

4   Scoop up tablespoonfuls of dough and arrange about
    2½ inches apart on the baking sheets. Bake for 10 to 12
    minutes, or until the cookies appear set. Let cool on the
    baking sheets for 2 minutes, then transfer to a wire rack to
    cool completely.

Candy Bar–Topped Brownies   MAKES 32

12 tablespoons (6 ounces) unsalted butter

1½ cups granulated sugar

3 tablespoons caramel-flavored iced coffee
    mix, such as Starbucks Via

¾ cup unsweetened natural cocoa powder

1½ teaspoons vanilla extract

3 large eggs

½ teaspoon salt

½ teaspoon baking powder

1⅓ cups (6 ounces) all-purpose flour

6 regular-size chocolate, caramel, nougat bars, such
    as Milky Way, chopped (see Baker's Notes)

1   Preheat the oven to 350°F and place a rack in the center.
    Line a 9 by 13-inch metal pan with nonstick foil.

2   In a large, microwave-safe mixing bowl, microwave the
    butter on high for 30 seconds, or until melted. Whisk in
    the sugar, then whisk in the coffee powder, cocoa powder,
    vanilla, and eggs. When the mixture is smooth, add the

Hubble Declares More Galaxies

For years, astronomers
believed the Milky Way
was the only galaxy. Things
changed on this day in 1924
when Edwin Hubble an-
nounced he'd found another
one. Using the powerful
Hooker telescope and calculations based on those by a
scientist named Henrietta
Swan Leavitt, Hubble mea-
sured the distance to several
variable stars in the Andromeda Nebula. His calculations
showed that these stars, called
Cepheids, were much farther
away than scientists thought,
proving that Andromeda was
not a nebula but a galaxy of
stars as big as our own Milky
Way. More galaxies have been
found since then.

salt and baking powder and whisk thoroughly, breaking up any lumps in the baking powder and taking care that it is thoroughly distributed; scrape the sides of the bowl and stir (do not beat) in the flour.

3 Pour into the pan and spread to the edges. Bake for 22 to 25 minutes, or until a toothpick inserted in the center comes out with moist crumbs. Let cool slightly in the pan. Scatter the candy bar chunks over the warm brownies and let the brownies cool completely in the pan. When cool, give them a quick chill for easy slicing. Lift from the pan, set on a cutting board, and with a big chef's knife, cut into thirty-two squares.

Baker's Notes: I like the dramatic effect of a brownie piled high with roughly chopped candy. The warm brownie melts the chocolate just enough that it adheres to the top of the brownie, so no extra ganache, icing, or melted chocolate is required. To complement the caramel flavor of the candy bar, I incorporated a few tablespoons of dry, lightly sweetened Starbucks Via caramel-flavored iced coffee mix. As for the candy, you get nicer slices of candy bar when you chill the bars, then make three cuts lengthwise followed by ½-inch-spaced crosswise cuts. And finally, this recipe halves nicely. Just use an 8-inch metal pan and 1 large egg plus 2 tablespoons of beaten egg, and remove the brownies from the oven at 22 minutes.

DECEMBER 31

New Year's Eve

Congratulations! You've made it through a whole year of cookies. It's time to celebrate, and whether you're ringing in the New Year with friends or staying home and doing it with the family, you'll need a sweet treat to keep you up until the ball drops.

This cookie, a favorite with our Girl Scout troop, is perfect for stashing in a tin and carrying just about anywhere.

Peanut Butter Toffee Chunk Cookies MAKES ABOUT 26

1¼ cups (5.6 ounces) all-purpose flour

½ teaspoon baking soda

½ teaspoon salt

8 tablespoons (4 ounces) unsalted
    butter, melted and cooled

½ cup firmly packed light brown sugar

½ cup plus 2 tablespoons granulated sugar

¼ cup natural creamy peanut butter

1 large egg

1 teaspoon vanilla extract

4 ounces toffee bars, such as Heath or Skor, roughly chopped

¼ cup roasted peanuts, chopped

1 teaspoon ground cinnamon

1 Preheat the oven to 350°F and place a rack in the center. Line two baking sheets with nonstick foil or parchment paper.

2 Mix the flour, baking soda, and salt together in a medium-size bowl; set aside.

3 With a wooden spoon, mix the melted butter, brown sugar, and ½ cup of the granulated sugar until combined. Stir in the peanut butter, egg, and vanilla. Gradually stir in the flour mixture. Stir in the toffee and peanuts. Chill the dough for 30 minutes, or just until it's easy to handle.

4 Stir together the remaining 2 tablespoons of granulated sugar and the cinnamon. Scoop up level tablespoonfuls of dough and shape into balls. Roll the balls gently in the cinnamon sugar. Arrange about 2 inches apart on the prepared baking sheets and flatten slightly.

5 Bake one sheet at a time for 8 to 10 minutes, or until the edges are set but the centers are still soft (they will look underdone). Let cool on the baking sheets for 4 minutes, then transfer to a wire rack to cool completely.

Other Events on This Day: The game of Monopoly was patented in 1935.

Acknowledgments

Thanks to Lane, Iris, Diane, Lisa, Elizabeth, and Dave for bringing this book to life.

To Holly and Allan for the inspiration.

To Katrina, Catie, Suzanne, Melissa, Sue, Cindy, Pat, Marisa, and Beth for recipe testing.

To Lisa L. for her sugar cookie recipe, Lisa M. for her sandwich cookies, Lisa E. for her chocolate almond shortbread, Lisa G. for the cinnamon roll in a waffle iron tip, Lizzie for helping me get the facts straight on all things Elvis, Louise for introducing me to alfajores, Janet for her honey cookies, Josie for her pistachio bars, Gloria for her chocolate banana brownies, Therese for her enthusiasm, Dr. Gerald Adair and Martha Adair and Roger and his family for their wonderful shortbread, Cheri for her ranger cookie expertise, Kristen for her chocolate cookie recipe, Melissa and Jenn for helping me determine that I prefer matcha straight rather than in cookies, Joe and Susan and Elaine for guiding me through the world of millionaire shortbread bars, Nicole at BakingBites.com, John Day for being my number one fan and for instilling curiosity toward just about everything; Ann Sorbera, Pat Day, and Maureen Ginsberg for enthusiasm and support, and my dogs for forcing me to leave the house and walk them. Woof!

Most of all, thanks to Emma and Todd for being my two best friends (and putting up with the state of our kitchen and the crazy number of cookies coming out of it).

Metric Conversions and Equivalents

METRIC CONVERSION FORMULAS

TO CONVERT	MULTIPLY
Ounces to grams	Ounces by 28.35
Pounds to kilograms	Pounds by 0.454
Teaspoons to milliliters	Teaspoons by 4.93
Tablespoons to milliliters	Tablespoons by 14.79
Fluid ounces to milliliters	Fluid ounces by 29.57
Cups to milliliters	Cups by 236.59
Cups to liters	Cups by 0.236
Pints to liters	Pints by 0.473
Quarts to liters	Quarts by 0.946
Inches to centimeters	Inches by 2.54

APPROXIMATE METRIC EQUIVALENTS

LENGTH

⅛ inch	3 millimeters
¼ inch	6 millimeters
½ inch	1.25 centimeters
1 inch	2.5 centimeters
2 inches	5 centimeters
4 inches	10 centimeters
6 inches	15¼ centimeters
12 inches (1 foot)	30 centimeters

WEIGHT

¼ ounce	7 grams
½ ounce	14 grams
¾ ounce	21 grams
1 ounce	28 grams
1¼ ounces	35 grams
1½ ounces	42.5 grams
1⅔ ounces	45 grams
2 ounces	57 grams
3 ounces	85 grams
4 ounces (¼ pound)	113 grams
5 ounces	142 grams
6 ounces	170 grams
7 ounces	198 grams
8 ounces (½ pound)	227 grams
16 ounces (1 pound)	454 grams
35¼ ounces (2.2 pounds)	1 kilogram

VOLUME

¼ teaspoon	1 milliliter
½ teaspoon	2.5 milliliters
¾ teaspoon	4 milliliters
1 teaspoon	5 milliliters
1¼ teaspoons	6 milliliters
1½ teaspoons	7.5 milliliters
1¾ teaspoons	8.5 milliliters
2 teaspoons	10 milliliters
1 tablespoon (½ fluid ounce)	15 milliliters
2 tablespoons (1 fluid ounce)	30 milliliters
¼ cup	60 milliliters
⅓ cup	80 milliliters
½ cup (4 fluid ounces)	120 milliliters
⅔ cup	160 milliliters
¾ cup	180 milliliters
1 cup (8 fluid ounces)	240 milliliters
1¼ cups	300 milliliters
1½ cups (12 fluid ounces)	360 milliliters
1⅔ cups	400 milliliters
2 cups (1 pint)	460 milliliters
4 cups (1 quart)	0.95 liter
1 quart plus ¼ cup	1 liter
4 quarts (1 gallon)	3.8 liters

COMMON INGREDIENTS AND THEIR APPROXIMATE EQUIVALENTS

1 cup all-purpose flour = 140 grams

1 stick butter (4 ounces • ½ cup • 8 tablespoons) = 110 grams

1 cup butter (8 ounces • 2 sticks • 16 tablespoons) = 220 grams

1 cup brown sugar, firmly packed = 225 grams

1 cup granulated sugar = 200 grams

OVEN TEMPERATURES

To convert Fahrenheit to Celsius, subtract 32 from Fahrenheit, multiply the result by 5, then divide by 9.

DESCRIPTION	FAHRENHEIT	CELSIUS	BRITISH GAS MARK
Very cool	200°	95°	0
Very cool	225°	110°	¼
Very cool	250°	120°	½
Cool	275°	135°	1
Cool	300°	150°	2
Warm	325°	165°	3
Moderate	350°	175°	4
Moderately hot	375°	190°	5
Fairly hot	400°	200°	6
Hot	425°	220°	7
Very hot	450°	230°	8
Very hot	475°	245°	9

Information compiled from a variety of sources, including *Recipes into Type* by Joan Whitman and Dolores Simon (Newton, MA: Biscuit Books, 2000); *The New Food Lover's Companion* by Sharon Tyler Herbst (Hauppauge, NY: Barron's, 1995); and *Rosemary Brown's Big Kitchen Instruction Book* (Kansas City, MO: Andrews McMeel, 1998).

Cookies by Type

CUT-OUTS

DROPS/ROUNDS

SHAPED

SLICE AND BAKE

Bars, Brownies, Brittles, and Other Pan Cookies by Pan Size

MINI MUFFIN PAN

STANDARD MUFFIN PAN

Cookies by Batch Size

VERY SMALL (YIELDS 1 TO 12)

SMALL
(YIELDS 14 TO 27)

Chocolate Almond Oat Cookies (14) 169

Sturdy Gingerbread Men (15) 49

Mini Phyllo Pear Pies (15) 364

Pomegranate Swirl Cheesecake Bars (16) 1

Black Bean Brownies (16) 7

Whole Wheat and Pecan Apricot Bars (16) 10

Sweet-and-Salty Corn Chip Candy (16) 16

Lamingtons (16) 30

Raspberry Thumbprint Scones (16) 33

Toasted Oat Breakfast Bars (16) 36

Double Chocolate Hazelnut Cheesecake Bars (16) 42

Apple Orange Bars (16) 43

Favorite Cream Cheese Brownies (16) 47

One-Bowl Peppermint Patty Brownies (16) 48

Peanut Butter Rocky Road Bars (16) 63

Josie's Chocolate Chip Cherry Pistachio Bars (16) 65

Cookie Chunk Brownies (16) 74

Scottish Oat Cookies (16) 79

Birdseed Bars (16) 91

Viennese Raspberry Bars (16) 101

Mock Apple Crumb Pie Bars (16) 104

Hard-Boiled Egg Chocolate Chip Cookies (16) 107

Pareve Brownies (16) 111

Sour Cream Blueberry Pie Bars (16) 113

Hazelnut Chocolate Marshmallow Puffs (16) 129

Caramel Pretzel Blondies (16) 131

Double Chocolate Raspberry Chipotle Bars (16) 139

Apple Crumb Bars (16) 149

Cherry Cobbler Bars (16) 154

Strawberry Malt Swirl Brownies (16) 158

Dried Cherry Chocolate Trail Bars (16 or 24) 174

Applesauce Cake Bars with Cream Cheese Frosting (16) 176

Black Cow Brownies (16) 181

S'mores Bars (16) 199

Kryptonite Macarons (16) 205

Strawberry Malt-Topped Brownies (16) 213

Millionaire Bars (16)

Jumbo Hazelnut Chocolate Cookies (16) 224

Mango Cream Pie Bars (16) 257

Nutty Shortbread Bars (16) 258

Chocolate Truffle Cookies (16) 286

Bakewell Bars (16) 300

Small-Batch Vegan Molasses Cookies (16) 324

Layered Pumpkin Cheesecake Brownies (16) 332

Hello Dollies (16) 357

Rugelach (16) 371

Spiked Brownies (16) 376

Chai-Chocolate Banana Tea Bars (16) 385

Maple Oat Bars (16) 386

Cranberry Streusel Bars (16) 388

Glazed Bourbon Whiskey Cookies (18) 19

Green Egg Cookies (18) 69

Strawberries and Cream Cookies (18) 92

Mini Cherry Cheesecakes (18) 128

Spiced Prune Bars with Penuche Icing (18) 232

Oatmeal Sandwich Cookies (18) 254

Lizzie's Dog Biscuits (18) 268

1787 Date Bars (18) 291

Crunchy Nugget Chocolate Chip Cookies (18) 331

Death by Giant Chocolate Cookies (18) 333

Butterfly Wings (18 to 20) 377

Peanut Browned-Butter Banana Bacon Cookies (20) 9

Milk Chocolate Chunk Walnut Cookies (20) 13

Cherry Coconut Pecan Biscotti (20) 60

Palm Sugar Cantucci (20) 86

Irish Cream Cheesecake Brownies (20) 87

Matzo Brittle with Spiced Pecan Topping (20) 97

Dinosaur Food (20) 132

Coffee Lover's Biscotti (20) 163

Zucchini Bread Cookies (20) 250

Mulled Apple Cider Cookies (20) 304

Surprise Mint Cookies (20) 308

Noodle Cookies (20) 311

Peanut Butter Haystacks (20) 311

Jalapeño and Cranberry Biscotti (20) 343

Vegan Almond and Bittersweet Chocolate Cookies (20) 344

Cranberry, White Chip, and Ginger Cookie Bark (20) 358

Pilgrim Hat Cookies (20) 360

Mississippi Mud Cups (20) 378

Eggnog Sandwich Cookies (20) 393

One-Bowl Thin and Buttery Chocolate Chip Cookies (22) 93

Double Trouble Chocolate and Potato Chip Cookies (22) 231

Double Peanut Butter Truffle Cookies (22) 396

HAL-Shaped Frosted Fudge Brownies (24) 14

MEDIUM (YIELDS 28 TO 56)

Speculoos (36) 374

Graham Crackers (40) 211

Three-Step Cookies (40) 50

Hal's Pumpkin Biscuits (40) 62

Mini Tofu Chocolate Pies (40) 121

Macadamia White Chocolate
Pineapple Cookies (40) 183

Spiced Dried Plum Cookies (40) 263

Flourless Peanut Butter Cookies
(40) 282

Banana Pudding Cookies (42) 37

Radium Chip Pistachio Cookies
(42) 124

Iced Root Beer Cookies (42) 153

Biscochitos (42) 166

Spiced Oatmeal and Currant
Cookies (42) 290

Fortune Cookies (45) 302

Bones of the Dead Cookies (45) 339

One-Bowl Cranberry Oat Cookies
(48) 7

Chinese Almond Cookies (48) 40

Mocha Truffle Brownies (48) 52

Mint Thins (48) 81

Split-Second Pecan Cookies (48)
118

Brazil Nut Cookies (48) 127

Accordion Cookies (48) 142

Oat Florentines (48) 168

Easy Macaroons (48) 170

Chocolate-Dipped Cookies (48) 198

Malted Milk and Candy Cookies
(48) 234

Chocolate Almond Shortbread
(48) 77

Raspberries and Cream Cookies
(48) 249

Left-Handed Chocolate Cookies
(48) 255

Chocolate Cookie Truffles (48) 279

Chocolate Rum Balls (48) 292

Checkerboard Cookies (48) 297

Cherry Cashew Cookies (48) 298

Good Morning Butterscotch
Cookies (48) 314

Bring in the Chips Cookies (48) 323

Pumpkin Cheesecake Cookies (48)
325

Peanut Butter Oat Chocolate Chunk
Cookies (48) 380

Mandel Bread (48) 383

Wine Cookies (48) 387

Pfeffernüsse (48) 392

Hazelnut Mocha Cookies (48) 398

Chocolate Peanut Raisin Clusters
(48) 95

Sesame, White Chip, and Oat
Cookies (48) 338

Carrot Cake Eyeballs (50) 145

Cinnamon Snail Cookies (50 to 60)
162

Chocolate Malt Snowballs (50) 372

Aztec Chocolate Cookies (52) 317

Sour Cherry Oatmeal Cookies (56)
98

LARGE
(YIELDS 60 TO 100)

Rum Scotchies (60) 120

Old-Fashioned Oatmeal Cookies
(60) 135

Sparkling Star Cutouts (60) 143

Jazzy Gelatin Spritz Cookies (60)
167

Oat and Coconut White Chocolate
Candy Cookies (60) 225

Peanut Butter Chip Chocolate
Cookies (60) 357

Candied Fruit and Bourbon Cookies
(60) 360

Dr. Keen's Scottish Shortbread
(60) 29

Ambrosia Cookies (60) 381

No-Bake Peanut Butter Pie Bites
(64) 27

Triple Chocolate Bites (64) 215

Crispy Peanut Butter Balls (70) 59

Cheddar Cheese Cookies (72) 24

Soft Trail Mix Cookies (72) 45

Gluten-Free Cheddar Animal
Crackers (84) 122

Mini Ginger Cookies (90) 210

Ten-at-a-Time Cookies (100) 384

MISCELLANEOUS
BATCH SIZES

Best-Ever Almond Butter Crunch
(1¼ pounds) 203

Caramel Corn (6 cups) 189

Chipotle Beer Brittle (1 pound) 347

Cookienola (1 pound) 146

Cookie Jar Cookie Mix (jar) 367

Granola (4½ cups) 177

Peppermint Cookie Bark
(1½ pounds) 395

Convenient Cookies

FROM A MIX

Black and White and Red All Over Cookies 278

Chocolate-Cherry Sour Cream Bars 61

Chocolate Chip Pecan Dulce de Leche Bars 64

Colorful Confetti Cookies 321

Crème Brûlée Bars 117

Double Peanut Butter Truffle Cookies 396

Easy Café au Lait Brownies 56

Easy Oatmeal Biscotti 240

Irish Cream Cheesecake Brownies 87

Orange Blossom Bars 201

Payroll Bars 280

Peach Bars 345

Quick Cherry Dream Bars 191

White Chocolate Raspberry Cheesecake Bars 244

ONE-BOWL

Black Bean Brownies 7

Dinosaur Food 132

Fabulous Four-Ingredient Bars 44

Janet's One-Bowl Honey Cookies 285

Monster Cookies 147

One-Bowl Honey and Oat Cookies 155

One-Bowl Cranberry Oat Cookies 7

One-Bowl German Chocolate Chunk Cookies 85

One-Bowl Thin and Buttery Chocolate Chip Cookies 93

One-Bowl White Chocolate Macadamia Cookies 397

Peanut Butter–Oat Candy Bar Cookies 41

VERY EASY

Big-as-a-Fist Breakfast Cookies 293

Buckeyes 68

Butterfly Wings 377

Chocolate Cookie Truffles 279

Chocolate Peanut Raisin Clusters 95

Dinosaur Food 132

Dr. Keen's Scottish Shortbread 29

Easy Baklava Cups 354

Easy Macaroons 170

Fabulous Four-Ingredient Bars 44

Flourless Peanut Butter Cookies 282

Frozen Mousse Balls 57

Left-Handed Chocolate Cookies 255

Lighter-Than-Air Mini Chip Cookies 242

Magic Wands 242

Microwave Brownies 2

Microwave S'mores 252

Mini Cherry Cheesecakes 128

Mini Phyllo Pear Pies 364

Mud Bars 173

No-Bake Peanut Butter Pie Bites 27

Pecan Dainties 35

Pilgrim Hat Cookies 360

Stir-and-Bake Peanut Butter Protein Cookies 67

Three-Step Cookies 50

Toasted Oat Breakfast Bars 36

NO-BAKE

Best-Ever Almond Butter Crunch 203

Buckeyes 68

Chocolate-Covered Wafer Cookies 196

Chocolate Peanut Raisin Clusters 95

Chocolate Rum Balls 292

Chocolate Salami 281

Chocolate Tiffins 134

Crispy Peanut Butter Balls 59

Dinosaur Food 132

Fabulous Four-Ingredient Bars 44

Frozen Mousse Balls 57

Left-Handed Chocolate Cookies 255

Maple Nut Triangles 160

Marshmallow and Peanut Butter Crispy Rice Treats 292

Mud Bars 173

Nanaimo Bars 207

No-Bake Honey Bars 327

No-Bake Peanut Butter Pie Bites 27

No-Bake Wheat and Peanut Butter Bars 320

Noodle Cookies 311

Peanut Butter Haystacks 311

Power Pellets 286

Red, White, and Blue Crispy Rice Treats 211

Three-Step Cookies 50

Toasted Oat Breakfast Bars 36

Two-Ingredient Peanut Butter Cup Cookies 356

White Chocolate Lemon Raspberry Dessert Pizza 349

Cookies for Special Diets

CAN BE MADE GLUTEN FREE

Best-Ever Almond Butter Crunch 203

Birdseed Bars 91

Bones of the Dead Cookies 339

Buckeyes 68

Chocolate Pecan Chewies 302

Chocolate Truffle Cookies 286

Chocolate Peanut Raisin Clusters 95

Easy Macaroons 170

Fabulous Four-Ingredient Bars 44

Flourless Peanut Butter Cookies 282

Gluten-Free Cheddar Animal Crackers 122

Granola 177

Lighter-Than-Air Mini Chip Cookies 242

Maple Nut Triangles 160

Marshmallow and Peanut Butter Crispy Rice Treats 292

Monster Cookies 147

Mud Bars 173

Red, White, and Blue Crispy Rice Treats 211

Sunflower Seed Butter Monsters 299

Toasted Oat Breakfast Bars 36

EGG FREE

Hermit Bars 335

VEGAN

Small-Batch Vegan Molasses Cookies 324

Vegan Almond and Bittersweet Chocolate Cookies 344

Makes a Great Gift

Almond Ginger Toasts 394

Almond Toasts 54

Best-Ever Almond Butter Crunch 203

Birdseed Bars 91

Buckeyes 68

Caramel Corn 189

Cherry Coconut Pecan Biscotti 60

Chocolate Peanut Raisin Clusters 95

Cookie Jar Cookie Mix 367

Crispy Peanut Butter Balls 59

Dr. Keen's Scottish Shortbread 29

Granola 177

Hal's Pumpkin Biscuits 62

Hard-Boiled Egg Chocolate Chip Cookies 107

Kryptonite Macarons 205

Matzo Brittle with Spiced Pecan Topping 97

Monster-Size Sugar Cookies 217

Mud Bars 173

No-Sharing Chocolate Chip Cookies 119

Palm Sugar Cantucci 86

Put-Your-Pet-on-a-Cookie 114

Scottish Oat Cookies 79

Snowballs 66

Three-Step Cookies 50

Bake Sale Favorites

Aztec Chocolate Cookies 317

"Big as a Boat" Oatmeal Cookies 245

Black and White and Red All Over Cookies 278

Blue Sky Sugar Cookies 327

Candy-Coated Chocolate Cookies 116

Chipotle Beer Brittle 347

Chocolate Chip Dream Bars 20

Chocolate Cookie Truffles 279

Chocolate Pecan Chewies 302

Colorful Confetti Cookies 321

Colossal Ginger Cookies 247

Cow Chip Cookies 223

Cowboy Cookies 366

Creamy Lemon Bars 346

Death by Giant Chocolate Cookies 333

Double Chocolate Almond Biscotti 277

Double Peanut Butter Truffle Cookies 396

Breakfast Cookies

Very Unusual Cookies

Index